The Definition and Measurement of Poverty

Westview Special Studies in Applied Social Research

The Definition and Measurement of Poverty
Volume 1: *A Review*
Volume 2: *Annotated Bibliography*

Sharon M. Oster, Elizabeth E. Lake,
and Conchita Gene Oksman

Are the poor, as one writer suggests, only those without enough to eat? Or does poverty instead consist of "the inability to buy a beer when everyone else has one"? These two volumes provide a comprehensive summary and annotated bibliography of the issues associated with the definition and measurement of poverty. The discussion is organized around eleven topics in the areas of economics, political science, and sociology. Included are such diverse subjects as the historical evolution of poverty definitions (How did Karl Marx and Adam Smith define poverty?); the "index number" problem; and regional differences in poverty measurement. The annotated bibliography, including both articles and books, primarily covers material written after 1950.

Sharon M. Oster, currently assistant professor of economics at Yale University, has done extensive work in the areas of environmental economics, industrial location, and problems of labor market discrimination. Elizabeth E. Lake, an economist at Urban Systems Research & Engineering (USR&E), performs research in income distribution, regional economics, and public finance. Conchita Gene Oksman has been a consultant at USR&E for four years. Her research focuses on the area of social welfare.

Other Titles in This Series

Guidance Manual to Providing Neighborhood Services, Stephen J. Fitzsimmons, Barbara C. Sampson, and M. Brigid O'Farrell

Other Urban Systems Research and Engineering, Inc., studies published by Westview Press:

Housing for the Elderly: An Evaluation of the Effectiveness of Congregate Projects, Irene K. Malozemoff, John G. Anderson, and Lidia V. Rosenbaum

Improving Environmental Quality through Land Use Ordinances, Michael A. Alford and James S. Hudson

The Definition and Measurement of Poverty

Volume 2: Annotated Bibliography

An Urban Systems Research Report
by Sharon M. Oster, Elizabeth E. Lake, and Conchita Gene Oksman

Routledge
Taylor & Francis Group
LONDON AND NEW YORK

First published 1978 by Westview Press, Inc.

Published 2018 by Routledge
52 Vanderbilt Avenue, New York, NY 10017
2 Park Square, Milton Park, Abingdon, Oxon OX14 4RN

Routledge is an imprint of the Taylor & Francis Group, an informa business

Library of Congress Cataloging in Publication Data
Oster, Sharon
The definition and measurement of poverty.
(Westview special studies in applied social research)
"Contract number 135-75-HEW-OS."
CONTENTS: v.1. A review.--v.2. Annotated bibliography.
1. Poor--United States. 2. Poor--United States--Bibliography. I. Lake, Elizabeth E., joint author. II. Oksman, Conchita Gene, joint author. III. Title.
HC110.P6088 301.44'1 77-5233
ISBN 13: 978-0-367-01775-0 (hbk)

ISBN 13 :978-0-367-16762-2 (pbk)

CONTENTS

BIBLIOGRAPHIES AND ABSTRACTS USED FOR LITERATURE SEARCH

INDICES AND ANNOTATED BIBLIOGRAPHIES

History of Economic Thought and Analysis, Emma Fundaburk (Scarecrow Press, New Jersey), 1973. A bibliography of history of thought.

Human Migration: A Guide to Migration Literature in English, 1955-1962 (J. J. Mangalam)

Index of Bibliographies, Council of Planning Librarians

Index of Economic Journals (Richard Irwin, Illinois)

International Political Science Abstracts (Blackwell, Oxford)

Journal of Economic Literature (American Economic Association)

List of Bibliographies, Regional Science Research Institute

Poverty and Health in the U.S.

Poverty and Human Resources Abstracts (Institute of Labor and Industrial Relations, University of Michigan)

Poverty in Canada and the United States, Benjamin Schlesinger (University of Toronto Press), 1966

Poverty in the United States During the Sixties (Institute of Government Studies, Berkeley), 1970

Public Administration Review

Publications in the Social and Behavioral Sciences

Research in Education Document Resumés

"Research on Household Behavior," Robert Ferber (literature review), American Economics Review

Rural Urban Migration Research in the U.S. (U.S. Department of Health, Education, and Welfare, 1975)

Social Indicators and Societal Monitoring

Social Science Citation Index

Sociological Abstracts (American Sociologists Association: New York)

PERIODICALS (*Separately* checked for the last 5 years to discover recent articles omitted in the indices above)

American Economic Review and American Economics Review Papers and Proceedings

American Journal of Economics and Sociology

American Journal of Sociology

American Sociological Review

Annals of the American Academy of Political and Social Science

Conference Board Record

Econometrica

Employment and Earnings Monthly Report on the Labor Force, published monthly by the Bureau of Labor Statistics

Journal of Human Relations

Journal of Human Resources

Journal of Law and Economics

Journal of Political Economy

Journal of Public Economics

Journal of Social Policy

Monthly Labor Review

Public Interest

Quarterly Journal of Economics

Review of Economics and Statistics

Review of Economic Studies

Rural Sociology

Social and Economic Studies

Social Forces

Social Problems

Social Research

Social Science Quarterly

Socio-Economic Planning Sciences

Sociological Quarterly

Sociology

Studies in Household Economic Behavior

Welfare in Review

DOCTORAL AND MASTERS THESES (last five years)

Harvard University Doctoral Theses 1970-1974 in Economics, Sociology, and Planning

Massachusetts Institute of Technology Doctoral and Masters Theses, 1970-1975 in Economics and Planning (no Sociology Department)

ANNOTATED BIBLIOGRAPHY

A NOTE ON THE USE OF THE ANNOTATED BIBLIOGRAPHY

Chapters of volume 1 of this work to which the annotations correspond are noted in Roman numerals in parentheses directly under the citation. Those works which are among the most relevant literature reviewed are indicated by an asterisk (*) before the name of the author(s).

Chapter titles and their numerical designations are as follows:

II.	Historical Definitions of Poverty: An Overview
III.	Index Numbers
IV.	Adjustments for Family Size and Composition
V.	Regional Cost of Living Differences as a Function of Public Sector Differences
VI.	Regional Cost of Living Differences as a Function of Private Sector Differences
VII.	Wealth/Assets and Consumption as Measures of Poverty
VIII.	Is Leisure a Resource?
IX.	Determinants of the Turn-over Rates of Poor Families
X.	Social and Economic Proxies for Poverty
XI.	Social Indicators
XII.	State Administrative Definitions of Poverty

The annotated bibliography is followed by an index, which is arranged according to the chapter divisions of volume 1 of this book. The index lists the literature in the bibliography relevant to each chapter.

Aaron, Henry. "The Foundations of the War on Poverty Re-examined." American Economic Review 57 (No. 5, 1967).

(IX,X)

Response to an article by Lowell Galloway, "The Foundations of the 'War on Poverty'" suggesting that the percentage of families living in poverty would decline considerably by 1970 or 1980. This conclusion was based on a regression of the logarithm of the percentage of families with incomes below $3,000 in 1963 dollars on median family income and the unemployment rate. Aaron states that: (1) aggregate poverty statistics are inherently incapable of providing evidence for or against the backwash thesis (that poverty will not largely disappear with growth). (2) Galloway's results are sensitive to the functional form of his regression: the semilogarithmic transformation tends to overstate the impact of rising incomes on the poverty percentage. (3) Galloway's results are sensitive to his data: if the semilogarithmic regression is run separately for the percentage of white and non-white families living in poverty, it appears that white poverty is more sensitive to economic growth, but less sensitive to the unemployment rate than is non-white poverty.

Aaron, Henry, and McGuire, Martin. "Public Goods and Income Distribution." Econometrica 38(1970): 907-920.

(II,V,X)

The impact of public goods on the distribution of income cannot be adequately assessed without recourse to a consumer's utility function for public goods. Different assumptions about preferences are shown to result in widely differing results. Under certain assumptions doubt is cast on the common assumption that public goods equalize the distribution of income. Different utility functions lead to the top income bracket paying net taxes of $10,000 per family or receiving net transfers of over $8,000. Not only income divisions but also other economic, social and demographic divisions ought to be considered in future studies of the impact of public spending.

*Abel-Smith, Brian, and Bagley, Christopher. "The Problem of Establishing Equivalent Standards of Living for Families of Different Composition." In The Concept of Poverty, edited by Peter Townsend. London: Heinemann Educational Books Ltd., 1970.

(IV)

A discussion of various problems in establishing equivalent standards of living for families of different sizes and age composition. Noting limitations and differences in methodology, Abel-Smith and Bagley describe the family adjustment methods of Townsend, Rowntree, the U.S. Bureau of Labor Statistics (City Worker's Family Budget), Nicholson, and Orshansky. The percentage of expenditure on food is cited as the best method of establishing equivalent standards of living for households of different composition. It is based on actual behavior of consumers rather than on their assumed behavior, it can be easily recalculated as new data on consumer expenditure patterns become available, and it is theoretically capable of greater refinements.

Abt Associates, Inc. The Causes of Rural to Urban Migration Among the Poor. Cambridge, Massachusetts: 1970.

(V,VI)

Chapter 9 of this study analyzes the effect perceptions concerning educational quality and accessibility have on rural-urban migration. As compared with other areas, especially job market conditions, respondents were not particularly critical of the educational system of rural areas. Less than half of the total sample tended to feel that educational problems were significant. Overall, about half of the people interviewed felt that education was better in the city than in rural areas. This rate is about the same as that for housing, less than that for health or jobs. The people who felt that the city had more to offer in the way of education were not necessarily the same ones who perceived problems in the rural system. They tended to be young people, people of low income, and people of greater educational attainment--as opposed to the problem perceivers, who were little differentiated by demographic characteristics. Migration was not at all related to the feeling that there were problems in rural education, although general problem perceivers were much more prone to go there than those who saw no particular urban advantage.

(Taken partially from the chapter)

Abt Associates, Inc. "Economic Structure." In The Causes of Rural to Urban Migration Among the Poor. Cambridge, Massachusetts: 1970.

(VI)

An analysis of some of the economic causes and microeconomic effects of migration. Perceptions of labor market opportunities in rural areas do not explain migration behavior. Non-migrants actually tended to be more critical of rural job conditions than migrants. Perceptions of urban-rural employment differences have a stronger relation to migration behavior, but they only explain a small portion of that behavior since almost all rural individuals perceive the urban areas offer better job opportunities. The only occupational factor that strongly differentiated migrants from non-migrants was the tendency for those with farming backgrounds to migrate. A much lower percentage of migrants than non-migrants has been in the labor force in rural areas, suggesting that young people migrate as part of their life cycle transition to economic self-sufficiency and family launching. All groups of migrants experienced income gains. Those with occupational backgrounds in agriculture and industry experienced the largest relative gains. Those with more than nine years of schooling gained more from migration than those with less education, but there was no important difference in income gains to the group with 9-11 years of school and those who had completed or gone beyond high school.

(Partially taken from the paper)

*Ackerman, Bernbaum, et al. "The Extent of Income Inequality in the United States." In The Capitalist System, edited by Edwards Reich and Weisskopf, 1970.

(II)

An analysis of the extent of income inequality in the United States from the post-war period until 1969. Inequality is calibrated on the basis of the relative shares of total income held by the lowest versus highest 20% of the population. In 1969, the lowest 20% received slightly less than 6% of total income, while the top 20% received over 40% of total income.

The effect of the income tax on reducing inequality is positive, albeit modest: in 1969, the share of the top 20% was reduced about 2% by income taxes. Wealth is distributed more unequally than is income: the top 1% of the population held 31% of its total wealth and 61% of corporate stock. Inequalities by race and sex still persist.

*Adelman, Irma, and Morris, Cynthia. "Factor Analysis of the Interrelationship Between Social and Political Variables and the Per Capita Gross National Product." Quarterly Journal of Economics 79(1965).

(X)

An analysis of the interaction of various types of social and political change with the level of economic development. Factor analysis is applied to per capita income and a large number of social and political indexes for 74 less developed countries in the period 1957-62. Adelman and Morris find that 66% of the inter-country variation in levels of economic development are associated with differences in non-economic characteristics. Among the socio-political factors considered were: size of the agricultural sector, degree of cultural and ethnic homogeneity, middle class, modernness of outlook, mobility, democracy, freedom of the press, political freedom, labor movement strength, political strength of the military, administrative efficiency, nationalism, and stability. Two aspects of socio-political change (derived from the variables above) exhibited a strong association with per capita GNP: socio-cultural factors, and westernization of political institutions.

Afriat, S.N. "The Theory of International Comparison of Real Income and Prices." In International Comparison of Prices and Outputs, edited by D.J. Daly. New York: National Bureau of Economic Research, 1972.

(III)

This paper develops a mathematical exposition of index number theory, specifically examining the analysis of value and cost in relation to utility, price indexes and marginal price indexes. The general problem considered is how to determine a correspondence between individual incomes in different countries that yield equal utility or real output at the prices that prevail. Although the discussion concentrates on comparisons between countries, the author emphasizes that comparisons between two time periods in the same place can be dealt with within the same theoretical framework as interspacial comparisons.

The problems of aggregation are central to the validity (or invalidity) of price index theory. It is recognized that preference relations are determined by circumstances and vary between individuals, times and places. Nevertheless, aggregate price index comparisons assume that there is a common preference structure for all. The proportion of income spent on a particular good is assumed to be determined by the price structure and nothing else -- it does not vary with income. Unfortunately, this assumption is very unrealistic, but it underlies the theory of index numbers and without it, the concept of an aggregate price index is meaningless.

Ahlbrandt, Roger S., Jr.; Brophy, Paul D.; and Farkas, William. "Current Issues Explored." *Journal of Housing* (January 1974): 11-14.

(V)

A paper on whether the number of families living below the poverty line should become the criterion for allocating federal funds for housing. The paper stresses the importance of the surrounding environment in determining the quality of housing services, a factor which the present housing programs do not take into consideration. The authors take issue with the traditional method of defining housing need only in terms of substandard housing, that is housing which is overcrowded, lacking some or all plumbing facilities, and dilapidated. It is suggested that rent-to-income ratios be used as a factor in the allocation of housing resources. However, while analyzing housing needs from this perspective (e.g., ability to pay) enables decision-makers to determine the *number* of people spending in excess of a normal percentage (25%) of their income toward shelter, it does not enable decision-makers to determine the number of people living in physically substandard conditions who are paying less than a normal percentage of their income for shelter. The authors conclude that a more direct *measure* of determining housing need is the number of people below the poverty level.

Aigner and Heins. "A Social Welfare View of the Measurement of Income Inequality." *Review of Income and Wealth* (March 1967).

(II)

Usual measures of income inequality, including the Gini index and coefficient of variation, measure income inequality without reference to explicit normative judgments. Without such judgments, it is not possible to say anything about whether any given change in such indices is good or bad. Aigner and Heins suggest an index of equality based on a Social Welfare function, which has as its arguments *incomes* of members of the population. In order to use this index, however, one must be able to specify the shape of the Social Welfare function--that is, use some alternative technique to decide how much equality society really desires.

Alan, Thomas J. Financing Rural Education. New Mexico: New Mexico State University, ERIC Clearinghouse on Rural Education and Small Schools, March 1974.

(V)

Well-financed and appropriately organized school districts are essential if rural education is to be improved. Since all three levels of government (local, state and federal) participate in providing revenues for rural education, coordination among them is necessary. In many states, the local property tax still provides a major portion of educational funding. In such states, property tax administration is of prime importance, since a poorly administered system limits the availability of revenues. In much of rural America, therefore, property tax reform is a matter of some urgency. If rural students are to be provided with an education appropriate for life in modern society, the quality of their schooling should not be based on local tax-paying ability. Considering the states' responsibility for the support of education, movement toward full state funding is recommended. Statewide planning is also needed to ensure that revenues provided by the state are used effectively. State leadership in the planning activities of local and regional authorities is an important element in the development of improved rural educational systems. Federal categorical support of programs designed to improve rural education should be continued. Within this complex financial and organizational system, the rural educator plays the key role. Therefore, administrators and school board members in rural communities should be provided with financial and technical assistance to permit them to meet the needs of their students.

Aldous, Jean, and Hill, Reuben. "Breaking the Poverty Cycle." Social Work 14 (1969): 3-12.

(IX)

Analysis of the changing balance of needs and resources over the family life span highlights two periods when poverty-prone families would benefit most from an income maintenance program: (1) the childbearing stage (most vulnerable to stress owing to insufficiencies of instrumental resources), and (2) the period of adolescence when families face acutely the social placement of their offspring. Income supplements at these two points would tend to keep families intact in the early years and would break the current cycle of transmitting poverty patterns from generation to generation.

*Alexander, Kenneth O. "Employment Shifts in Areas of Persistent Unemployment." Industrial and Labor Relations Review 22(1968): 73-85.

(X)

In this article, the author presents an analysis of total, regional, and industrial employment shifts in local labor markets in Michigan, Minnesota, and Wisconsin during the period 1950-1960, distinguishing between counties of "persistent unemployment" (PU) and all others.

"Persistent" unemployment (PU) is a classification used by the Bureau of Employment Security (BES) for identifying areas with long-term employment problems. This is to be distinguished from "substantial" unemployment which is a BES classification for areas currently experiencing an abnormally high unemployment rate. In this study, "persistent" unemployment was used as a criterion for selecting study areas because, in the first place, it is an eligibility criterion for Economic Development Act related assistance and for Federal procurement preference; and, in the second place, it refers to the most severe unemployment areas relative to the nation as a whole.

The study found that the larger PU counties experienced smaller shifts of employment due to industrial mix and larger shifts due to regional share than did the smaller PU counties. The author draws the implication for federal policy that perhaps more attention in area development programs should be directed to the stimulation of the existing manufacturing base in the larger PU counties, thus bringing people to jobs, rather than continue the present emphasis on bringing jobs to people in the smaller, more rural PU counties.

(Partially taken from editor's note)

Alix, Ernest K., and Lantz, Herman R. "Socio-Economic Status and Low Occupational Aspirations: Resignation as an Orientational Variable." Social Science Quarterly 54 (December 1973): 596-607.

(XI)

A test of "resignation" as an orientational variable in determining linkages between SES and occupational aspirations. Alix and Lantz offer the resignation concept as an orientation state which constitutes an obstacle to mobility.

Resignation is treated as a social-psychological orientation which represents "an accommodation to a history of economic failure, disappointment, and frustration." Four hypotheses were formulated in an attempt to assess the effect of resignation on the SES/occupational aspirations relationship. Questionnaires were administered to 1,754 fifth through twelfth graders; resignation was measured by a 15-item index. It was found that:

(1) the proportion of children with high occupational aspirations does vary positively with SES;

(2) the proportion of children with high resignation does vary negatively with SES; and

(3) the proportion of children with high occupational aspirations does vary negatively with level of resignation.

These findings have important bearings on how poor people could be motivated to become involved in government-sponsored programs and on whether permanent change regarding the aspirations of the poor could result from poverty programs. The authors contend that the nature of resignation is such that the resigned poor probably would not change their way of life unless they can be convinced and assured that something better will take its place.

Alker, Hayward R., Jr., and Russett, Bruce M. "On Measuring Inequality." Behavioral Science 9(July 1964): 207-218.

(II)

This article is a multidisciplinary summary of different measures of inequality. Thirteen different measures are defined and discussed: largest/smallest, ratio of advantage, percent of value held by top X% of the population, the Pareto coefficient, the mean deviation, the average ratio of advantage, the standard deviation, the skewness of a distribution, the minimal majority, the Lorenz Curve, the Gini Index, the equal share index and the Schutz coefficient.

The authors conclude that measures of extremes (the first four above) tend to be misleading and should be used with great caution. They found that the equal share index could give essential information when used in conjunction with either the Gini or the Schutz measure, both of which were found to be very good summary measures. Finally, they conclude by saying that a major source of error in measuring inequality was the improper grouping of data.

Allen, R.B.D. "Some Observations on the Theory and Practice of Price Index Numbers." Review of Economic Studies 3 (1935-36): 57-66.

(III)

This article presents a discussion on the theoretical problems of price index numbers, developing the previous works of Konyus and Staehle. Consider a particular expenditure level or standard of living (e_o) in an initial situation (o) - a particular year or place. What are the limits of the index number $I_{(e_o)}$ determining the equivalent expenditure in another situation (1). There will be a unique bundle of goods q_o consumed at e_o given a particular price system p_o. The ratio between the value of q_o when priced at the different systems of prices, p_o and p_1, will determine the upper limit of $I_{(e_o)}$. Now, determine the bundle q, in situation 1 so that it costs as much as q_o, both costs at p_o prices. The lower limit of $I_{(e_o)}$ is determined by the ratio of q_1 priced at p_o and q_1 priced at p_1.

$$\frac{\Sigma\ p_1\ q_1}{\Sigma\ p_o\ q_1} < I_{(e_o)} < \frac{\Sigma\ p_1\ q_o}{\Sigma\ p_o\ q_o}$$

Using this theory, a cost-of-living index number can be found within limits for any standard of living. The standard can be determined by calculating the entire expenditure in one situation. Allen concludes with a practical application comparing the cost of living under Swedish prices in 1923 and German prices in 1927-28.

Allen, Vernon L., ed. Psychological Factors in Poverty. Chicago: Markham Publishing Co., 1970.

(XI)

A collection of works exploring recent theoretical and empirical developments in behavioral science that relate to problems of poverty. Several articles focus on issues related to the learning process and its importance to socialization among persons born in poverty. Another group of papers address the question of the potential contribution of a hereditary component to poverty. Behavioral concomitants to poverty are also discussed; these include motivational and educational problems and impairments in personality functioning. Various intervention strategies are presented.

Amemiva, Takesho and Boskin, Michael. "Regression Analysis when the Dependent Variable is Truncated Log-Normal, with An Application to the Determinants of the Duration of Welfare Dependency." International Economic Review 15 (No. 2, June 1974): 485-496.

(IX)

A new statistical technique for use when a dependent variable is positive and truncated is developed in this article. One such variable is the duration of welfare dependency (in months) for a five year sample of California Welfare recipients. A number of economic and demographic variables were tested to see if they affected this variable. Non-wage income (excluding welfare), and dichotomous variables measuring health, age, and the presence of preschool children all had no significant effect. The expected wage and length of unemployment based on personal characteristics of the head of household both were significant; the former large and negative, the latter smaller and positive. The type of estimate used gave a larger and more accurate weight to the expected wage than did two alternatives.

American Chamber of Commerce Research Association. "Announcing the ACCRA Cost of Living Index." Chicago: Chicago Association of Commerce and Industry, 1965.

(III)

The Consumer Price Index measures price changes over time, but it does not allow for inter-city comparisons. This index, developed by the American Chamber of Commerce Researchers Association, does not have continuity over time, but it does allow direct comparison of the cost of living in the 150 participating cities.

The index is computed on a base of well chosen product and service prices carefully weighted in proportion to the cost-of-living dollar expenditure pattern. All items are priced by following explicit specifications and procedural instructions. The items are keyed to the concept of an executive's 4-person family, whose salary is $15,000 to $16,000. Prices are collected in more than 150 cities each calendar quarter and are combined into 6 component indexes for Food, Housing, Utilities, Transportation, Health and Miscellaneous Services. The weighted component indexes are totaled to an "All Items" Index.

Because the index has only a limited number of prices, it can only show that the cost of living in one city is more or less expensive than in another city. The index cannot show how much more or less expensive it is.

(Partially taken from article)

Anderson, Martin. The Federal Bulldozer: A Critical Analysis of Urban Renewal 1949-1962. Cambridge, Massachusetts: Massachusetts Institute of Technology Press, 1964.

(V)

This book traces the development of the Urban Renewal Program from the post World War II era to the early sixties. The author contends that the federal government is less effective than the private sector in effecting positive social change through urban renewal projects. Those low income people displaced because of eminent domain are often forced to move to less desirable neighborhoods and homes. This is especially true for minority groups. Thus, the end result of intercity relocation is destructive rather than constructive. The author concludes that "the federal urban renewal program is very costly, destructive of personal liberty, and is not capable of achieving the goals put forth by Congress."

(Partially taken from
Poverty Studies in the Sixties)

Anderson, Odin W. "Infant Mortality and Social and Cultural Factors: Historical Trends and Current Patterns." In Patients, Physicians, and Illness, edited by E. Gartly Jaco. New York: Free Press, 1958.

(XI)

Since the beginning of the century, the number of infant deaths occurring before one year of age has decreased remarkably. It is possible to separate factors affecting a specific infant mortality rate into broad categories--biological, social, and cultural--and to demonstrate how certain social and cultural factors seem to affect biological ones. Among biological factors are age, sex, hereditary predisposition to disease, and mortality; social indices include class, occupation, income level, and education; cultural influences are those such as religion, customs, and attitude toward the value of human life.

Odin Anderson explores contemporary and traditional patterns of infant mortality as they relate to various conditions, reveals some interesting exceptions to these trends, and suggests new directions for future research.

Anderson, Theodore R. "Intermetropolitan Migration: A Correlation Analysis." American Journal of Sociology 61(1956): 459-462.

(VI)

Variations in the rates of in-migration, out-migration, net migration, and total migratory activity between metropolises in the northeastern and north-central regions of the United States between 1935 and 1940 may be substantially explained by four independent measures derived from two theories of migration. The independent measures were (1) the percentage of unemployed in the labor force, (2) the mean rent, (3) the population size, and (4) the location of the metropolis. Net migration can be explained purely in terms of the push-pull theory, while each of the other rates is explained by a combination of the push-pull and size-distance theories.

(From the article)

*Anderson, W.H. "Trickling Down: The Relationship Between Economic Growth and the Extent of Poverty Among American Families." Quarterly Journal of Economics 78 (1964): 511-525.

(II,V,IX)

This study of income growth and distribution presents statistical evidence that poverty cannot be eliminated through economic growth alone. The income distribution and economic growth relationship is divided into three states: (1) when the great masses of people are poor, few people become affluent as income rises; (2) as the median income rises near the poverty line, people move into affluence quite quickly; (3) finally, when the masses become affluent, more income growth means fewer people move into affluence. The results of looking cross-sectionally at American families single out the the white and Black non-farm, male-headed (under 65 years old) families as being affected by this income distribution/economic growth relationship. The farm and female-headed families are considered isolated from economic growth. Anderson suggests that only a change in the shape of the poverty curve can reduce the incidence of poverty.

Ando, Albert, and Modigliani, Franco. "The 'Life Cyle' Hypothesis of Savings: Aggregate Implications and Tests." American Economic Review 53 (March 1963): 55-84.

(VII)

A clear restatement of the derivation of the "Life Cycle" theory of consumption is followed by a number of empirical tests and a discussion of some of the implications of the theory. The theory basically says that current consumption is a weighted average of current income, expected future income, and current assets. A number of simplifying assumptions permit the theory to be tested empirically. The tests are successful, and the long run marginal propensity to consume out of income is calculated to be about .7. The coefficient of assets is significant and positive, indicating that consumers view assets as a possible source of income for consumption. The theory is then shown to be capable of explaining the observed long-term stability of the savings-income ratio, unlike the (now outdated) Keynesian consumption function.

*Antonovsky, Aaron. "Social Class and Illness: A Reconsideration." Sociological Inquiry 37 (1967): 311-322.

(XI)

A critique of Kadushin's contention that "in recent years... there is very little association between becoming ill and social class, although the lower classes still 'feel' more sick." Antonovsky's detailed re-examination defines the problems in Kaduskin's interpretations of ten studies used to support his conclusion, presented in "Social Class and the Experience of Ill Health." While Kadushin has called attention to the fact that there are intervening variables affecting social class and illness and that these variables have changed in the twentieth century, the data is far from conclusive in demonstrating that class differences in disease no longer exist. Antonovsky delineates several theoretical and methodological problems in Kadushin's analysis. However, data does not necessarily support a permanent inverse relationship between class and illness; sociologists must first provide an adequate conceptualization of class.

Antonovsky, Aaron. "Social Class, Life Expectancy, and Overall Mortality." Milbank Memorial Fund Quarterly (April 1967): 31-73.

(XI)

Discusses studies of life expectancy by social class. Studies show wide class differences in mortality rates during the early 19th century. However, in the latter half of the century, the gap began to diminish. Currently, the trend in closing of the class gap has slowed to a rate of almost zero.

Author observes that all but three of the 30-odd studies considered show a positive relationship between class status and life expectancy, with lowest classes generally having the highest death rate. Two of the three studies contradicting this point are of questionable use in that the gross classification method used in both may have obscured subtle differences within the sample population. The third contradictory study focussed on a population with the lowest death rate ever recorded; the findings of this study are questionable when applied to the population as a whole. However, "it suggests the extremely important hypothesis that as the overall death rate is lowered, class differentials may similarly decline."

Further, Antonovsky discusses implications of the variable class gap. The trend in the late nineteenth century toward a narrowing gap is attributed primarily to lower death rates among the upper classes. More substantial progress among the upper classes in reducing the mortality rate can be explained by the fact that they have received a greater proportion of benefits from recent improvements in access to and quality of medical care.

Appel, Gary L., and Schlenker, Robert E. "An Analysis of Michigan's Experience with Work Incentives." Monthly Labor Review 94(September 1971).

(II,X,XI)

Between July 1964 and July 1970, a new financial work incentive program went into effect for Michigan women receiving AFDC benefits. At the same time, employment increased significantly for this group. There is an attempt in this article to determine whether the incentive program was responsible for the employment increase. The work incentive was in effect a reduced average tax rate. Most AFDC mothers are unemployed so this effective increase in wage rate causes a substitution effect with no off-setting income effect. Thus, in theory, there should be a positive influence on employment rates. Some of the factors that make isolation of this mechanism difficult are: the structure of the program itself (turnover and increases in participants for example), personal and family characteristics (e.g.

education, health, family size), and other background effects such as the local unemployment situation. When local unemployment trends were examined for thirteen separate geographic areas, they were found to indicate declining labor markets; so the observed increases would have had to occur in spite of a depressed employment situation. Similarly, an examination of the employment patterns of those entering and leaving the program showed that the incoming participants, who were in greater numbers than withdrawals, were more likely to be unemployed. Therefore, these two processes worked against the observed increase. After making corrections for workers above the pre-incentive breakeven point, who were only counted because of the reduced tax rate, there are still statistically significant increases. Factors relating to personal attitudes are among the influences which could not be treated. Nevertheless, it is felt that, "The hypothesis that the work incentive caused most of the increase cannot be rejected even though it is not proved beyond a doubt."

Armstrong, Anne. "Infant Mortality--Some Possible Determinants." Canadian Journal of Public Health 57 (June 1966): 263-268.

(XI)

Seeks to explain wide variation in infant mortality rates among countries. Formulates a statistical model which supports hypothesis that two variables, standards of living and availability of health services, are important determinants of the infant mortality rate. Model uses a country's per capita income and ratio of hospital beds to population as indicators of standard of living and standard of health services.

Ashenfelter, Orley; and Heckman, James. "The Estimation of Income and Substitution Effects in a Model of Family Labor Supply." Econometrica 42(January 1974): 73-85.

(II)

The classical theory of labor supply behavior for the family implicitly contains several restrictions on the labor supply functions of the husband and wife. In this paper, these restrictions are formulated in a way that can be tested using the empirical data of the 1960 U.S. Census of Population. These tests are carried out, and it is shown that the data does not contradict the theoretical restraints. This implies that somewhat greater faith can be placed in the application of the theory to the real world.

Atkinson, A.B. "Poverty and Income Inequality in Britain." In Poverty, Inequality and Class Structure, edited by Dorothy Wedderburn. London: Cambridge University Press, 1974.

(II,IV,VI)

A survey of earlier work on measuring poverty and inequality in Britain. Atkinson argues that the poor should be defined as those people whose income falls below an acceptable minimum relative to the general income level. Poverty thresholds should ideally be constructed to provide uniform standards in real terms: thus adjustments should be made for family size and region. The wide divergence in measures of the number of people in poverty under different definitions is explored. Finally, the demographic attributes of Britain's poor are reviewed.

Ausubel, David P. Drug Addiction: Physiological, Psychological, and Sociological Aspects. New York: Random House, 1958.

(XI)

An integrated study of characteristics of drug addiction - pharmacological, psychiatric, psychological, and educational. The book deals, for the most part, with opiate addiction and discusses other drugs such as alcohol, barbiturates, cocaine, and marijuana for comparative purposes.

Attempts to relate social factors such as age, sex, race, ethnic origin, occupation, religion, socio-economic status, place of residence, and educational level, to causes of addiction have proved inconclusive.

Examination of socio-economic conditions demonstrates that they "affect the incidence of drug addiction primarily by influencing the availability of drugs to those individuals already predisposed on other grounds." Thus, medical personnel and residents of urban areas with port facilities show a high incidence of addiction. The addict is more likely to live in a poor neighborhood, to have an erratic employment history, and to be in a lower income bracket. The disproportionate number of addicts from the lower classes can be attributed to greater availability of drugs in slum areas.

Bach, G.L., and Stephenson, James B. "Inflation and the Redistribution of Wealth." Review of Economics and Statistics 56 (1974): 1-13.

(II, III)

"The redistributional effects of inflation are very complex, requiring analysis cutting across broad functional income groups to individuals or smaller groups." Recent inflation has shifted income from business (profits) to wage and salary earners. The effect of inflation on the redistribution of wealth from creditors to debtors since W.W. II is estimated to be between $360 and $600 million. Furthermore, in 1973, the amount of monetary assets subject to inflation erosion is larger than ever. The primary direction of the creditor to debtor transfer of wealth has been from households to the government (taxpayers). "Although inflation benefited nonfinancial corporations as net debtors, it harmed them through undercharging of depreciation." (Only the purchase price of machinery is depreciated, not the higher--due to inflation--replacement cost of machinery. This causes an overstatement of profits.) The net effect of these two opposing factors is unclear. "Among households, inflation transfers purchasing power from older to young people, and from the very poor and the very rich to the middle and upper-middle income groups." Overall, the generally accepted conclusion that inflation hurts the poor and helps the rich has not been substantiated.

Bacon, Lloyd. "Migration, Poverty, and the Rural South." Social Forces 51(March 1973): 348-355.

(VI)

The 1967 Survey of Economic Opportunity data are employed to test hypotheses about differences in migration selectivity depending on the structural distance traversed in the migration process. Theoretically, the greater the structural distance crossed in the migration process, the more rigorous would be the selectivity. Conversely, where migration involves movement between similar places, little selectivity would be expected. Structural distance was defined as movement across both regional and rural urban axes. Selectivity was defined by the relative incidence of poverty among the various residence and migration categories. Analysis of movement into and out of the rural South revealed empirical relationships between variables consistent with the theory employed, although important exceptions were found. These exceptions required a modification of the theory.

(Author abstract)

Bacon, Lloyd. "Poverty Among Interregional Rural-to-Urban Migrants." Rural Sociology 36(1971): 125-140.

(VI)

Migration and residence data from the 1967 Survey of Economic Opportunity are used to examine the differential incidence of poverty among people of rural origins. Migration within and between the South and the North (the census Northeast, North Central, and West aggregated) is analyzed for Negro-white patterns of movement and associated proportions in poverty. Poverty status, the dependent variable, is operationally defined as a measure of how successfully adults in various residence and migration categories have coped with their environments. A social systems framework is utilized, and a set of theoretical propositions is induced from the findings. These propositions are statements of relationships between social distances traversed and differential selectivity operative in migration.

(From the article)

Baetz, Reuben. "Income Security for Canadians?" Canadian Welfare (May/June 1973).

(II)

Baetz, in a summary of the papers collected in Guaranteed Annual Income: An Integrated Approach, identifies two schools of thought regarding measurement of poverty. One defines in absolute dollar terms some level of income necessary for providing a minimum standard of living. Another school regards poverty in more relative terms, and sees GAI's objective as the reduction of the disparities in the current distribution of income among the entire population. The author subsequently presents a list of criteria for developing a GAI program.

Bahr, Richard C. "Price Indexes by Size of City Show Increases from 8.8 to 10.4 Percent." Monthly Labor Review 96 (December 1973).

(VI)

The Consumer Price Index for five different sized urban population groups is presented for the first three quarters of 1973, together with comparable figures for the preceding year. The rate of increase for food prices increased for all population groups. The housing index rate of increase was also highest in the third quarter for all groups except the $50,000-$250,000 category. In contrast, the rates of increase were lower for apparel and upkeep in most groups and for health and recreation in all groups during the third quarter. In the transportation category, the prices themselves actually declined for all groups "largely because of decreases in new and used car prices."

Bailey, Margaret; Haberman, Paul; and Allesne, Harold. "The Epidemiology of Alcoholism in an Urban Residential Area." Quarterly Journal of Studies on Alcohol 26 (1965): 19-40.

(XI)

A survey of alcoholism prevalence was undertaken in the Washington Heights Health District in Manhatten as part of a more general survey conducted in 1960-61 by Columbia University. Interviews yielded an overall alcoholism prevalance rate of 1.9%, with a ratio of 3.6 males to one female. The most vulnerable sub-groups in the population were found to be widowers and divorced or separated persons of both sexes. Blacks had a higher percentage than whites, with Black females seeming to be particularly susceptible. Except for the low percentage of Jews, religion seemed to be less associated with alcoholism prevalence than race. The analysis of socio-economic variables revealed some concentration of alcoholics among the group with the least education. The alcoholics reported lower personal earnings, poorer housing, greater occupational and residential mobility, and more chronic physical illness than adults in general. On various psychological measures, they revealed marked evidence of emotional strain and impairment, especially regarding guilt and depression. The findings appear to be descriptive of an urban, noninstitutional sample of persons presumed to be alcoholics, who are functioning in the community but whose socio-economic status is vulnerable and who are under great psychological strain.

(Partially taken from Sociological Abstracts)

Bailey, Martin J. "The Welfare Cost of Inflationary Finance." The Journal of Political Economy 64 (1956): 93-110.

(III)

An analysis of the welfare implications of inflationary government finance. The opposition to inflation is usually centered around its redistributive and disruptive effects -- the hardships created for people on fixed incomes and the misallocation of resources due to greater uncertainty. Bailey examined data compiled by Philip Cagan concerning seven cases of post-World War I hyperinflation. Based on this examination, Bailey argues that there would have been substantial welfare losses even in situations of anticipated inflation with cost-of-living escalators designed to avoid redistributive and disruptive effects. When the value of money drops, people switch their holdings from liquid to real assets. As inflation accelerates, this process consumes increasing amounts of time, since people will make more trips to the bank, spend their money as soon as they receive it, and eventually engage in barter transactions. This inefficient use of time represents a loss of real utility even if the monetary value of an individual's assets keep up with inflation.

Baker, Edwin. "Utility and Rights: Two Justifications for State Action Increasing Equality." Yale Law Journal 84(November 1974): 239-259.

(II)

This article develops and compares philosophical justifications for government intervention in the market in order to bring about a guaranteed income or minimum satisfaction of "just wants" for every member of the society. Baker presents two rationales for this intervention. One is derived from the utilitarian theory. This justification, Baker claims, means that total societal utility is maximized by distributing wealth where equality is greater than it would be if the total wealth of the society, not utility, were maximized. The other argument for income distribution is based on Ronald Dworkins "theory of rights" and proposes that, in order to guarantee certain rights to each member of the society, total utility may be reduced.

Based on the two assumptions that wealth and equality vary inversely and that every individual has a diminishing marginal utility for wealth, Baker develops a two person model to determine the exact degree of equality needed to maximize total society utility. The result, which he labels as "B-type" solution, indicates that utility maximization exists under conditions of less than maximum wealth and less than maximum equality, or in essence "establishes a minimum income." Comparing these two approaches Baker finds that applied together they provide a better solution than either approach separately.

Ball, R.J., and Drake, Pamela S. "The Relationship between Aggregate Consumption and Wealth." International Economic Review 5 (January 1964): 63-81.

(VII)

This article reopens the question of the basis of the consumption function. A new consumption theory is derived from the assumption that people's views are short-range and that their utility is dependent on both their current consumption and the amount of wealth that they hold. This reduces to an equation that says that current consumption is the weighted sum of current income and past consumption, the weights adding to one. This is equivalent to many other proposed consumption functions, except for the restriction on the weights. The theory is tested empirically with inconclusive results. The hypothesis that the two weights add to one is shown to be defensible.

Banerjee, Kali S. Cost of Living Index Numbers: Practice, Precision and Theory. New York: Marcel Dekker, 1975.

(III)

A monograph designed to introduce the practice and theory of index numbers to beginners. It presents a nonmathematical illustration of the computation of cost-of-living index numbers as well as the basic concepts of econometrics that are necessary for understanding them. Areas discussed are: formal tests basic to the theory of index numbers, the chain index, the true index, components of error associated with index numbers, how index numbers can be constructed to compare two places at one point in time, and some statistical problems associated with sampling and precision.

Banfield, Edward C. "The Problem of Unemployment" and "Several Kinds of Poverty." In The Unheavenly City. Boston: Little, Brown and Co., 1970.

(II,IV,X)

These two essays comprise two chapters of a book by the author. The first contends "that automation and technological change are not creating a serious unemployment problem and are not likely to; that the unskilled, far from facing a hopeless future, will probably maintain and improve their position relative to the skilled; and that the Negro will benefit from this trend." Increasing the minimum wage and educational levels of the unskilled will probably do them more harm than good. Those who are unemployed are in that position because the price of their services (cost/productivity) is so high that it is unprofitable to employ them.

The second chapter first lays out four levels of poverty--destitution, want, hardship, and relative deprivation--which span the range from real to psychological poverty. The author finds that almost everybody has both the opportunity and resources for warm clothing, uncrowded housing, education, entertainment, and so on, and that "if one is willing to live just above the level of want... one can do so with little effort." "Many--perhaps most--of those with reported incomes below the official poverty line are not undergoing hardship." Finally, "lower class poverty... is 'inwardly caused' (by psychological inability to provide for the future, and all that this implies)."

Little empirical evidence is given to substantiate these theories.

Baratz, Morton S., and Grigsby, William G. The Meaning and Measurement of Poverty. Philadelphia: Institute for Environmental Studies, University of Pennsylvania, September 1968.

(II,VII)

This monograph presents a broad spectrum of views on poverty. The report is divided into two parts: "Conceptualization of Poverty" and the "Definition and Measurement of Poverty." Each of these areas is then subdivided according to the various ways of conceptualizing and measuring poverty. For example, poverty can be conceptualized as economic insufficiency, economic inequality, economic dependence, self-perceived deprivation, inadequate consumption, and multiple deprivation. Under economic insufficiency, poverty is defined as a lack of monetary claims and the ability to buy the quantities which are adequate to provide an acceptable level of living. A person or family is judged to suffer economic insufficiency, not by reference to self-perceived needs, but in relation to some socially acceptable minimum level of consumption. An analysis of this conception of poverty shows that it is good in that it focuses on the specific deprivation. On the other hand, a significant flaw in the conception is its faulty premise that a family with the financial ability to acquire the socially acceptable minimum level of consumption will almost always consume in a socially acceptable pattern.

(Poverty and Human Resources Abstracts)

Barr, Richard H. Expenditures for Public Elementary and Secondary Education 1971-72. Washington, D.C.: National Center for Educational Statistics (DHEW/OE), 1974.

(V)

The information in this report is directed to both the general information needs of educational researchers and the more specialized needs of personnel administering programs under P.L. 81-874--School Assistance in Federally Affected Areas--and P.L. 89-10--the Elementary and Secondary Education Act of 1965. For this reason, this publication contains two types of current operating expenditure data for public elementary and secondary education at the local level: (1) total current expenditures and (2) current expenditures as defined by P.L. 81-874 and P.L. 89-10. Data are presented in tables by state. The appendix contains a sample of the state fiscal report form for fiscal year 1972.

(Taken from the report)

Barth, Michael C. "Migration and Income Maintenance." In The President's Commission on Income Maintenance Programs, Technical Studies, 1970.

(V,VI)

A review of literature and studies on the effects of income maintenance programs on migration patterns, and an assessment of the potential impact of income maintenance-induced migration on the national economy. Areas investigated are: the implications of past and present migration patterns in the United States, the findings of existing migration studies which have some bearing on income maintenance-induced migration, descriptions of potential migrants to isolate possible effects of migration on the labor supply, and the potential effects of interregional migration on the national economy, and special migrant groups. A national income maintenance program with portable benefits and the facilitation of job search for those unemployed who are seeking work are suggested as possible directions for future policy.

Barth, Michael; Orr, Larry L; and Palmer, John L. "Policy Implications: A Positive View." In Work Incentives and Income Guarantees, edited by Joseph A. Pechman and P. Michael Timpane. Washington, D.C.: The Brookings Institution, 1975.

(II)

In this evaluation, the New Jersey negative income tax experiment is credited with generating a substantial body of knowledge relating to programs involving cash transfers scaled according to recipients income and with providing an example of the use and value of social experimentation as a tool of policy research. One anticipated consequence of the study is that opposition to income-related transfer programs which is based on a fear of reduced work effort should cease. Moreover, the modest degree of work reduction was not found to be very sensitive to the particular tax rate or guarantee chosen, so that policy decisions about these parameters can stress other criteria. For example, high tax rates are considered here to insure a minimum guarantee level and to concentrate effort at the lower end of the distribution; whereas lower tax rates are seen to effect a change in the income distribution over a much broader range. The experiment also provided information on the practical mechanics of how such a negative tax program could be administered. Finally, the New Jersey study was the first major controlled social experiment. "It opened up an entirely new methodology of policy research." The study developed specific statistical techniques and established a prototype for several subsequent government-sponsored policy research experiments.

*Bauer, Raymond A., ed. Social Indicators. Cambridge, Massachusetts: The Massachusetts Institute of Technology Press, 1966.

(XI)

This volume is devoted to the topic of social indicators--statistics, statistical series, and all other forms of evidence that tell us something about our social well-being. The authors examine the present state of social indicators, pointing out the gaps in social statistics, and the flaws in their present use. This examination leads to a series of proposals for improvements in the system, and a discussion of how social indicators could be used to evaluate social programs. The use of social indicators in defining poverty is examined, though only peripherally, by Bertram M. Gross. His views are summarized in the following:

> A sound approach to the measurement of "material well-being," however, can never be made in terms of income (or expenditures from it) alone. Whether we are concerned with establishing minima or calculating the extent of opulence, it is essential to recognize that the material well-being of individuals and families

> is three-dimensional. Full command over material resources is an aggregate of (1) income, (2) assets, and (3) public services that are not bought. To some extent these are interchangeable. More assets in the form of savings, insurance, and property may make up for deficiencies in income and assets. We must begin to think of poverty in terms of income poverty, asset poverty, and public service poverty, with minimum standards for each developed in terms of a country's productive capacity and adjusted to rising price levels. Opulence and gross inequities in distribution of full command over resources must also be calculated in three-dimensional terms. (p. 227)

* Baumol, William J. "An Overview of the Results on Consumption, Health, and Social Behavior." The Journal of Human Resources 9 (Spring 1974): 253-264.

(XI)

This paper examines the general effects of graduated work incentives on the life style of beneficiaries and represents partial results of the Graduated Work Incentive Experiment, known also as the New Jersey-Pennsylvania negative income tax experiment, initiated in 1967. Prior hypotheses implied, on one extreme, that a large portion of payments would be wasted by the recipients; a view at the other extreme suggested that life style would be much improved. Baumol concludes that a guaranteed income does not significantly affect living patterns or substantially change attitudes toward consumption. Family size, health, social activities, spending choices, and many social and psychological behaviors appear to be relatively unaffected by the support program. The single major change produced by the program was improved housing standards and increased home ownership.

Bawden, D. Lee. "Income Maintenance and the Rural Poor: An Experimental Approach." American Journal of Agricultural Economics 52(August 1970): 438-441.

(II,VI)

Notes on the experimental design and rationale behind two experiments (ongoing at the time of publication), one in an urban setting and one rural, involving tests of various negative income tax plans. The test objectives were to investigate program costs, to evaluate possible changes in attitudes and behavior among the poor resulting from these payments, and to assess the effect of the program on rate and composition of migration with particular attention to differing responses across age groups. Urban-rural differences in types of employment, in work response to alternative employment opportunities, and in proportion of self-employed people necessitated the separation of studies. Test results were to be compared and contrasted.

Bawden, D. Lee; Cain, Glen G.; and Hausman, Leonard J. "The Family Assistance Plan: An Analysis and Evaluation." Public Policy 19 (Spring 1971).

(II,IV)

Article reviews the Nixon Administration's Family Assistance bill. Some changes are recommended: (1) establish a more explicitly uniform administrative structure within the federal government, which will limit discretionary authority at the local level; (2) eliminate or curtail a number of related programs and provisions, like the food stamps program, child care and other social services, and the work test; (3) treat income from various sources more uniformly for tax purposes; and (4) increase Family Assistance Plan payment levels--eventually to the point of reducing all existing categorical aid programs.

Beale, Calvin. "Rural-Urban Migration of Blacks: Past and Future." American Journal of Agricultural Economics 53 (1971): 302-307.

(VI)

This article presents a broad view of black migration and migrants including overall numbers of black migrants, their characteristics, where they came from, where they ended up, and what happened to them after migrating. Black rural-urban migrants, despite an educational disadvantage, have succeeded in earning average family incomes nearly equal to those of black urban natives. Black migrants do not appear to have a significantly higher reliance on welfare than natives. Furthermore, the economic and educational status of the migrants is far superior to those of blacks left behind, although black urban migrants are poorer than their white counterparts.

In the future, the flow of black rural-urban migrants will be much smaller since only one-fourth of the total black population lives in rural areas (compared with more than one-half in 1940). Also, non-farm rural employment is supporting larger numbers of rural blacks than before. Nevertheless, black rural-urban migration is likely to continue since "the economic status and opportunities of rural blacks is still so inferior to that of the urban population."

Bearwood, Roger. "The Southern Roots of Urban Crisis." Fortune 78 (August 1968): 80-87, 151-156.

(V,VI)

The author discusses the gap between the living conditions of the black, rural poor and those of others. In 1966 the median income for southern rural Blacks was $3,422 as compared to $5,746 for Blacks elsewhere. 75% of rural southern Blacks live in substandard housing as compared to 15% in northern areas. These conditions have spawned a large number of migrants for the following reasons:

1) greater job opportunity,

2) chance to avoid physical violence,

3) higher welfare payments.

Those who migrate go to urban areas--primarily north and west though many rural Blacks are migrating to southern urban areas. The urban areas are unprepared to deal with a large number of people needing public assistance and thus the inequalities in the southern rural areas are having an impact nationally.

*Becker, G. "An Economic Analysis of Fertility." In Demographic and Economic Change in Developed Countries. Princeton: Princeton Press, 1960.

(IV)

An economic analysis of factors determining fertility which asserts that income and demand for children are positively related. Author draws an analogy between children and consumer goods and argues that, like durable goods, children are an investment and a source of utility. Generally, as with durable goods, demand for quantity and higher quality of children (seen purely as a result of added expenditure per child) increases with income. (Quality and quantity are seen as decision variables in a consumer choice.)

Uses empirical evidence to support this hypothesis. Past studies indicate a greater degree of success with contraceptive techniques and child-spacing among higher-income groups. These findings support implications in fertility rates that income and actual fertility are negatively related, while income and desired fertility are positively related. Further, author holds that conformance of business cycle with cyclical fluctuations in birth rate (a measurement for fertility rate) indicates correlation between economic status and fecundity.

Becker, Gary. <u>Human Capital</u>. New York: National Bureau of Economic Research, 1964.

(VI)

This book develops a general theory of investment in human capital. Education, on the job training, migration and health can be considered investments in human capital. Such investments tend to "raise observed earnings at older ages because returns are part of earnings then, and lower them at younger ages, because costs are deducted from earnings at that time." The net effect is to raise the life time earnings of individuals as well as raise national productivity as a whole. "Since these common effects are produced by very different kinds of investment in human capital, a basis is provided for a unified and comprehensive theory." Human capital theory helps explain the fact that substantial income growth remains after the growth in physical capital and labor have been accounted for.

Becker's theoretical analysis is supported by empirical evidence on rates of return to human capital investments covering a wide variety of groups and time periods. In particular, the effects of education on the shapes of age-earnings and age-wealth profiles are examined.

*Becker, Gary. "A Theory of Marriage." <u>Journal of Political Economy</u> 82 (March/April 1974): 511-526.

(IV)

In a two-part series Becker presents an analysis of the "marriage market." Using a simplified model of marriage which is based on the assumptions that each person attempts to find another mate who maximizes their well-being and that the "marriage market" is in the state of equilibrium, Becker argues that the gain from marriage compared to remaining single has a positive relationship to income, differences in wages, and level of "nonmarket-productivity augmenting-variables" (e.g., education, or beauty). Findings include an explanation of why people who care for each other have a higher incidence of marrying each other than other similar types, an analysis of which marriages are most likely to terminate in separation or divorce, a description of how the inequality among men has a significant correlation to the incidence of polygamy and how the selection of mates over years has been along income lines.

Beckerman, Wilfred. International Comparisons of Real Incomes. Paris: Development Centre of the Organization for Economic Co-operation and Development, 1966.

(XI)

A state-of-the-art review of measuring and comparing real incomes across countries. Discusses difficulties of conversion by exchange rates of currency since these reflect equilibrium in foreign transactions rather than internal purchasing power; notes also that cross-national differences in tastes and felt "needs" affect the relationship between gross output and social welfare.

Surveys the major works which use national accounts concepts (including international price comparisons), and those based on non-monetary indicators attempting to proxy level-of-living. Proposes a new method--the "Modified Non-Monetary Indicator" Method-- choosing indicators that correlate highly with some national accounts aggregates, and using them for countries where national accounts data is inadequate.

Bedger, Jean E.; Gelperin, Abraham; and Jacobs, Eveline E. "Socio-economic Characteristics in Relation to Maternal and Child Health." Public Health Reports 81 (September 1966): 829-833.

(XI)

A study in Chicago and suburban Cook County sought to determine the causes of an increasing infant mortality rate. The study consisted of four phases: 1) Analysis of socioeconomic factors and their relationship to local health conditions, 2) interviews with agencies concerned with health problems, 3) collection of data on incidence and prevalence of illness and disability among infants, and 4) the proposed superimposition of services over needs. This study verified the supposition that socioeconomic status and infant mortality are inversely related. It was also seen that the number of premature births in lowest-income groups (per 1000) is twice that of the highest income, and the rate of illegitimate births in the lowest class is eight times that of the highest. Also, it was determined that non-white population and income were inversely related in Chicago. The authors conclude that there is a definite relationship between socioeconomic needs and health needs by area in Chicago and in suburban Cook County.

(Taken from Poverty and Health in the United States)

Behrens, Jean; and Smolensky, Eugene. "Alternative Definitions of Income Distribution." Institute for Research on Poverty Reprint Series 132 (1974).

(II)

Income redistribution is defined as the difference between some "primary" distribution and the distribution that actually prevails with government fiscal intervention. The four definitions of income redistribution discussed here differ only in their definitions of this primary state, called the counterfactual. Under the zero-government counterfactual the private sector distribution of income becomes the primary distribution, defining equals and unequals. Under the second counterfactual, benefit taxation -- where taxes paid by each individual equals benefits received -- is included in the primary distribution. Thus, government allocations, though not redistributions, are included. A variant of this definition excludes recipient benefits from transfers, since the beneficiaries are not taxed for their benefits. The taxpayers, on the other hand, are assumed to gain an offsetting benefit from granting the transfers. In the author's own definition, the primary distribution includes both government's allocative and its redistributive actions based on some optimal ability-to-pay basis. Under this last definition, redistribution is an unambiguous move away from the optimum.

Beilin, Harry. "The Pattern of Postponability and its Relation to Social Class Mobility." Journal of Social Psychology 44 (August 1956): 33-48.

(XI)

Discusses a theory of class values which suggests that a distinct pattern of postponement of current gratifications "differentiates the person in the lower socio-economic group who is potentially mobile from the one who will remain at appreciably the same level that characterized his youth."

Theory tested by administering an open-ended questionnaire to white, male graduating high school students with Otis IQ's of 110 or over. A topical autobiography was used to verify questionnaire responses.

Study concludes that modification and clarification of the hypothesis are necessary. Author suggests that postponement is an unconscious deferring process, not a conscious decision (as implicit in the original hypothesis). Further, pattern of behavior suggested by the original hypothesis exists essentially from the observer's frame of reference.

Bell, Carolyn Shaw. "Should Every Job Support a Family?" The Public Interest 40 (Summer 1975): 109-118.

(II)

"Income has two standards of measurement. One refers to an individual worker--the amount a job pays. The other refers to the household where the individual worker lives--the amount needed to provide that household with a given standard of living... ' Until we learn to disentangle these two kinds of measurement, we shall be unable to solve some serious problems of income distribution which confront us."

In today's economy, individual earnings can not be determined by looking at family needs. If we were to take the Bureau of Labor Statistics lower-level budget, which just covers the income needed to support a family of four, and if we were to assume a single wage earner for that family, we would need a minimum wage of $4.50--yet this would still fail to provide a decent living for this family. Moreover, no specific wage can be calculated that, when paid to individual earners, will provide the same standard of living to families of different sizes.

"A policy of promoting full employment, instead of merely reducing employment, has not been accepted because we cling to the notion that every job, and perhaps especially those created by the federal government, should pay enough to support a family." Yet in 1973, only two out of five families depended upon a single earner, and presently, of all women with children, 43% are in the labor force, and 33% of women with children under six years of age are working.

Bendavid, Avrom. Regional Economic Analysis for Practitioners. New York: Praeger Publishers, 1972.

(VI)

This text represents one of the first attempts to approach the techniques of regional analysis with an emphasis on the limited resources and data available in developing countries. Frequently researchers in these areas do not have access to computers and highly trained staffs. This book is therefore aimed at practitioners with some background in methods of regional analysis who have a need for more information on the practical application of various techniques under conditions of limited manpower, scarce data and limited financial resources.

The author begins with a general introduction to thinking in regional terms and progresses to a discussion of information gathering for the compilation of a standard data compendium. He provides several examples of alternative formats for organizing the data according to the needs of the practitioner. A detailed section on the organization and presentation of data is also included.

Techniques which are examined include social accounting and an analysis of flows both within a regional economy and between economies. Alternative measures of income are studied with respect to their strengths and deficiencies. The discussion then turns to an analysis of the flows between regions. Particular attention is paid to the difficulties of gathering data on flows when accurate record-keeping practices are not used.

Bendix, Reinhard, and Lipset, Seymour Martin, eds. Class, Status, and Power. New York: The Free Press, 1966.

(II,IX,XI)

A reader devoted to a comprehensive treatment of literature on social stratification. Historical, methodological, and comparative articles are emphasized which reflect the impact of historical change upon American sociological thinking. The 74 articles are divided into the following major areas:

1) Theories of Class Structure

2) Historical and Comparative Studies

3) Power and Status Relations

4) Differential Class Behavior

5) Social Mobility

6) Pending Issues.

Bentzel, Ragnar. "The Social Significance of Income Distribution Statistics." Review of Income and Wealth 16 (1970): 253-264.

(II)

"In both political discussions and scientific literature the income distribution has come to occupy a central position for the consideration of social welfare and economic equalization. It has been assumed that an individual's income reflects his consumption opportunities and therefore his standard of living or economic welfare. The thesis of this paper is, however, that there are reasons for being quite pessimistic about drawing meaningful conclusions from income distribution data. As illustrated by the use of Swedish data, the distribution of income gives an extremely incomplete picture of the distribution of consumption for a wide variety of definitional and statistical reasons. The distribution of consumption, furthermore, cannot be transformed into a corresponding distribution of welfare, since there is no well defined concept of welfare. The treatment of public consumption in empirical analysis of the distribution of welfare also raises problems. The paper closes with the presentation of the conceptual basis for an alternative to the traditional method of analyzing the distribution of income." This alternative studies income and consumption distributions from the welfare point of view, making welfare distribution the central emphasis or consideration.

(Partially taken from article)

Berg, Alan. "Priority of Nutrition in National Development." Nutrition Review 28 (August 1970): 199-203.

(XI)

A short essay on nutrition as a national development variable. Toward this purpose in the United States nutrition must shift from a welfare focus to a development focus. The correlation between nutrition and income is mentioned as not strong. Cases are cited where a modest increase in income will actually cause a decrease in nutrition. In these cases, as shown through examples in India, nutrition could be a better indicator for national development than income. The acceptance of nutrition as a national development variable in this country could only be gained through a high quality, well-funded and policy specific program, Berg contends.

Berger, Alan S., and Simon, William. "Black Families and the Moynihan Report: A Research Evaluation." Social Problems 22 (December 1974): 145-162.

(XI)

Article challenges the major conclusion of the Moynihan Report that the Black family socializes children very differently from the way that the white family socializes children, and these patterns produce anti-social behavior and lower levels of occupational attainment. Berger and Simon's study employs data collected from a random sample of the 14-18 year old population of Illinois and examines the joint effects of race, gender, social class, and family organization on a number of indicators of family interaction, antisocial behavior patterns, educational aspirations, and gender role conceptions. Few differences were found in the ways that families treat their children, and these differences were not concentrated in the lower class. Even in the lower-class broken family, there was no indication that Black families are dramatically different from white families. Thus, in terms of delinquency, educational expectations, perceptions of the education desired by the parents, self conceptions, and notions of appropriate gender role behavior of adults, the empirical evidence does not provide adequate support for the conclusions of the Moynihan Report.

Bergson, Abram. "A Note on Consumer's Surplus." Journal of Economic Literature 13 (March 1975): 38-44.

(III)

Consumer surplus theory as originally developed by Marshall assumed cardinally measureable utility. Hicks supplanted cardinality with ordinality of utility measurement, but "retained cardinally scaled metrics of consumer's surplus." Samuelson, in his Foundations of Economic Analysis, argued that economists should answer problems in welfare-economics in terms of the consumer's ordinal preference field (indifference map), instead of seeking cardinally scaled metrics of consumer surplus referring to the demand schedule for the product in question.

Bergson argues that, while ordinally scaled measures suffice for utility, in general, cardinality is needed when measuring consumer gains or losses. Nevertheless, "at least where the concern is with a single household or groups of households with similar tastes and incomes, a more accurate calculation might often be feasible by using the procedure urged by Samuelson: that is, by reference to indifference maps."

*Bergstrom, Theodore C., and Goodman, Robert P. "Private Demands for Public Goods." American Economic Review 63(1973): 280-296.

(V,VI)

Private demand for public goods cannot be observed directly. By assuming that municipalities' actual choices reflect those of the consumer with the median income for this community, the authors estimate demand functions from observation of a large number of municipalities.

Renters apparently do not believe that they pay the entire property tax on their housing, so they are more inclined to vote for more public expenditure than are homeowners of the same income. Large public expenditures seem to be needed to attract commerce and industry.

It may be that once some critical city size is reached, city size becomes largely a matter of indifference from an efficiency viewpoint over a fairly large range of sizes. Some corroborating evidence is provided by the fact that in metropolitan areas, contiguous municipalities frequently differ substantially and seemingly arbitrarily in size.

Berman, Jules H. "The Means Test: Welfare Provisions of the 1965 Social Security Amendments." The Social Service Review 50 (No. 2, 1966).

(VII)

Predicts that the more liberal means test for medical services under Title XIX will result in liberalizing of means tests for other services. Deploring the severity and inflexibility of present eligibility criteria, the article discusses need for further liberalization of residence requirements, responsibility of relatives, assessment of income and resources, and administrative complexities in order to strengthen the process of giving aid by better meeting needs of people dependent on public assistance programs.

(Partially taken from Poverty and Human Resources Abstracts)

* Berry, Brian J. L., and Horton, Frank E. Geographical Perspectives on Urban Systems. Englewood Cliffs, New Jersey: Prentice-Hall, Inc., 1970.

(VI)

This textbook provides an introduction to the study of urban geography. It reviews and develops the study of cities within the framework of ideas provided by urban location theorists. Several issues are analyzed that are relevant to the comparison of cities: the distribution of city sizes, types of cities and their functions, and the hierarchical framework of interurban influence on non-urban or suburban areas and the comparison of regions. The authors discuss the theories and techniques of studying urban and regional growth: trade theory, location theory and export theory. They also examine the influence of cities on adjacent areas by looking at population, education, income, employment and other economic characteristics of regions in relation to their distances from urban centers. They find that median family income of an area drops and the percentage of families with incomes under the poverty line rises the farther the area is from a city.

Berry, R., and Soligo, R. "Rural-Urban Migration, Agricultural Output and the Supply Price of Labor in a Labor Surplus Economy." Oxford Economic Papers 20 (1968): 230-249.

(VI)

The economics of surplus labor studies the effect of transfers of labor from the traditional or agricultural sector to the modern or urban sector. A common characteristic of surplus labor models is that, due to the very low marginal product of labor, up to some extent, a transfer of labor away from the agricultural sector will not result in a fall in agricultural production. Another frequent feature of these models is that the modern sector faces a horizontal supply curve of labor. Berry and Soligo, using a simple one-good model of the agricultural sector, test these hypotheses for the case in which peasant proprietorship, sharecropping or fixed rentals predominate as the form of tenancy; and the case in which wage labor predominates. They find that in both cases, barring government intervention or changes in tastes, the two hypotheses will only be true if very specific and implausible assumptions are made about the worker's indifference map between work and leisure.

Berry, W.T.C. "Nutritional Surveillance in Affluent Nations." Nutrition Review 30 (June 1972): 127-131.

(XI)

A discussion of the issues of nutritional appraisal in affluent countries, using Britain's experiments as examples. Problems cited include the heavy reliance on nutritional education and the small degree of actual malnutrition in affluent countries, and the complexity of using the many criteria which are needed for nutritional study. Interaction between the economist and nutritionist is needed for national program and prediction purposes. Britain's nutrition system includes a family survey and a national food survey which records foods purchased and analyzes them for their nutritional and dietary value. Nutrition appraisal discussion centers around malnutrition of need and not malnutrition of excess. Also addresses some other nutrition-related measures, such as morbidity rates, infant mortality, and child growth rates.

Bertrand, Alvin L. "Symposium: Views on American Poverty: II--Poverty as Relative Deprivation: A Sociological View." Journal of Human Relations 15 (1967): 155-158.

(II)

The sharp focus in recent years on the underprivileged is noted. It is stated that a sociological definition of poverty should be oriented to what has been designated as relative deprivation, where deprivation is a state of mind. Poverty is then defined as "having too little of what is considered to be the basic necessities of life within our society." This approach is discussed in its relativeness, and the arbitrary measure of poverty used by the Government is considered. Some facts on poverty are pointed out: (1) it is with us all the time and is thus often taken for granted; (2) all agree that it is evil, but there is no consensus as to who the enemy is. At times, the poor themselves are blamed for their condition; (3) its victims are seldom as concerned over their plight as are individuals who are not poverty-striken. Several reasons for the great concern over poverty are suggested: it is related to national growth and progress; it is a causal factor in other problems (crime, juvenile delinquency, unemployment, etc.); we want to assuage our national conscience; we wish to maintain a world image of affluence. It is concluded that a vigorous program must be designed which would present the outside world to the poor in a more realistic fashion.

(Partially taken from Sociological Abstracts)

Billingsley, Andrew. "Black Family Structure: Myths and Realities." Studies in Public Welfare, U.S. Joint Economic Committee, Paper No. 12, Part II.

(XI)

Attempts to dispel three myths about black family structure. The paper contends that, contrary to popular belief that black families are largely broken families, the overwhelming majority are two-parent families. Further, the majority of families with a female head perform the child-rearing functions well. Lastly, the author contends that the conventional categorization of families as either one-parent or two-parent is too simplistic; black households display a large variety of family compositions.

Birch, David, and Saenger, Eugene. "The Poor in Massachusetts." In The State and the Poor, edited by Samuel Beer and Richard Barringer. Cambridge: Winthrop Publishers, Inc., 1970.

(II)

This article describes the poor in Massachusetts, employing both a relative as well as an absolute concept of poverty. According to a relative scale, the poor are those who have the least opportunity, i.e., those families in the lowest 20% of income. The authors cite problems raised by the relative approach: (1) the definition may include people who are not severely deprived; and (2) regardless of the success of anti-poverty efforts, 20% of the population will remain "poor." The absolute scale establishes a fixed cut-off point for income, below which a family is defined as poor. Using both types of definitions, the article examines the social and demographic characteristics of the poor in Massachusetts.

Bird, Alan B., and McCoy, John L. "White Americans in Rural Poverty." Agricultural Economics Report No. 124, U.S. Department of Agriculture. Washington, D.C.: U.S. Government Printing Office, November 1967.

(III, VI)

Bird delineates the special problems faced by poor whites living in rural areas:

- lack of education
- lack of marketable skills
- isolation
- lack of organization
- relative anonymity.

He contends that many of the federally funded programs designed to aid the poor do not reach this segment because:

1) antipoverty programs tend to be identified as programs for Blacks, and
2) arbitrary income definitions of poverty exclude many who are just above the poverty guideline, but who need aid.

Bird suggests many methods of remediation:

1) national programs for income and employment opportunities,
2) eradication of the belief that poverty programs are primarily for Blacks, and
3) better education and training programs for children.

Bird, Ronald. Inadequate Housing and Poverty Status of Households. Statistical Bulletin No. 520. Washington, D.C.: U.S. Department of Agriculture, Rural Development Service, 1973.

(V)

A study of inadequate housing and the poverty status of households in areas served by the Farmers Home Administration (FmHA) programs. The study area included rural areas and places with 2,500 to 10,000 population located outside urbanized areas. Poverty levels used were those developed by the Bureau of the Census for the 1970 Census.

The objectives of this study were to determine (by race for each state for areas served by FHA housing programs): (1) how many rural households are living in poverty, (2) how many households living in poverty reside in inadequate housing, and (3) how many households not living in poverty are residing in inadequate housing.

(Partially taken from the study)

Bird, Ronald; Beverly, Lucia; and Simmons, Anne. Status of Rural Housing in the United States. Washington, D.C.: U.S. Department of Agriculture, Economic Research Service, 1968.

(V)

An analysis of rural housing conditions in the United States, based on 1960 Census data. Rural housing has improved considerably since 1960, but the condition of housing occupied by the rural poor may not have improved very much. It is estimated that from 1960 to 1966 there were 3.7 million rural homes built and about 15.6 million rural homes repaired. However, over 95 percent of the homes built were constructed by families with incomes over $6,000 a year. Also, most of the repairs were of a minor nature and made to standard homes. It is estimated that less than 150,000 rural homes that lacked plumbing in 1960 had complete plumbing added between 1960 and 1966.

Only 10 percent of the new homes built in rural areas from 1960 to 1966 were constructed as a result of a direct or insured loan made by a federal agency or a federal land bank. Only about 6 percent of the home repairs were financed with the help of a federal agency. Perhaps most significant was the finding that nearly two-thirds of the occupants of substandard housing in rural areas in 1960 had family incomes of less than $3,000 a year.

(Partially taken from the study)

*Bird, Ronald, and Perciful, Julia B. Housing Conditions in Areas Served by Farmers Home Administration Housing Programs, 1970. By States. Washington, D.C.: U.S. Department of Agriculture Economic Research Service, 1972.

(V)

An analysis of housing conditions in areas served by the Farmers Home Administration using the 1970 Census data. In the past decade housing in areas served by the Farmers Home Administration (FmHA) improved about as much as in more urbanized areas, as shown by analyses of selected housing data. Nonetheless, FmHA areas contained a high percentage of the nation's inadequate housing. FmHA areas contained only 32 percent of the nation's occupied units in 1970. Included in that 32 percent, however, were 68 percent of the nation's occupied units which lacked complete plumbing and 38 percent of the nation's crowded units. Of those units which lacked complete plumbing or were crowded, or both, 48 percent were in FmHA areas. Of Black housing which lacked complete plumbing, 68 percent was in FmHA areas.

(Taken from the study)

Bish, Robert L. The Public Economy of Metropolitan Areas. Chicago: Markham, 1971.

(II,VI)

Bish derives a theoretical structure for the analysis of metropolitan municipal structures. He finds no a priori grounds for the allegation that suburban commuters "exploit" the central cities, since commuters add to the urban tax base through their purchases there. Since tastes vary, different kinds and levels of public services should be provided in different municipalities to achieve allocative efficiency. Redistribution is another issue, but is apparently favored by voters. It would be best achieved through a program of national negative income taxation.

*Blanco, Cicely. "The Determinants of Interstate Population Movements." Journal of Regional Science 5(Summer 1963): 77-84.

(VI,X)

Availability of jobs is the principle factor which determines the direction and amount of interstate migration. A study done at the Netherlands Economic Institute demonstrates that 86% of the variation in the rate of civilian migration between states from

1950-1957 can be explained by two factors: change in the level of unemployment in areas (85%), and changes in the number of federal and military personnel in each state (1%). A series of multiple correlation analyses is done on factors such as unemployment levels and changes, wage rates, geographic distances, level of education, climate, racial prejudice, and changes in location of military personnel. Regional differences in racial prejudice, education, wage levels and climate do not appear to have any direct significance. Reducing unemployment differences may not be a suitable strategy for achieving a greater equality of regional per capita income.

*Blau, Peter M., and Duncan, Otis Dudley. The American Occupational Structure. New York: John Wiley and Sons, 1967.

(VI,IX)

An analysis of the American occupational structure and patterns of intergenerational mobility. Blacks are found to be handicapped by having poorer parents, less education and inferior early career experiences than whites, yet these factors do not account for the total gap in occupational status. Investment in education does not pay off well for Blacks. The handicap of southerners is largely produced by inadequate occupational preparation, while the somewhat superior performance of white ethnic groups probably rests on selective experience and motivation. Migrants from farm to city achieve higher occupational status than those remaining on the farm, but do not achieve a status as high as the city-born. The large family is not conducive to occupational success. Those from broken families have lower educational levels and hence lower occupational status.

Rural migrants to cities have replaced immigrants as catalysts to upward mobility. Technological advances free labor for white-collar work. The U.S. rate of upward mobility remains high.

Blendon, R.J., and Gaus, Clifton R. "Problems in Developing Health Services in Poverty Areas: The Johns Hopkins Experience." Journal of Medical Education 46(June 1971): 477-484.

(V)

Describes problems encountered by Johns Hopkins Medical Institution in attempting to establish a model prepaid group medical practice in a low-income area of Baltimore. Financial support was needed for capitalization payments, developmental expenditures, and facilities renovation and construction. In seeking government funding sources to meet these needs, the East Baltimore Medical Plan was confronted with fragmented government programs and inconsistent administrative policies. The most serious difficulties generated by fragmentation were variations in eligibility criteria and benefit levels and diversity in the sources of administrative fiscal control. Compounding the problems associated with complexities in administrative control were conflicting agency aims and funding commitments.

The article affords a close look at existing limitations on public medical care and is, therefore, pertinent to a study of quality and level of service provided.

Blevins, Audie L., Jr. "Migration Rates in Twelve Southern Metropolitan Areas: A "Push-Pull" Analysis." Social Science Quarterly 50(1969): 337-353.

(VI)

Twelve Southern Standard Metropolitan Statistical Areas (SMSA) are analyzed to determine why some metropolitan areas gain more migrants than others. The census survival rate method is used, with age, sex and racial factors examined, in an attempt to test the "push-pull" theory of migration. (SMSA's with high income levels and a large percentage of the labor force working tend to have high in-migrant rates, while SMSA's without these characteristics tend to have high out-migrant rates.) No specific trend is found for any of the migration differentials (age, sex, race, and education), although net migration by educational grouping is found selective in the extremes (greater than 11 or less than 5 years of school completed). Generally, occupational variables are found to have more influence on migration than do either median income, length of employment, or percentage of working force employed. Non-white migrants are more responsive to economic and occupational variables, while white migrants are more responsive to social variables. Both regression and statistical analyses support the "push-pull" theory.

Blevins, A.L. "Socioeconomic Differences Between Migrants and Non-migrants." Rural Sociology 36 (1971): 509-520.

(VI)

One hundred forty-four rural residents and 144 rural-to-urban migrants were matched on age, education, and rural background. The sample included Anglos, Mexican Americans, and Negroes. It was found that urban migrants surpassed rural nonmigrants on all measures of financial well-being (for example, migrants' incomes were double those of non-migrants). On the basis of these findings, it is suggested that urban planners as well as politicians should be cognizant of the gains made by poor migrants upon moving to an urban area, and that no restrictions should be placed on such migration because of its potential for improving the financial condition of migrants.

(Taken from the article)

Blinder, Alan. "A Micro Simulation Model of the Size Distribution of Income." Journal of Economics and Business 27(November 1974): 1-10.

(II)

An attempt at constructing a total model of size distribution of both income and wealth is presented in this article. Initially a unified framework for an economic theory of size distribution is presented in its embryonic form. Next, a highly simplistic "life cycle" model of household behavior is laid out. This provides the main base for the rest of the simulation model. In order to replicate the actual income distribution in the United States, potential wage was based on a sample of 25-29 year olds; inherited wealth was derived from inheritance data for the cohort between 55 and 64; and differences in tastes were based on elasticities of time pressures and leisure preferences, and bequests. The simulation was conducted on 400 individuals under three makeshift economies: equalitarian, inequality of economy, stratified society. The results showed that the distributions of income in the stratified South is much less equal, that the negative income effect of the lump sum tax on work effort explains the unimportance of inequality of opportunity on overall inequality, and that the dispersion of wages is the single most important cause of income inequality.

Blinder, Alan. "The Economics of Brushing Teeth." Journal of Political Economy 82 (July/August 1974): 887-891.

(IV)

A description of a new economic model of human behavior is introduced and tested. Blinder presents a "mother told me so" theory, which is rooted in the assumption that the mother's decision concerning her instructions to her child on the frequency of brushing teeth is governed by income maximization for the child. He then develops a more sophisticated equation derived from this human capital hypothesis. The basic thrust of this derivation is that the ratio of brushing to nonbrushing time is equated to the partial elasticity of the wage with respect to brushing time. The model is tested using a cross-section study of Americans conducted by the Fuller Brush Institute. Results indicated a high correlation between people in jobs in which wages are highly sensitive to brushing and people who devote more time to brushing. Blinder hopes that his study will inspire a renewed interest in these types of questions by economists.

* Blum, Zahava D., and Rossi, Peter H. "Appendix: Social Class Research and Images of the Poor: A Bibliographic Review." In On Understanding Poverty, edited by Daniel P. Moynihan. New York: Basic Books, Inc., 1968.

(II,XI)

A literature review of the articles contained in On Understanding Poverty (referenced elsewhere). In addition, it includes a discussion of the types of poor, for example "respectable" vs. "disrespectable" or the "happenstance" poor vs. the "chronic" poor. The authors arrive at a broad definition of the poor--those with low income who cannot attain the minimum level of living and who pose problems to society at large. Methods and criteria used in the Moynihan book in evaluating and defining poverty are reviewed. Areas explored include: community organization and participation, mortality and medical services, delinquency, family behavior, parental practices, achievement and aspiration levels, personality adjustments, intellectual performance and linguistic behavior, and values and ideology (societal evaluations).

Blumberg, Leonard, and Bell, Robert A. "Urban Migration and Kinship Ties." Social Problems 6(1959): 328-333.

(VI)

Data on Negro migrants into Philadelphia is used to discuss the theme, "Family and kinship are more important for some population elements in (the) urban community than for others, and hence the dysfunctional rural-to-urban 'adjustment' analysis may be limited in its application."

Family, kin, and close friendships have much deeper personal roots for migrants into the urban community than might have been anticipated. This seems to be true for all migrants, both recent and past, and both Black and white migrants. However, if the migrant achieves vertical social mobility, an element in the mobility achievement is to modify, if not drop, many of his old family ties. This estrangement is facilitated when vertical social mobility is accompanied by migration. The class-mobile, middle-class migrant breaks kinship ties. The lower-class migrant, especially from the rural South, strives to reinforce them, or to create pseudo-kin relationships.

(Annotation taken partially from Mangalam, J.J. Human Migration: A Guide to Migration Literature in English, 1955-1962. Lexington: University of Kentucky Press, 1968)

*Blumen, I.; Kogan, M; and McCarthy, Phillip. The Industrial Mobility of Labor as a Probability Process. Ithaca, New York: Cornell University, 1955.

(IX)

This paper analyzes the possibility of finding a probability model that will describe the movement of workers through the U.S. industrial structure. The study uses Social Security data, specifically, the Continuous Work History Sample of the Bureau of Old-Age and Survivors Insurance. Several models are examined, including models of short term movement and a simple probability model that analyzes the question, "If one takes all workers in a given industry at a specific point in time, what can be said about their industry locations two or three years later and what can be said about their interindustry movement between these two points in time?" It was found that the most accurate models were models that take into account continuity of employment and a worker's attachment to an industry as well as other aspects of the worker's personal history. In all the models, age and sex were found to be important variables.

Bodsworth, Fred. "What Happens to Family Allowances?" Maclean's Magazine 67 (December 1, 1954).

(IV)

A report on the status of Canada's family allowance system or the "baby bonus," to which it is popularly referred, after its tenth year in existence. Family vignettes highlight characteristics of the program; government officials offer comments on the merits and detractions of the program thus far. A history of family allowance legislation provides a context for comparison.

Questions by the program's skeptics are explored: "Have ten years of family allowances proved them to be the commendable and enlightened legislation their creators foresaw? Or do they constitute a grandiose economic monstrosity that lends itself to waste and fraud? How are they administered and how much does it cost? Do you know whether you yourself win or lose in the income-tax family allowance seesaw?"

The author concludes that the program will remain a permanent fixture as a poverty-reducing measure.

Boek, Walter E.; Sussman, Marvin B.; and Yankauer, Alfred. "Social Class and Child Care Practices." Marriage and Family Living 20 (1958): 326-333.

(XI)

An analysis of some child care practices as associated with social class. Data is based on part of a 1955-56 project of larger scope sponsored by the New York State Department of Health. The Warner Index of Status Characteristics, recognizing five classes--I, II, III, IV, and V from upper to lower--was utilized, and 1,433 upstate New York families were interviewed. The authors note class differences in family planning, feeding practices, literature use, and mother's occupational and educational aspirations for the child.

Bogue, Donald J. "Internal Migration." In The Study of Population, edited by Philip M. Hauser and Otis Dudley Duncan. Chicago: University of Chicago Press, 1959.

(VI)

This chapter of The Study of Population was funded by the Rockefeller Foundation and summarizes some methodological lessons of migration research which were acquired as a part of a long-range program of research in population distribution. Issues are dealt with in a very general way and include: the problem of defining internal migration, definitions of concepts and terms, methods of measuring migration, and a broad summary of existing knowledge on migration and migration streams. Some basic economic equations of migration are presented, and the strengths and weaknesses of some economic generalizations concerning migration are dealt with in a general way.

Bogue, Donald J., and Beale, Calvin L. "Recent Population Trends in the United States and Their Causes." In <u>Our Changing Rural Society: Perspectives and Trends</u>, edited by James H. Copp. Ames, Iowa: Iowa State University Press, 1964.

(VI)

Population changes affect the country's economic, political, and social life and must be considered by policy analysts in their plans for future developments. Using data from the 1960 Census of Population and other sources, the authors review, with particular attention to rural areas, significant shifts between 1950 and 1960 in population growth, distribution, and composition, as well as causative factors. Though dramatic, these shifts must be viewed within the context of cumulative effects over decades and not as isolated phenomena.

Distributive trends are discussed by category, among which are regional, metropolitan-nonmetropolitan, rural-urban, and county by population size. Socio-economic and demographic characteristics provide a framework for presenting composition trends. Causes of these shifts are attributed to numerous patterns and developments in our society relating, for example, to migration, business, and education.

Changes in the basic demography of the population have occurred rapidly, and their implications are far reaching.

Bogue, Donald J., and Hagood, Margaret. "Differential Migration in the Corn and Cotton Belts." <u>Scripps Foundation for Research in Population Problems</u> 6(1953): 1-127.

(V,VI)

This monograph summarizes the results of special experimental tabulations which were made from 1940 census materials in an effort to evaluate differential migration statistics in the United States, their costs and the special technical problems arising from their use. The non-metropolitan portion of the Corn Belt and the old Corn Belt were selected as the two loci of the study based on the fact that they were such different areas. By cross tabulating the variables which were hypothesized to influence migration, the authors were able to arrive at nine generalizations about migration. Among these are that internal migration is selective of persons with particular combinations of traits, that migration can be highly selective with respect to a given characteristic in one area and mildly selective in another area, migrants who leave prosperous agricultural communities with good schools have no problem adjusting to city life, and that factors other than economic opportunity underlie the movement of population.

Booth, Charles. Labour and the Life of the People. (Second Series, Vol. 2) New York: AMS Press, Inc., 1970.

(II,III,IV)

Written in 1902, this study starts with a definition of the poor as "those whose earnings are small because of irregularity of employment and those whose work, though regular, is ill-paid. They are further defined as those whose means are barely sufficient for decent independent life." Interviews and 1891 census data for the city of London are then used to determine what income and housing conditions correlated with this definition. An income of 18 to 21 shillings per week for a "moderate sized family" is set as the minimum income upon which a thrifty family can decently exist. When housing is used as a measure of poverty, Booth concludes that two or more persons per room in a dwelling is crowded and therefore presumably poor. Three or more persons per room is counted as very poor. While it is admitted that there are limitations upon this measure, on an average it seems to provide a reasonably fair measure of poverty. There is also a very good correlation between occupation and standard of living.

*Borcherding, Thomas E., and Deacon, Robert T. "The Demand for the Services of Non-Federal Governments." American Economic Review 62(1972): 891-901.

(V)

The authors develop a general model of the demand for public goods with its theoretical basis in the theory of collective decision-making. Quality variations were handled by assuming the quality of labor in the service sector to be directly proportional to the quality of labor in manufacturing. Furthermore, since the outputs, the capital and the firms in that latter sector are all very mobile, the observed differences in wages reflect quality differences alone.

The total land area and the degree of urbanization of a city had little effect on demand for public goods which was largely accounted for by the traditional demand function arguments of cost and income.

Boshia, Michael J. "The Negative Income Tax and the Supply of Work Effort." National Tax Journal 20(December 1967): 353-367.

(II)

This article provides a number of theoretical reasons why a negative income tax (NIT) might not affect work effort and attempts to empirically measure a maximum work incentive effect among poor urban Negroes. The standard analysis of the NIT rests on two assumptions the author finds dubious. First, that the poor are on their labor supply curve (have as much work as they want), and second, that their wages will not change if the negative income tax is put into effect. His objection to the first assumption rests on his empirical results; many of the poor do want to work more than they actually do. His objection to the second rests on the dynamic effects of higher income; it may result in better health and education, allowing the poor worker to work longer hours or obtain a higher paying job.

The empirical work is based on a small (109-person) sample of individuals living in the West Oakland ghetto. Less than 12% of those working indicated that an increased outside income (from the negative income tax) would induce them to reduce their hours worked. This is an upper limit. The total reduction in work effort came to less than 8%, again an upper limit. Thus, a negative income tax will not, according to the author, cause a large reduction in work effort.

Boulding, Kenneth. "Reflections on Poverty." The Social Welfare Forum, 1961. Proceedings of the National Conference on Social Welfare. New York: Columbia University Press, 1961.

(II)

Boulding feels that chronic poverty is the product of subcultural systems. Redistributive transfer payments would not eliminate poverty in Boulding's sense; they might even extend the mendicant class. Police and social workers may be part of a system which perpetuates the underclass. Boulding's definition excludes those who have low incomes due to personal misfortune, and centers around members of poor societies.

Boulding, Kenneth E. "Social Justice in Social Dynamics." In Social Justice, edited by Richard B. Brandt. Englewood Cliffs, New Jersey: Prentice Hall, Inc., 1962.

(II)

An examination of social justice, or peoples' concepts of social justice, in terms of its role in determining the dynamic processes and evolution of a society. According to Boulding, society changes because people become discontent when there is a disparity between some ideal or vision of what society should be and the reality of what society actually is. Poverty is discussed mainly in terms of its role in causing discontent. One important point is that the very poor are too concerned with survival to show discontent, while the above subsistence level poor may show a great deal of discontent; hence, peoples'concepts of how badly off they are is not proportionate to how poor they actually are. Also important is the point that economic inequality is seen not as a problem of distribution but rather of relative growth. Therefore, inequality should not be solved by redistributing wealth but by making the poor more productive. No definition of poverty is explicitly offered, but Boulding clearly thinks in terms of relative income levels.

Bowen, William G., and Finegan, T.A. "Labor Force Participation and Unemployment." In Employment Policy and the Labor Market, edited by Arthur M. Ross. Los Angeles: University of California Press, 1965.

(X)

This essay presents the findings of a study, the objectives of which were to estimate the effects of differences in local labor market conditions (as determined by the overall unemployment rate) on the labor force participation rates of various subsets of the population, to see whether this relationship has changed over time, and to note the effects on labor force participation of factors such as educational attainment, other non-labor income, color, etc. The major substantive conclusion of the study is that "to the extent that high unemployment has induced some additional family members to enter the labor force, this tendency has been more than offset by the negative effect of high unemployment on labor force participation." Whereas in 1940 an unemployment rate of one percent above average for a city was associated with an overall labor force participation rate of about .75 percent below average. Factors such as educational attainment, enrollment in school, and father's income also showed changes in their effect on labor force participation over time. Cross-sectional analysis and single equation multiple-regression techniques are used, and the study uses supply and demand variables in an original way.

Bowles, Gladys K. "Strengths, Limitations, and Uses of the Surveys of Economic Opportunity as Sources of Data for the Study of Rural Poverty on Labor Markets." Presented to the Conference on Rural Labor Markets, Austin, Texas, October 30, 1970.

(VI)

The 1966 and 1967 Surveys of Economic Opportunity (SEO) conducted by the Bureau of the Census, covering income, assets, liabilities and other economic information, "were designed so that estimates of the poor would have a higher reliability than those obtained from the regular Current Population Surveys (CPS)." The SEO surveys were found to be most useful for several reasons: (1) "they are large samples from which population parameters can be measured;" (2) new analytical categories can be obtained from the data; (3) the SEO contains data not available elsewhere; and (4) SEO's are relatively inexpensive. Although the surveys are not without errors and inconsistencies, overall they are accurate and useful.

*Bowles, Gladys K.; Bacon, A. Lloyd; and Ritchey, P. Neal. Poverty Dimensions of Rural-Urban Migration: A Statistical Report. Washington, D.C.: U.S. Government Printing Office, 1973.

(VI)

A collection of statistics drawn from the 1967 Survey of Economic Opportunity concerning questions of poverty associated with rural to urban migration. The report presents information on the total of poor households, families and populations; the migration status and regional and environmental residence history of urban and rural populations; poverty characteristics of employment in various industries; and personal characteristics of migrants as compared with the characteristics of their urban hosts and of people remaining in rural areas. These characteristics include education, marital status, fertility, health, receipt of public assistance, employment, occupation, assets, liabilities, and net worth.

Bowles, Samuel. "Migration as Investment: Empirical Tests of the Human Investment Approach to Geographical Mobility." Review of Economics and Statistics 52 (1970): 356-62.

(VI)

This article presents a simple model of migration as "a response to economic incentives arising from disequilibria across spacially separated labor markets." The model is tested empirically using data on net migration out of the U.S. South. "The results suggest that the present value of the expected income gain from moving out of the South is positively related to the probability of moving and provides a better explanation of migration than the more convential measure based on regional differences in current incomes. Further, the level of schooling appears to increase the effect of income gain on the probability of moving." This suggests that people with more education adapt more successfully to economic disequilibria. Age appears to reduce the effect of income gain on the probability of moving. "Blacks appear to be less responsive to the income gain from moving than whites. This finding is consistent with the notion that the stability of an unequal income distribution may be explained in part by socially generated attitudes--risk aversion and high rates of time preference, for example--which inhibit Blacks from taking advantage of those avenues for higher incomes, such as education and geographical mobility, ordinarily used by whites from upper and middle income backgrounds."

Bowles, Samuel, and Nelson, Valerie I. "The 'Inheritance of IQ' and the Intergenerational Reproduction of Economic Inequality." Review of Economics and Statistics 56 (February 1974): 39-51.

(IX)

If the heritability of IQ is used as a mechanism to explain the transmission of economic status from one generation to the next, then first of all, IQ, as measured on standard intelligence tests, must be highly heritable; and secondly, IQ must be a major determinant of income or occupational status. This article examines the latter requirement. Occupational status, schooling, and income are the three measures of intergenerational status employed. The childhood IQ of an individual is determined by a combination of "genotypic IQ" and "socio-economic background" of the parents. The model consists of a set of four recursive equations, and the correlation between the status measures and the socio-economic background of the parents is decomposed into a genetic inheritance portion and a portion due to other mechanisms. A 1962 Current Population Survey provided the data for a cross-section of age groups. Childhood IQ is found to have a substantial influence on years of schooling and considerably less direct effect on income and occupational status. The IQ influence on these latter two measures is largely indirect and occurs via years of schooling. The authors conclude that, "Genetic inheritance of IQ is a relatively minor mechanism for the inter-generational transmission of social and economic status...If childhood IQ were totally unimportant in the process of intergenerational status transmission, the degree of intergenerational immobility (as measured by the intergenerational status correlations) would be lowered by, at most, 13%."

Brackett, Jean. "New BLS Budgets Provide Yardsticks for Measuring Family Living Costs." Monthly Labor Review 92 (April 1969): 3-16.

(III,IV,V,VI)

Newly implemented procedures for determining standard budgets include separate estimates of dollar expenditures for low, moderate and high income levels, and special indices that measure comparative living costs for family types and geographical variations. Brackett highlights the new indices for comparing living costs. Within each region, intercity indices reflect variation among areas in price levels, regional differences in quantities and kinds of items needed to provide the specified standard of living, and fluctuations in state and local taxes. She also explores the criteria for the lower, moderate, and high level budgets. Lower budget figures are based on U.S. Department of Agriculture (USDA) low-cost food plan for the consumption index, rental housing cost for the shelter index, replacement rates for clothing costs, and estimated medical and transportation costs. Brackett contends that the new lower budget level does not attempt to measure the cut-off point between those with enough versus those with insufficient income, but rather provides a more realistic figure for those working with the problems of inadequate income.

Brackett, Jean. "Urban Family Budgets Updated to Autumn, 1972." Monthly Labor Review 96 (August 1973): 70-77.

(III,IV,VI)

A statistical report of the Bureau of Labor Statistics' three hypothetical budgets for a precisely defined family of four in 1972. Budgets reflect three levels of living based on estimates of costs for specified types and amounts of goods and services rather than actual expenditures by families. Estimated budgets are $7,386 at the lower level; $11,446 at the intermediate level; $16,558 at the higher level.

Price changes between 1971 and 1972, as reported in the Consumer Price Index, are applied to the 1971 budget for each main class of goods and services. Area indices reflect differential area price levels as well as regional variations in consumption patterns, differences in climate, and types of transportation and taxes.

Bradford, David F., and Kelijian, Harry H. "An Econometric Model of Flight to the Suburbs." Journal of Political Economy 81 (1973): 566-590.

(VI)

This paper analyzes the movements of the middle-class and the poor from the city to the suburbs using econometric techniques. The authors find that the likelihood a middle-class family of given income will reside in the suburbs increases as the percentage of poor families living in the central cities 10 years earlier decreases, and as the fiscal surplus generated for middle-class families by the central-city public budget decreases. The likelihood that a poor family will live in the suburbs increases as the proportion of old housing increases, as the proportion of central city old housing decreases, and as the fiscal surplus for poor families in the central city decreases. The racial composition of the central city does not appear to affect these choices once other variables have been accounted for. Policy implications are that income redistribution within the central city will be self-defeating, causing only more polarization, but that reductions in poverty that do not change the distribution of income would substantially increase the numbers of middle-class families choosing to remain in the city. The authors assume that a dollar of city government expenditure yields an equal benefit to all families on average.

*Brady, Dorothy. "Family Budgets: A Historical Survey." In Monthly Labor Review, 1948.

(II,IV,VI)

This historical survey begins with Aristotle's observation that social satisfaction does not rest on material needs alone and proceeds through the inception of statistical studies of family living in the nineteenth century to the study by the Commissioner of Labor in 1907 of living conditions, the cost of a "fair standard of living," and the cost of a "minimum standard of living." The latter studies were the first budgets in this country expressed in quantities of goods and services to which prices were applied to determine the total cost of the budget. The depression decade, which might have been the impetus for conceptual and administrative advances in this area, instead excused the use of inadequate budget estimates, which failed to account for variations in the cost of goods and services from place to place.

Brady, Dorothy S. "Individual Incomes and the Structure of Consumer Units." American Economic Review 48 (May 1958): 269-278.

(VII)

The relationship between income and family size is discussed. If the scale of requirements is relatively invariant, then larger families will be cheaper on a per-capita basis than smaller ones. Many individuals may not have enough income to live independently, but do earn more than their incremental cost to a family. If these individuals join an already existing family unit, both will be better off. This is the economic justification of "doubling-up". One form of doubling-up will occur whenever parental income is below a certain level (above which they can support independent children) and their children's income is below another level (above which they could support independent parents). As incomes increase (either because of business cycle changes or because of the increased earnings of children as they grow older), 'undoubling' will occur. These changes in family composition must be taken into account for realistic policy decisions involving the poor.

Brady, Dorothy S. "Measurement and Interpretation of the Income Distribution of the U.S." Income and Wealth Series VI. London, 1957.

(VII)

A consideration of some of the methodological problems involved in the study of income. The concept of the family and of normal, as opposed to temporary, income changes over time invalidates time series comparisons. The income provided by a working wife causes problems when it allows low income couples to live independently. The relative cost of living makes comparisons among different income groups, different geographical areas, and different temporal periods difficult and perhaps misleading. The problem of transitory income receives the majority of attention. The use of social and economic characteristic groups, occupational groups, and the study of stable income groups are all examined as means of dealing with this problem.

Brady, Dorothy S. "Research on the Size Distribution of Income." Studies on Income and Wealth 13 (1951): 3-60.

(VI,VII)

A discussion of the methodological problems involved in calculating the size distribution of income. Among the problems discussed:

1. The Recipient Unit: long-run social and demographic changes alter the nature of the 'economic family' making time series and international comparisons difficult.

2. Income: 12-month period too short because of transitory components. Solutions include:

   a. group averages for homogeneous groups
   b. some notion of expenditures
   c. average over larger time--but watch for family formation and dissolution
   d. change the income definition to best fit what you are interested in: use only stable income for constant expenditures; use a broad definition of income for variable expenses and welfare.

3. Price Level: income differences frequently reflect geographic price level differences and differences in needs. Climactic and non-money factors must be standardized.

Bramhall, David F., and Bryce, Harrington L. "Interstate Migration and Labor-Force Age Population." Industrial and Labor Relations Review 22(1969): 576-583.

(VI)

Interstate migration is an important phenomenon in the United States, with significant effects for individual states in terms of population growth and economic development. This article examines factors associated with the migration of population of working age, the largest component of such migration. It finds that migration from a state is closely linked to the relative size of different age groups within the population rather than to economic conditions. Immigration rates into states, on the other hand, are importantly determined by employment opportunities. Other findings are that the propensity of nonwhites of labor-force age to migrate is less than that of whites, and whites are generally more responsive to changes in employment opportunities among states than are nonwhites.

(From article)

Branch, Edna G. "Urban Family Budgets Updated to Autumn 1974." Monthly Labor Review (June 1975): 42.

(III,IV,VI)

A description of the Bureau of Labor Statistics' autumn 1974 updates of urban family budgets. The three hypothetical budgets for lower, intermediate, and higher level families of four were respectively $9,198, $14,333, and $20,777 per annum. The budgets were updated by applying Consumer Price Index regional price changes to the autumn 1973 cost for each main class of goods and services. The method of updating is approximate because the Consumer Price Index is based on spending patterns of urban wage earners without regard to family size, composition, and level of living. The last direct pricing was done in 1909. Food price increases had the greatest impact on the lower level families, because food comprises a greater portion of their total budget.

These budgets do not reflect minimum or subsistance level of living nor are they based on actual family expenditures. Rather they are based on estimates of costs of goods and services that are thought to be consumed by families of the three different levels. The budgets are for a precisely defined urban family of four consisting of a 38-year-old husband, employed for 15 years; a non-working wife; a boy of 13; and a girl of 8.

Differences in budgets across regions are also described. They are based on differentials in price levels, consumption patterns, climate, transportation facilities, and taxes. Budget costs were lowest in small cities in the South and highest in the Northeast, however these differences were smallest for the lower level budgets.

Brazer, Harvey. "Tax Policy and Children's Allowances." In Children's Allowances and the Economic Welfare of Children, edited by E.M. Burns. New York: Citizen's Committee for Children of New York, Inc., 1968.

(IV)

An examination of children's allowances and brief consideration of two alternatives designed to achieve the same goals--tax credit and the negative income tax.

The author devoted the major portion of the discussion to cost of the program and methods of reducing net costs by including the allowance as taxable income or by substituting the allowance for present income tax deductions for dependents. Brazer proposes that both these measures be applied and that tax-payers be required to add to their tax liabilities as otherwise computed an amount equal to a proportion of children's allowances received.

*Bremner, Robert H. <u>From the Depths: A Discovery of Poverty in the United States</u>. New York: New York University Press, 1956.

(II)

A history of social policy towards poverty in the United States. Traces changes in people's perceptions of the causes of poverty and the resulting actions taken to eliminate poverty.

Poverty initially became a concern in this country in the early 19th century. During this period, the problem was attributed primarily to immigration--hence the establishment of immigration laws. Later with the rise of industrialization and urbanization and the consequent birth of the urban slum, poverty was thought to be due to sloth and sinfulness. The cure was spiritual rehabilitation.

In the late 19th and early 20th century, the work of social workers and statisticians directed attention away from moral considerations and towards economic factors such as occupation and wages. Throughout the 19th century, the definition of the poor included only those who did not have enough money to survive. In the early 20th century, the definition was extended to those who had enough to survive but not enough to be secure. The major causes were believed to be accident, illness, premature death, old age, and unemployment.

Concern for poverty became most widespread in the country after the Depression. It was expressed in the form of a variety of programs designed to protect the income of the worker, the sick, and the aged.

Brennan, Michael J.; Taft, Philip; and Schupok, Mark B. <u>The Economics of Age</u>. New York: W. W. Nastaz and Company, Inc., 1967.

(IV,VI,X)

The number and proportion of older people in the American labor force have become progressively larger, though labor force participation by older people has declined. The attempt is made here to treat age as an economic variable. Three aspects of employment and earnings by age are investigated: industries, regions, and occupations. Labor demand and supply equations are estimated in order to distinguish age-related factors that operate across industries. "On the demand side of the labor market, declining productivity with advancing age, greater pension costs, and to a lesser extent, substitution of female workers lessen the demand for older males. On the supply side, increasing immobility with age prevents a proportionate rise in the income of old and young alike." Migration to new geographic regions offers smaller pecuniary returns to older persons and is complicated by such things as marital status and the individual's sense of his established place in the community. Thus regional and job immobility are in part responsible for the relatively low economic status of older workers which cannot be totally explained by changes in individual productivity, discrimination in hiring practices, and female substitution. Finally, occupation age-related patterns are explained. For example, the shift away from the agricultural and self-employed sectors is partly responsible for the declining participation rate of older people in the labor force. A concluding discussion on public policy centers on efforts to raise productivity rather than concentrating on more conventional relief and assistance programs.

*Bressler, Barry. "Income Distributions, Relative Poverty, and Family Size, 1947-71." Quarterly Review of Economics and Business 14 (Spring 1974): 27-37.

(II,IV)

"Income distributions are only meaningful when all families are standardized for differences in size." A procedure for making such an adjustment is suggested; and the consequences for measures of inequality, quintile shares, relative poverty, and income distribution trends are examined. The ratio of the estimated income needs (Orshansky) for a family of four to the estimated income need of every other size family is computed giving an adjustment factor for each family size. Comparisons between adjusted and unadjusted income distributions for selected years in the interval 1947 to 1971 indicate that Gini ratios are 2.4 to 10.9 percent higher for the adjusted distributions. However, the adjusted figures indicate a trend of greater reduction in equality during this period. Similarly the unadjusted figures overestimate the income share of the lowest fifth and underestimate that of the highest fifth, yet the adjusted figures imply a more rapid trend toward equalization since they show that the share of the lowest fifth increased by 17.8 percent as compared with a 10.4 rise indicated by the unadjusted figures. If a measure of relative poverty is employed, such as the number of families falling below half the median income, it is found that the unadjusted figures may either underestimate or overestimate the proportion in poverty as compared with the adjusted incomes (+10.9 to -7.2 percent differences), though the trends toward reduction in relative poverty are greater for the adjusted distributions. The adjusted data showed that the proportion of families with incomes below one-half the median was reduced by 23.5 percent compared with 11.5 percent based on unadjusted figures.

Bretzfelder, Robert B. "State and Regional Income, First Half 1974: Current-Dollar Income Rises, Real Income Decline." <u>Survey of Current Business</u> 54(October 1974): 17-18.

(VI)

A presentation of total state and regional personal income statistics from 1971-1974 and a brief analysis of the causes of income trends and their relative change in relation to price changes. In 1974 real income rose in only seven states. Price rises exceeded income gains in all nine census regions. Much of the interregional income variation can be traced directly to farming. Changes in farm income among agricultural states ranged from gains of 200 percent to losses of 80 percent. Manufacturing income changes ranged from gains of 10 percent to losses of 10 percent. Weakness was concentrated in states involved in auto manufacturing.

Briar, Scott. "Welfare From Below: Recipients' Views of the Welfare System." <u>California Law Review</u> 54(1966): 370-385.

(V)

This study evaluates the public welfare system in a county in California through direct interviews with recipients. Interviewers were matched ethnically with recipients, spending from three to seven hours with them, the better to obtain more sincere responses. The study found that recipients regarded welfare more as a charity than as the right that it is under California law. Each felt he deserved welfare but many felt others were "cheating" and should be caught by all available means. Recipients believe themselves at the mercy of an impersonal benevolent autocracy.

Bridges, Benjamin T. "Imputed Income From Owner Occupied Housing." Social Security Administration, Office of Research & Statistics. <u>Research and Statistics Note # 3,</u> January 1967.

(VII)

Several methods of imputing income from owner occupied buildings are discussed in this article. The incidence of two methods, both involving owners equity, are analyzed in depth. Other methods--rental on comparable housing less expenses, net savings in housing costs, and net return on a low-risk asset with the same value--are discussed peripherally. The two methods analyzed in depth are a constant rate of return on owners equity and an imputation based on a (higher) rate of return on the value of the building less an empirically determined interest rate on the outstanding mortgage. The two methods gave similar aggregate imputations, but the first gave larger imputed values to middle and higher income groups and to the young than did the second.

Bridges, Benjamin. "Net Worth of the Aged." Social Security Administration, Office of Research & Statistics. Research and Statistics Note #14, 1967.

(VII)

A comparison of the 1963 Federal Reserve Survey of Financial Characteristics of Consumers and the 1963 Social Security Administration Survey of the Aged Population. Differences in the definition of the two populations meant that an aged (65 or more years old) family member living with a non-aged head of household would be counted as an aged individual in the Social Security Administration (SSA) study but not in the Federal Reserve study. There were problems in the under reporting of assets in the SSA study that did not exist in the Federal Reserve study.

The two studies did tend to agree on the distribution of assets among the aged, though the low-income poor had fewer assets in the SSA study. A comparison of the two methods used to compute 'potential income' (income plus some fraction of assets) showed the Federal Reserve method, which involves a 4% imputation on the value of the home and a 5-year amortization period, caused a larger increase in 'income' than the SSA method which assumed that all assets except the home earned 4% and were amortized over the individual's actuarial lifetime. This last method is more useful for policy purposes, since the liquidation of the home causes drastic lifestyle changes.

Brimmer, Andrew F. "Inflation and Income Distribution in The United States." Review of Economics and Statistics (1971): 37-48.

(III)

Between 1961 and 1965, the U.S. economy experienced a period of rising real output and relatively stable prices, whereas, by 1969, the rise in the Gross National Product represented primarily price increases and very little growth in output. Basically, this inflation occurred at a time when the economy was already close to full employment. The accelerated activity due to the war "stimulated economic activity in those regions of the country where the rate of growth had been lagging," particularly in the Mid-West and Middle Atlantic states. In general, the 1965-1969 period reinforced the long run trend towards greater equality although notably, there was a decrease in the real income of the aged, of semi-skilled manufacturing factory workers and some other groups. The money gains of these groups were completely eroded by higher taxes and prices. The rise in equality seems to have been largely due to a sharp rise in the number of multi-earner families. Nonwhites as a group gained, but the distribution within the nonwhite community remained very much the same. Nevertheless, the period between 1965 and 1969 saw real gains for many regions, some marginal groups and lagging industries. It is important to design anti-inflation policy that will not sacrifice these gains.

Brooks, Mary E. "Commentary - The Equity Concept in Land Use Decisions." Future Land Use, edited by R.W. Burchell and D. Lisrokin. New Jersey: Center for Urban Policy Research at Rutgers University, 1975.

(V)

The article considers growth control and environmental quality issues in relationship to housing equity. Land use controls at the local level have been considered to resolve each of these problems. In addition, attempts to resolve one issue have often made it difficult to solve others. For example, environmental legislation at the metropolitan or state level often increases the cost of land, thus making it difficult to produce lower cost housing. Growth controls and forms of exclusionary zoning have also often limited the access of lower income families to suburban areas by limiting the availability of housing at a reasonable price.

Since the actions of localities affect regional growth, environment and housing equity, regional factors should be considered in evaluating local ordinances. Brooks suggests that local ordinances should be considered as devices to exclude low and moderate income households unless the locality can demonstrate responsiveness to regional housing needs and if it does not provide for housing for employee households with existing or anticipated jobs in the jurisdiction.

Brown, C.V., and Levin. "The Effects of Income Taxation on Overtime: Results of a National Survey." Economic Journal 84(December 1974): 823-848.

(II)

Brown and Levin conducted a survey to show the net effect of income tax on overtime worked. The survey was performed on 2,000 weekly paid workers in Britain; the study was conducted at the University of Sterling, England. The net impact of the income tax was expressed to be quite small -- perhaps on the average of an extra one-half hour per week for men. Approximately 15% of the males questioned cited tax as the main incentive to work overtime and 11% claimed tax as a disincentive to more overtime work. Married men were more likely than single men to claim that tax had made them work more. The inclusion of nontaxpayers and employees who had no influence on the overtime workload partially explains the high incidence of men (74%) and women (93%) claiming no effects.

Brown, T. M. "Habit Persistence and Lags in Consumer Behavior," Econometrica 20 (No. 3, July 1952): 355-371.

(VII)

A number of theories of the consumption function are tested using Canadian data which lists wage and non-wage income separately. The theory the author chooses to analyze in depth holds current consumption to be a function of current income and past consumption. This implies that changes in consumption lag changes in income by continuously decreasing amounts over time. It also implies that the short run multiplier is smaller than the long run multiplier: it takes a while for any changes to make themselves felt. The proposed equation fits the data well but leads to few testable conclusions.

Browning, Edgar K. "Alternative Programs for Income Distribution: The NIT and the N.W.S." American Economic Review 43(March 1973): 38-51.

(II)

A comparison of the labor supply effects and economic efficiency of two methods of income maintenance: the negative income tax (NIT) and the negative wage subsidy (NWS). The NIT proposes to grant any individual with less than a base level income a fraction of the difference between that base level and his current income. The negative wage subsidy would instead grant any individual with a wage less than a base wage level a fraction of the difference between his current wage and the base wage -- in short, a wage subsidy.

The article then shows that the NWS leads to a larger national income than the NIT, inasmuch as it offers a much greater incentive to work. The NIT theoretically results in less labor and higher wages for low paid jobs; the NWS, on the other hand, may result in more labor, a lower market wage rate, and a higher take-home wage rate. The article concludes by offering three plausible reasons why the NWS should have a lower economic welfare cost than the NIT. It should be noted that the NWS plan requires the repeal of the Federal Minimum Wage Law to work effectively.

Browning, Edgar K. "Incentive and Disincentive Experimentation for Income Maintenance Policy Purposes: Note." American Economic Review 61(September, 1971): 709-712.

(II)

One proposal to test the work disincentive effect of a negative income tax is to take a random sample of people eligible for the tax, divide it in two, give one group the income they would receive from such a tax, the other nothing, and then compare their work effort. This article shows that an estimate of the work disincentive effect arrived at through this process would be erroneous. A national negative income tax would cause a national reduction in hours worked. This reduction in labor supply would cause wages to rise. The rise in wages would cause either more or less work, depending on the relative strengths of the income (higher wages mean more income and a desire for more leisure) and substitution effects (leisure now costs more in foregone earnings). A small experimental negative income tax would not measure this kind of effect.

*Bryce, Harrington. "Identifying Socio-economic Differences Between High and Low Income Metropolitan Areas." Socio-economic Planning Sciences 7(1973).

(X,XI)

Discriminant analysis is applied in order to identify vectors of socio-economic indicators which could describe some non-income aspects of well-being in high and low income cities. Two hundred cities were studied, evenly divided into low and high income areas; data was taken from the 1960 Census. Five demographic indicators were examined: percent non-white, death rate, outmigration, fertility rate, and non-white dependency rate. Of these, the death rate was most important in describing demographic differences in high -- versus low -- income areas. Three industry-employment indicators were considered: specialization of employment, concentration of non-whites in low-paying industries and an index of non-farm occupational mix. All indicators were important, with the concentration of non-whites most significant. Bryce considered four housing indicators: percent vacant rentals, percent families with two cars, percent homes with adequate plumbing, and percent people in group quarters. All are moderately significant. Educational indicators were also important, particularly the percent of adults with four or more years of college.

*Budd, Edward. "Postwar Changes in the Size Distribution of Income in the United States." American Economic Review 60(1970): 247-260.

(II)

The development and application of a method for comparing changes in size distribution of incomes is presented in this article. By comparing the mean income of any quintile relative to the mean income of the distribution as a whole, one shows the changes in inequality within the distribution rather than the total change represented by most analysis techniques. Budd then analyzes change in income size distribution, from 1944-1967 using various statistical series. To accomplish this he employs his new method and a comprehensive interpolation of the Lorenz curve. The major conclusion he draws from this analysis is that the middle and upper part of the distribution have gained relative to the lower and upper tail groups. The changes in relative mean incomes, are, however, quite small but do reflect the real changes rather than the deficiencies of our data sources.

Budd, Edward C., and Seiders, David F. "Micro Aspects of Macro Performance: The Impact of Inflation on the Distribution of Income and Wealth." American Economic Review (May 1971): 128-138.

(II,III)

This paper uses data from the Survey of Financial Characteristics of Consumers conducted by the Bureau of the Census for income during 1962 and asset holdings and liabilities as of the end of 1962 to analyse the following question: "given the historical evidence on the extent to which economic decisions have become adjusted to inflation," how would a 2% and a 5% change in the rate of inflation affect the size distribution of wealth and income among households classified by size of income or net worth? Unlike many other studies of this question, this "model abstracts from the changes in the level of real output and employment that may be associated with changes in the rate of inflation."

The authors found that the distribution of real net worth was shifted slightly downward, while the distribution of real income inclusive of corporate profits before tax was shifted slightly upwards. The distributions of real money income, real income inclusive of undistributed profits, and real income inclusive of undistributed profits and inflation induced real capital gains and losses all shifted from high income and low income groups to middle income groups. Overall, the redistributive effects of the simulated inflations were quite modest. It was concluded that "if the rather mild redistributive effects noted (in the paper) for income are deemed to be undesirable ones, they can be mitigated by modifications of existing transfer and tax policies."

Burchinal, Lee G. Rural Youth in Crisis: Facts, Myths, and Social Change. Background papers prepared for the National Committee for Children and Youth. Condensation of the papers by the U.S. Department of Health, Education and Welfare. Washington, D.C.: U.S. Government Printing Office, 1965.

(VI)

The author contends that rural youth are at a distinct disadvantage in an increasingly urbanized culture. Employment opportunities are fewer in rural areas because, particularly for farm youth, the only technical skills they possess are becoming obsolete. For those who migrate to urban areas, the problems often remain and intensify. Rural youth often have not the knowledge necessary to function effectively in an urban area. Those who are most likely to succeed are those who have an education beyond high school or who have a marketable skill.

Burchinal theorizes that the four major reasons for migration to an urban area are:

1) educational opportunity

2) greater job opportunity

3) recreational opportunity

4) lack of opportunity at home.

He contends that only those who are to some extent urbanized (i.e., skilled, internally motivated and willing to change) are apt to succeed at the transition.

The author concludes by suggesting that, if the gap between rural and urban opportunities is to be narrowed, the opportunities for education in rural areas should be increased and federally funded programs to reeducate rural youth be developed.

Burchinal, Lee G., and Siff, Hilda. "Rural Poverty." Journal of Marriage and the Family 26(November 1964): 399-405.

(VI)

Rural poverty in the United States, though less dramatically visible to an urban-oriented society, remains a serious problem for urban areas which must receive rural migrants as well as for rural areas themselves. Some of the more salient characteristics of the rural population are presented and relate to residential and employment patterns, migration, internal distribution, and other demographic factors. The prevalence of poverty among groups in this population and rural community problems serve as evidence of the need for remedial programs. The authors outline directions which these programs must take.

(Partially taken from an introductory summary)

Burke, Kenneth. Permanence and Change. New York: New Republic, Inc., 1935.

(IX)

A philosophical exploration. Our thoughts and acts are affected by our interests. Our orientation, or Weltanschaung, tends to become a self-perpetuating structure, creating the measures by which it shall be measured. It moves to form a closed circle, though individual and class divergencies ever tend to break the regularity of this circle. Those who have power degrade people, and condemn them for being degraded. Their very "morality" is involved in their privileges: their means and purposes are adjusted to them, their concepts of the good life are grounded in them.

*Burns, Eveline M., ed. "Childhood Poverty and the Children's Allowance." In Children's Allowances and the Economic Welfare of Children. New York: Citizen's Committee for Children of New York, Inc., 1968.

(IV)

"Poverty among children is permitted to persist despite general recognition of its lasting effects on personal development and despite acknowledgement that children cannot be blamed for their economic disadvantages or expected to overcome them." Current measures aimed at saving children from the devastating consequences of poverty involve improvement of the adult economic situation and thereby affect dependent children indirectly; programs are again largely inadequate because they do little to alleviate poverty owing to family size.

Burns further examines the deficiencies of present systems and presents the feasibility and implications of devices which might help poor children, such as social insurance improvement, public assistance expansion, and the negative income tax.

The measure toward which the least attention has been paid in the United States and to which the author devotes considerable discussion is the children's or family allowance, effective today in nearly all industrialized countries. Among advantages are the simplified administrative management owing to absence of an income or eligibility test and uniform allowance amount; the removal of the stigma associated with receiving assistance; and the channeling of money to families who suffer income inadequacy due to family size. Possible problems are considered in detail, among which are the belief that the allowance will stimulate procreation, the problem of its effect on initiative, and the possibility that parents will misallocate monies for goods and services not in the best interest of the child.

Policy decisions would require a tremendous research effort; the article outlines the numerous, related areas needing investigation. Though the author does not view the child allowance as a panacea, she feels it has great promise as a deterrent to poverty and urges careful study of the program's potential.

Burns, Eveline M., ed. Children's Allowances and the Economic Welfare of Children: The Report of a Conference. New York: Citizen's Committee for Children of New York, Inc., 1968.

(IV)

A report of the 1967 Children's Allowances Conference, sponsored by the Citizen's Committee for Children. The Conference dealt with the family allowance program as a means of enhancing the well-being of poor children. Contributors examine existing programs and address themselves to issues which provide for the reader a clear understanding of the program and an appraisal of its effectiveness.

Burns, Eveline M. "Children's Allowances: A New Scheme for Attacking Poverty." AAUW Journal (American Association of University Women) 62 (October 1968): 21-23.

(IV)

Children are dependent upon adults for their livelihood and have no control over their economic status. This article emphasizes the need in the United States for a system of Children's Allowances, similar to those operating in many other industrialized countries, to counteract the devastating effects of poverty on children. The advantages of this kind of program over others much less effective, such as the negative income tax and the Aid to Families with Dependent Children (AFDC) system, are pointed out. Burns addresses arguments to popular objections to Children's Allowances.

Cain, Glen G., and Mincer, Jacob. "Urban Poverty and Labor Force Participation: Comment." American Economic Review 59(March 1969): 185-194.

(X)

This is a comment on the article by Mooney ("Urban Poverty and Labor Force Participation," AER, March 1967) relating unemployment rates and labor force participation of urban poor. The authors find that the cross section regression estimates shown in the original study are not translatable directly into aggregate time series behavior; thus a wide range of time series behavior can be shown to be consistent with the cross-section results. Moreover, it is proposed that the labor supply functions of the poor and non-poor groups differ in the opposite direction from that initially stated. The difference in white and non-white mobility is another significant factor not accounted for. If, as is generally believed, white families can more easily move out of poverty areas in response to better job opportunities, then the remaining white labor force will show a weaker participation response. "The net effect of unemployment for segments of the poverty population and for non-whites is probably negative, but the effects are unlikely to be larger than those for the non-poor and white groups."

Callahan, John J. School Finance Reform in the States: What Should Be Done? Paper presented at National Educational Finance Project Annual Meeting, Atlanta, Georgia, April 2, 1973.

(V)

This document examines the effect that alternative ways of reforming school finance would have on major city school districts. Using census data, the authors attempt to show that parity between tax effort and revenue yield will not in itself insure fiscal justice for most major city schools. The paper considers the higher costs of educational inputs in urban areas; the economic status of the population as between urban, suburban, and rural areas; the problem of municipal overburden; the additional educational needs of urban children; and fiscal capacity. Numerous tables throughout the paper outline the problem on a city-by-city basis. The document concludes with some recommendations for creating an adequate mechanism for the financing of education.

(Taken from the paper)

Callahan, John J., et al. Urban Schools and School Finance Reform: Promise and Reality. National Urban Coalition, Washington, D.C., 1973.

(V)

This study focuses on how central city school districts can benefit from educational finance reform. The publication is designed for use by both those charged with the responsibility for education matters and by the general public. The document begins with a discussion of the fiscal impact of several popular alternative school finance reforms, including traditional percentage equalization, district power equalization, and full state funding of education. Next, it details the factors that affect city school finances, those to be considered in any significant school finance reform intending to aid urban school districts. The study examines what states have done in response to urban fiscal needs and presents an analysis of a suggested school finance reform measure, which can provide more broad-gauged fiscal equity--particularly for urban schools. The document concludes with suggested general policies that could be followed by large city and other fiscally disadvantaged school districts to make the most of future reform opportunities.

(Taken from the report)

Callaway, Lowell E.; Gilbert, R.F.; and Smith, P.E. "The Economics of Labor Mobility: An Empirical Analysis." Western Economic Journal 5(1967): 211-223.

(VI)

At attempt to empirically measure, using differential analyses and linear regressions, the relative impact of various quantifiable economic variables on gross and net interstate labor movements. While per capita income differences are a significant determinant of interstate population movements, many of the reasons underlying labor migration between states must be explained by other, possibly non-economic, factors. Distance seems to be at least as important an explanatory variable as income differentials. Results obtained from welfare and unemployment differentials were not impressive. This study found no conclusive answers to the following two questions: (1) Is interstate labor force migration sufficiently heavy to have a significant effect upon relative sizes of labor supplies in the states? (2) Have changes in the geographical distribution of labor tended to equalize wages and incomes?

*Campbell, Angus, and Converse, Philip E. The Human Meaning of Social Change. New York: Russell Sage Foundation, 1972.

(XI)

As a complement to social indicators which focus on social structural changes, this volume delineates the social psychological concomitants of these changes. Among the topics considered are the use of time, community integration, family networks, job satisfaction, leisure, political and criminal behavior. Attitudes of and toward American Blacks are studied, and the Marxian concepts of alienation and engagement are approached through the measurement of feelings of powerlessness. The procedures that ought to be used in measuring these phenomena, rather than actual conclusions, are stressed throughout.

*Campbell, Arthur A. "The Role of Family Planning in the Reduction of Poverty." Journal of Marriage and Family 30 (1968): 236-245.

(IV,IX)

One of the major burdens of the poor is the large number of children dependent on them. The prevention of unwanted births would have a substantial economic impact on families living in poverty. Using conservative assumptions, the costs of family planning programs are estimated to average $300 to prevent every unwanted birth that would otherwise have occurred. Over the years, however, the avoidance of an unwanted child would save the family an average of $8,000 in the costs of child care. It would also enable couples to add an average of $600 to their annual incomes over a four-year period by making it possible for some of the wives to work. When all of these savings and added earnings are discounted, the total economic benefits average $7,800 for every $300 spent on family planning services. The ratio of benefits to costs is 26-1.

Cantor, Norman L. "The Law and Poor People's Access to Health Care." Law and Contemporary Problems 35(1970): 901-922.

(V)

The poor receive inadequate medical care, and litigation is one possible avenue to the improvement of this situation. The poor are less healthy than the nonpoor, yet receive less care. Indigent patients are turned away from private hospitals into the hands of municipal hospitals, even when in such critical condition that they die en route. Such economic discrimination may be found unconstitutional since it constitutes a deprivation of life without due process of law and is an insidious form of discrimination under the equal protection clause.

Recent precedent suggests that any improvement that comes about will have to take place through the political system. Furthermore, the judicial approach has an inherent limitation in that it can require only dollar expenditures, not the restructuring of the health-care delivery system that is necessary to provide adequate access for the poor.

Caplovitz, David. The Poor Pay More. New York: The Free Press, 1967.

(V)

Authoritative documentation of the poor as exploited participants in consumer society with its phenomenon of consumer credit.

Deceptive and fraudulent marketing practices have increased with the advent of installment payments; the consumer must no longer be able to afford an expensive purchase to make it. Laws enforce contract payment and the methods of obtaining the customer's signature are ignored. The poor have thus become victims of abusive practices accompanying this method of selling; family economic disaster often results.

The book is based on a study conducted in 1960 through intensive interviews with families living in low-income housing projects in the neighborhoods of three sponsoring settlement houses in New York City. The author contends that the situation created by exploitative schemes and breakdown in credit transaction has worsened in New York City since the time of the study and that the problems and practices illustrate a general condition of urban areas.

The book initially shows how merchants of high-cost durables are able to operate in low-income areas; the major part of the book deals with the consumer behavior of low-income families. The needs for, uses of, and affects of credit and poor are considered in detail. Subsequent chapters address themselves to observations of families bordering on insolvency, difficulties in dealings with merchants, reactions to troubles, and knowledge by consumers of community help programs. A final chapter presents conclusions: theoretical observations and practical recommendations.

Carliner, Geoffrey. "Difference in Earning and Education Among Ethnic Groups." The Discussion Papers of the Institute for Research and Poverty. Madison, Wisconsin: University of Wisconsin Press, July 1973.

(IX,X,XI)

A paper analyzing the differences in education and earning levels among a national sample of men of seven European ethnic groups: five Spanish heritage groups, Blacks and a miscellaneous group. The initial theory is that economic and social mobility differences among ethnic groups (excluding Blacks) should decrease from one generation to the next. Education is cited as a better measure of mobility for this case because it represents direct discrimination and not secondary effects, such as differences in training and work experience, visible in the earning measure. Results indicate relatively little change in education achievement of the European ethnic groups, and dramatic increases in the educational achievement level of Blacks and Chicanos. Large differences in earnings among ethnic groups does not seem to be a function of age, education, marital status or location except for the generational advance of the European groups.

Carliner, Geoffrey. "Returns to Education for Blacks, Anglos and Five Spanish Groups." Institute for Research on Poverty, University of Wisconsin. Working Paper 250 - 75. January 1975.

(IX,X)

Data from the 1971 Current Population Survey is used to estimate returns to various personal characteristics for five Spanish surname ethnic groups, as well as for Blacks and non-Spanish Whites. Returns to education were 30% higher for men of Cuban and Central or South American origin than for non-Spanish Whites, Puerto Rican men, or "other Spanish" men. Black and Chicano men had lower returns to education than those of non-Spanish White men. Differences persist despite corrections for nativity, language, age, education and marital status.

Carlson, Michael D. "The 1972-73 Consumer Expenditure Survey." Monthly Labor Review (December 1972): 16-23.

(III)

The Bureau of Labor Statistics periodically conducts surveys to determine the consumer expenditure behavior of the population. The 1972-73 survey is the first since 1960-61. The primary purpose of the surveys is to revise the "market basket" and the expenditure weights used to determine the Consumer Price Index. Other uses of the surveys are becoming increasingly important, including evaluation of economic policies, econometric analysis of consumer demand and income, social welfare planning, compiling national consumer accounts and standard family budgets, supplying data for market research and providing information for consumer counseling. "The 1972-73 Consumer Expenditure Survey consists of two separate surveys each with its own questionnaire and sample: (1) a quarterly panel survey in which each consumer unit in the sample is visited by an interviewer every 3 months over 15 months; and (2) a diary or record-keeping survey completed at home by the respondent for two 1-week periods. This design differed markedly from that of all previous surveys, including the most recent."

This article includes a note on the history of the consumer expenditure surveys from their inception in 1888.

"The Case for a Family Allowance." New York Times, 5 February 1967.

(IV)

Presents testimony by Daniel P. Moynihan excerpted from a Senatorial seminar investigating solutions to problems of the urban poor. Moynihan cites the necessity of a system of income maintenance to assuage the discrepancy between wages and costs of raising a family; the family allowance system is a "straight-forward and rational investment in the welfare of the dependent children of the present generation."

Moynihan emphasizes the major difference between the family allowance system and most social welfare programs: the issue of need is not considered.

He feels that the government concentrates more on doing things for the poor than it does on giving them money. Policy must change, if one accepts the definition of being poor as having too little money.

Caudill, Harry M. Night Comes to the Cumberlands. Boston: Little, Brown and Co., 1963.

(II,V,VI)

This study of the Cumberland Plateau region of Kentucky traces the social and industrial history of its inhabitants to the present-day deteriorated and impoverished condition of the area. Industrial developments and the manner in which they affected mining and logging and, concomitantly, the economic situation are described. As jobs became scarce in the Cumberlands, the self-reliance and initiative of its inhabitants deteriorated into self-pity and hopelessness, resulting in the rise of the welfare state (to which Caudill devotes a chapter). Poverty as described here is more than an economic state; it affects and is expressed by every facet of life, not merely for a selected number of unfortunate individuals, but for the majority of the population in the area. A spectrum of changes is proposed, from court reform to welfare improvements to resettlement.

*Cebula, Richard J. "Local Government Policies and Migrations: An Analysis for SMSA's in the United States, 1965-1970." Public Choice 19(1974): 85-93.

(V,VI)

Regression analysis is used to determine the effect of several local government policies on migration decisions. These policies include level of property taxes, welfare benefits, and non-welfare public expenditure. Per capita income, the level of air pollution and the amount of sunshine are also considered. Regressions are run separately for Blacks and whites. For Blacks, statistically significant coefficients (at .05 level) were found for the welfare payments variable and the public expenditure variable. Black migration into a metropolitan area varies directly with the level of these variables. For whites, statistically significant coefficients were found for all variables except the public expenditure variables. Inmigration by whites varies indirectly with the level of property taxes, welfare payments and pollution, and varies directly with the level of per capita income and sunshine. The author concludes that local government policy does have a major impact on individuals' locational decisions. Local government should exercise care in the establishment of policy since, from the national point of view, such policy could lead to a significant misallocation of human resources.

Cebula, Richard, and Vedeer, Richard. "A Note on Migration, Economic Opportunity and the Quality of Life." Journal of Regional Science 13(August 1973): 205-211.

(V,VI)

Treating the decision to migrate as an investment decision, this study examines whether migration could be caused by environmental factors. Cebula and Vedder use net "in-migration" statistics to empirically test the impact of certain social, economic, and environmental variables on labor migration. All variables except air pollution were found to have a statistically significant impact on migration rates in all of the 39 SMSA's examined. Change in per-capita income was by far the most important factor, representing more than 44% of the total variation in net migration rates. Unemployment, coldness of climate and availability of health services were also found to be important factors in the migration decision. The author concludes "that migrants, at least from 1960-1968, behaved in the manner consistent with the predictions of economic theory, attempting to maximize the net positive benefits of migration."

Center for Rural Manpower and Public Affairs. Manpower Services in Rural America. Michigan: Michigan State University, 1973.

(V)

A summary of the proceedings of the conference on manpower services in rural America is presented. Issues range from the types of manpower services needed and their delivery to strategies to gain public support of state and local government. Problems, such as low density and long distance travel, make the rural public services dilemma unique. Furthermore, manpower tends to be thought of as an urban problem and most delivery systems are designed toward this end.

In an article by Kenneth Rainey, rural access to urban areas is discussed. Rainey claims that the three cost factors that influence the delivery of services in rural areas are distance, density and technology. The major portion of the remainder of the book presents the applied side of the rural service program. Job banks, volunteer and paraprofessional work force, cooperative extension programs and the Comprehensive Employment and Training Act of 1973 are presented and analyzed as programs to help solve the rural service crisis.

Chaiklin, Harris. "Motivating the Poor." In Poverty in Canada and the United States, edited by B. Schlesinger. Toronto: University of Toronto Press, 1966.

(II)

Examines the conventional wisdom concerning the social characteristics and pathologies of the poor. This paper focuses on the thesis that the poor are no different from the nonpoor in their motivation to participate adequately in our society. Social welfare has not presented a balanced and clear-cut appraisal of the needs of the poor. The question to be answered is, "What material level of living is necessary before services which are aimed at 'motivating' people have a chance of success?" The problem is to bridge the gap between what the poor desire and what is available to them. Material needs must be satisfied before a successful attempt to motivate can be made. Among the nations of the Western world the U.S. has the most punitive system of public welfare.

(Partially taken from Poverty and Human Resources Abstracts)

Champernowne, D.G. "A Comparison of Measures of Inequality of Income Distribution." Economic Journal (December 1974): 787-816.

(II,VIII)

A comparison of the performance of several "indexes of inequality" in measuring the following three aspects or dimensions of inequality: (1) inequality due to extreme relative wealth, (2) inequality among the less extreme incomes, and (3) inequality due to extreme poverty. Six general indexes of inequality were chosen for comparison: (1) the coefficient of variation of income, (2) the standard deviation of the logarithm of income, (3) the proportion by which the geometric mean income falls below the arithmetic mean income, (4) the proportion by which the harmonic mean income falls below the arithmetic mean income, (5) the Gini coefficient of inequality, and (6) Theil's entropy coefficient of inequality. In addition, five specialist indexes which are sensitive to one or another of the three types of inequality mentioned above are considered.

Three techniques of comparison are used. One contrasts the rankings of 40 hypothetical income distributions by the six general inequality indexes, the second makes use of contour maps and the third compares the indexes by means of triangular diagrams.

No index was found to be best in all circumstances. Which index is most appropriate depends on the type of inequality in which one is most interested. It was emphasized that whether inequality was judged to be increasing or decreasing often depended on the index chosen.

Chapin, Robert Coit. The Standard of Living Among Workingmens' Families in New York City. New York: Charities Publication Committee, 1909.

(II,III,VII)

After looking at how diet, housing, fuel, health care, and income contribute to individual welfare, the author concludes that income is the most accurate and consistent measure for a definition of poverty. Eight hundred dollars, if spent judiciously, is found to be the lowest annual income necessary to support an average non-dependent family in 1909 "without a lowering of the standard of living below the normal demands of health, working efficiency, and social decency." Independence, health, working efficiency, and social decency are included as indicators of well-being because these are necessary if individuals are to possess the means to achieve social mobility and individual betterment.

Chapman, William. "Semantics of Poverty Studied." Washington Post 31 March 1973.

(II)

This Washington Post article describes the reasons a Nixon Administration task force was tried to redefine "poverty." The current definition had several weaknesses. (1) It overstates the extent of poverty because it does not include non cash income such as food stamps and Medicare benefits. (2) It discriminates against big city residents because it does not take into account the high urban cost of living. (3) "Poverty" is a politically loaded term. As one Administration official said, "Poverty is a value-laden term. We try to avoid value laden terms. We like neutral terms." (4) Finally, under the current definition, poverty in the US actually increased between 1970 and 1971.

Chase, Richard. <u>An Evaluation of the Reduction in Poverty Among Various Demographic Groups 1947 to 1963</u>. Arlington: Institute for Defense Analysis, 1966.

(IX)

This study traces poverty reduction for various demographic groups between 1947 and 1963 and correlates these trends with the rate of overall economic growth. Poverty is concentrated among farm families and those with nonwhite, aged or female heads and became even more so over the period studied. Changes in the level of poverty incidence among these groups are not so closely associated with the level of economic activity as they are for the general population. Unable to better their condition even in times of economic growth, these groups constitute a "backwash" poor population and require selective and specific anti-poverty programs.

*Chase, Richard, and Laber, Gene. "Economic Growth as an Anti-Poverty Tool: A Further Consideration of the Backwash Debate." <u>Social Science Quarterly</u> 50 (December 1969): 604-608.

(IX)

An explanation and conclusion on the results of a multivariate regression model of poverty incidence on median family income and unemployment for eight poverty family subgroups in America between 1947 and 1966. The "backwash thesis," or the argument that the recent deceleration in poverty reduction rate was caused by a "hard core" group of poor who are unaffected by normal economic growth, is examined through a double log equation using poverty incidence, overall annual unemployment rate and overall median family income. Results indicate that in almost all cases for small subgroups of the poor the poverty reduction rate responds less to income growth than in larger population classifications. Also smaller population subgroupings, except non-whites, respond to some unspecified independent variable. Chase and Laber maintain that this support of the backwash theory provides evidence that the elimination of poverty can only be achieved through selective and focussed anti-poverty programs.

Chilman, Catherine S., ed. Approaches to the Measurement of Family Change. U.S. Department of Health, Education, and Welfare. Welfare Administration Division of Research, Research Report #4, June 1966.

(IV,IX)

A collection of four papers by Joseph Langey and Catherine Chilman, Leonard Kogan and Ann Shyne, Ivan Nye and William Rushing, and Marvin Sussman. All of the papers deal with the measurement of changes in family welfare, particularly those associated with social services. The Langey and Chilman paper describes an ideal experiment to measure family welfare change and then considers a number of problems that have prevented this ideal from being realized in existing empirical work. The Kogan and Shyne paper recounts the history of one particular measure of change: the CSS movement scale. This scale measures the improvement in individuals who are part of welfare families. The scale measures only change relative to the starting point; research is continuing in an attempt to devise an absolute scale. The Ivan and Nye paper presents an analysis of the proper way to develop a family measurement instrument. 'Family Integration' is used as an example and the many steps leading to a statistical instrument designed to measure this concept are detailed. The final paper, by Sussman, contains a broad overview of the problem and a description of a series of experiments designed to yield useful new techniques and data.

Chilman, Catherine S. "Child-Rearing and Family Relationship Patterns of the Very Poor." Welfare in Review 3 (January 1965): 9-19.

(IX,XI)

Among the causative factors associated with intergenerational poverty are the ways in which parents in the very poor families, as distinct from the stable working class families, rear their children and relate to each other. This article highlights the findings of past research in this area, and compares these findings with those of studies concerned with "ideal" patterns of child rearing and family life. Though highly critical of past research efforts, especially their lack of precision and use of middle-class values as criteria, Chilman feels that data indicate that child-rearing patterns and family life styles of low-income parents seem more conducive to "poor emotional health, school failure, social rejection, inadequate impulse control (lack of good character)...family breakdown...and collateral areas of behavioral malfunctioning." Finally, the implications of this data for service programs and further research are indicated.

(Partially taken from Poverty in Canada and the U.S.)

*Chilman, Catherine. "Population Dynamics in the U.S.: Implications for Family Planning Programs." <u>Welfare in Review</u> 4 (June 1966): 1-13.

(IV,IX)

Discusses implications of the high national birthrate and demonstrates that it is both a result of and a contributory factor to poverty. The socio-economic conditions of poverty play an important role in creating multi-child families, while large family size combined with low family income creates serious "per capita" poverty.

Data presented on fertility rates, contraceptive effectiveness, fatherless family rates, and illegitimacy rates reveal that women at the lowest socio-economic levels have greater difficulty in planning and spacing the birth of their children. Among this low-income group, non-white women have the most difficulty in limiting the size of their families (their difficulties with family planning are attributed to socio-economic problems).

Chipman, John S. "Homothetic Preferences and Aggregation." <u>Journal of Economic Theory</u> 8 (1974): 26-38.

(III)

The article presents a mathematical analysis of the conditions under which aggregation of demand functions ("community indifference curves") is valid. It is possible to derive aggregate demand functions from individual demand functions, but only with the acceptance of some strong assumptions concerning individual preferences. First, it must be assumed that individual preferences are homothetic ("each comsumer prefers a bundle x to a bundle y if and only if he prefers λx to λy for all $\lambda > 0$"). Further, assuming that all income is spent, it follows that individual demand curves are homogeneous in income. If it is also assumed that such demand curves are differentiable, it can be concluded that they will have unitary income elasticity. The converse is also true, and its application to aggregate demand functions is important. If aggregate demand has unitary elasticity and is generated by preferences defined for aggregate bundles, then the preference relation is homothetic.

Chipman presents several proofs that aggregation of demand functions is possible in two situations: (1) if preferences are homothetic and identical, or (2) if preferences are homothetic and income proportional ("invariant with respect to changes in prices and aggregate income").

Chiswick, Barry R., and Mincer, Jacob. "Time Series Changes in Personal Income Inequality in the United States from 1934, with Projections to 1985." Journal of Political Economy 80 (Supplement; May/June 1972): 34-66.

(II,IX)

A human capital earnings function is constructed and used in an analysis of time series changes in income inequality. "The model relates income inequality to the distributions of age, schooling, employment, and rates of return, and to the intercorrelation among these variables." Changes in relative income inequality during the post-war period are attributed primarily to changes in the distribution of employment. Changes in the distribution of age and schooling are seen to play a much smaller role. "The stronger influence has been the business cycle through its effects on the dispersion of weeks of employment." A projection of changes in income inequality from 1965 to 1985 "on the assumption that age-specific employment is the same in both years" yields no net change for 25- to 64-year-old males. This prediction assumes that the rate of return to schooling is constant during this period. "A substantial decline in inequality in the future during years of full employment could occur if there is a reduced dispersion in full employment weeks worked or if there is a decline in the rate of return to human capital."

*Clark, Harold. "Education and Poverty." In The Disadvantaged Poor: Education and Employment. Task Force on Economic Growth and Opportunity, Washington, D.C.: 1966.

(II,XI)

A review of the major empirical literature on the relationship between education and income. Early enthusiasm that increased education would eliminate poverty and improve the income distribution has been, at least to some extent, dampened. Early empirical work, which simply indicated the higher median income associated with higher education is somewhat misleading: people with a lot of education also tend to have greater ability, parental connections and other attributes which themselves influence income. Moreover, frequently people acquire the "wrong" kind of education--i.e., learn skills not needed in the marketplace--and this does not help to increase income. A summary discussion of the relationship between education and poverty is included.

*Clawson, Marion. "Rural Poverty in the United States." Journal of Farm Economics 49(December 1967): 1227-1234.

(V)

The author contends that rural poverty is less visible than urban poverty and therefore, the rural poor are less likely to benefit from federal programs. Only one-fourth of the rural poor receive direct aid from the government in terms of loans, hot lunch programs, welfare benefits, etc. When rural poor migrate to urban areas they band together and discover that through their numbers they can exert more force. The author feels that because of the disparity between the services available to the rural and urban areas, the government is tacitly saying to the rural poor that if they want recognition and aid they must go to the nearest large city and learn to riot.

Clawson feels that in the future more and more people will migrate to urban areas. In order to avoid the feeling on the part of these people that only in urban areas can their needs be met, a greater effort must be made to locate and serve the rural poor.

*Clawson, Marion, and Knetsch, Jack L. Economics of Outdoor Recreation. Baltimore: The John Hopkins Press, 1966.

(VI)

This general study of outdoor recreation provides a method of valuing the economic worth of a public good: outdoor recreation areas. A demand curve is derived from the willingness of users to incur costs (dollars, time and travel) in order to enjoy the recreational experience. The sum of the maximum prices which various users would pay for use of the facility--the area under the demand curve--is the measure of total user benefit. A simple sum of these expenditures does not capture the true economic worth of the facility any more than the market value of the fish caught measures the value of fishing. Market value estimates of the worth of public recreational facilities suffer from their use of private facilities' prices as their guideline. These prices are greatly affected by the existence of free public facilities. Also, multiplication by the number of visitors at zero charge will lead to a great overstatement of value since at a positive charge the number of visitors would decline sharply. The direct interview method requires skillful interviewing to avoid biases and the results of this costly method are difficult to compare with studies done elsewhere.

Cloward, Richard A., and Jones, James A. "Social Class: Educational Attitudes and Participation." In <u>Education in Depressed Areas</u>, edited by A. Harry Passow. New York: Teachers College Press, 1966.

(XI)

A discussion of the relationship between academic achievement and socio-economic position. Schools in depressed areas are depicted as having inferior facilities, higher teacher turnover, inexperienced staffs, shortages of materials. They therefore do not offer equal educational opportunity. Cloward and Jones then discuss attitudes toward education among various social classes based on their interviews with 988 residents of New York City's lower East Side. Their tentative conclusion is the lower income people have lower occupational aspirations which relate to lower educational aspirations. Cloward and Jones also suggest that lower income people's characteristically lower participation rates in school activities affects their diminished evaluations of the importance of education.

Cohen, Wilbur J. "The Quality of Life and Social Indicators." <u>National Bureau Report, Supplement to Number Nine</u>. New York: National Bureau of Economic Research, March 1972.

(XI)

This essay, taken from remarks made at the National Bureau of Economic Research's Fiftieth Anniversary Human Capital Colloquium, notes that between 1950 and 1970, the percent of the Gross National Product expended on health, education, and welfare from all public and private sources has increased from 13.5% to 21.6%. As a result, the extent of poverty, as defined by the census report, has declined over the last ten years, as has infant mortality.

Another major occurrence has been a shift from pure economic to quality-of-life analysis in social science research. This change has enabled us to see that the nation's social problems can not be effectively dealt with until the nation's number one social problem, poverty, has been eradicated. At this time the major anti-poverty program is Social Security, without which 11 million Americans would be impoverished. This policy of guaranteed income in old age should be extended to include a general income guarantee program for all ages. Additionally, and especially given a general increase in leisure time and the fact that factors other than income are playing an increasing role in job choice and determination of lifestyle, expenditure should be increased in the areas of education, and child care for parents who work or attend school.

Coleman, James. Equality of Educational Opportunity. 1966.

(XI)

A study of the quality of education for black and white students. Survey reveals relatively poor school facilities in predominantly black schools. However, study asserts that elements of school quality have less of an impact on achievement levels of pupils than the social composition of the schools; the educational backgrounds of students (the educational strength of their home environments) appeared to be a significant factor in a child's school performance.

In the survey, the impact of both school characteristics and educational background of students appeared to have a greater impact on minority groups than on whites. Improving the school of a minority pupil, therefore, would have a greater effect than improving the school of a white child.

Study asserts that integration would seem to have a beneficial effect in improving the social composition of schools.

Coll, Blanche D. "Deprivation in Childhood: Its Relation to the Cycle of Poverty." Welfare in Review 3 (March 1965): 1-10.

(XI)

A paper on the reasons poor children often fail in school. The major factors contributing to school failures are:

(1) economic deprivation--poverty-stricken children often go to school suffering from quantitative (caloric) and/or qualitative (nutritive) deficiencies;

(2) illness--children of poor families are more likely to be out of school due to chronic conditions (paralysis), visual and hearing impairments, orthopedic impairments, and lack of preventive care;

(3) emotional deprivation--a child who is separated from the "normal family setting" may have depressed intellectual functioning; and

(4) cultural deprivation--children of the poor are ill-prepared to assimilate the lessons which educators have geared to children from middle-class homes.

Coll then discusses the research and programs designed by the Welfare Administration which are aimed at preventing and alleviating the damage caused by these deprivations in childhood.

Coll, Blanche D. Perspectives in Public Welfare: A History, DHEW, Social and Rehabilitation Service. Washington, D.C.: U.S. Government Printing Office, 1969.

(II)

A history of social welfare attitudes and policies; it traces a persistent malignment of and repressive attitude towards public assistance through United States history and English heritage. The prevailing attitudinal barriers to an adequate and humane relief system include a tendency to blame poverty on personal failure rather than economics and social conditions, a fear of fostering dependency through aid, and a belief that relief, especially to people in their own homes rather than in workhouses, is a temptation to slothfulness.

Countervailing "sets of mind" to these negative attitudes include a persistent aversion to indoor relief based on a belief that workhouses are demoralizing and inefficient. In addition, there has been a gradual recognition of the role of economic and social conditions in causing poverty and a shift of the onus of poverty from the individual to the society which allows it to persist.

Community Council of Greater New York. Annual Price Survey--Family Budget Costs, October 1973. New York: Community Council, 1974.

(III,IV)

The committee's annual publication of current data on budget costs for families living at a moderate level in New York; costs reflect October 1973 prices.

Part I summarizes and analyzes living costs in New York City, showing cost changes between October 1972 and October 1973 for two family types: the index family of four (employed father, housewife mother, boy 13, girl 8), and the retired elderly couple. The section also contains a brief analysis of budget costs for other family types, giving special attention to comparative food costs for seven family types.

Part II represents the updated cost tables from two Committee publications, Family Budget Standard and How to Measure Ability to Pay for Social and Health Services.

Part III lists retail prices for various goods and services integral with and related to the cost data in Parts I and II.

Part IV contains the appendices, including select cost schedules that may be helpful to report users.

(Partially excerpted from the Preface)

Conference on Economic Progress. Poverty and Deprivation in the U.S. Washington, D.C.: Conference on Economic Progress, 1962.

(II)

Because income is seen by the Conference on Economic Progress as by far the most important determinant of level of living, poverty is defined as characterizing households with less than $4,000 annual income, and deprivation characterizes households with between $4,000 and $6,000 annual income. Given these definitions, 43%, or 78 million, of the residents of the United States in 1962 still lived in poverty or deprivation and were underserviced in education, health services, housing, social security, minimum wage laws, and relief from unemployment. Regionally, the South was in the worst shape with 80% of its non-white population and 68% of its total population living in poverty or deprivation. Satisfactory economic growth depends on distribution keeping pace with our ever-growing productive powers. This requires expansion of both private consumption and public programs devoted to the general welfare.

Congressional Quarterly. "U.S. Poor Result of Many Factors." The Christian Science Monitor, 18 April 1966.

(II,IV,V)

Problems in administering antipoverty programs arise because poverty is relative. It can depend on where you live, how large your family is, and which federal or state agency is administering the program. Not all federal agencies (e.g. Veteran's Administration and Office of Education) employ the OEO definition of poverty. A brief summary of the various income criteria employed in administering programs is presented.

(Partially taken from Poverty and Human Resources Abstracts)

Conlisk, John. "Can Equalization of Opportunity Reduce Social Mobility?" American Economic Review 64 (1974): 80-90.

(IV,IX,XI)

It has been suggested by some psychologists that equalizing opportunity would only emphasize the importance of hereditary factors and so reduce social mobility. This hypothesis is investigated here using a linear model of three different equations with income, IQ, and genetic potential variables defined on successive generations of a single family. One interpretation of equalization would be to reduce the importance of parental income in the model by reducing the appropriate coefficients. This kind of equalization implies a lowering of the parent-child income correlation and hence increased mobility. (Parent-child income correlation is considered a measure of immobility.) Equalization of opportunity not associated with parental affluence is interpreted as a reduction in the variance of a "noise" term; and this does in fact result in greater parent-child income correlation, that is reduced mobility. Thus these two types of equalization are found to have opposite effects on mobility. Another objective of equalizing opportunity might be to reduce income inequality. In this case, the two alternate interpretations of equalization produce the same result. Both reduce the variance of income and so reduce income inequality.

Conlisk, John. "Simple Dynamic Effects in Work-Leisure Choice: A Skeptical Comment on the Static Theory." Journal of Human Resources (Summer 1968).

(II)

A dynamic model of the effect of increasing the poverty threshold on work-effort. In the usual static model, increases in the poverty floor (income guarantees) reduce work. In a dynamic model, however, this result may not hold. Work behavior is characterized via three equations. A work supply equation is specified in which work effort depends on income guarantees (-), motivation (+), and wages (indeterminate). Motivation, in turn, is assumed to be a positive function of past income. This assumption is justified by the arguments that high past incomes accustom people to high living standards and thus increase future motivation; high incomes improve health and thus improve motivation; and high incomes independently increase motivation. Since increases in income guarantees increase over-all income, they will also increase motivation. Depending upon the specification of the model, this motivation effect may swamp the negative work effect and result in an increase in work effort as a result of income guarantee increases.

Conrad, Alfred H. "Redistribution Through Government Budgets in the United States, 1950." In Income Redistribution and Social Policy, edited by Alan T. Peacock. London: Jonathan Cape, 1954.

(II)

The question addressed by this essay is: "To what extent were individual incomes in the system redistributed by the government in the course of collecting and spending more than one-fifth of the Gross National Product in 1950?" The direct effects of the budget are measured on the concentration of redistribution in terms of benefits and redistributed income; secondary effects are also discussed; and the question of the extent to which redistribution is the result of social policy or simply coincident with traditional government function is considered.

Analysis of tax collection and budgetary expenditure patterns for 1950 reveal that the top income groups paid a larger proportion of taxes than was accounted for by their share in the income totals; the lower income groups were benefitted disproportionately by transfers and partial benefits while the higher groups were benefitted disproportionately by general government expenditures for the military, foreign assistance, and general government services; and that in the final distribution, the lower four of seven income brackets gain a net benefit from government expenditures while the upper three brackets experience a net loss. Both the tax burden and transfer payments are clearly progressive.

Redistribution results in inflation control and also in the stabilization of government expenditure (to the extent that Congress accepts redistribution as a positive goal). Conversely, "the growth of government expenditure reduces consumer sovereignty and in that reduces welfare."

Cooter, R., and Helpman, E. "Optimal Income Taxation for Transfer Payments Under Different Social Welfare Criteria." Quarterly Journal of Economics 88(November 1974): 556-70.

(II)

Social welfare functions (SWF) are applied to this study to find the optimal income tax redistribution level. A simulation which uses U.S. data and makes three assumptions about the ability distribution is tested. The optimal tax rate under each SWF increases with inequality of ability. The more egalitarian the SWF, the higher the marginal rates. Specific parameters marked the trade off point for equity/efficiency. The inclusion of Musgrave's data on the government's redistribution in this model resulted in the finding that the United States system appeared to maximize the median individual's utility.

Coser, Lewis A. "The Sociology of Poverty." Social Problems 13 (Fall 1965): 146-148.

(II)

Poverty is dealt with as a social category that emerges through societal definition; it can be best understood sociologically not in terms of low income or deprivation but rather in terms of our social response to such deprivation. The central feature of this social response is that individuals, associations, etc., attempt to correct this state of deprivation.

The dynamics upon which this definition of poverty is based are well-illustrated by the recent phenomenon of the emergence of "the other America." The growing scholarly and social concern with poverty has led to the belief that a greater number of persons than previously imagined deserve assistance.

Given the basic proposition that persons are referred to as poor when they are assigned a position of receiving or being entitled to receive assistance, the question arises: What are the terms upon which such relief is granted, and what are the consequences of those terms?

The relationship between the grantor-worker and the recipient is basically one of unilateral dependence rather than interdependence. Here lies the crux of the problem, for only by abolition of the unilateral relationship of dependence can the problem of poverty be solved. Results from recent experiments carried out, for example, in Mobilization for Youth programs have established the value of nonprofessionals as workers in breaking down unilateral dependence. In short, the task is to create a relationship in which the person in need is required and enabled to make a social contribution in a joint undertaking of mutual aid.

(Partially taken from Poverty and Human Resources Abstracts)

* Council of Economic Advisors. "The Problem of Poverty in America." In The Economics of Poverty, edited by Burton A. Weisbrod. Englewood Cliffs: Prentice Hall, 1965, taken from the Economic Report of the President Together with the Annual Report of the Council of Economic Advisers.

(II,IX)

A statistical portrait of the poor in America (1962) in terms of distribution by region, race, age, education and the incidence of a variety of special characteristics. These descriptive features, it is hoped, will serve not merely to identify the poor but will provide insight into the best means of eliminating poverty. This is viewed as a real possibility; for while acknowledging that there will always be inequality, the study defines poverty as "the inability to satisfy minimum needs" and translates this into a $3,000 yearly income (before taxes in 1962 prices) for a typical family. The figure is a conservative average of the minimum budgets from other studies. A different threshold would of course produce a different estimate of the size of the problem, "but the analysis of the sources of poverty and of the programs needed to cope with it would remain substantially unchanged." Postwar trends are of special interest here. The decline in poverty since 1947 is considered primarily a consequence of economic growth as it has not involved any substantial change in the income distribution. However a projection of even the most rapid growth rate during this period, without any redistribution, is found to imply an unacceptable residue of poverty by 1980.

Council of Economic Advisors. "Some Economic Tasks of the Great Society." In The Economics of Poverty, edited by Burton A. Weisbrod. Englewood Cliffs: Prentice-Hall, 1965.

(II,III)

Some of the results of the 1964 CEA report, based on a poverty level of $3,000 yearly income for a typical family of four, are revised here using Social Security Administration estimates of minimum income needs for families differentiated by size and age in urban and rural areas. The new criteria estimate essentially the same total number of poor, but suggest that the group as a whole has a different composition. In particular, there are fewer elderly families and more large families; the number of children in poverty rises by a third from 11 to 15 million. A more comprehensive standard of poverty would take account of a family's assets; however, since the median net asset holding of poor families only amounted to $2,760, this refinement would not alter the results very much. Only some older families who had built up substantial savings would be reclassified. A survey of families with incomes less than $3,000 in the 1962 found that nineteen percent had moved to incomes over $3,000 in the following year. Of these, two-fifths moved only into the $3,000 to $4,000 bracket.

Coward, Barbara E.; Feagin, Joe R.; and Williams, J. Allen. "The Culture of Poverty Debate: Some Additional Data." Social Problems 21 (June 1974): 621-634.

(XI)

Article examines Oscar Lewis's four major culture of poverty dimensions: the attitudes, values and character structure of the individual; the nature of the family; the nature of the slum community; and the relationship between the culture and the larger society. In reviewing the literature on the culture of poverty, Coward, Feagin and Williams observe that despite various conceptual disagreements with Lewis, few researchers have tested Lewis's generalizations with empirical studies. The authors then discuss their own study of a sample of 271 Black respondents. Some support for Lewis's culture of poverty was found in less than half of the cases; and in several cases their findings were in direct opposition to the culture of poverty predictions. In addition, those traits that did lend support to Lewis's argument, the authors suggest, are better classified as situational conditions of poverty. These findings call into question the use of the culture of poverty perspective as a basis for policy decisions.

Crockett, Jean. "Income and Asset Effects on Consumption: Aggregate and Cross Section." In Models of Income Determination, Studies in Income and Wealth 28 (1964): 97-136.

(VII)

This study of the relationship between income, assets, and consumption uses new statistical methods to isolate the effects of the transitory and permanent components of income. An attempt is made to differentiate actual and equilibrium asset holdings. An equilibrium income trend is computed, with the remainder of actual income defined as the transitory component.

Cummings, Laurie D. "The Employed Poor: Their Characteristics and Occupations." Monthly Labor Review 88(July 1965): 828-835.

(X)

The purpose of this study is to show the current status of those who are poor yet working throughout the year at a full-time job. Using the 1960 census, it identifies the specific jobs paying low wages to show the characteristics of workers holding these jobs. Those characteristic features of low-wage workers analyzed in this report include occupation, age, education, family responsibility, color, and residence.

(Partially taken from Poverty in Canada and the United States)

Currie, J.M.; Murphy, J.A.; and Schmitz, A. "The Concept of Economic Surplus and its Use in Economic Analysis." Economic Journal 81 (December 1971): 741-799.

(II,III)

A broad review article of the concept of economic surplus: its historical development, its basic principles, and some of its applications. The concept dates back to Ricardo who argued that since land was a "free gift of nature," all earnings of land constituted a surplus or rent. Since Ricardo, the concept has been developed by Marshall, Dupuit, Hicks, Henderson, Mishan, Patinkin, Bishop, and many others.

The theory of economic surplus is based on the hypothesis that when a consumer makes a purchase, or a producer a sale, he "receives something which has a greater direct or indirect utility to him than the utility of the thing he gives up." The authors discuss several theoretical questions basic to the theory. These include: consumers' surplus; compensating variation and surplus, and equivalent variation and surplus as they pertain to consumers and producers; compensated supply and demand curves; and the advantage of defining the surplus collected by producers as economic rent as opposed to producers' surplus. Several applications of the theory are made in the general areas of the misallocation of resources in a closed economy, international trade, price instability and investment.

The article discusses some of the controversy surrounding the concept of economic surplus. It is emphasized that when evaluating the usefulness of this concept, its limitations should be kept in mind. It can only help determine the effect of an economic change. It is the responsibility of the "decision-maker" to determine whether the change is desirable. The authors conclude that while it is easy to criticize the use of the concept of economic surplus as a policy making tool, it is hard to find a suitable alternative.

Dajani, Jarir S., and Egan, M. Michael. "Income Distribution Effects of the Atlanta Transit System." Transportation Research Record 516. Washington, D.C.: Transportation Research Board, 1974.

(V)

This paper reports on a pilot study to evaluate the income-distribution effects of the proposed Atlanta transit system. The incidence of benefits and costs to each of 8 traffic zones is estimated. The zones have annual incomes per family varying between $5,000 and $18,000. Benefits accruing to each zone as a result of savings in time, vehicle ownership, and operating costs, transit fares, parking and accidents, are estimated and compared to transit fares and additional sales taxes that must be paid by the residents of that zone. The net benefits accruing to each zone seem to be more, both per family and per trip, in zones where family incomes are lower. This pattern, however, is strongly influenced by both the location of the zone relative to the closest transit station and the level of interaction between the zone and the central business district. Other factors affecting the distribution of income in the Atlanta metropolitan area are also discussed.

(Author abstract)

Daly, Herman E. "A Marxian-Malthusian View of Poverty and Development." Population Studies 25 (1971): 25-37.

(II)

"The names of Marx and Malthus often are linked in disjunction but never in conjunction. Nevertheless, the thesis argued in this paper is that the two historically dominant theories of poverty, the Marxian and the Malthusian, are not inconsistent, but complementary; that a union of the two yields a basic fourfold typology of social classes by differential ownership of property and differential fertility; that this typology can also be viewed as a way of disaggregating the meaningless average of 'GNP per head' in a way which gives social content (i.e., a distributional dimension) to the concept; that the typology provides more satisfactory definitions of 'development' and 'overpopulation'; and that these four categories are improved, or usefully supplemented, by replacing the flow of income by the stock of wealth in each case. Also the universality of the typology is discussed along with some preliminary empirical considerations."*

Daly defines poverty as low Y/P for a class where Y is income and P is population size. Class is defined in terms of underlying social force functions (differential property ownership and differential fertility) which largely determine the size of Y/P. Hence the poor have a lower income and more children.

* Summary of paper written by Daly.

Danley, Robert A., and Ramsey, Charles E. Standardization and Application of a Level of Living Scale for Farm and Nonfarm Families, Memoir #362. Ithaca, New York: Cornell Agricultural Experimental Station, 1958.

(V,VI)

The authors develop a sociometric index designed to allow comparisons of farm and nonfarm rural families on the basis of their social status, degree of isolation, and their health. From an original battery of fifty household items, nine were chosen which best predicted family heads' education, occupational status and organization memberships. Although originally developed in Oklahoma, the scale performed well in New York.

Younger and older segments of the rural population area were found to have differing values. A family's level of living was found to be better correlated with the characteristics of the wife than of the husband.

*Darby, Michael R. "The Permanent Income Theory of Consumption--A Restatement." The Quarterly Journal of Economics 88(1974): 228-250.

(VII)

This paper defends the permanent income hypothesis by re-examining data that had seemed to contradict it. Permanent income is defined as the long-run expected yield from wealth, including human capital. The desired rate of consumption is held to be a stable, linear function of permanent income. Earlier empirical studies had found that current income had a great weight in determining consumption, but Darby shows that the econometric techniques used suffered from severe upward bias. By adjusting for changes in households' inventories induced by the receipt of transitory income, Darby estimates the weight of current income to be about 0.1 on an annual basis. In non-statistical terms, this means that consumption is not closely associated with current income.

David, Martin. "Lifetime Income Variability and Income Profiles." <u>Proceedings of the American Statistical Association</u> (1971).

(VII)

An analysis of the pattern of income received by individuals in Wisconsin from 1947 to 1959. Tax returns are used to determine both the magnitude and causes of income variability. Two models of income dynamics are tested: a simple trend model versus an autoregressive specification. If income positions persist strongly from year to year, the autoregressive model should perform better than the simple trend version. It does not, which suggests that income variability is more prevalent than had previously been hypothesized. Variability is particularly apparent in the incomes of older professionals, managerial workers and the self-employed. David's results suggest that "transitory" (short-run) poverty may be fairly widespread.

*David, Martin. "Measurement of the Cost of Living Including the Public Sector." <u>Annals of Economic and Social Measurement</u> (Winter 1975): 133-152.

(V)

This paper analyses the problems in constructing a Cost of Living (COL) Index that makes adequate allowance for changes in the quality and relative importance of government services in the consumer's consumption patterns. A proposal for attitudinal measures of COL is developed. In addition, a strategy for using existing expenditure and government data is presented.

(Taken from editor's note)

*David, Martin. "Welfare Income and Budget Needs." <u>Review of Economics and Statistics</u> 41 (No. 4, November 1959): 393-399.

(II,IV,VII)

This paper begins with the statements that disposable personal income is a poor measure of individual welfare because non-money income is not measured and families have different compositions, and that Per-Capita Disposable Income is a poor measure because it ignores the effects of returns to scale within the family. Two new measures of family welfare are then proposed. The first consists of the disposable income of the family, plus home grown food, plus an imputed rent for home-ownership, the whole sum divided by the minimum needs of a family of that size and type as determined by the Welfare and Health Council of New York. The second measure is identical except that the value of all family held liquid assets is added to the other sources of income.

A comparison of these measures of welfare with disposable income is made using the 1956 Survey of Consumer Finances. Many families with inadequate incomes according to these welfare measures had money incomes of more than $2000 or even $3000; others with money incomes below these figures had more than enough income to meet their needs, again according to these measures. From 14% to 24% of all spending units were mislabeled in terms of these systems if money income below $1000, $2000, or $3000 is used as the criterion for poverty.

Davidson, Chandler, and Gaitz, Charles M. "'Are the Poor Different?': A Comparison of Work Behavior and Attitudes Among the Urban Poor and Nonpoor." Social Problems 22 (December 1974): 229-246.

(II)

Is poverty the result of a work orientation peculiar to the poor? To answer this, a secondary analysis of data obtained from a stratified sample of the Houston population was conducted. Ethnicity (Black, Mexican American, Anglo) and sex were controlled, and age was standardized. The findings cast doubt on the "culture of poverty" hypothesis insofar as it pertains to work habits and attitudes. The assumption that the poor work less than the nonpoor was found to be unwarranted in the cases of Mexican American males and of women of all ethnic groups. The employment rate among Mexican American impoverished males was higher than among the Anglo nonpoor. No significant differences in attitudes toward work were found to exist between the poor and nonpoor within any ethnic group. Contrary to a popular view, the minority poor were found to be as work-oriented as the Anglo nonpoor.

*Davis, Karen. "Equal Treatment and Unequal Benefits: The Medicare Program." The Brookings Institution, Washington, D.C.: November 1973.

(V)

Explores magnitude of variation in Medicare benefits by income-class, race, and region. Disparities in regional benefits may be explained primarily by availability of physicians and medical resources, and costs of medical care. Author notes that financing and provider reimbursement provisions of Medicare tend to perpetuate rather than remedy these disparities.

*Davis, Karen. <u>The Effect of Medical Care Financing on Racial and Geographic Barriers to Medical Care</u>. Cambridge, Massachusetts: Harvard University Press, 1974.

(V)

Benefits from Medicare and Medicaid have not been equally shared by all the poor; gains have been disproportionately low for Blacks and residents of rural areas. The primary factor contributing to disparities in benefits between Blacks and whites is racial discrimination. Barriers to adequate health care in rural areas include limited medical resources, transportation problems, ancillary problems which reduce effectiveness of medical treatment, and an inability to attract needed health manpower.

Author points out that Medicare and Medicaid have failed to address and counteract these problems. If a program of national health insurance is to replace these current programs, special efforts must be designed to overcome the prevailing inequities and barriers to adequate delivery of health care to the poor.

Davis, Karen. "Lessons of Medicare and Medicaid for National Health Insurance." The Brookings Institution, Washington, D.C.: 1974.

(V)

A summary of problems inherent in the Medicaid program which presents rationale for national health insurance. Problems include: barriers in access to adequate medical services; high costs generated by inflationary impact of Medicaid and other insurance programs; inadequate financial protection under maximum liability provisions of program; adverse incentives to covered persons; and variation in states' benefit programs.

Discussion of access difficulties is especially pertinent to the issue of regional variation in level and quality of public service provision. Variations are primarily a result of differences in price of medical care and availability of medical resources.

Davis, Karen. "Medicaid: Its Impact on the Poor." The Brookings Institution, Washington, D.C.: May 1974.

(V)

Measures Medicaid's success in meeting its stated goals of ensuring the poor quality medical care and relieving them of the financial burden of medical care costs. In assessing Medicaid's impact, the author discusses utilization patterns, quality, and convenience of medical care and distribution of benefits by state, race, and place of residence.

Author points out that apparent gains in access to medical care are misleading. Especially in states with restrictive eligibility criteria, large numbers of needy persons are excluded from the Medicaid program. Further, discriminatory and residential barriers to utilization of services impede health care delivery under Medicaid. Southern Blacks and rural residents are most affected by these hindrances.

DeJong, Gordon F., and Donnelly, William L. "Public Welfare and Migration." Southwestern Social Science Quarterly 54(September 1973): 329-344.

(V,VI)

"Do differential AFDC payment levels predict, at least in part, non-white migration to U.S. cities?"

The article focuses on migration theory as it applies to non-whites. Most Standard Metropolitan Statistical Areas (SMSA), the unit of analysis for this study, have experienced net migration gains in non-whites during recent decades. It is necessary, therefore, for the author to examine those factors which stimulate or deter migration; these "push-pull" factors as determined in numerous studies are reviewed. Major findings indicate that real or perceived differences in economic and social situations, the existence of familial or friendly ties in the area, and the lure of expanded social and cultural activities of metropolitan locations serve as major influences in defining attractiveness.

The level of AFDC payment per family as a significant variable in the motivation to migrate is not borne out by the research. To interpret this resource as a primary cause of net migration is questionable; the destination of migration for non-whites is likely to be a city which offers the greatest opportunities. It is more often coincidental that nonwhite migration tends to be to large cities which provide more liberal AFDC benefits.

deJouvenel, Bertrand. "The Ethnics of Redistribution." In Inequality and Poverty, edited by Edward C. Budd. New York: W.W. Norton and Company, Inc., 1967.

(II)

Equalizing income is seen to have certain consequences for cultural values. For example, such redistribution would put consumers of "artistic and cultural goods" at a disadvantage; and low-demand, high-priced cultural activities would be deprived of patrons with the means to support them. The goal of maximizing individual satisfactions, insofar as it implies equal income, may well conflict with cultural objectives. Moreover, deJouvenal argues that those advocates of equalization who put the burden of maintaining such cultural activity on the state not only confer great power in this way but contradict their own goals as well. They tamper with the market values and resource allocation resulting from the income distribution which was to have effected greatest total satisfaction. "Those who spontaneously correct their schemes of redistribution by schemes for such support are in fact denying that the ideal allocation of resources and activities is that which maximizes the sum of satisfactions."

Dernberg, Thomas, and Strand, Kenneth. "Hidden Unemployment: A Quantitative Analysis by Sex." The American Economic Review 56(1966): 71-95.

(X)

At the trough of the business cycle, some workers may become discouraged and leave the labor force. Later in recession there are "additional worker" pressures to rejoin the labor force. For males 25-64 labor force participation does not depend on the business cycle, but for females and young males a rise in employment brings about a rise in labor force participation. An increase in employment of 1,000 brings forth additional labor force participation of 454, on the average, so that the fall in unemployment is only 546. Thus, the unemployment rate in 1962 including hidden unemployment was 8.5 percent, while actual figures showed only 5.6 percent.

Deutsch, Martin. Minority Group and Class Status as Related to Social and Personality Factors in Scholastic Achievement. Monograph Number 2. Ithaca, New York: The Society for Applied Anthropology, 1960.

(XI)

Environmental factors affect the development process; a child's self-concept and perceptions of reality are determined by the conditions under which he lives and grows up. The relationship between life conditions, development and learning are well-established.

This 3-year study, conducted in the schools and community of an all-Negro area in a major northern city, focused on (1) interrelationships among social environment, class, ethnic and racial factors, and group behavior of children; and (2) the inherent implications for scholastic achievement, for school organization to better meet needs, and for values and attitudes for teachers in working with these children.

"In an affluent society whose goal is success and whose measurement is consumption, the lower class child starts the race to that goal with an assortment of disadvantages. Economic uncertainty, slum living, crowded homes, and small value given to intellectual activity are not an adequate foundation for achievement." The lower-class child, and especially the lower-class minority child, lives in an environment which fosters a negative self-concept and produces other deleterious effects. The majority of Negroes are members of lower socio-economic groups and are, therefore, subject to the damaging aspects associated with this status. Perhaps an understanding of man's increasing alienation from his work and from his fellow man might begin with a study of the progressive alienation of the Negro child in the white world.

Dewey, John. The Public and Its Problems. Denver: Alan Swallow, 1954 (1st pub. 1927).

(II)

Dewey suggests that since the industrial revolution language and conditions have changed, but actual transformation in ideas and ideals has not occurred. Dewey reminds us that the physician might "cure" the disease--that is, cause its present alarming symptoms to subside--but since he does not modify the causes his treatment may even affect them for the worse. These thoughts and Dewey's concern about the inability of all but the elite to affect the ideas and ideals of society have relevance as a concept of poverty. Those who are unable to "communicate" are unable to share in political power and are therefore in poverty.

(Baratz and Grigsby, 1966)

Dickinson, Jonathan. "Labor Supply of Family Members." In 5,000 American Families -- Patterns of Economic Progress, Vol. 7. Ann Arbor, Michigan: Survey Research Center, Institute of Social Research, University of Michigan, 1974.

(II)

This work reports on the labor supply characteristics of a population of 5,000 families that have been intensively studied for five years. The major conclusions from this study are:

1) Education and occupation strongly influence the probability of becoming involuntarily unemployed; education increases earnings largely by decreasing unemployment and increasing the ease of finding a second job.

2) Few workers have complete control over the number of hours they can work. The work disincentive effects of a negative income tax will be substantially diluted when 30% of the working population cannot decrease its hours and another 40% currently desires greater hours.

3) Labor supply is 'backward bending' for most workers: an additional dollar an hour in wages will reduce work effort by roughly 50 hours.

4) There is a strong positive relationship between wage rates and hours worked for married women. An income supplementation program with a high marginal tax rate will substantially reduce the number of hours worked by married women; an equalization of male and female wage rates would substantially increase it.

Diewert, W.E. "Functional Forms for Revenue and Factor Requirements Functions." International Economic Review 15 (1974): 119-129.

(III)

This article addresses the problem of finding functional forms for demand and supply equations for applied econometric work which are (1) consistent with the assumed optimizing behavior of producers or consumers, (2) sufficiently "flexible" so that technology or tastes may be adequately approximated, and (3) sufficiently "simple" so that existing econometric techniques may be used to estimate unknown parameters. One necessary condition is that factor requirements functions (these functions give the minimal amount of input x needed to produce the vector outputs, $(y_1, \ldots, y_m)$) used for supply equations is that the curvature is consistent with constant returns to scale. This condition is satisfied, at least about a point, by functional forms which can attain an arbitrary set of elasticities of substitution at a given vector of output prices and at a given vector of outputs. To develop these functional forms, the author characterizes multiple output, single input technologies in three ways: (1) in terms of a factor requirements function, (2) in terms of a revenue function, and (3) in terms of production possibilities sets. Finally, he shows how systems of supply functions may be easily derived using the theoretical results developed in the article.

Diewert, W.E. "Harberger's Welfare Indicator and Revealed Preference Theory." Stanford University Institute for Mathematical Studies in the Social Sciences, <u>Technical Report #104</u> (August 1973).

(III)

Diewart finds Harberger's welfare indicator to be consistent with Samuelson's weak axiom in revealed preference theory. Given two different price and quantity situations, Harberger holds welfare to have increased or decreased as the following expression is positive or negative:

$$H(p^1,p^2,x^1,x^2) = p^{1T}(x^2 - x^1) + 1/2(p^2 - p^1)^T(x^2 - x^1)$$

where p refers to price, x to quantity, numerical superscripts to time periods and p^T is the vector of all prices in the period. This indicator does not resolve the zone of indeterminacy since it can be made positive or negative by simply scaling prices in either period. Once normalized by using prices divided by expenditure in that period, the Harberger indicator is equal to the negative of Hick's normalized welfare indicator.

Diewert, W.E. "Homogeneous Weak Separability and Exact Index Numbers." Stanford University Institute for Studies in the Social Sciences <u>Technical Report #122</u> (January 1974).

(III)

Diewert obtains a family of superlative index numbers which includes the Fisher-Konyus form. The quantity index is found to be consistent with revealed preference theory and with a linear aggregator function (infinite substitutability between the goods to be aggregated). Fisher's ideal index numbers are consistent with Leontief aggregator function (zero substitutability between the commodities to be aggregated). The Fisher price index is $(p^{1T}x^1p^{1T}x^o/p^{oT}x^1p^{oT}x^o)^{\frac{1}{2}}$ and his quantity index is $(x^{1T}p^1x^{1T}p^o/x^{oT}p^1x^{oT}p^o)^{\frac{1}{2}}$, where p and x are prices and quantities, the numerical superscripts refer to periods and "T" is the symbol for a price or quantity vector for the period.

Donabedian, Evidis; Rosenfeld, Leonard S.; and Southern, E.M. "Infant Mortality and Socioeconomic Status in a Metropolitan Community." Public Health Reports 80 (December 1965): 1083-1095.

(XI)

Data were obtained on the socioeconomic characteristics of 90 census tracts in a part of metropolitan Boston and on the fetal and infant deaths occurring to mothers who resided in the tracts studied. These were used to plot the geographic distribution of perinatal mortality in the study areas, and to study the relationships between the various mortality rates and socioeconomic status. The findings show a fivefold difference in perinatal mortality between the census tracts with the highest and the lowest socioeconomic status and a sharp geographic localization of the areas of highest mortality. All segments of mortality decreased markedly as socioeconomic status improved, except for deaths during the first week of life which remained at an even level.

(Poverty and Health in the United States)

Douglas, Paul H.; Hitch, Curtice N.; and Atkins, Willard E. The Worker in Modern Economic Society. Chicago: University of Chicago Press, 1923.

(II)

"Broadly speaking, a standard of living for any group of people is such a sum of accustomed goods and services as they consider absolutely essential to their maintenance." Given this as a basic definition, "poverty level" is taken to mean "a level at which the income, even though expended with ordinary prudence is insufficient for even the physical upkeep of a family of moderate size." In 1923, for the larger American cities, this is found to be an income range of between $1,000 and $1,100 for a family of five. The minimum subsistence level, at which income is sufficient for complete physical and natural upkeep of a bare kind but insufficient for emergencies or social pleasures requiring money, is between $1,000 and $1,400. Not until an income level of $2,100 is reached is a family considered to live in comfort.

Downs, Anthony. Who Are the Urban Poor? Supplementary Paper Number 26, Committee for Economic Development, 1970.

(V,VI)

Presents some characteristics of the urban poor and discusses the concept of poverty, which, in this paper, rests on a food-based budget of the Social Security Administration.

A look at the extent of poverty in 1968 reveals that while there were twice as many poor whites in the United States, the incidence of poverty among non-whites was three times that of the white population. Metropolitan areas accounted for 51% of the nation's poor. Further analysis of urban poverty is possible by dividing the population into six specific groups. The data show greatest prevalence of poverty among children under eighteen years of age, the elderly, and households headed by females (under age 64). The author examines the causes of poverty in all six groups as well as trends and significant results of this condition.

Issues related to public policy are addressed, including social institutions as possible reinforcers and promoters of poverty, future population changes, and factual findings on which sound decisions can be based.

Duesenberry, James S. Income, Saving and the Theory of Consumer Behavior. Cambridge, Massachusetts: Harvard University Press, 1949.

(VII)

An empirical study that seeks to demonstrate the invalidity of the fundamental assumptions of aggregate demand theory that (1) every individual's consumption behavior is independent of that of every other individual and (2) that consumption relations are reversible in time. The study is based on three sets of data: (1) the data on aggregate savings and income in the period 1869-1929 collected by Kuznets; (2) the budget studies of 1935-36 and 1941-42; and (3) the yearly data on aggregate savings and income for the period since 1929 published by the Department of Commerce. The author summarizes his conclusions as follows:

(1) In periods of steadily rising income the aggregate savings ratio tends to be independent of income.

(2) The savings ratio will be affected by changes in interest rates, income expectations, the distribution of income, the rate of growth of income, and the age distribution of population.

(3) On balance, changes in these variables have not been sufficiently large to have had much effect on the savings ratio.

(4) Over the trade cycle the savings ratio is dependent on the ratio of current income to previous peak income.

(5) The effect of the two hypotheses taken together can be expressed by the equation $S_t/Y_t = 0.25Y_t/Y_o - 0.196$, where S_t = current savings, Y_t = current disposable income, and Y_o = previous peak disposable income.

(6) The hypotheses just stated are consistent with all the available data.

Duncan, Otis D. "Inheritance of Poverty or Inheritance of Race?" In On Understanding Poverty, edited by Daniel Moynihan. New York: Basic Books, 1968.

(IX)

An attack on the "inheritance of poverty" literature. Duncan argues that Negroes in particular "are poor mainly because they are 'Negroes' and are defined and treated as such by our society and that their poverty stems largely not from the legacy of poverty but from the legacy of race." Path analysis is used to trace the effects of family social and economic background on income, education, and occupational achievement. Data was taken from Duncan and Blau's 1962 study of occupational mobility. Duncan finds that parental socio-economic status (including income, education, and occupation) are significantly less important in determining Negro income and education that that of whites. Thus, "the Negro family is... relatively less able than the white to pass on to the next generation any advantage."

Duncan, Otis Dudley. "A Socioeconomic Index for All Occupations," and "Properties and Characteristics of the Socioeconomic Index." In Occupations and Social Status, edited by Albert J. Reiss, Jr. New York: The Free Press, 1965.

(XI)

These two essays deal with the construction of an occupational socioeconomic index (SEI) from census information on detailed occupational characteristics. The first considers the index in relation to National Opinion Research Center (NORC) materials on occupational prestige, and the second considers the index in more general terms as a measure of socio-economic status. The SEI combines available information on education and income level by occupation, and is found, with exceptions, to be comparable to NORC occupational prestige scores for the occupations covered by both measures. The SEI is potentially useful for stratifying a population of individuals or as a research instrument for investigating occupational structure. However, the authors note that it is advisable to supplement the SEI with other measures because of the limited correlation between the index and variables of income and education on the individual level. This is the case because variation in education can only account for one-third of the variation in occupational socio-economic status, and occupational socio-economic status can account for only one-fifth of individual variation in income. There also may be problems of stability and comparability of the index over time.

*Duncan, Otis Dudley, and Hodge, Robert. "Educational and Occupational Mobility: A Regression Analysis." American Journal of Sociology (May 1963): 629-644.

(IX,XI)

Regression analysis of occupational mobility is made feasible by recent work providing socio-economic status scores for detailed occupations. Data from the Chicago portion of the 1951 Six-City Survey of Labor Mobility reveal correlations of about .3 between respondents' occupational scores and those of their fathers, while respondents' educational attainment has a somewhat greater influence, as indicated by correlations of .4 or .5. Sons of farmers and non-whites were handicapped by comparison with respondents of non-farm origin and whites. Despite rising levels of educational attainment accompanied by decreasing dispersion of number of school years completed, evident in intercohort comparisons, education was no less important as a determinant of occupational status in 1950 than in 1940.

*Dunlop, John T. "Poverty: Definitions and Measurement." In The Concept of Poverty, Task Force on Economic Growth and Opportunity, Chamber of Commerce of the United States. Washington, D.C.: Library of Congress No. 65-21323, 1965.

(II)

A general discussion of problems in definition and measurement of poverty, the structure of poverty, and approaches to mitigating poverty. Issues raised on definition and measurement include the question of absolute versus relative measures of poverty; the distinction between family income and income of unrelated (single) individuals; the use of annual income versus assets, consumption, or income in-kind; the distinction between families who suffer a severe hardship in income in one particular year and those who are permanently poor; and the concept of insular or community poverty versus personal poverty. A discussion of the structure of poverty examines the various subgroups that comprise the poor population. They are the aged, the sick and disabled, the unemployed, the uneducated, the racial minorities, the agrarian population, and those in regional concentrations of poverty. The life cycle of income is also emphasized and described.

Durbin, Elizabeth. Welfare Income and Employment. New York: Praeger, 1969.

(II,X)

An analysis of public welfare programs in New York City. The choice between working and going on welfare is partially conditioned by the relative economic benefits from each. Where payments are cut by one dollar for each dollar earned, there is little incentive to work. Work requirements should produce more willing workers at lower wages. The 90% increase in the city caseload between 1958 and 1967 was attributed to (1) a higher ratio of acceptances to applications for welfare after 1963; (2) an increase in the Basic Allowances in 1966, automatically increasing the size of the eligible population; and (3) the increased real value of welfare payments and their greater accessibility, which apparently offset the effects of improved labor market conditions over the period. These effects were deemed more important than the in-migration of groups tending to be poor.

*Eldridge, Hope T., and Thomas, Dorothy Swaine. Demographic Analyses and Interrelations. Vol. III of Population Redistribution and Economic Growth United States, 1870-1950. Philadelphia: American Philosophical Society, 1964.

(VI)

This volume presents information on population growth and redistribution in the United States from 1870-1950, including a general view. Natural increase and migration, net migration of native whites and Blacks and of foreign born, streams of migration, differentials by age and sex, and urban growth and population redistribution are discussed. Statistical analyses and charts are presented for all of these areas.

Since 1880, the association between temporal variations in the rate and level of economic growth and the volume of internal migration and population redistribution has been impressively close. Both dispersion and urbanization have been essential to the development of a single integrated economy and social system occupying the available territory. Given the statistical evidence of growth and population redistribution, it is possible to hypothesize that migrants, because of factors of selectivity and detachment, have enabled a greater rate of industrial growth and economic development than would have been possible if urban industry had had to depend upon only the resident urban populations for labor.

Elesh, David. "Poverty Theories and Income Maintenance: Validity and Policy Relevance." Social Science Quarterly 54 (September 1973): 359-373.

(II,XI)

Two types of theories of poverty are cultural and structural. Cultural theories find the explanation for poverty in the traits of the poor themselves. Structural theories explain poverty in terms of the conditions under which the poor live. The extent of agreement between the two theories in terms of ten traits is presented. Both types of theorists believe that successive generations of the same family remain poor. The frame of reference for both theories extends across national, cultural, ethnic, and racial boundaries. No one would deny that both culture and structure play some role in poverty, but it can be questioned as to whether the roles currently assigned to them are accurate. Most importantly, the theories are not able to explain the large variations in the presumed characteristics among the poor. In relation to programs of income maintenance, two points are made: in practice, the policy implications of the two are marginally different. Despite their generality and universal applicability to poverty policy, they have little to say about income maintenance programs. To the extent to which the poverty syndrome can be identified and is affected by income maintenance, the cultural theory is undermined, but the meaning of income maintenance for the structural theory is not so clear. It is useful to consider the effects of both cash and in-kind transfers on the employment, education and health service markets. The implication for income maintenance programs is that responses would increase with succeeding generations. The two major competing theories of poverty can offer little guidance for poverty policy, but suggest a number of dimensions along which poverty could be more usefully analyzed for the purposes of both theory construction and policy formation.

(Taken from Sociological Abstracts)

*Elinson, Jack. "Toward Sociomedical Health Indicators." Social Indicators Research 1 (1974): 60-71.

(XI)

An exploration of the status and usefulness of sociomedical health indicators. Mortality data--life expectancy at birth, the infant mortality rate, the death rate--are the statistics that are generally used as indicators of the level of health. However, in economically-developed countries, these indicators have remained static and no longer adequately measure health status. Sociomedical indicators are suggested as an alternative. They measure other objective conditions of health status and social values of what health is. Current attempts to develop sociomedical health indicators include: measures of social disability; typologies of presenting symptoms, which have been used to estimate probable needs for care; measures which focus on behavioral expressions of sickness; research based on operational definitions of "positive mental health," "happiness" and perceived quality of life; and assessments of met and unmet needs for health care, which are measures of social capacity to care for the sick.

Ellickson, B.C. "Jurisdictional Fragmentation and Residential Choice." American Economic Review 6 (1971): 334-339.

(V)

Metropolitan areas today contain many political jurisdictions. Different individual choices of where to reside and differing packages of public goods supplied simultaneously determine one another. Ellickson develops a model which reveals under what conditions suburban communities will become stratified by wealth. Collusion may be necessary to keep wealthy communities exclusive. Low income households in a heterogeneous community can be expected to vote against decentralization while the residents of wealthy jurisdictions will resist annexation to less wealthy communities.

Ellickson, B.C. Metropolitan Residential Location and the Local Public Sector. Unpublished doctoral dissertation, Massachusetts Institute of Technology, 1970.

(V)

Ellickson argues that decentralization of the consumption of public goods within the metropolitan area (as distinct from political decision-making) is necessary for allocative efficiency. It seems right that households cluster together on the basis of income and tastes to form homogeneous neighborhoods. Then to the extent that local public services may be viewed as simply additional characteristics of neighborhood environment, variation in the quality of these services will be desirable as well. As for political decision-making, decentralization here is undesirable on principles of distributive justice, for it allows higher-income households to block majority rule within the states, a violation of the "one man--one vote" principle.

Ellis, John M. "Socio-Economic Differentials in Mortality from Chronic Diseases." In Patients, Physicians, and Illness, edited by E. Gartly Jaco. New York: Free Press, 1958.

(XI)

Results of a Houston study supporting the author's hypothesis that there exists an inverse relationship between mortality and socio-economic status for both infectious and chronic diseases. This conclusion contrasts with the popular view that chronic disease bears no relationship to social class; chronic disease is not influenced by poor environmental conditions which are a predominant factor in death from infectious diseases.

In studying death rates for the seven leading diseases (two infectious, five chronic) in Houston mortality, Ellis implies that differentials are due, in part, to inaccessibility of the lower classes to information emphasizing early diagnosis and treatment and to the inability to afford treatment. He urges further research into the subject and more effort by public health organizations to reduce class differentials.

Elteto, O., and Frigyes, E. "New Income Inequality Measures as Efficient Tools for Causal Analysis and Planning." Econometrica 36 (April 1968): 383-396.

(II)

A new system of inequality measures is proposed which is particularly suited to exhibit the effect of different contributing economic factors. The population is divided into those above the mean income and those below, and the mean income of these two groups is also computed. The proposed inequality indices are ratios of mean incomes: $u = m/m_1$ $v = m2/m_1$ $w = m2/m$ (where m = mean income for total distribution, m_1 = mean for the low group, and m2 = mean for the total group). Ease of computation is noted as an advantage, and a geometric interpretation is given. For a lognormal distribution, the system achieves added simplification since in this case u = w. The indices are found to be particularly useful for analysis when average income is perceived as the product of several related factors. The expression in this paper, for example, decomposes per capita income into factors representing average wage, fraction of labor force utilized, fraction of labor force in the population, and ratio of total income to wage income. In this form, the logarithms of the inequality indices themselves show the relative significance of the components. Data from a 1962 survey of households in Hungary are used to give a practical illustration of some of these features.

Enke, Stephen. "On the Economics of Leisure." Journal of Economic Issues 2 (December 1968): 437-441.

(VIII)

The author utilizes a broadened definition of leisure to divide time into work, leisure (discretionary time) and non-discretionary time. He then discusses the economic implications of this new division, particularly the tradeoffs between the different activities. He concludes by observing that as work takes up less and less time, the problems of leisure will become more and more important.

Environmental Protection Agency. The Quality of Life Concept: A Potential New Tool for Decision-Makers. Washington, D.C.: Office of Research and Monitoring, Environmental Studies Division, 1973.

(XI)

The results of a symposium on the subject of quality of life, including articles by participants in the conference. The book stresses the importance of quantitative indicators of the quality of life for policy-making purposes. Poverty is not addressed, except as it provides an indicator for a national (as opposed to individual) quality of life measurement. However, the possibilities and uses for, and the philosophical and technical (quantitative) problems raised by the development of social indicators of a particular condition, whether it be quality of life or poverty, are illuminated.

*Epstein, Lenore. "Measuring the Size of the Low-Income Population." In Six Papers on the Size Distribution of Wealth and Income, edited by Soltow. New York: National Bureau of Economic Research, 1969.

(II)

A study of the effect of the definition of the recipient unit, reconstruction of families, and the time reference period on the size of the low income population. Epstein suggests that the Census "family" is too broad for use as a base from which poverty is measured; an alternative family definition in which "related adults" (other than spouse or unmarried children) are excluded is suggested. The net effect of this change is to increase the number of aged, the number of mother-child families, and the number of disabled persons counted as poor. Members of each of these 3 groups frequently live in extended households and their poverty is masked by the higher income of the rest of the household. Using consumption expenditures rather than income as a poverty measure leaves the total count of the poor unchanged, but does alter the mix of the poor. In particular, when income is used as a poverty threshold, young people (who are frequently suffering only temporary poverty) are over-represented in the count; the use of expenditure data corrects this since young people tend to overspend in anticipation of an expected higher future income.

Epstein, Lenore A. "Some Effects of Low Income on Children and Their Families." Social Security Bulletin 24 (February 1961): 12-16.

(IV, XI)

A number of estimates of the percentage of children in the United States whose families are poor are presented. The consensus figure is 20-25%. These are followed by a survey of the literature linking income and the quantity and quality of food, housing, medical care, and education. Poor children receive inferior amounts of these goods, thus increasing the probability that they will be poor as adults.

Epstein, Lenore, and Murray, Janet. "The Aged Population of the United States." Department of Health, Education, and Welfare, Social Security Administration, Office of Research and Statistics. Research Report # 19, 1967.

(VII)

This is the official final report of the 1963 Social Security Administration Survey of the Aged. A total of 7500 individuals and couples with at least one member over 62 responded. A complete demographic portrait of the aged is presented in the report. The principal sources of income for these families are examined and a positive correlation between high median income and income from earnings is noted. The interrelationships among social security benefits, public relief, earnings, and total income are examined in depth. The distribution of wealth among the aged is discussed and the high correlation between assets and income noted. Over 60% of the individuals in the lowest income third had less than $500 in financial assets. Financial assets were found to play a determining role in the decision to live with relatives rather than independently.

Fair, Ray C. "The Optimal Distribution of Income." <u>Quarterly Journal of Economics</u> 53 (November 1971): 551-579.

II)

This article attempts to calculate a range of optimal income distributions given different (and extreme) assumptions about the distribution of abilities among people, the distribution of industriousness (desire for income as opposed to leisure) among people, and the relationships between productivity (wages) and ability supplemented by education. The values chosen for these assumptions covered both extremes: the author hoped that the true optimal income distribution for the United States (based on a consensus of what is a fair distribution among people of equal abilities) would be within the range of values calculated.

The calculations were quite complex and involved a large model of an economic system. It was assumed that individuals maximized their own utility by choosing optimal values of education and hours of work and that the government constructed a tax schedule that optimized a social welfare function given individual optimization of utility. This social welfare function is society's choice as to what the best distribution of utility is; it was chosen so that its largest values came when every individual had roughly equal amounts of utility.

The resulting after-tax income distributions were optimal in that they maximized this social welfare function given the range of individual abilities, preferences, and productivities. Those calculations made with individuals of widely different abilities, preferences and productivities produced a less equal optimal income distribution than those made with individuals with similar abilities, preferences and productivities.

The actual income distribution of the United States appears to be very unequal. Only the most extreme choice of all variables produced an optimal income distribution more unequal. The article concludes with a list of reasons the actual income distribution might be less equal than the optimal one and then a warning from the author: the results are based on empirical data on the relationships between ability, education and productivity that is subject to doubt; the article should be read for its analysis and not for its results.

Fane, C.G. "Index Linking and Inflation." <u>National Institute of Economics Review</u> 70 (November 1974): 40-44.

(III)

Inflation affects both the total product of an economy (the "social cost" of inflation) and the distribution of that product among individuals. The social cost is largely a result of inflation induced uncertainty. The real value of long term contracts or debts can not be predicted in an economy with a fluctuating inflation rate. Assuming that borrowers and lenders are risk averse, this uncertainty makes both groups worse off than if the real values of debts were known. Inflation also influences the redistributive effects of taxation. An income tax in an inflationary period also acts as a tax on wealth. For instance, a 10% rise in share values accompanied by a 10% inflation represents no real gain, but for tax purposes it is treated as a 10% capital gain. Due to this and the interaction of inflation with other factors present in the British economy in the 1970's, equities have failed to be a hedge against inflation. Since wages and salaries have kept up or exceeded inflation during the early 1970's in England, inflation has probably distributed wealth away from people with investment incomes and towards those with earned incomes. Even if this redistribution is desirable, it could be achieved more efficiently and with less uncertainty by direct taxation at known rates. These uncertain and harmful effects of inflation could be mitigated by linking taxes, wages, government securities, mortgages, annuities, alimony, and other long term financial arrangements to an average price index. Learning to live with a relatively high rate of inflation, 10% or higher, with widespread use of cost index linking, would be better than suffering the harmful effects of a recession engineered to bring the inflation rate down to the lower levels of the 1950's and early 1960's.

Featherman, David, and Carter, T. Michael. "Discontinuities in Schooling and the Socioeconomic Life Cycle." Institute for Research on Poverty, University of Wisconsin, Working Paper 238 - 74. November 1974.

(IX)

An analysis of causes and consequences of discontinuities in schooling--age-grade retardation and temporary dropouts. Panel data on 340 men drawn from high schools in Michigan in 1957 and re-interviewed in 1972 were used. Mental ability emerges as the strongest cause of discontinuity, although parental occupational status is also important. Discontinuities were found to reduce future income and educational opportunity.

Featherman, David; Hauser, Robert; and Sewell, William. "Toward Comparable Data in Inequality and Stratification: Perspectives on the Second Generation of National Mobility Studies." American Sociologist 9 (1974).

(II)

A report on current empirical research on occupational mobility. Early literature in this area simply provided data on the extent of mobility; more recently, however, studies have begun to inquire into the causes of mobility. Additional work is necessary in this area, particularly in merging research on social indicators and mobility. A synopsis of mobility reports given in Rome (1972) at the International Sociological Association's meeting on social stratification is provided.

The Federal Budget and "The General Welfare". Conference on Economic Progress, Washington, D.C., 1962.

(II)

Poverty is considered to be a relative phenomenon: "A level of family living regarded as being above poverty decades ago may not be above 'poverty' today."

This 1960 study advocates more federal spending in all areas of social welfare: education, health, old age, unemployment and poverty. A full employment economy, the study argues, could produce enough tax revenue to finance massive programs while keeping defense spending at current levels.

Federal Energy Administration. Project Independence Report. Washington, D.C.: U.S. Government Printing Office, November 1974.

(V,VI)

The Project Independence Report is an evaluation of the nation's energy problem; it assesses the "base case" situation through 1985 if current policies continue and evaluates the implications of a wide range of major energy policy alternatives. Three broad options are considered: increasing domestic energy supply, conserving energy and managing energy demand, and establishing standby alternative energy programs. These strategies are evaluated in terms of their impact on the development of alternative energy sources; vulnerability to import disruptions; economic growth, inflation, and unemployment; environmental effects; and regional and social impacts.

Chapter VI, "Economic and Social Impacts," is of special interest in considering the interrelationship of poverty and energy. This chapter notes that higher income families use more energy but spend a lower proportion of their consumption budget for energy consumption than lower income families. Also, in colder regions, lower income families are at a disadvantage compared with higher income families in the same region and with families in warmer regions. Increases in energy prices generally bear more heavily on the poor since the energy related expenses of running a home--heating, lighting, and cooking--are a larger portion of a low income family's budget than of a high income family's budget. Gasoline purchases to operate a motor vehicle consume an increasing percentage of after tax income at annual income levels up to $6,000. Thereafter, the proportion of income spent on gasoline declines from about 5% at $6,000 to about 2% at $20,000.

*Feld, Barbara. "The Subemployment Index -- A New Measure." The Conference Board Record (July 1968): 26-30.

(X)

An examination of the Department of Labor's (DOL) new index of unemployment. In order to analyze areas within a city where unemployment is concentrated, DOL needed a new tool which would present a more realistic picture of employment problems. In addition to the traditional definition of unemployment, the "subemployment term" includes persons working part-time but wanting full-time work, heads of households and other members under 65 working full-time but still having a poverty income, half of the non-participant male group and an estimate of those absent. Preliminary results using the new measure indicate higher unemployment rates in all 10 slum areas when compared with their respective metropolitan areas. The poverty level measure also indicated higher rates in the slum areas than was the national norm. Feld however, argues that the poverty index is inconsistent with the normal income criterion for poverty and that a variable index, such as the one the Social Security Administration uses, would be a better measure.

Ferber, Robert. "Research on Household Behavior." American Economic Review (1962): 19-23.

(VII)

A survey of the principal empirical research on household behavior during the mid-fifties to early sixties. The literature surveyed falls into the following categories:

(1) theories of spending and saving;

(2) influence of variables other than income on spending and saving;

(3) determination of asset holdings;

(4) determination of specific expenditures;

(5) decision processes.

Ferguson, Robert. "Employment and the War on Poverty in the United States." International Labor Review (March 1970): 247-267.

(X)

A look at employment as a key factor in the reduction of poverty between 1949 and 1967. Using the $3,000 standard as an index for poverty, Ferguson finds that the percentage of low income families declines as more family heads gain full-time employment. The decline in the unemployment rate (1961-1968) and a major shift in higher paying jobs have also lowered the poverty incidence. Self-employment, particularly in agriculture is still one of the main contributors to poverty and provides potential for further reduction of poverty. A large number of those presently unemployed and not in the labor force are also poor. Many of them are too old or lack skills and education to seek employment. Ferguson recommends an expansion of the social welfare program and improvement in the quality of education as solutions for the further reduction in the poverty level.

*Ferguson, Robert. Unemployment: Its Scope, Measurement, and Effect on Poverty. Ithaca, New York: New York State School of Industrial and Labor Relations, 1971.

(X)

The relationship between unemployment and poverty is discussed. Using unemployment and poverty indices from the past 20 years Ferguson explains that unemployment, whether temporary or long-term, is a major cause of poverty. He singles out the elderly, female-headed families, farm workers disabled and Blacks as suffering most from this causal relationship. The "hidden unemployed", or those not counted as being in the labor force represent over 40 percent of those jobless and in poverty. Ferguson explains that unemployment, especially among the poor, will continue to be a problem until access to education and training is open to all. Racial discrimination, inadequate housing, and discriminatory hiring practices are also barriers preventing the poor from becoming employed.

Ferman, Louis A.; Kornbluh, Joyce L.; and Haber, Alan, eds. Poverty in America. Ann Arbor: The University of Michigan Press, 1965.

(II - XII)

A collection of 48 articles which focus on the definitions and prevalence of poverty, the structure of poverty, the relationship of poverty to the political economy, sustaining conditions of poverty, the life and values of the poor, and policies and programs to ameliorate poverty. Also included are a series of selected bibliographies. Articles relevant to the definition and measurement of poverty are annotated separately.

Fishelson, Gideon. "Simple Dynamic Effects on Work-Leisure Choice: A Rejoinder to the Skeptical Comment on the Static Theory." Journal of Human Resources (Spring 1971).

(VIII)

A criticism of Conlisk's paper "Simple Dynamic Effects in Work-Leisure Choice," which argues that raising the poverty floor might increase work effort. Fishelson also defines a variable termed "motivation" which affects work supply; here, however, motivation depends on future expected income, not on past income as in the Conlisk model. Fishelson's re-specification of the motivation equation, coupled with several additional modifications, changes Conlisk's results considerably. In particular, an increase in the income guarantee will increase work effort only in young age groups; for older people, the usual negative relation is preserved.

Fisher, Franklin M., and Shell, Karl. "Taste and Quality Change in the Pure Theory of the True Cost-of-Living Index." In Price Indexes and Quality Change, edited by Zvi Griliches. Cambridge, Massachusetts: Harvard University Press, 1971.

(III)

A major weakness in the theory of price index numbers is its treatment of taste and quality changes. Quality changes are considered either as the introduction of a new good or a price reduction. Change in tastes are ignored -- the consumer is assumed to have an unchanging indifference map and knowledge of all products and qualities, even those not yet introduced. This weakness is largely due to a misinterpretation of the theory of true costs-of-living indexes. The theory is erroneously thought to answer the question, "How much would it cost at today's prices to make the consumer just as well off as he was yesterday?" This question can only be answered by resorting to arbitrary comparisons of utility over time. A similar question that can be answered is, "How much income is required today to make me just indifferent between facing yesterday's budget constraint and facing a budget constraint defined by today's prices and the income in question?" With the correct interpretation of the theory, the assumption of unchanging indifference maps can be dropped, allowing the authors to develop a rigorous formulation of the theory involved with changing tastes. They conclude by showing what kind of information is needed to handle the treatment of the introduction of new goods and quality changes in a satisfactory manner.

Fisher, Irving. Theory of Interest, Chapter 5. New York, 1930.

(VII)

Fisher's thesis was that an individual with a variable income throughout his life would even out his consumption by means of lending and borrowing; these transactions depending on the market rate of interest. He also studies the interaction of saving decisions with investment decisions to determine market interest rates. His work is important because it provided one foundation of theory in saving and interest which led to the life cycle of saving and consumption theories of Brumberg, Modigliani, Tobin, Friedman and others.

Fisher, Janet. "Income, Spending, and Saving Patterns of Consumer Units in Different Age Groups." Studies in Income and Wealth 15 (1952).

(VII)

An account of income, asset and saving distributions over the life cycle. Income was found to increase with age, peaking in late middle age. Its distribution became more unequal with increasing age. Liquid assets follow the same pattern but start later. Income and liquid assets are shown to be a joint variable: about 25% of those with less than $1,000 in income had zero or negative assets. The demand for durables is shown to decrease with age and be replaced by a demand for household goods. Finally, the expenditures of the elderly are shown to vary less sharply than their incomes: the income elasticity of saving increases with age.

Fisher, Janet A. "Measuring the Adequacy of Retirement Incomes." In Aging and the Economy, edited by J. L. Orbach and Clark Tibbetts. Ann Arbor: University of Michigan Press, 1963.

(IV,VII)

Fisher's study focuses on the problem of distribution of income and financial assets within the older population. Her findings of greater income and asset inequality within the older population than within other age groups pointedly demonstrates the need for close examination of the oft-quoted statistics of the high average assets of the aged. When the top 20 percent of the aged population possess 78 percent of the group's total liquid assets and the bottom 30 percent have none at all, of what meaning is the average liquid asset? When this factor is taken in conjunction with the income distribution figures, we are left with a total picture which still emphasizes a very large proportion of the older population with severely limited incomes and little or no assets which are of any value in providing for current living needs.

(From the Introduction)

Fishman, Leo, ed. Poverty Amid Affluence. New Haven: Yale University Press, 1966.

(II,III)

This collection of conference papers covers historical and contemporary conceptions of poverty, poverty as a social phenomenon, special cases of poverty (e.g. the Negro, Appalachia), and various approaches to the elimination of poverty.

In general, the authors define poverty in ways convenient for their purposes. The Council of Economic Adviser's $3,000 poverty line proved especially useful because of the massive data available from the 1960 Census, although a measure that took family size, age, sex and permanent income into account would have been more accurate. Other authors stress the unique social organization of poor communities, showing how they perpetuate apathy and depression leading to poor performance at school and on the job.

Fleisher, Belton. "The Effect of Income on Delinquency." American Economic Review 56 (March 1966).

(XI)

A regression analysis of the effects of economic factors on delinquency. Establishes a direct correlation between income and delinquency. This relationship is expressed in terms of supply and demand; income positively affects number or value of delinquency opportunities (supply), and income negatively affects propensity to be delinquent (demand). Social factors of importance in the demand component are personality traits and family characteristics. "Demand" effect of income most pronounced among groups displaying these social traits to a high degree.

Ford Foundation Energy Policy Project. A Time to Choose: America's Energy Future. Ballinger, 1974.

(VI)

A Time to Choose is the final report of the Ford Foundation's Energy Policy Project which explored the range of energy choices open to the United States and identified possible energy policies. The report projects three energy use scenarios to the year 2000 and considers questions of energy supply and demand and the impacts of various levels of energy used. Chapter 5, "The American Energy Consumer: Rich, Poor, and In-between," is of special interest to considering the impact of energy policy on the poor.

Consideration of the relationship between income and energy consumption is based on a survey of household energy consumption in 1972-1973 undertaken by the Washington Center for Metropolitan Studies (WCMS). Although high income households use more energy than low income households, the variations in energy levels among the different income groups are less pronounced than the differences in income. While the average household income among the poor is about one-tenth as large as that of the well-off, poor families use almost half as much energy as families who are well-off. This means that energy, like other necessities such as food and housing, eats up a considerably larger share of a poor family's budget than an affluent family. Poor families spent roughly 15% of their income annually on natural gas, electricity, and gasoline, while lower-, middle-, and upper-middle income groups spent seven percent and six percent respectively; the well-off spent about 4% of family income on energy.

Forrester, Jay W. Urban Dynamics. Cambridge: MIT Press, 1969.

(V,VI)

Urban Dynamics is a model using the simulation language DYNAMO to model urban growth. It considers three population groups, three industrial levels, and three types of housing; and models changes related to "natural" influences and local policies. The model results show little effectiveness for housing and social service programs, but great multipliers for industrial development. The reason for these results is simple: an implicit assumption is that there is a great mass of poor rural people waiting to move into the city whenever it becomes attractive. Social programs improve attractiveness, create in-migration, and are stopped. Development programs create jobs filled by upper class people, and succeed. The model is rooted in the assumptions of its developers; while useful as a demonstration tool of the interrelationships involved in a city, it adds little insight.

*Forsyth, F. G. "The Relationship Between Family Size and Expenditure." Journal of the Royal Statistical Society. Ser. A, 123 (1960): Part A.

(IV)

The use of "adult equivalent scales," in which any family member can be expressed as a proportion of a "standard" family member for the purpose of explaining the relation between family size and family expenditure, has been examined by Allan (1942) and by Prais and Houthakker (1955). Forsyth uses previously unavailable household survey data to examine the equivalent scale hypotheses for families composed only of two adults and children under sixteen.

Weekly expenditures in twelve categories are regressed on mean aggregate expenditure for families of four different sizes using four alternative function forms; these yielding different regression coefficients for each family type and expenditure category. These regression coefficients are then used in the estimation of a family composition parameter for each commodity. Comparison of predicted and actual expenditures for families of different size lead Forsyth to conclude that the "equivalent scale hypothesis" is not effective in explaining family expenditure differences.

Foster, C.D., and Neuburger, H.C.I. "The Ambiguity of the Consumer's Surplus Measure of Welfare Change." <u>Oxford Economic Papers</u> 26 (1974): 66-77.

(III)

There are three commonly-used measures of the welfare effects of price changes, government programs, etc. (1) The Marshallian method measures the area under the relevant section of the demand curve. (2) The equivalent variation (EV) is measured by the amount of money that will yield the same level of utility before the change as would be brought about by the change. (3) The compensating variation (CV) is measured by the amount of money needed after the change has been made to bring an individual back to his original utility level.

For the purpose of ordinal utility rankings of alternative programs or changes, the EV and CV measures are theoretically more correct than the Marshallian method. Marshall accepted the unlikely assumptions that there is a constant marginal utility of money, and that consumers will not change their patterns of consumption in response to a price change (or will change them insignificantly). Of the two "variations," only the EV is "always an admissible index for the analysis of welfare changes, while only the CV is "always an admissible index of Pareto optimal compensations." Unfortunately, knowledge of incomes and price elasticities are necessary for the calculation of both the EV and the CV. Since the Marshallian method only requires knowledge of conventional Marshall demand curves, it is always more practical to use this method. In principle, the three methods do not necessarily yield the same ordinal rankings, but, in practice, they usually do.

Franke, Walter. "The Long-Term Unemployed." In In Aid of the Unemployed. Baltimore, Maryland: Johns Hopkins Press, 1965.

(X)

An analysis of long-term unemployment and prospective federal programs to curb employment problems. The extent of hardship coming from long-term unemployment is examined by looking at such variables as sex, age, breadwinner status and number of dependents. The older workers, married men and women and non-whites are shown as experiencing the highest percentages of long-term unemployment. In geographical terms long-term unemployment did not seem to be higher in depressed areas than other areas. However, in areas dominated by a single industry, long-term unemployment caused by an industry move or shut-down is severe. The total analysis indicates that persistent unemployment is related to national economic trends and that by minimizing recessionary swings and increasing the national growth rate the federal government can partially help to solve the problems of long-term unemployment. Rapid growth of the labor force and the rapid increase in technology are two reasons cited for the inadequacy of the federal initiatives.

Franklin, N.N. "The Concept and Measurement of 'Minimum Living Standards'." International Labour Review 95 (1967): 271-298.

(II)

Human needs include both biological necessities and social needs determined by the community. Turn-of-century studies in Britain by Rowntree used only physical subsistence standards to set a poverty line. In 1954, Townsend calculated a poverty line by multiplying the cost of a minimally adequate diet by a multiple obtained by surveying the poorest 25% of all those actually able to secure adequate nutrition. Current U.S. standards are calculated in a similar fashion.

Standards in less-developed countries, used mainly to set minimum wages, are based on minimum requirements for utter necessities.

Yet there are no clear-cut medical minimum food requirements, and non-food needs are even less well-defined. Social necessities are too complex to specify, but generally increase the more affluent the community. Galbraith has suggested that anyone much poorer than others in his community is poor.

Franklin, N.N. "Employment and Unemployment: Views and Policies, 1919-1969." International Labour Review 99(March 1969): 293-314.

(II,X)

Prior to the First World War, two major causes of unemployment were recognized: (a) seasonal and cyclical fluctuations in the demand for labor, and (b) deficiencies in the employment market organization that prevented employers and workers from efficiently coming in contact with one another. "The idea that the demand for labor as a whole might fail to keep pace with the supply had been raised only to be dismissed in orthodox circles." The post-war depression stimulated some measures to institute public employment exchanges and compulsory unemployment insurance, but it was the Great Depression of 1929-1933 that exposed the inadequacy of current theories. "The ten years following the publication of Keynes's General Theory in 1936 saw a remarkable growth of understanding of the problems of unemployment in developed countries." The ideas that deficiency of demand may be more than a cyclic phenomenon and that major government fiscal actions may be necessary to raise effective demand to a full employment level were given added credibility by "the great object lesson of the Second World War." "In country after country, as government wartime expenditure mounted, unemployment melted like snow in a hot sun." The role of government in maintaining demand is now more acknowledged, and a more common problem of the past thirty years in managing demand for employment has been to insure that "demand should not be so excessive in relation to available supplies as to generate intolerable inflationary pressure."

*Freeman, Howard, and Sheldon, Eleanor. "Notes on Social Indicators: Promise and Potential." Policy Science 1 (1970): 97-110.

(XI)

An overview of the utility and claims of social indicators. Evaluation of three possible uses for indicators is explored: goal setting, program evaluation and social balance sheet development. Authors contend that the use of these social measures should be done cautiously and only as part of the total social policy decision-making process. They suggest possible uses of social indicators to be descriptive reporting, social change analysis and predicting future social events. The embryonic stage of social statistics and the absence of social theories which define the variables of a social system are two central reasons given for limited use of social indicators.

Freeman, Richard B. "Changes in the Labor Market of Black Americans, 1948-1972." Brookings Papers on Economic Activity (No. 3, 1973): 67-120.

(IX)

The income and occupational position of Blacks improved significantly relative to that of whites during the 1960's. Apparently this improvement took place largely as a result of governmental and related antidiscriminatory activity associated with the 1964 Civil Rights Act. Young Black men and young Black male college graduates experienced especially large economic gains relative to whites; white older men made much smaller relative gains. This suggests that the gains of the decade went mainly to men starting their careers during the period and thus were not handicapped by inexperience or lack of on-the-job training relative to their white counterparts. On the other hand, Black male employment is strongly cyclical, rising relatively in expansions and falling in recessions. Black women experienced the largest relative gains of any group of Black workers. This occurred as a result of their movement into higher paying occupations. The supply of Blacks to occupations was significantly influenced by income opportunities. Supply elasticities rose as high as 1.6 for younger Blacks. When economic opportunities improved, Blacks responded by moving into jobs at many occupational levels that previously had been closed to them.

Friedman, Barry, and Hausman, Leonard. "Income Conditioning in a System of Transfer Programs." American Economic Review 64 (No. 2, 1974): 175-180.

(II)

It is normally assumed that income subsidy programs are superior to commodity subsidy programs. This article shows that this is not necessarily true. Given an income subsidy program whose subsidy depends on the income of the recipient (is income conditioned), an offsetting small transfer from the income subsidy program (taken to be a negative income tax) to a commodity subsidy program (wage or rent subsidies) will result in a greater work effort from the recipient while at the same time increasing his utility. This suggests that a mix of subsidy programs would be the most effective way to combat poverty. The article concludes with a discussion of some of the problems involved in coordinating such a mix of programs.

Friedman, John, and Alonso, William. Regional Development and Planning: A Reader. Cambridge, Massachusetts: The MIT Press, 1964.

(VI)

This volume is a collection of 35 articles about regional development and planning. The articles are organized within a loose framework provided by the editors and are grouped into four areas: space and planning, location and spatial organization, the theory of regional development and national policy for regional development.

Development areas can be classified into four general categories: metropolitan regions with high potential for further economic expansion; development axes or corridors along transport routes between metropolitan areas; frontier regions or nonmetropolitan regions with growth potential due to new technologies, resources or national objectives; and depressed areas. Three approaches to regional development are analysed. The first is mainly historical and focuses on a given region. The rest of the country is treated as one unit. The second looks at the nation as a whole. "The question is therefore not why a given area, arbitrarily defined, has fared in a certain way, but why particular patterns and sequences of spatial organization have accompanied the evolution of the national economy." And the third analyzes internal migration.

The editors suggest four criteria for testing the consequences of specific policy proposals: 1) national economic integration, 2) economic efficiency, 3) maximization of opportunities for growth of the national economy, and 4) attainment of interregional balance in living conditions.

Friedman, Milton. Capitalism and Freedom. Chicago: The University of Chicago Press, 1962.

(II)

Friedman argues that competitive capitalism--the organization of the bulk of economic activity through private enterprise operating in a free market--is a system of economic freedom and a necessary condition for political freedom. The role of government in a free system should be limited to the preservation of law and order, the enforcement of private contracts, and the encouragement of private markets. Economic inequality, i.e., income distribution, takes two forms: temporary and long-term. The former occurs in societies with great mobility and change, such as in the U.S.; the latter in societies with great rigidity such as in Communist countries. Although at any one time, the income distribution in the U.S. may be wide, in the long-run it is narrower than in Communist countries. Poverty is defined as relative lack of money which may be ameliorated by raising the incomes of the poor to a minimum standard. The negative income tax is favored because it provides the poor individual with that which he needs most--cash. This definition minimizes government interference in poor people's lives. It also leads to the most efficient means for mitigating poverty--simply giving people money. Finally, it isolates poverty from other factors such as race, group membership, occupation, etc. Economic progress, which can be attributed to the capitalist system, has been a major factor in the elimination of absolute poverty.

Friedman, Milton. "Discussion of the Inflationary Gap." In <u>Essays on Positive Economics</u> by Milton Friedman. New York: University of Chicago Press, 1953.

(III)

This essay is a discussion of the inflationary gap or the "difference between expected expenditure and the value of goods expected to be available." Friedman argues against the hypothesis that fully anticipated inflation has no negative effect on economic welfare. In particular he argues that price rises reduce the value of fixed government obligation. This is equivalent to a tax on the holding of such obligation and tends to reduce the amount of real income. This in turn reduces demand and tends to close the inflationary gap. A demand reduction, however, results in a reallocation of resources leading to a loss of economic welfare.

The government can use several policies to close the inflationary gap: stimulation of savings, taxation, rationing some goods, restricting consumer credit, reduction of expenditures, wage freezes, etc. Quantitative estimates of the contribution of each tool are needed to obtain the optimum combination of policies.

*Friedman, Milton. "A Method of Comparing Incomes of Families Differing in Composition." <u>Studies in Income and Wealth</u> (1952).

(IV)

In order to investigate consumption patterns and rank families by relative economic status, we need a means of comparing the incomes of families differing in age and sex composition. "Ammain scales" (adult male maintenance) for items consumed by the individual can be directly calculated for each category of consumption by choosing one family member as the unit of comparison. If the ratio of each family member's consumption in the category to the amount consumed by the base member is independent of family size and income, the result is an ammain scale. For items consumed by the family as a whole we need compare two families who are "equally well off", as defined by some dietary scale or by a statistical analysis of multiple correlation. These families should differ in composition by exactly one family member, thus the additional expenditure needed to leave the family equally well off can be calculated.

*Friedman, M. A Theory of the Consumption Function. Princeton: Princeton University Press, 1957.

(VII)

Post-war empirical studies of consumption gave rise to a paradox which this book attempts to resolve. Cross-sectional data show that units with relatively high incomes save a larger percentage of their incomes than do those with lower incomes (the poorest group actually dissaves). Yet when incomes rise generally with economic growth, the average propensity to save, rather than rising as would be expected, remains remarkably constant. Friedman hypothesizes that a unit's consumption is a function of its "permanent income" and that windfall gains tend to be saved while transitory losses are compensated for out of savings. In any given time period, those suffering temporary losses of income will be concentrated in the lowest income groups and will be observed to dissave, while those currently reaping windfall gains, who will be concentrated in the higher income groups, will seem to have a higher propensity to save. Long-run economic growth, however, will change permanent income and so induce proportionately higher consumption. This is consistent with the wide variety of evidence Friedman marshals.

*Friedman, Rose. Poverty Definition and Perspective. Washington, D.C.: American Enterprise Institute, February 1965.

(II,IV,V)

An examination of definitions and descriptions of poverty. Poverty definitions vary widely depending upon the level of living prevalent in the reference county. In the 18th and 19th centuries, as well as in many present underdeveloped countries, subsistence constituted the relevant poverty line. By the early 20th century, the poverty line had moved up from adequate income to eliminate hunger to adequate income to provide a "nutritionally sound" diet, as well as to cover other essential needs. More recently, the relative concept of poverty has become popular. Friedman then criticizes the Council of Economic Advisor (CEA) definition of poverty on the grounds that it ignores need differences produced by differences in family size and composition, regional and rural-urban differences in prices, and differences in percentage of budget spent on food at different income levels in its choice of a multiplier factor to transform food budgets to total needs. Friedman's re-estimate of poverty suggests that only 10% of all families are poor, as opposed to the CEA's estimate of 20%.

*Fuchs, Victor R. "Redefining Poverty and Redistributing Income." Public Interest 8 (Summer 1967): 88-95.

(II)

It is proposed that any family whose income is less than 50% of the median family income be defined as poor. This poverty standard allows for changes with the growth of real national income and has several other advantages. By a fixed standard it would seem that poverty has declined considerably since WWII, but defined in relation to contemporary standards there has not been any decrease in the entire postwar period. The United States has formulated many policies aimed at achieving efficiency in the use of resources, stability of employment and prices, and growth of real output, but has tended to ignore policies aimed at an equitable distribution of income. The author contends that poverty in the United States in the 1960's is a matter of economic and social distance (a relative rather than absolute perspective), and that the gap between the average family and those at the bottom is large enough to justify the use of a poverty standard that changes with the growth of real national income. This standard: (1) is not subject to political manipulation; (2) can be adjusted to take account of family size and composition; and (3) adjusts itself to reflect current conceptions of material needs.

(Partially taken from Poverty and Human Resources Abstracts)

*Fuchs, Victor R. "Toward A Theory of Poverty." In The Concept of Poverty, Task Force on Economic Growth and Opportunity, Chamber of Commerce of the United States. Washington, D.C.: Library of Congress #65-21323, 1965.

(II)

A look at poverty in terms of problems of definition, analysis, and policy. Focus is on economic poverty, although existence of other forms is recognized. Problems are raised about the use of annual income data to measure poverty. Absolute versus relative definitions of poverty are compared, with the conclusion that, since absolute standards constantly change, relative standards are more appropriate for present and future policy. More observations are made about the status of absolute versus relative poverty in America and its implications for policy. Demographic characteristics of the poor are enumerated. Regional differences are discussed. Consequences of poverty and policy are also analyzed.

Fuz, J.K. Welfare Economics in English Utopias. Netherlands: Martinus Nijhoff, 1952.

(II)

A study of welfare measures advocated in the early Utopian literature, beginning with Francis Bacon (1629) and ending with Robert Wallace (1761). A wide variety of "optimal" income distributions are advocated in this literature. Bacon suggests that revenue should be "varied by discretion according to the number and dignity of the family" (Nova Atlantis). Mandeville, in discussing poverty suggests that "to make the society happy and people easy under the meanest circumstances, it is requisite that great numbers of them should be ignorant as well as poor" (Fable of the Bees). Wallace, on the other hand, argues that "not only poverty, but the fear of it...(should be) ...banished" (Various Prospects). Finally, Bellers adds an adage of some interest: "the Poor without Imployment are like rough diamonds, their worth is unknown" (Proposals for Raising a College of Industry).

Galbraith, John K. The Affluent Society. Boston: Houghton, Mifflin Co., 1968.

(II)

Many central economic ideas have been rendered obsolete by America's transformation into an affluent society. It is the first nation in history in which poverty is not the norm for the vast majority. New products are held to create their own demand (the "dependence effect"). Poverty is loosely defined as a lack of sufficient food, shelter and clothing, with "sufficiency" determined by the community's idea of a decent standard of living. Poverty in America, the author contends, consists primarily of "case poverty" (stemming from some handicap or circumstance peculiar to the individual) and "insular poverty" (characteristic of areas such as Appalachia where everyone is poor and poverty cannot be attributed to individual deficiency).

*Gallaway, Lowell. "On the Importance of 'Picking One's Parents.'" Quarterly Review of Economics and Business (Summer 1966).

(IX,XI)

A critical analysis of the "vicious-cycle of poverty" assumption. Using data collected by the Department of Commerce study of Lifetime Occupational Mobility (1962), Gallaway estimates the degree of intergenerational occupational mobility among males aged 25-64. An "economic opportunity index" is developed which summarizes the probability of sons remaining in their fathers' occupations; the index varies from 0--no relationship between father and son occupations--and 1--sons perfectly inherit fathers' positions. In addition to the aggregate opportunity index, Gallaway constructs separate transition probabilities by occupation. Gallaway's conclusion is that the data provides "a strong argument against the idea that the economic status of parents is a major determinant of the economic success of offspring."

Gallaway, Lowell E. "The Negro and Poverty." The Journal of Business 40 (January 1967): 27-35.

(XI)

Article evaluates the relative contributions to Negro poverty of educational differences between Negroes and whites and a composite of all other elements correlated with race. Gallaway uses stochastic analysis to determine the income transition probabilities (movement from non-poverty to poverty status or vice versa) for Negroes and white males separately between the years 1955-56. The incidence of poverty among Negroes is 2.5 times that of whites, and Negroes are more likely to move from non-poverty to poverty status. Negroes, therefore, have lower income opportunity. Gallaway then demonstrates that educational differences and race are important factors which correlate with the Negroes' diminished income opportunity. Improving educational levels among Negroes could make a substantial contribution to eliminating their poverty. Race, likewise, and all the composite factors associated with it--discrimination in labor markets, social attitudes of Negroes, etc.--must also be dealt with effectively if the greater relative incidence of poverty among Negroes is to be eliminated.

* Gans, Herbert J. "Culture and Class in the Study of Poverty: An Approach to Anti-Poverty Research." In <u>On Understanding Poverty</u>, edited by Daniel P. Moynihan. New York: Basic Books, Inc., 1968.

(II)

A criticism of the poverty research which has been performed by middle-class members of an affluent society who tend to view the poor as "deserving" or "undeserving". Gans endorses the viewpoint of the poor as the economically and politically deprived who have adapted to their deprivation.

The deficiencies of the cultural view of social and personal change of the poor, the lack of homogeneity within the poor class, the use of overly behavioral definitions, and the systematic view of the interrelationships of poverty are explored. Gans proposes an alternative research method which involves viewing poverty as behavioral patterns, norms, and aspirations and testing their validity as a function of their persistence in changing conditions.

Gans, Herbert J. "Income Grants and 'Dirty Work'." <u>The Public Interest</u> 6 (Winter, 1967): 110-113.

(II)

The underpaid people who do "dirty work," and those who earn only $50 a week might be lured away from work by income grants or a negative income tax. The problem which would arise in this situation, however, is not one inherent in the concept of income grants, etc., but one inherent in "dirty," underpaid jobs. The fear that underlies opposition to these economic programs is that if they were present there would be nobody who would fill these jobs, which are presently relegated in a vast majority to Blacks. In response to this fear the author states that "products and services which can exist only through subsidization by low wages should not exist." A study is quoted which found that social pathology, which was only correlated .07 with unemployment, was correlated .64 with unskilled "low status" jobs. "More attention must be paid to the elimination of dirty, dead end, and low-paid jobs, even as the society struggles to eliminate unemployment."

Gans, Herbert. More Equality. New York: Vintage Books, 1974.

(II)

A collection of essays dealing with the problems of achieving greater equality and the likely social, economic and political consequences of increased equality. In determining the optimal distribution of income, it is necessary to make a trade-off between efficiency considerations and ethical/normative considerations. Some variance in income is necessary, for example, to provide incentives for sorting people properly across jobs and to generate effort; thus, perfect income equality is not advocated. On normative grounds, no person should have less income than is necessary to provide for the socially accepted standard of living. Gans identifies this acceptable standard (on the basis of Gallup surveys) at 60-70 percent of society's median income.

Garfinkel, Irwin, and Haveman, Robert. "Earnings Capacity and the Target Efficiency of Alternative Transfer Programs." American Economic Review 64 (May 1974): 196-204.

(III, V, IX)

In this paper, the authors developed an alternative indicator of family economic status using a measure of earning capacity. This measure is intended to eliminate the influence of people's taste for work, as well as the distortions of temporary fluctuations in income. Regression analysis was used to estimate the effects on various demographic characteristics (age, years of school, race, marital status, location, weeks worked and part-time/full-time employment status) on earning capacity. The regression coefficients were applied to the demographic characteristics of each of 50,000 families to arrive at an estimate of their earnings capacity. The earnings capacity poor is thus identified and compared to the poverty population as defined by the standard annual income definition. Some interesting findings: female headed families were as high among the earnings capacity poor as among income poor, indicating that even if a substantial number of female heads worked more, they would still be poor. Also the working poor constituted a larger percentage of the earnings capacity poor than they did the income poor, emphasizing the inequity in failure to provide assistance to them. A comparison of the target groups that each measure would identify for several alternative income transfer programs was also illuminating.

*Gastwirth, Joseph L. "Estimating the Number of Hidden Unemployed." Monthly Labor Review (March 1973): 17.

(X)

An analysis of econometric methods for estimating the number of "hidden unemployed." The "hidden unemployed" are also known as "discouraged workers," those people who are not looking for work because they think there are no jobs available for them. They are not included in the unemployment rate; however, the Bureau of Labor Statistics (BLS) does collect data on them. The present study observes that there are wide discrepancies between the BLS survey estimates of the "hidden unemployed" and econometric model estimates and offers some explanations for the differences. Critical assumptions underlying the model are also examined. Some reasons for the discrepancy in one model were: (1) prediction equations varied with the time period, hence recent data would have to be used; (2) the elasticity of married women's labor force participation is very large, hence contradicting the model's assumption that primary labor markets (men 25-55 years old) and secondary labor markets (women and men age 16-24) were independent of one another. (3) The models assume that present labor force behavior is entirely predicted by past behavior, when, in fact, the basic labor force behavior appears to be correlated with general economic trends. In conclusion, the researchers indicated a need for dynamic or recursive models which will be more responsive to economic and social trends in labor force behavior.

Gastwirth, Joseph L. "Large Sample Theory of Some Measures of Income Inequality." Econometrica 42 (January 1974).

(II)

"In order to draw valid conclusions from actual samples, one needs to know the sampling distribution of the statistic used to estimate the measure of inequality." This paper presents methods to determine the large sample distribution of the mean deviation, the Pietra ratio, and the measures of Elteto and Frigyes.

*Gastwirth, Joseph L. <u>On the Estimation of the Lorenz Curve and Gini Index</u>. Technical Report No. 147. Baltimore, Md.: Johns Hopkins University, November 1970.

(II,III)

"Most of the measures of income inequality are derived from the Lorenz curve; indeed J. Morgan states that the Gini index is the best single measure of inequality. The aim of the present article is to review some of the theoretical properties of the Lorenz curve, relating them to characteristics of the frequency function underlying the income distribution and using them to develop methods of obtaining accurate bounds on the Gini index which do not depend on curve fitting. In the process some myths concerning the Gini index are laid to rest such as:

a) its relative insensitivity
b) difficulty in computation
c) problems related to the inclusion of negative incomes.

"The basic idea of our approach is to obtain upper and lower bounds to the Gini index from data which is grouped in intervals and the mean income in each group is known." An advantage of the methods used is that they are readily modified to incorporate negative incomes. More significantly, the bounds derived by one of the methods used in this essay are usually accurate enough to distinguish between the IRS income distributions for consecutive years.

Geary, R.C. "A Note on 'A Constant Utility Index of the Cost of Living'." <u>Review of Economic Studies</u> 18 (1949): 65-66.

(III)

Income (r) can be expressed as the sum of prices (p) and quantities (x).

$$r = \sum_{i-1}^{n} p_i x_i$$

Income can be expressed in terms of prices alone if the Slutsky equation is satisfied and if the demand equation has the form:

$$x_i = \Sigma a_{ij} \frac{p_i}{p_i} + \beta_i \frac{r}{p_i}$$

Geary shows that using the "intuitive" hyperbolic form of the utility function, the demand equation can be derived in the above form; and using the maximum utility property

$$\left(\frac{\partial u}{\partial x_i} = kp_i\right),$$

the income can be found in terms of p_i alone without resorting to the Slutsky equation. Although this is theoretically possible, "it remains to be seen whether the conditions under which the Slutsky equation holds are more plausible than the assumption that the utility function has hyperbolic form.

"The General Principles on Which Scales for Family Allowances are Determined." International Social Security Review 18 (July-September 1965), (Report XVII).

(IV)

A study of the calculation and fixing procedure for family allowance rates in 39 countries. Discusses the effect of factors associated with the children in calculation of the grant: age, number, seniority and residence of the child. Also, considers influence of factors regarding the breadwinner: nature and sector of occupational activity, working hours, residence, marital status, etc. Some variance among countries is noted on all the above counts, but it is concluded that most countries prefer the rule of uniformity.

Report also explores variance in methods of fixing rates. Observes two alternative forms: lump sum payment and percentage of a reference (for example, occupational income or minimum wage) basis. Observes that lump sum scheme is used in 29 out of 39 countries.

George, Henry. Progress and Poverty. New York: Robert Schalkenbach Foundation, 1929.

(II)

A late nineteenth century study of the causes of industrial depressions and the persistence of poverty. The conventional Malthusian doctrine that poverty persists because of population pressures is first examined and rejected. George than suggests that it is the private ownership of land that holds wages down to a subsistence level, and in fact "as land increases in value, poverty deepens." Quite naturally, George considers the only viable solution to the poverty problem to be the abolition of privately owned land. The effects of this action are then analyzed.

Girao, J.A.; Tomek, W.F.; and Mount, T.D. "The Effect of Income Instability on Farmers' Consumption and Investment." Review of Economics and Statistics 56(1974): 141-149.

(VI)

The hypothesis that income stability would help farmers make better consumption and investment decisions is analyzed. Five consumption models are used. Two are based on Friedman's permanent income hypothesis; the third is derived by combining expectations and partial adjustments models; the fourth is based on Ando and Modigliani's life cycle hypothesis; and the fifth is derived from the Duesenberry-Eckstein-Fromm formulation of the relative income hypothesis. The rate of investment is considered to be determined by "the intersection of the marginal efficiency of investment and the marginal cost of funds schedule." Two gross investment measures are used: total fixed investment and investment in machinery and equipment. The authors conclude that income instability has little effect on consumption, but it does appear to influence investment. In unstable conditions, farmer's investment decisions are more short-run and less responsive to savings and to changes in sales than in stable conditions.

Gladwin, Thomas. "The Anthropologist's View of Poverty." In The Social Welfare Forum, The National Conference on Social Welfare. New York: Columbia University, 1961.

(XI)

The poor may be viewed as a subculture, characterized by shared patterns of behavior, thinking, and feeling which differ in some respects from those of the larger culture. Our commitment to eliminate hard-core poverty involves a re-examination of our values and requires our acceptance of and respect for the poor. Our subjective assumptions about the "undeserving poor," that they are shiftless and do not want to try to help themselves, serve as a critical barrier to respect.

Two attributes which require understanding and upon which social workers should focus when dealing with "multiproblem" families involve their perception of reality--their lack of control over destiny and absence of future time perspective. Gladwin asks, "Why should they work hard and make sacrifices toward a goal which others control and which will be withheld from them?" Why delay gratification when the chance may never come again?

An effective program to abolish poverty and its threats to society must be one of culture change.

*Glantz, Frederic B. "The Determinants of the Interregional Migration of the Economically Disadvantaged." Federal Reserve Bank of Boston Report . 52, January 1973.

(VI)

Migration is often seen as a labor market adjustment mechanism--labor migrates from low-wage, high-unemployment areas to high-wage, low-unemployment areas. For the economically disadvantaged, in addition to job opportunities, other factors appear to be significant determinants of migration. "The disadvantaged migrate to areas about which information is more readily available to them--larger areas and areas with high concentrations of disadvantaged residents." The data also suggests that the poor also migrate to areas with higher welfare payments per recipient although the evidence is not completely consistent. Between 1955 and 1960 higher welfare was not a significant attraction to migrants.

"It appears that the determinants of the migration of the economically disadvantaged is a special case of the determinants of the migration of labor. Labor migrates in response to interregional differences in economic opportunity--defined to include income from non-labor sources. The lower the migrants' economic status (defined by earnings potential) the more importance he attaches to interregional differences in nonlabor income in his migration decision."

Glantz, Frederic B. "Migration and Economic Opportunity: The Case of the Poor." New England Economic Review (March-April 1973): 14-19.

(VI)

An explanation of migration patterns of the poor. Employment opportunities and wage rates are considerations in migration, as explained by classical economic theory; however, non-labor sources of maximizing income, such as interregional welfare payment differentials, may also influence the decision to migrate. Noneconomic factors may be further catalysts: friends and family often provide information as well as temporary support and shelter, and population size is related to the amount of information available to the public and to the area's attractiveness through its social and recreational activities.

The study's hypothesis--that migrants attempt to maximize income from all sources--was tested empirically and validated. A technical appendix discusses in detail the statistical analysis.

The author concludes with a word on the implications of migration for economic efficiency and recommends uniform national standards for welfare payments to disallow welfare payments as an incentive to migrate and thereby eliminate misallocation of funds.

Glazer, Nathan. "Paradoxes of American Poverty." The Public Interest 1 (1965): 71-81.

(II)

The social phenomenon of poverty in America is contrasted with poverty in Europe. The U.S. poverty line is the wage of the respectable working class in Western Europe. In Europe, necessities like housing and medical care are provided publicly while the United States relies on the free market. Thus public assistance in Europe is a mere adaptation to "ill-fitting planks in the national floor" (i.e., an adequate standard of living), while in the United States anti-poverty programs are devoted more to manpower training than to a guaranteed minimum income. The numbers of Black and Spanish-speaking people among the poor make poverty such a social problem, in contrast to Britain where much less attention is paid. The ethnic and cultural divisions between the staff of social programs and their clients necessitate community action pressure groups to change the bureaucracy from the outside. These groups sometimes have federal funding. This, too, is unknown in Europe.

Glazer, Nora, and Creedon, Carol, eds. Children and Poverty. Chicago: Rand McNally and Co., 1969.

(XI)

A collection of essays on the interconnections between social institutions and the social and psychological characteristics of poor children in the United States. Causes of poverty, characteristics of the poor, and the impact of social institutions in remedying poverty are considered.

Goldman, Nathan. "Social Breakdown." Annals of the American Academy of Political and Social Science (September 1967).

(XI)

Poverty is one among many symptoms (e.g., family breakdown, alcoholism, mental disorder, sexual deviation) of moral and social disintegration. However, available data on these problems are either so deficient or so incomplete that accurate appraisal of the situation is impossible, and some of these problems seem to be more or less socially sanctioned adjustments to strains in the social system rather than maladjustments in themselves. To achieve our goal of maximizing the social health of U.S. society, these problems can be considered as indicators of strain, and our national resources must be focused on the reduction of these strains. Standard definitions or criteria of social problems must be established, and the scope and accuracy of data-collection increased. Information-gathering on the local or state level would need to be coordinated on a nationwide basis to provide a useful set of indicators of the social state of the nation.

Goldsmith, Selma. "Changes in the Size Distribution of Income." The American Economic Review 47 (1957): 504-518.

(II)

This article discusses changes in the relative income distribution between 1929 and 1955 and the influence of various definitions and concepts on these changes. Between 1929 and 1948 the share of the top 5 percent of income-earners declined 40 percent. For the lowest 40 percent of consumer units the greatest relative gains were made during World War II, with no relative changes since that time. From 1929 to 1955 the share of wages in national income rose steadily from 61 percent to 73 percent. Rural-urban and other regional differences narrowed over the period. The share of the top income groups may be understated due to capital gains, executive fringe benefits and underreporting.

Goldsmith, Selma; Jazi, George; Kaitz, Hyman; and Liebenberg, Maurice. "Size Distribution of Income Since the Mid-Thirties." The Review of Economics and Statistics 36 (1954): 1-32.

(II)

The article examines pre- and post-tax income distribution from 1935 to 1950. Real income nearly doubled over this period, greatly reducing the number of families in the lowest absolute income brackets. The relative distribution of income became more equal between 1935 and 1944, and stayed constant thereafter. The change was mainly due to a decline in the share of the top income group, although its absolute income rose. Federal income taxes were found to reduce the Gini index of inequality by 4-1/2 percent in 1941 and by 6 percent in 1950. This difference is mainly due to changes in the tax structure.

Goldstein, G.S., and Moses, L.N. "A Survey of Urban Economics." Journal of Economic Literature 11 (1973): 471-515.

(V,VI)

Modern urban economics dates back to the first two decades of the 20th century. At the time, researchers focused on the internal structure of the developing U.S. city. In the 30's urban economists, particularly Hoover and Isard, applied broader economic concepts and theory, including location theory, to the study of cities. In the 60's Alonso and Wingo developed the analysis of urban land use. In their models, cities consisted of a central business district surrounded by circular rings, each with a different land use: finance, retailing, housing, etc. The object was to show how competition determines the price of urban space with given techniques, costs of transportation, and prices of products and factors. More recently, several objections have been raised to these models, particularly their abstraction from institutions (i.e. government) and their static nature. Concerning the latter, models of urban growth have been developed but these have neglected land use. Urban simulation models attempt to analyze problems of growth and land use change, but they have many weaknesses.

Goodrich, Carter, et al. Migration and Economic Opportunity. Philadelphia: University of Pennsylvania Press, 1936.

(VI)

What shifts in migration, if any, would contribute to the more effective utilization of our human and material resources? This is the major question which the study addresses in its discussion of the relationship between migration and economic opportunity.

The book initially examines the need for migration by contrasting regional economic levels, by studying migration impacts in four regions, and by analyzing the changing demand for manpower. The second section focuses on migration measures by reviewing unguided migrations in the United States and attempts at guided movements in three other countries. A critique of government control over migration is presented, followed by new data and interpretations which offer fresh directions for migration policy.

Gordon, David. Theories of Poverty and Underdevelopment. Lexington, Massachusetts: D.C. Heath & Co., 1972.

(X)

A review of three alternative economic explanations of ghetto employment problems -- orthodox theory, the dual labor market theory, and radical economic theory. The development of a sub-employment index in 1966 under the aegis of the Department of Labor is reviewed; Gordon suggests that this development stimulated revisions of Manpower programs. Parallel with this statistical development were changes in economic theory. In particular, dual labor market theory and radical theory emerged as challenges to conventional models of labor force behavior. Inherent in these alternative models is the notion that the labor market is stratified, that labor is not easily mobile across jobs. Empirical evidence to support or refute the stratification hypothesis, however, is scanty.

Gordon, Jerome B. "Socioeconomic Status: A Re-examination of Its Dimensions." Journal of Human Resources 4 (1969): 343-359.

(II)

A statistical re-examination of several existing techniques used to derive socio-economic status (SES) scores from census and other survey sources. Gordon defines SES as the position of the individual in some status ordering as determined by the individual's characteristics, i.e., his education, income, position in community, market place, etc. Gordon used multiple regression to answer the following questions about the Duncan, N.O.R.C. (National Opinion Research Corporation), and Census SES scoring system: (1) is there any benefit from including more variables in the construction of the SES index? and (2) how should the determinants of SES be weighted? Results suggest that factors such as job training and entry requirements, age, and labor force supply phenomena, number of hours worked per week, are relatively unimportant in explaining the variations of SES. On the other hand, measures of full employment do provide greater precision in determining SES. In terms of weighting, education should be weighted more than employment. The analysis raised doubts as to whether the model was actually multiplicative rather than additive, and a Cobb-Douglas production function for estimating SES was proposed.

Gordon, Margaret S., ed. Poverty in America. Berkeley, California: Chandler Publishing Company, 1965.

(II, X)

Proceedings of a national conference held at Berkeley in February 1965. Areas discussed included the nature of poverty in the United states, some views on anti-poverty programs, income distribution policies, education policies, full employment and labor market policies, income maintenance policies, welfare services and rehabilitation, urban renewal policies, area redevelopment and rural poverty, the role of the poor, and a program to combat poverty in America. Papers relevant to the study of poverty definition and measurement are summarized below.

R.A. Gordon, "An Economist's View of Poverty."

A review of economic definitions of poverty beginning in 1904 that reveals that the poverty line has been steadily rising, irrespective of price changes. From the fifties to the mid-sixties it rose by 20-30 percent. From 1935 to 1960 it rose by 40-75 percent. In addition, the incidence of poverty has declined since the 1920's. Statistical comparison of the Council of Economic Advisors' single standard of $3,000 per family with HEW's more flexible standard which takes into account basic differences in need (e.g. size of family), reveals differences in the composition of the poverty group identified by the two measures but yields the same estimate of the number of poor.

H.P. Miller, "Changes in the Number and Composition of the Poor."

A close examination of concepts and statistical measures of poverty to ascertain changes in the number and composition of the poor.

There has been a slowdown in recent years in the rate at which poverty is being reduced. If $3,000 is used as the poverty line, certain handicapping characteristics, notably old age, or absence of an earner or of a male head, have become increasingly prominent in the poor population. However, if the composition of the poor is examined, using a $2,000 poverty line for 1951 and a $3,000 poverty line for 1963, much smaller changes in the composition of the poor are found.

The use of contemporary definitions of poverty suggests that there has been little change in the composition of the poor, whereas the use of a fixed poverty line suggests that there has been a great deal of change. The magnitude of poverty and the characteristics of the poor depend to a large extent on the location of the poverty line. A static view of the poverty line may represent sound strategy for a short-term viewpoint; however, it is fraught with peril for historical analysis.

Recently T.W. Schultz has attempted to use the elasticity concept borrowed from the theory of demand to explain the relationship between the rise in per capita income and the rise in the poverty line. If it is true, as Schultz alleges, that the percentage change in income exceeds the percentage change in the perceived poverty line then we might expect on that account alone to find a decrease in the incidence of poverty over time in a growing society.

Figures suggest that the incidence of poverty has been sharply reduced regardless of the poverty level used. The most marked reduction appears to have taken place for those groups nearest the bottom of the income distribution. In view of the stability of income distribution since the early 1940's, it appears that the rise in the deprivation line has more closely approximated the rise in average incomes than has been the case for the subsistence poverty line. The reduction in the incidence of poverty appears greater if the 1960 poverty lines are used for the earlier years.

Estimates prepared by Smolensky suggest that about one-third of the families were in poverty in 1935 and about one-fifth were in poverty in 1959, using a variable poverty line centered around a $3,000 value for 1959. The estimates prepared by Ruth Mack suggest a much sharper reduction in poverty during the past 30 years than those prepared by Smolensky.

(Poverty and Human Resources Abstract--edited by USR&E)

Robert J. Lampman, "Income Distribution and Poverty."

An in-depth analysis of how income is distributed in all sectors of the American economy including analysis of both the top and bottom levels of the economy, approaching the difference between income inequality and poverty. Income inequality traditionally has referred to the sharing of arbitrarily defined income among arbitrarily defined income receiving units. Poverty, on the other hand, may be defined by relating an absolute real income level to family size and other indications of need. Inequality has not changed dramatically in recent years. Poverty, on the other hand, is retreating.

Gotbaum, Victor H. "New Careers and the Employed Poor." In Up From Poverty. New York: Harper and Row Publishers, 1965.

(X)

New careers without career ladders and incentives fail to aid the poor in this country. Gotbaum maintains that the majority of the poor in this country are employed, and that career opportunities must be opened up at all levels to aid those in working poverty. A short description of the career opportunity and training program conducted by public employees union in the New York City municipal hospital system is included. Incentive payments for training, clear career ladder steps and promotional titles were the major provisions of this program. Gotbaum contends that these types of programs make it easier for the unemployed as well as employed to find work, hold jobs and lead meaningful careers in public employment.

Graham, Saxon. "Socio-Economic Status, Illness, and the Use of Medical Services." In Patients, Physicians, and Illness, edited by E. Gartly Jaco. New York: The Free Press, 1958.

(XI)

A paper examining social stratification, illness, and use of physicians and hospitals in Butler County, Pennsylvania, in 1954. It is against the conditions of America's greater economic prosperity, medical advances, and the more widespread utilization of health insurance that traditional relationships between class and health are tested. Findings of numerous, previous studies, revealing an inverse relationship between class and illness and a lower rate of physician consultation and hospital use by the lower socio-economic classes, are not borne out by this research effort; in actuality, class differences were insignificant. The author suggests that the issue be pursued in future studies.

Graham, Saxon, and Reeder, Leo G. "Social Factors in the Chronic Diseases." In Handbook of Medical Sociology, edited by Howard E. Freeman et al. Englewood Cliffs, New Jersey: Prentice-Hall, Inc., 1972.

(XI)

Graham and Reeder study the two largest categories of chronic disease, cardiovascular disease and cancer, and the sociological factors in their development, prevention, and therapy. Prevention and therapy require an understanding of ways that diseases develop; scientific studies must be supplemented by knowledge of the social aspects of life since prevention and treatment often necessitate a change in behavior.

Chronic diseases place tremendous burdens on society and the individual. For example, men of lower class standing with coronary heart disease experience the most severe disruptions regarding long-term disability and loss or reduction of income. In addition to the personal consequences of disability, chronic diseases pose tremendous economic problems for the community which must direct some of its resources to sustain and treat those persons whose services have been lost. Disease itself has an impact on the social structure, influencing socio-economic status and life style.

Studies have shown that social class can be related to various diseases. Though the single etiology approach cannot be applied, statistics show a high correlation between socio-economic status and chronic diseases such as hypertension, coronary artery disease, and certain cancers. Health surveys report more serious illness among the poor than among the general population. Social class may, therefore, be a gross indicator of other variables related to health and behavior.

The authors discuss other topics: familial characteristics, and ethnicity and religion as they relate to chronic disease; social stress, its measurement and sources; the recovery process and rehabilitation; and finally, prevention of chronic diseases.

Grant, W. Vance, and Lind, C. George. Digest of Educational Statistics, 1973 Edition. National Center for Educational Statistics (DHEW/OE), Washington, D.C., 1974.

(XI)

The twelfth in a series of annual publications, this document provides an abstract of statistical information covering American education from kindergarten through graduate school. Subjects on which statistics are provided include the number of schools and colleges and information on enrollments, teachers, graduates, educational attainment, finances, federal funds for education, libraries, international education, and research and development. The digest is divided according to (1) levels of education, (2) elementary and secondary education, (3) higher education, (4) federal programs for education and related activities, and (5) selected statistics related to education in the United States. Innovations include trend data on high school enrollments in foreign languages; expanded coverage of the field of adult education; statistics from the Bureau of Labor Statistics on the number of librarians; salaries of instructional staff in colleges and universities by type of institution, academic rank, and sex; and summary data from the National Longitudinal Study of the High School Class of 1972. Of particular relevance to the study of geographic differences in availability and quality of public education is information provided on per pupil expenditures by state.

(Partially taken from the report)

Green, Christopher. "Negative Taxes and Monetary Incentives to Work: The Static Theory." Journal of Human Resources 3 (Summer 1966): 280-289.

(VIII)

The author presents a clear, thorough account of the classical analysis of the Negative Income Tax. Using the standard income/leisure indifference map and normal and National Income Tax budget constraints, it is shown that if leisure is a positive good (more of it is "bought" as income increases), an individual subject to the Negative Income Tax will work less. An individual who makes enough money to receive no National Income Tax payments may work the same amount or less, depending upon his tastes (his indifference map).

Green, Christopher. Negative Taxes and the Poverty Problem. Washington, D.C.: The Brookings Institution, 1967.

(II)

Presents rationales for some form of income-conditioned grant which would provide universal income maintenance coverage. Author discusses relevance of negative taxation to present income maintenance programs such as public assistance, social insurance, and family allowances. These existing programs are seen as limited; they are directed only to specific categories of disadvantaged poor.

Author describes a variety of transfer-by-taxation plans including a "social dividend" program (an income guarantee based on a combination of negative and positive taxes) and a negative taxation scheme. Technical and administrative problems are associated with both of these schemes, but they are not unworkable.

Presents hypothetical plans for income-conditioned grants and uses these as basis for estimating costs and benefits of negative taxation programs.

Green, Christopher, and Tella, Alfred. "Effect of Nonemployment Income and Wage Rates on the Work Incentives of the Poor." Review of Economics and Statistics 61 (November 1969): 399-408.

(II)

This article provides an empirical estimate of the degree that work effort will be reduced by a sample negative income tax. Data from the Census's Current Population Survey of 1965 and 1966 was used to calculate the average annual number of hours worked for low income workers with and without nonemployment income. Those without such income worked longer, on the average. These figures were used to calculate substitution and income effects for different income classes. Those workers with no nonemployment income had a higher wage rate than those with nonemployment income in the same income class; a comparison gave the substitution effect. A comparison of workers with the same wage rates and different incomes gave the income effect.

The conclusion reached was that a negative income tax which raised family income by $600-$1,000 while reducing the marginal wage rate 25%-50% would lead to a 11.5% decrease in hours worked.

*Greenwood, Michael J. "Research on Internal Migration in the United States: A Survey." The Journal of Economic Literature. 13 (June 1975): 397-422.

(VI)

The economic literature on migration is reviewed and overall conclusions outlined. The literature is organized into two categories: (1) the "determinants" of migration, and (2) the consequences of migration.

The chief determinant of migration appears to be actual real income differentials. These include real wage differentials as well as differential access to various amenities such as availability of family and friends, pleasant climate, etc. It has been found that migration decreases with increased distance. The data suggest that this is due to greater psychic and informational costs as migratory distance grows. Personal characteristics such as age, race and education also influence migration decisions. More research is needed to determine the effect of welfare level differentials on migration.

Relatively little work has been done on the consequence of migration. Presumably, migration is a mechanism for geographically reallocating labor supplies. This should tend to reduce interregional wage differentials. The empirical evidence is inconclusive concerning this thesis. Apparently, the convergence of interregional mean incomes depends importantly on externalities associated with migration. The application of the concept of human capital to the problem of externalities has helped clarify the effect of migration on regional factor and product markets.

Recently, greater emphasis has been placed on "the estimation of simultaneous equation models of the determinants and consequences of migration."

Greenwood, Michael J., and Gormely, Patrick J. "A Comparison of Determinants of White and Nonwhite Interstate Migration." Demography 8 (February 1971): 141-155.

(VI)

The primary objective of this study is to present an explanation of the interstate migratory movements of white and nonwhite persons which occurred over the period 1955-1960. The study is similar to several other recent studies in that we estimate the magnitudes in which various factors have influenced interstate or interregional migration in the United States. It differs from earlier studies in two important respects. First, we estimate and compare the magnitudes in which certain factors have influenced both white and nonwhite interstate migration. Second, unlike previous studies, many of which have made "country-wide" estimates of the determinants of migration, we have disaggregated data to the state level and obtained white and nonwhite "migration elasticities" for every state. These elasticities are in turn used to test several additional hypotheses relating to racial and regional differences in the elasticities themselves. We argue that discrimination against nonwhites and/or differences in "social milieu" between the South and the nonsouth provide a unifying explanation for most of the observed differences in white and nonwhite migration elasticities.

(Abstract taken from the journal)

Griliches, Zvi. "Hedonic Price Indexes Revisited." In Price Indexes and Quality Change by Zvi Griliches. Cambridge, Massachusetts: Harvard University Press, 1971.

(III)

The "hedonic" approach to price indexes is based on the idea that different models of a commodity can be understood in terms of a small number of basic characteristics (size, power, etc.). "In practice, the following questions are asked: (1) What are the relevant characteristics? (2) What is the form of the relationship between prices and characteristics? (3) How does one estimate pure price changes from such data?" This approach has several advantages. It allows more direct comparison with other commodities, it greatly reduces the number of variables, and in terms of those variables, "the demand relations, the relation between prices and quantities purchased, are more stable, (and) explain a larger fraction of the observed variance...".

Grimstead, Mary Jo; Green, Bernard L.; and Redfern, J. Martin. "Social and Labor Adjustment of Rural Blacks in the Mississippi Delta: A Case Study of Madison, Arkansas." U.S. Department of Agriculture, Economic Research Service.

(VI,XI)

In a study of socioeconomic factors affecting employability of the rural poor residents of Madison, Arkansas, a primarily Black community of about 985 in the Mississippi Delta, the poor residents did not exhibit the degree of hopelessness, fatalism, and search for immediate rewards--the "culture of poverty"--often attributed to deprived populations. As a group, Blacks were more willing to work, to move, or to commute to find employment--and they held better images of work--than their white counterparts. Although not necessarily representative of the Black population of the rural South, Madison may provide a model for predicting behavior and attitudinal patterns in other rural southern communities where employment opportunities in industry are increasing, income levels are rising, and Blacks are gaining political power and social status.

(From the article)

Gross, Bertram, and Moses, Stanley. "Measuring the Real Work Force: 25 Million Unemployed." Social Policy 3 (September/October 1972): 5-10.

(VII)

The average rate of official unemployment in the U.S. for 1971, as reported by the Department of Labor, was 5.7%, but the definition of unemployment used in arriving at this percentage does not include those who, whether for reasons of discouragement or other reasons, were not actively seeking work. When these individuals are added, the estimate for real unemployment jumps to 24.6% for the nation. "Labor force definitions have been constructed so as to exclude millions of people in order to understate the dimensions of unemployment and the extent to which the economic system has failed to generate adequate and suitable job opportunities." Unemployment defined realistically would include: "all those who are not working and are able and willing to work for pay." This definition should be augmented by an understanding that a suitable job is one which is regular, fair, fulfilling, nonexploitative, and peaceful (in reference to foreign military and business relations).

The authors call for restatement of a policy of guaranteed full employment by the government. An explanatory table is included to demonstrate how the authors arrived at their measurement of "real unemployment."

Gurin, Douglas B. "Improving Job Access for the Urban Poor." Highway Research Record 473. Washington, D.C.: Highway Research Board, 1973.

(V)

Transportation planners are beginning to learn that different population groups have different travel needs. This paper summarizes what has been learned about the work-related travel requirements of the metropolitan poor. It begins with a description of likely travelers, the already motivated poor; their preference for good jobs paying more than the minimum wage; and the types of available jobs, most of which are unpleasant jobs paying unacceptable wages. The needs likely to be faced by poor people when they have to travel--in search of work, to apply for a job, and to commute--require flexibly routed and scheduled vehicles. The suitability of buses, car pools, and private autos to meet these needs is considered, and their availability and service inadequacies are identified. Programs are recommended to reduce the need to travel for work-related purposes, to foster self-help transportation by facilitating car ownership among non car-owning households, and to provide better transport options such as taxis or dial-a-bus systems for those who cannot help themselves.

The article suggests that the routing and scheduling flexibility requirements of the unskilled poor when they travel to look and apply for jobs are met most satisfactorily by the private automobile or by publicly provided modes with similar performance capability and availability. For urban, suburban, and rural poor, suitable job opportunities are often located in dispersed, relatively inaccessible locations, making it difficult to find jobs without an automobile or flexible public transportation.

(Partially taken from the article)

Gursslin, Orville R.; Hunt, Raymond G.; and Roach, Jack L. "Social Class and the Mental Health Movement." In <u>Mental Health of the Poor</u>, edited by Frank Riessman, Jerome Cohen and Arthur Pearl. New York: The Free Press of Glencoe, 1964.

(XI)

Article describes ways that the mental health movement is unwittingly propagating a middle-class ethic under the guise of science. The dominant themes of twenty-seven mental health pamphlets are cited. The disjunction between these themes and the lower-class orientation are then presented. Gursslin, Hunt, and Roach conclude that to the extent that the mental health movement is successful in advancing a middle-class health prototype as a desirable model to emulate, it may have a considerable personally disorganizing effect upon those lower-class people who attempt to simulate this prototype. Lower-class people who take on forms of behavior implied in the mental health model may find themselves alienated from lower-class society as well as subjected to other stresses of upwardly mobile, middle-class types.

Guthrie, Harold W. "Intergenerational Transfers of Wealth and the Theory of Savings." The Journal of Business 36 (No. 1, January 1963): 97-108.

(VII)

Modern theories of saving and consumption do not consider intergenerational transfers of wealth. Yet empirically wealth increases over time and is handed down from one generation to the next. This article contains the results of a small sample of established families and their parents. They were asked their feelings concerning inheritances, bequests, and other transfers of income and wealth between generations. The major results were:

1. Most families, especially those of moderate means, felt that education would be their major means of transferring wealth to succeeding generations.
2. Older people feel that they should be financially independent of their children.
3. Despite this feeling, more than a quarter of the younger generation families helped support their parents.

Further research might suggest the way in which these feelings and the resulting actions of individuals could be incorporated into a more realistic theory of consumption and savings.

Guthrie, Harold W. The Prospect of Equality of Income Between White and Black Families Under Varying Rates of Unemployment. Madison, Wisconsin: University of Wisconsin Press, 1970.

(II,X)

Through the use of a growth-unemployment model, income changes are analyzed for black and white families under different rates of unemployment. The model uses as input data income level information gathered from the results of social conditions and changes over the past two decades. Projecting this data into the future gives results which are discouraging for those wanting rapid movement toward income equality for blacks and whites. Only weak statistical evidence suggests that poor blacks and whites are adversely affected by high levels of unemployment. Based on this result, Guthrie attributes the recent relative gains by black families to conditions other than labor market. Other results indicate that at a stable 3.5 percent unemployment rate, equality of incomes for a middle range of incomes could be achieved in 25 years, that growth rates among black families are higher than among white families in all groupings and that a stable unemployment rate of 4.5 percent would require an extra 25 years in order to achieve equality of income among blacks and whites.

Guthrie, Harold W., and Orcutt, Guy H. "Microanalytic Simulation of Household Behavior." Annals of Economic and Social Measurement 1 (1972): 141-170.

(II,IX)

In order for a social policy to be effective and equitable, policy makers need to know what its effects will be on all segments of the population. This paper gives a progress report on the micro-analytic model being developed at The Urban Institute for simulating the distributive effects of alternative socio-economic policies. A sample of individuals and families representing the U.S. population is moved forward in time by a recursive set of functions which predict annual changes in demographic status, earning behavior and wealth accumulation. A macro model of output and price movements provides an environment for the model. This paper includes descriptions of the auxiliary macro model, the demographic functions predicting births and marital status changes, and the system of computer programs for developing, implementing, and using substantive models.

Guthrie, James W., et al. Schools and Inequality. Cambridge, Massachusetts: Massachusetts Institute of Technology Press, 1971.

(IX,XI)

Present educational finance policies can be construed to be in violation of the Equal Protection Clause of the United States Constitution's Fourteenth Amendment. Assisted by the National Urban Coalition, the authors of this book have compiled a great deal of information and analysis on school services in the State of Michigan--information which may typify such services throughout the country. One purpose of the book is to define equality of educational opportunity by exposing the roots of financial inequality. It sets up a conceptual chain that links socio-economic status, school services, and school achievement with success in later life, showing that poor neighborhoods have poor schools and that good education in America is a prerogative of the middle and upper classes. The book concludes with specific proposals for financing schools for equal opportunity and suggests means for implementing such a program, stating that a significant change would be to shift state support from school districts to individual schools as units of expenditure.

(Taken from the book)

Haagstrom, Warren C. "The Power of the Poor." In Mental Health of the Poor, edited by Frank Riessman, Jerome Cohen, and Arthur Pearl. London: Collier-MacMillan Limited, 1964.

(II)

An attempt to single out one aspect of poverty that is both damaging to people and self-perpetuating. Haagstrom's thesis is that it is the powerlessness of poverty rather than income per se that makes people disadvantaged and unable to improve their situations. Lack of money is a form of powerlessness common to all poor people, but there are numerous cases of low income people who are not psychologically crippled by lack of money and do exert control over their lives. Haagstrom tries to get at the complexities of the psychology of powerlessness and the difficulty of stopping the vicious cycle of poverty. He concludes that the poor should be encouraged to initiate and control action programs which have an interdependent rather than dependent relationship with the institutions of the larger community.

*Haber, Alan. "Poverty Budgets: How Much is Enough." Poverty and Human Resources Abstracts 1-2 (No. 3, 1966).

(II,III,IV)

Author challenges usefulness of Social Security Administration's (SSA) Poverty Index, or minimum non-poverty budget, as a poverty measure and social policy guide. Essentially, the index is deceptive as a measure of well-being. It is based on the assumption that family food expenditures are accurate indicators of economic well-being, yet the actual level of food expenditures from which the budget is calculated (the USDA's "economy diet plan" for emergency financial situations) is seriously deficient. In addition, the SSA index reflects unrealistic assumptions about the life conditions of poor families, and it takes no direct account of human needs other than food.

Further, author discusses limitations in the Bureau of Labor Statistics (BLS) "moderate but adequate" standard of living. The BLS standard is based on the current distribution of expenses and does not attempt to reallocate to "overcome past neglects" in the minimum budget. Further, the BLS budget makes no provisions for contingency savings.

Author suggests an alternative measure of poverty which accounts for social and psychological needs of poor families, as well as for their material well-being. He holds that a budget that allows for social participation is vital in order to affect the realities of social isolation and inequality.

Hall, Robert E. "Effects of the Experimental Negative Income Tax on Labor Supply." In Work Incentives and Income Guarantees, edited by Joseph A. Pechman and P. Michael Timpane. Washington, D.C.: The Brookings Institution, 1975.

(II)

The labor supply results of the New Jersey negative income tax experiment are analyzed here. Emphasis is placed on the importance of the distribution of unobserved labor supply determinants, and a theoretical model is proposed to better accommodate the differential appeal of the negative tax. It is also noted that the experiment made no effort to treat the issue of choice that families make in deciding whether to earn above or below the breakeven level and thus whether or not to be covered by the tax. The anomalous response from Blacks and Spanish-speaking groups is questioned because of the high attrition rate in these samples. With regard to the basic results of the experiment, it is argued that there are small but clearly positive reductions in average hours of work among those offered the negative income tax. "The statistical reliability of the estimate is sufficiently high to make it implausible that there is actually no effect at all." In the future, it is suggested that the experiment could be designed more efficiently by gathering as much data as possible on the subjects before and after the program and thus allowing the subjects to serve as their own controls.

Hall, Robert E. "Wage Income and Hours of Work in the United States." In Income Maintenance and Labor Supply, edited by Glen G. Cain and Harold W. Watts. Chicago: Rand McNally College Publishing Company, 1973.

(II)

An empirical study using a special census conducted in 1966. The major results: (1) both black and white husbands worked full time and had only weak reactions to changes in income and wages; (2) black husbands worked fewer hours than white husbands in the same family income group; (3) the number of hours worked by husbands aged 60 or above seemed very sensitive to wages and income; (4) black wives worked substantially longer hours than did white wives from families of the same income group, enough to make up for the difference in incomes earned by their husbands; (5) the hours worked by wives were sensitive to wages and income; (6) teenagers not in school worked very little relative to all other groups; and (7) race and sex differences had an important impact on the hours worked by husbands and wives, but had little impact on the hours of singles.

*Halloran, Daniel. "Progress Against Poverty: The Governmental Approach." Public Administration Review 28 (1968).

(II)

The author argues that the concept of poverty is a relative one. The standard of living which is considered impoverished varies from place to place and from time to time. In early American society widespread poverty did not exist, and the poverty which did exist did not put a serious strain on local governmental resources. In the latter part of the nineteenth century, poverty in the United States became a serious problem and local governments could no longer handle it alone. In the first three decades of the twentieth century poverty existed on a scale which increasingly required the assistance of state governments. The poverty ushered in by the Great Depression in the 1930's was unique, and the impact upon government and politics in the United States was significant. The present situation is that of a persistent core of poverty surrounded by affluence. The War on Poverty attempts to uncover and strike at the roots of poverty, and to destroy its causes instead of treating its symptoms. The anti-poverty program of 1964 and the reasons for the limited success of the War on Poverty are discussed. The author contends that despite disagreements among American economists over the means to achieve a new economic structure and over the exact nature of that structure, their current thinking constitutes the final state in the evolution of Keynesian economics. Open and free discussion of the contemporary problem of poverty, rather than fruitless ideological controversy, is called for.

(Partially taken from Public Administration Review)

Hamburger, William. "The Relationship of Consumption to Wealth and the Wage Role." Econometrica (January 1955): 1-17.

(VII)

Another theory of consumption. Consumption is considered a function of lifetime resources, lifetime needs, and the interest rate. Lifetime resources are defined to be the sum of human wealth and property wealth. Human wealth is held to be proportional to the wage rate, property wealth to the net value of wealth held by the human sector. This model gave a very good fit to empirical findings. According to it, the average wage earner discounts human wealth quite quickly: the discounted present value of future earnings is only some six times current earnings. This approach assumes that consumption is determined by anticipated lifetime consumption power, which is best expressed in terms of wealth and the wage rate. If these assumptions are correct, disposable personal income grossly underweights the influence of income from wealth.

Hamilton, William L.; Collignon, Frederick C.; and Carlson, Carole E. The Causes of Rural to Urban Migration Among the Poor. OEO Contract No. B99-4841. Cambridge, Massachusetts: Abt Associates, 1970.

(VI)

The question, "Why do poor people move from rural to urban areas?", is analyzed using data collected from poor urban migrants in six major cities and a sample of poor current residents in rural areas. The analysis addresses the economic conditions, labor market characteristics, and "infrastructure" services of rural and urban areas; the decision process through which individuals decided to migrate; potential future migration patterns; and factors which could be significantly influenced by policy and program action. The study confirms findings that employment and economic factors tend to push potential migrants toward the cities, and that migrants tend to benefit economically from moving. The ownership of fixed assets, such as a home or farm, correlated very highly with decisions not to migrate. Data suggests that rural-to-urban migration is declining, but the problems created by urban influx and rural depopulation remain. Critical factors for future rural policy are identified as greater job opportunity, increased rural services, improved rural transportation, and asset ownership. Predictions for future migration are outlined.

Handel, Gerald, and Rainwater, Lee. "Persistence and Change in Working Class Life Style." Sociology and Social Research (April 1964): 281-288.

(XI)

Compares behavior and attitudes of American working-class and middle-class. Research on 298 working-class and 101 middle-class couples indicates a superficial similarity in the areas of education and housing; these surface approximations are essentially a result of adaptation to changes in the opportunity structure of American society rather than assimilation of middle-class values by the working class. Regarding family behavior, the authors distinguish between modern and traditional working-class families. The modern families increasingly resemble middle-class families largely in their tendency to a nuclear structure. In the area of consumer behavior, spending patterns for the two groups are alike for hard goods, but not for services.

Handler, Joel F., and Hollingsworth, Ellen Jane. The "Deserving Poor". Chicago: Markham, 1971.

(V,XII)

A study of the administration of AFDC in Wisconsin, based on questionnaires and interviews. As in about half the states, Wisconsin's welfare program is administered at the county level, although the state government has been lately exercising greater control. The bureaucratic structure allows flexibility at the field level, a flexibility unfortunately exercised as noninvolvement and a minimum of regulation with the result that AFDC is basically low-level income maintenance program and very little else. Illegal or questionable practices (e.g., failure to report earned income) were often ignored. On the other hand, there was little that caseworkers could do for their clients beyond health care advice, and the worker-client relationship remained superficial. Still, the great majority of recipients in this survey expressed positive attitudes toward the welfare program and the caseworker. AFDC was a regular source of income for them, higher than they could earn, and most recipients came from such harsh backgrounds that they expected little more.

Handlin, Oscar. "Poverty from the Civil War to World War II." In Poverty Amid Affluence, edited by Leo Fishman. New Haven and London: Yale University Press, 1966.

(II)

Handlin describes the changing American conception of poverty from 1860's through the 1930's. Inequality was assumed and when accepted, each family was presumed self-sufficient, and only those without households, e.g. orphans and the infirmed, were assisted publicly. Even when industrialization and the business cycle had created large numbers of urban poor, only actual starvation was a valid basis for social intervention. The early 20th century saw poverty attributed to societal rather than personal failure. Yet even the New Deal assumed poverty to be an inevitable part of the system. The concepts of full employment and of universal diffusion of adequate minimum incomes were not widely heard until the Second World War.

Hanlon, Richard A. "Differences in Reporting Family Income." Monthly Labor Review 96 (April 1973).

(IV,VII)

Surveys by the Bureau of Labor Statistics on family income in Portland and Miami were found to produce very different results depending on the design of the questionnaire. A housing survey using a single question to determine total income for the preceding twelve-month period produced consistently lower responses than a consumer expenditure survey using a battery of detailed questions. The housing survey conducted in January and February of 1970 asked respondents to specify one of nine income classes ranging from under \$3000 to 25,000 and over. The expenditure survey conducted from March to May of the same year requested detailed information about wages, dividends, interest from bonds, government benefit payments, etc. About 130 families took part in both surveys; of these, 43 percent of the Miami families and 50 percent of the Portland families should have been in a higher income class on the single question survey according to the tabulated results of the detailed survey. A least squares fit of the detailed income estimate as a function of the single question estimate produces for both cities a similar linear relation approximately parallel to the line representing agreement between the two techniques.

Thus, the amount of difference between the two estimates does not vary much over the range of income classes. On the average, the difference is about \$2000. The percent of underreporting is therefore greatest at the lower end of the income distribution.

*Hansen, Niles. "Improving Access to Economic Opportunity: A Study of Nonmetropolitan Labor Markets in an Urban Society." Center for Economic Development, Austin, Texas (unpublished) 1975.

(V,VI)

"This study is primarily concerned with the spatial organization of nonmetropolitan labor markets, and problems associated with giving workers and potential workers in nonmetropolitan areas greater access to manpower services and to more and better employment opportunities. The emphasis is on problems related to the frictions associated with distance, although it also is recognized that this access often is limited by social and political factors such as information diffusion and human resource development."

Specific government programs aimed at developing the rural labor force and access to rural employment opportunities are described and evaluated. These include federal programs to develop coordinated substate regional planning areas, the Comprehensive Employment and Training Act of 1973 and innovative programs for rural transportation.

*Hansen, Niles M. Intermediate-Size Cities as Growth Centers: Applications for Kentucky, The Piedmont Crescent, the Ozarks, and Texas. New York: Praeger Publishers, 1971.

(VI)

The market mechanism leads to geographic concentration of population and industry because of the external economies of agglomeration available to firms located near other firms, social overhead capital, and a large well-trained labor force. However, from a social point of view, such concentration and the crowding that accompanies it, may create external diseconomies such as pollution, congestion, etc. Since firms internalize the external economies but only partially internalize the diseconomies, market forces alone will lead to socially undesirable levels of concentration. This suggests that migration to large metropolitan areas should be discouraged while migration away from such areas should be encouraged. Efforts to develop stagnant rural areas as an alternative through industrial growth and public works have met with little success. "Firms that have tended to leave metropolitan areas have been characterized by stagnation or decline; they frequently seek cheap labor in areas with surplus agricultural populations."

Hansen suggests the development of "decentralized concentration" in intermediate-sized cities ("growth centers"). Such centers could provide the external economies of agglomeration without the social diseconomies. Policy in stagnant rural areas should concentrate on development of human resources (i.e., health, education and training) instead of public works and industrial development. This policy should be linked with efforts to encourage migration to the developing "growth centers."

Hansen, Niles M. "Regional Development and the Rural Poor." Journal of Human Resources 4 (Spring 1969).

(V,VI)

The regional policy of the President's Advisory Commission on Rural Poverty is based on the assumption that the social costs of bringing industry to relatively poor regions would be less than the social costs involved in the migration of workers and increased congestion and unemployment in industrial areas. However, there is no convincing evidence that central government programs can attract enough industry to the countryside to provide people everywhere with jobs in proximity to their places of residence. On the other hand, federal programs to influence the quality of human resources in lagging rural areas benefit the people of these regions and the nation as a whole. Opportunity cost considerations favor federal subsidies for investment in education, health, and training in lagging regions, as well as for relocation subsidies and information programs to facilitate rational migration towards intermediate regions where growth is rapid but where congestion poses no immediate threat.

(Taken from the article)

*Hansen, Niles. Rural Poverty and the Urban Crisis. Bloomington: Indiana University Press, 1970.

(V,VI)

This study examines the interrelationships among lagging rural, intermediate and congested urban regions and suggests policies which might be applied to each kind of region. Investments in human and physical capital and greater labor mobility are called for. Negroes leaving the South contribute to the problems of the northern cities. The key to the development of the South, the nation's most important problem area, lies in urbanization and in increasing the skills of the work force. Its workers, like those in Appalachia, are in declining or slow-growing sectors. The people of Appalachia tend to migrate out and their skill levels must be improved if they are to find good jobs. Federal regional assistance programs assume no out-migration and seem more concerned with areas than with people. The rural poor are not rooted to the land, but rather wish to acquire skills and higher incomes and are willing to move in response to opportunities. The intermediate-sized growth center is a possible solution to these problems which has hitherto been ignored.

Hansen, W., and Weisbrod, Burton. "Human Capital Investment, Schooling and Earnings: The Role of Experience." Institute for Research on Poverty, Discussion Papers. University of Wisconsin, October 1973.

(IX,X)

Hansen and Weisbrod examine the relationship between experience and future earnings. Using five classifications of experience--social, labor market, on the job, with the employer and in the skill--the earnings of 965 veterans is regressed with their schooling and experience. Annual income is used as the approximation of earning figure for the least-squares regression model. Results include: time spent right after high school and prior to taking their first job has no value on future earnings; duration of military service has no statistical significance on earnings; civilian work experiences and duration of current job are highly significant. Difficulties in using age as a measure of experience and in empirically estimating a multidimensional variable are also discussed. A regression model measuring the combined effect of school experience before and after military experience on future earnings shows more significant evidence.

Hansen, W. Lee; Weisbrod, Burton A.; and Scanlon, William J. "Schooling and Earnings of Low Achievers." American Economic Review 60 (1970): 409-418.

(IX, X, VI)

This study of a group of low-achievers estimates the extent to which their earnings are determined by their education versus the effects of training, age, color, and economic opportunity. Schooling explains very little of the variance in earnings, and even this significance may be due to its correlation with more fundamental variables. What one actually learns, in or out of school, is more important than schooling per se. Training programs or work experience may be more valuable than mere school attendance.

Hanushek, Eric. A. "Regional Differences in the Structure of Earnings." The Review of Economics and Statistics 55 (May 1973): 204-213.

(V)

Many studies attempting to measure the relationship between schooling and earnings of individuals have been seriously weakened by the assumption that earnings relationships are uniform across the country or across large numbers of states. The author tried to overcome this problem by considering major metropolitan areas as separate labor markets. Within these markets he used a model that assumes earnings to be a function of schooling, ability and experience. Large variations were found in the returns to these variables across labor markets. The choice of regions was found, in many cases, to explain as much of the variance in earnings as the marginal contribution of several years of schooling. Despite some sampling problems, these results suggest that "more attention should be given to disaggregate structural models which incorporate differences in individual labor markets."

Harberger, Arnold C. "Three Basic Postulates for Applied Welfare Economics: An Interpretive Essay." Journal of Economic Literature 9(1971): 785-979.

(III)

Some economists are skeptical concerning the use of applied welfare economics on one or more of the following grounds.

1) "Consumer-surplus analysis is valid only when the marginal utility of real income is constant.

2) "Consumer-surplus analysis does not take account of change in income distribution caused by the action(s) being analyzed.

3) "Consumer-surplus analysis is partial equilibrium in nature, and does not take account of the general-equilibrium consequences of the actions whose effects are being studied.

4) "Consumer-surplus analysis, though valid for small changes, is not for large changes.

5) "The concept of consumer surplus has been rendered obsolete by revealed-preference analysis."

These objections can all be satisfactorily dealt with if the following three basic postulates are accepted as providing a conventional framework for applied welfare economics:

1) "The competitive demand price for a given unit measures the value of that unit to the demander;

2) "The competitive supply price for a given unit measures the value of that unit to the supplier;

3) "When evaluating the net benefits or costs of a given action, the costs and benefits accruing to each member of the relevant group (e.g., a nation) should normally be added without regard to the individual(s) to whom they accrue."

Many programs or actions subjected to welfare-economic analysis may have characteristics beyond the scope of these postulates. Those characteristics, such as income-distributional and national defense aspects, may be the most important factors governing policy decisions, but they are outside of the expertise of economists. Economists are, therefore, not professionally qualified to judge the effects of policy on these factors.

Hardesty, John J. An Empirical Study of the Relationship Between Poverty and Economic Prosperity. University of California, San Diego, Ph.D. Thesis, 1970.

(IX)

A Ph.D. thesis that analyzes the degree to which economic prosperity has been responsible for the reduction in poverty. Econometric methods, specifically linear regression techniques, are used. Median family income and the unemployment rate are used as indexes of prosperity. Various functional form analyses are undertaken to determine the most appropriate form of the functional relationship linking poverty and economic prosperity. The major findings of the study are that: (1) continued economic prosperity (defined as a 4% unemployment rate and a continuous growth of median family income at a 2.93 percent annual rate) can be expected to reduce total poverty to 2 million families within 20 years; but beyond that, no additional reductions can be expected to take place. (2) While non-white, male-headed families benefit less from prosperity than do white, male-headed families, economic prosperity can still be expected to eventually eliminate poverty within the group. (3) The 2 million poor families in 1990 will all be female-headed. (4) Results are extremely sensitive to the definition of poverty adopted and other definitions considered show the number of poor to be increasing rather than decreasing over time.

*Harland, Douglas. "The Measurement of How Things Are." Canadian Welfare 48 (No. 2, 1972).

(II,XI)

The issue of poverty as a popular academic hobbyhorse appears to be yielding to interest in the quality of life. Measuring quality of life with social indicators is a natural development of previous poverty research. However, there remain profound theoretical and conceptual problems associated with defining and measuring general welfare. Income statistics can serve as useful proxy measures for policy planning and program evaluation, but social indicators to measure the non-economic dimensions of general welfare are not presently available. It is not clear that the basic ingredients of the good life can be delineated and measured to everyone's satisfaction, and it may be too early to consider the development of concise, comprehensive, and balanced statistics describing quality of life.

Harlem Youth Opportunities Unlimited. Youth in the Ghetto. New York: Century Printing Company, 1964.

(IX,XI)

Specific problems in the adjustment of Negro youth, such as dropping out of school, delinquency, and general hopelessness and despair, can be understood as the consequences of rejected minority status upon the personality development of children, and of the general psychological and physical violence associated with overt discrimination. Statistical correlations of juvenile delinquency, aid to dependent children (poverty), venereal disease among youth, and homicide form a configuration of social pathology in which it seems reasonable to assume that the factor which holds these four measures together is the fact that three of them represent aggression which is outwardly directed toward other residents of the ghetto. This aggression would seem to be a protest against inner feelings of powerlessness which characterize ghetto residents.

Underlying this social pathology are factors of education, employment, and family life. Low correlations occur between social pathology and unemployment, poor housing, and recent migration from the South; however, high correlations occur with unskilled jobs and broken homes. This would indicate that improved housing alone will have little effect on ghetto life. The far more important factors which programs must tackle are better jobs and income, better education, and better family adjustment.

*Harrington, Michael. The Other America: Poverty in the United States. New York: MacMillan Company, 1962.

(II)

Harrington divides the poor into four categories for his discussion: the classic poor, the intellectual-bohemian poor, the alcoholic poor, and the rural poor in the cities. While each group has its own origins and traits, they are similar in that the individuals which make them up are members of a cyclical "culture of poverty" which forms not a part of, but the whole lives of the poor. The "new poor" are forgotten victims of impersonal processes and are the first poor in history to be in a minority, invisible, and politically isolated--deserted by their more productive counterparts. The most fatal trait of the new poverty is that it is constructed to destroy aspiration. The definitions of poverty which have been advanced by other authors are reviewed, and descriptions of the poor are given to substantiate the definitions. It is concluded that the Federal Government is the only institution with the resources and breadth of influence capable of acting to abolish poverty.

Harrison, Bennett. "Rethinking the Case for Public Service Employment." Social Policy 3 (September/October 1972): 28-30.

(X)

"The present interest in--and widespread support for--decentralization of manpower programs bodes ill for the urban poor." The author, arguing a case for public service employment, cites a study of the Model Cities Program which he has recently completed which shows that the proportion of federally subsidized city jobs going to "model neighborhood" (i.e., ghetto) residents is systematically smaller in cities with powerful mayors and highly institutionalized personnel systems.

The strongest argument for public service employment is not based on efficiency or cost-effectiveness, but rather on the desperate shortage of "public goods and services," i.e., those items which have some degree of collective consumption or joint production associated with them. Another strong argument concerns the job satisfaction value of labor intensive, human service oriented public service jobs. A third involves the equity effects of public service employment as an anti-poverty policy. This latter is well documented, especially for the urban poor; the probability of a public employee's falling under any one of a number of "poverty thresholds" is only one-half as great as the probability for a similar worker who is privately employed. The problem of the "working poor" is basically a private sector problem.

Hassan, Zubain A.; Johnson, S.R.; and Finley, Robert M. "Further Evidence on the Structure of Consumer Demand in the U.S.: An Application of the Separability Hypothesis." Southern Economics Journal 41 (1974-75): 244-266.

(III)

Until recently, parameters of consumer demand functions were estimated by single equation least squares methods. Limitations of these methods led to studies using simultaneous equation methods for the estimates. These results were still limited in generality. Since demand equations contain all prices and incomes, the estimations needed the "addition of information in the form of exclusion restrictions." These required the use of highly specialized behavioral assumptions. Recently, the "advent of the various separability concepts has provided a more substantive behavioral underpinning for exclusion restrictions on sets of parameters in systems of demand equations."

The authors discuss the theoretical basis of the separability hypothesis and apply it to the estimation of parameters of consumer demand in the U.S. between 1929 and 1969, using a method that incorporates an additive utility function. They find that their empirical model is a workable approach to the estimation of price and income elasticities.

Haughton, James. "Nutritional Anemia of Infancy and Childhood." American Journal of Public Health (July 1963): 1121-1126.

(IV,XI)

Presents findings of a New York City Health Department study of the prevalence of nutritional anemia among children in a low-income area. Of the 286 preschool children studied, 75.5% were Puerto Rican, 15% Negro and 9.5% white. Results of the study show that 18.9 percent of those children had hemoglobin levels below 10 gm percent (a reasonable but not definitive test of anemia). Findings also indicate that although the dietary patterns of the three ethnic groups studied may differ, the percentage of children with hemoglobin levels under 10 gm percent was almost the same for each group.

While the author cautions that the study sample was limited, his findings indicate a high incidence of nutritional anemia among children in low socio-economic groups. Use of a screening process in child health centers to detect cases of true anemia among preschool children is suggested.

(Partially taken from Poverty and Health in the U.S., Medical Health Research Assn., N.Y.)

*Hauser, Robert, and Featherman, David. "White-Nonwhite Differentials in Occupational Mobility Among Men in the United States, 1962-1972." Demography 11 (1974).

(IX)

Intercohort shifts between 1962 and 1972 in the occupation distributions of white and nonwhite men are analyzed and compared at ages 35-44, 45-54, and 55-64. Both white and nonwhite occupation distributions were upgraded over the decade, but among the nonwhites the shifts away from the lowest status occupations were expressed partly in increasing rates of absence from the labor force. There are indications of especially rapid shifts in the occupation distributions of nonwhite men at ages 35-44. Among whites and nonwhites intercohort shifts in the occupation distribution can be attributed primarily to changing patterns of movement from first full-time civilian jobs to current occupations, rather than to changing occupational origin distributions or patterns of movement to first jobs.

The white and nonwhite occupation distributions did not show a clear pattern of convergence over the decade. They became less similar at ages 35-44 and more similar at older ages. White and nonwhite distributions were most likely to converge in those occupation groups where the share of whites was stable or declining, rather than in the groups whose share of the occupation distribution was increasing. Later cohorts of nonwhites would have a much more favorable occupational distribution if they had enjoyed the mobility patterns of whites in earlier cohorts. In 1972, as in 1962, the inferior occupational chances of non-whites are due primarily to the disadvantageous patterns of occupational mobility, rather than to impoverished social origins.

(Taken from the article)

*Heckman, James. "Life Cycle Consumption and Labor Supply: An Explanation of the Relationship Between Income and Consumption Over the Life Cycle." American Economic Review 64(1974): 188-194.

(VII)

A relationship between consumption and income receipts with an income and expenditure peak in the 45-54 age interval has been suggested by Lester Thurow based on an imperfect credit market that prevents consumers from borrowing as much against their future income as they desire. The same relationship has been analyzed by Keizo Nagotani in terms of the risk and uncertainty associated with the consumer's future income. This article proposes to account for the identical income-consumption relationship by assuming that individuals are free to determine the number of hours they will work. If market goods are taken as complementary to leisure time "in the sense that the marginal utility of leisure increases with increments in the consumption of goods," then the greatest gains in utility result from consuming market goods and leisure jointly. Consequently, when leisure price is high, the consumer economizes in both areas as well. "In this case, he works more and saves more at ages with higher wage rates than at other ages." If market goods are substituded for leisure "in the sense that a reduction in the consumption of leisure raises the marginal utility from consuming goods," then, during the same periods of high-priced leisure, the consumer gains more utility by economizing on leisure alone and spending on market goods. Formal specification of rates of interest and time preference and specification of a monotonically increasing wage pattern allow peaks in consumption and hours of work to occur in the middle years of the life cycle. By deriving these results without reference to credit market restrictions, the article questions the need for government intervention in the loan market as called for by Thurow's model.

Heien, D.M. "Income and Price Lags in Consumer Demand Analysis." Journal of the Royal Statistical Society 132(1969): 265-271.

(III)

Heien uses a new cybernetic lag-determination procedure to estimate short- and long-run income-elasticities for 13 categories of consumer expenditures. Inclusion of this flexible lag structure improved the goodness of fit of the regressions considerably.

Henderson, A.M. "The Cost of a Family." In Readings in Welfare Economics, edited by M.J. Farrell. MacMillan, 1973.

(IV)

Presents the author's attempt to determine the cost of a child to the family. The cost of the child may be viewed as the amount that family income would have to increase to compensate for child expenditures and leave the parents with the same amount to spend on themselves, or the amount that income available for parents would decrease if family income level remained constant.

Using calculations of the Ministry of Labour in 1937 and 1938, Henderson explains the association between income, total expenditure and family size. Figures indicate that dollar amounts spent on children fall with the standard of living of the family and that the family living standard decreases with additions in number of children if there is no increase in family income. He assesses family costs in view of price changes, rationing, and social service developments.

Analysis of the figures has implications for policy and suggests norms for fixing family allowances to offset the effects of children in depressing the family's standard of living.

*Henle, Peter. "Exploring the Distribution of Earned Income." Monthly Labor Review 95 (December 1972): 16-27.

(II)

The distribution of total earnings (including earnings of the self-employed) and the distribution of wage and salary income are examined for the years 1958 to 1970. During this period there is a trend toward inequality, as measured by quintile shares and Gini coefficients, for all wage and salary recipients, all year round full-time wage and salary recipients, and all earners. (The only exception to the trend is year full-time earners.) This data is broken down by occupation and industry as well. It is noted that if fringe benefits could be included, the inequality would be more pronounced since such benefits become more important at higher wage levels. Possible reasons for the trend are categorized as either changes in the personal characteristics of earners (age, schooling), changes in the characteristics of jobs (part-time/full-time ratio, new demand patterns, new technology), or changes in compensation rules that are not uniform. Some specific factors are suggested: (1) The growing importance of voluntary part-time work contributed a large group of low income workers. (2) An influx of young workers entered the lower end of the blue collar spectrum of occupations and industries. (3) Technological advances increased the number of highly paid professional and managerial personnel. (4) Earnings increases were greater for higher earning occupations. Many of these factors are seen as inevitable in an advanced economy and not really subject to control; so it is suggested that government programs which operate outside the earnings distribution (transfer payments, taxes) might be most effective for redistribution.

Hepner, Ray, and Maiden, Norma. "Growth Rate, Nutrient Intake and 'Mothering' as Determinants of Malnutrition in Disadvantaged Children." Nutrition Review 29 (October 1971): 219-223.

(XI)

A study of the growth rate, nutrient intake and morbidity rate of 9,000 urban disadvantaged children. The initial results showed most children grew and developed normally, but that an excess over expected number of children possessed growth failure, deviant laboratory values and borderline or deficient emotional-behavioral-intellectual status. The remainder of the article explores the emotional-cognitive relationship between mother and child and its controlling impact on nutrient intake.

Herman, Marylu. "The Poor: Their Medical Needs and the Health Services Available to Them." The Annals of the American Academy of Political and Social Science 399 (January 1972): 12-21.

(V,XI)

A study of the availability and use of health services by the poor. In spite of higher disease and mortality rates, the poor sector of the population makes fewer visits to physicians and is less likely to receive personal health counseling or preventive services than those of higher income levels. In addition, hospital admissions are as high for the poor as those with higher incomes, and tend to be for longer lengths of stay. Although private physicians are the most common source of medical care at all income levels, the poor make greater use of hospital clinics and emergency services. Low-income patients are unlikely to receive comprehensive care from private physicians and few public clinics are designed to provide such care.

Herman concludes that in order to bring the poor into the mainstream of medical care, adequate public support for their health services, combined with inducements to provide comprehensive care, are required.

Herzog, Elizabeth. "Some Assumptions About the Poor." Social Service Review 37 (December 1963): 389-401.

(II,XI)

A look at some assumptions about the poor and a review of some of the testimony for and against them. The first assumption is that there is a culture of poverty. Herzog describes the culture of poverty, reviews some literature on the subject, and concludes that it is a useful concept provided it is used with discrimination, with recognition that poverty is a subculture, and with awareness of stereotyping. Second and third are assumptions that family and sex patterns of the poor differ from those of the middle-class, and family and sex patterns of poor Blacks differ from those of poor whites. Differences were believed to exist between the poor and the middle-class but there was no sound evidence that such differences were racial.

Hess, Robert D. "The Transmission of Cognitive Strategies in Poor Families: The Socialization of Apathy and Underachievement." In Psychological Factors in Poverty, edited by Vernon L. Allen. Chicago: Markham Publishing Co., 1970.

(XI)

Discusses the nature of the learning environment (as represented by the mother) of the child from a poverty background. The paper shows "that social-class differences clearly emerged in the way the mother oriented the child toward authority figures. Likewise, expectations that the mother conveyed to her preschool child about school and her conception of the desired behavior of a child in school tended to vary by social-class level. Finally, differences among social-class levels were observed in techniques the mother used in teaching her child a specific and simple task. The ingenious experiments described by Hess show in miniature the nature of the learning environment (as represented by the mother) of the child from a poverty background. That the child is likely to encounter difficulties in school work is not surprising in view of his previous learning experiences. As Hess puts it, mother-child interaction among the lower class can be described as 'socialization of apathy and underachievement.'"

(Partially taken from the editor's introduction)

Hicks, John. <u>A Revision of Demand Theory</u>. Oxford: Clarendon Press, 1965.

(III)

Hicks presents an index-number theorem which shows that if prices and quantity consumed change with real income held the same, the Laspeyre price and quantity indices tend to be greater than their Paasche counterparts. If, however, tastes and preferences change over the period, or if there are large income effects, there is no way of telling which index will be greater.

The effect of a price change on the consumer's surplus may be considered in two ways. After a fall in the price of a good, the compensating surplus measures the amount the consumer would have to lose to arrive at his original indifference level, while the equivalent surplus measures the amount he would have to gain after the same price rise to remain indifferent. These measures are close together only if the commodity in question is readily substitutable and income effects are small.

Hicks, John. <u>Value and Capital</u>. Oxford: Clarendon Press, 1946.

(III)

Hicks shows that if the prices and quantities consumed change, but the consumer remains at the same indifference level (i.e., real income is unchanged), then Paasche's index number of prices (weighted by the quantities consumed in the second of the two situations) must be less than Laspeyre's (which is weighted by the quantities consumed in the first). He further distinguishes the compensating variation--the change in income which offsets a given change in prices, and the equivalent variation--the change in income, taking place in the initial price-situation, which induces the same change in utility as is induced by the price change.

Hicks, J.R. "The Valuation of Social Income." <u>Economica</u> 7 (1940): 105-124.

(V)

Goods provided by the public sector are difficult to value in national income because they have no market prices. Public goods may be excluded from national income, making this an unambiguous measure of private output, or they may be included at cost on the assumption that they are worth at least as much as was paid for them. This last alternative, however, blurs the distinction Hicks draws between income as a measure of welfare and as a measure of productivity. This results from the fact that there is no parallel to consumer indifference theory for producers.

From his discussion of economic index numbers Hicks concludes that if the observed expenditure ratio $\Sigma p_2 q_2 / \Sigma p_1 q_1$ (where p and q are prices and quantities in two periods with different prices) is greater than both the Paasche and Laspeyes indices, then there has clearly been a rise in national income. If it is less than both, income has fallen and in between the case is ambiguous.

*Hill, Herbert. "Demographic Change and Racial Ghettos: The Crisis of American Cities." Journal of Urban Law 44 (Winter 1966): 231-285.

(VI)

The author traces some of the demographic changes among Blacks for the years 1945-1965. He notes an acceleration in population growth, increased mobility, and rapid urbanization as the major forces behind the civil rights movement. Statistically, the Black population is increasing more rapidly than that of whites and, the former are more mobile. Fifty percent of the Black population now lives in the North. Because of greater publicity in urban areas due to the mass media, the Black situation received more recognition during the early and middle sixties. However, the author believes that the overall situation for Blacks did not significantly improve during this period.

Hill, Richard Child. "Separate and Unequal: Governmental Inequality in the Metropolis." The American Political Science Review 68 (1974): 1557-1568.

(VI)

Separate, incorporated municipalities in metropolitan areas are seen as institutional arrangements for promoting and protecting the unequal distribution of scarce fiscal resources, thus perpetuating class and status inequality within the metropolis. The empirical data of this study suggest several conclusions consistent with this view. "(1) Governmental inequality is rooted in income inequality among families in the metropolis. Family income inequality is translated through the dual mechanisms of residential segregation and political incoporation into inequality in the distribution of fiscal resources among municipal governments in the metropolis. (2) Racial discrimination is a basic component of the urban stratification system and underlies governmental inequality. (3) Inequality tends to be higher in older, larger and more densely populated metropolitan areas which indicate a demographic potential for municipal differentiation in urban space."

Hillery, George A., Jr.; Brown, James S.; and DeJong, Gordon F. "Migration Systems of the Southern Appalachians: Some Deomgraphic Observations." Rural Sociology 30 (March 1965): 33-48.

(VI)

This study discusses an analytical scheme for fitting together migration streams, representing separate migration patterns, into an integrated whole. Attention focuses on indicating the probable existence of "migration systems" on the demographic level, their conceptual form, the data necessary to study them, and some problems associated with such a study. Migration systems are illustrated by 1949-1950 migration data for State Economic Areas of the Southern Appalachians.

(Author abstract)

Hines, F. "Effects of Welfare Reform on the Rural Poor." Agricultural Finance Review 32 (1971): 22-34.

(II)

This article examines potential effects of the proposed Family Assistance Plan (FAP) on families by place of residence and characteristic of family head. Special attention is given to families of farm operators and hired farmworkers. Under FAP, benefits would increase $3.18 billion (26 percent) over current programs. Almost twice as many families would be eligible for basic FAP transfer as are eligible for the current Aid to Families With Dependent Children Program. Eligibility would increase fourfold among rural residents, compared with 50 percent for urban residents. The probability of a family being eligible for FAP would be closely related to the family head being female, of a minority race, or having a low educational attainment. Eligibility would extend to 18 percent of all farm operator families and 41 percent of all farm laborer families.

This article concentrates on the effects of the specific FAP provisions. Many other income support type proposals have been made with different specific provisions. The basic conclusions of this article would apply to any proposal similar to FAP.

(Partially taken from the article)

Hirsch, Werner Zvi. The Economics of State and Local Governments. New York: McGraw-Hill, 1972.

(V,VI)

This general textbook on the economics of state and local governments divides the costs they incur into agency and social costs. Agency costs are actual payments made by state and local governments to obtain the services of resources. Social costs entail all the resources required for the government activity, according to their best alternative uses.

Consolidation of local government services often does not lead to reduced average cost. This horizontal cost curve is favored by the fact that, because labor is the major input of local governments, few inputs are bought to secure major price concessions. Electricity, sewage and gas, capital-intensive exceptions, show declining average unit costs.

Hirsch, Werner Zvi. Urban Economic Analysis. New York: McGraw-Hill, 1973.

(V,VI)

In this textbook on urban economics Hirsch shows how the supply functions of certain urban services can be estimated. The long-run average unit cost of a given service is affected by the service quality, quantity, prices of factor inputs, service conditions affecting input requirements and the state of technology. Because these services are labor-intensive, wage and manpower quality differences will account for most interregional cost differences. Estimated cost functions for many public services are derived, giving, for example, inpatient hospital costs as a function of the number of admissions, the occupancy rates, patient-care expenses per inpatient operating expenses (a proxy for quality), and patient-days per personnel (a technology proxy). More complex frameworks are needed to assess the cost and value of more complex services. Police protection, for example, has six major goals, i.e., reducing violations of property rights, individual's rights, enforcing moral conduct and collective civil regulations, reducing traffic violations and providing non-crime services. Its activities are prevention, deterrence, apprehension, and noncrime services. Generalizations cannot be made for even in the "arts" category of "public recreation," the performing arts are labor-intensive while the visual arts are capital-intensive.

Hobbes, Thomas. Chapter 30. Leviathan. New York: E.P. Patton and Co., 1940.

(VII)

This chapter of Hobbes' work of political philosophy concerns the correct actions of the sovereign power. Sovereignty is absolute and should be maintained through education of the people in the virtues of the government. Only individual consciences stand higher than the rulings of Sovereign. Equity is a national law and so must be adhered to by the sovereign. This means equality in the administration of justice and also in the collection of taxes. Taxes represent the payment of the debt individuals owe to the state for its protection. For the imposition of taxes to be equal, they must be imposed according to the use individuals get from this protection. This is measured by consumption, not income: the frugal worker gets as much protection and should be taxed the same as the spend-thrift idler. Also discussed is the proper treatment of the poor, the choice of counselors, rewards and punishments, and the making of new laws.

Hobsbawn, E.J. "Poverty." In International Encyclopedia of the Social Sciences, edited by David L. Sills. New York: The MacMillan Co. and The Free Press, 1968.

(II)

Aside from the administrative "poverty line," the article distinguishes three types of poverty: (1) social poverty implies a relation of inferiority, dependence or exploitation as well as low income; (2) pauperism describes those unable to subsist without outside assistance; and (3) moral poverty defines whether poverty is morally acceptable and what status it confers on the poor. After an historical account of the origin and nature of the lowest social class, and of societal and governmental attitudes and actions, the article gives some alternative poverty definitions. Material poverty in a poor society is physiological subsistence, while a conventional minimum tending to rise with time is characteristic of advanced countries. Nonmaterial poverty--unequal rights, status and opportunities--is harder to measure or define. Measures of consumption are useful for comparisons, especially international ones. Income distribution may also be useful, although where nonmoney income is important, these statistics are faulty.

Hoch, Irving. "Income and City Size." Urban Studies 9 (1972): 299-328.

(VI)

This paper considers the relation between income and city size, under the basic hypotheses that there are net negative non-pecuniary returns with size, which tend to be balanced by increases in per capita money income. However, improvement in institutional arrangements, in particular, better pricing, can increase real income. Such improvement will probably increase city size. Empirical evidence, conforming to the hypotheses, is presented for money income, cost-of-living indexes, rent and transport cost, environment, crime, health and social problems. Generally, all measures increase with both size and density, which, in turn, is a function of size.

Hochman, Harold, and Rodgers, James. "Pareto Optimal Redistribution." American Economic Review 59 (September 1969): 542-57.

(II)

An exploration of the relationship of Pareto Optimality and redistribution of income. Hockman and Rodgers contend that the financiers (the public) of public welfare programs benefit in that they are safeguarded against any large future income variations and they gain through the interdependence of individual utility functions. Using this latter concept as a base from which to construct a model, the two authors experiment with many hypotheses on utility interdependence. They find that Pareto Optimality may in fact be required for the proper distribution of income. By calculating the patterns of tax burdens, transfers, and fiscal incidence in 1960 that would be Pareto Optimal, they are able to arrive at the utility interdependence of actual fiscal residues. As a result, progressive taxation is shown to be fully consistent with the Pareto criterion. The authors recommend that more empirical study be conducted on the public and private choice patterns. This, they indicate, may lead to a more individualistic fiscal structure in line with the nation's tradition.

Hollander, Jacob H. The Abolition of Poverty. Cambridge: The Riverside Press, 1914.

(II,X)

A theory of the principal causes of poverty is offered and programs for treating them are proposed. Poverty is described as principally an economic condition of not having enough food, clothing, and shelter to maintain a decent standard of living. Hollander sees the principal causes of poverty as being (a) underpayment, (b) unemployment, and (c) unemployability. Programs proposed to treat those causes and hence greatly reduce poverty in this country are respectively (a) a government regulated minimum wage program; (b) job banks, job training, and unemployment insurance; and (c) social insurance to protect and provide for unemployables. Hollander admits the possibility of other causes of poverty, but feels the need to begin treating the problem at an economic level. Other more subtle and complex aspects of poverty that may exist can be dealt with as they appear once these more basic problems are solved.

Holleb, Doris B. "Social Statistics for Social Policy." Planning: 1968. Chicago: American Society of Planning Officials, 1968.

(XI)

This essay proposes that social measurement be extended to: systematically record change in terms of explicit social goals (social indicators); and provide a framework for evaluating our social policies and programs in terms of their effectiveness in achieving these goals (social accounts). This is seen as a necessary remedy to the present situation in which policy makers find themselves simultaneously deluged with statistical data and starved for relevant data. While both socio-economic theory and governmental policy needs would seem at the present time up to the task of developing a set of social indicators, the outlook is not so bright for the development of a system of social accounts. Generally, the obstacles to the development of the latter fall into two categories: first, both our social theory and our social measurements are at the present time quite primitive; and second, there are real difficulties inherent in any attempt to evaluate social policies and programs in terms of their effectiveness in achieving social goals.

Hollingshead, August B., and Redlich, Frederick C. Social Class and Mental Illness. New York: John Wiley and Sons, 1958.

(XI)

This report on the classic New Haven study focuses on the relationship of social class to mental illness and its treatment. The authors conclude that each class demonstrates distinct types of mental illness, that each class responds to the existence of mental illness in its members in diverse ways, and that treatment methods vary according to class. Recommendations for improving psychiatric care are offered.

(Partially taken from Poverty in Canada and the United States)

Hollister, Robinson G., and Palmer, John L. The Impact of Inflation on the Poor. Institute for Research on Poverty Reprint #106, University of Wisconsin, 1973.

(III)

A statistical analysis of the effect of inflation on the economic well-being of the poor using official Social Security Administration criteria to define poverty. Areas examined are: (1) the "expenditure effect" or how the impact of inflation is conditioned by the ways in which the poor spend their incomes; (2) how inflationary effects are reflected in the sources of income of the poor; and (3) the impact of inflation on the assets of the poor and how that effects their welfare.

Hollister and Palmer conclude that the economic well-being of the poor rises relatively and absolutely during periods of inflation. (1) The "expenditure effect" of inflation hurts the poor less than the non-poor. (2) With respect to income, considerable gains to the poor exist in terms of wages and salary income. During periods of tight labor markets associated with inflation, income from transfer payments has kept up with or exceeded inflation, while only a small percentage of the aged-poor depend on "fixed incomes." (3) The negative wealth effects of inflation are estimated to be extremely limited for the poor.

*Honig, Marjorie. "The Impact of Welfare Payment Levels on Family Stability." Studies in Public Welfare, U.S. Joint Economic Committee, No. 12, Part I.

(IX,XI)

An empirical study which supports the theory that high welfare payments do encourage family splitting. Implicit in the argument is the contention that welfare creates the incentive to dissolve families for purposes of welfare eligibility. Data presented shows a direct correlation between a high AFDC payment level and high recipient and female headship of family rates. However, according to the statistics, male wages and unemployment rates may act as a countervailing factor to AFDC payments in this regard.

In light of these conclusions, the author recommends reversing the policy emphasis to reduce the family-splitting incentive. Policy changes would include extending the same AFDC benefits to two-parent families and improving the wage and employment opportunities for low-income males.

Hoover, Edgar M. An Introduction to Regional Economics. New York: Alfred A. Knopff, 1971.

(V,VI)

This book is an introductory text to the study of regional economics. An understanding of spatial and regional economics can be based on three variables (1) natural resource advantages (2) economies of concentration, and (3) costs of transport and communication. In particular the author discusses the following subjects: the location of individuals, economic activities and cities; cost of transportation; land use; and the spatial structure of urban areas. In addition, the concept of economic regions and their development are discussed. Regional development seems to depend on a variety of factors including both supply and demand characteristics for factors and final outputs. Interregional trade and factor movements as well as the location of large cities are influential in determining regional growth.

Houthakker, H.S. "Additive Preferences." <u>Econometrica</u> 28(1960): 244-257.

(III)

Houthakker considers two theoretically equivalent formulations of the utility function. The familiar direct utility function has commodity bundles as arguments and is constant on any indifference surface. But given the usual convexity assumptions, this utility function can be written "indirectly" as a function of prices and total expenditure. This is the relevant function for measuring welfare changes caused by price changes through index variables.

Houthakker compares these concepts empirically under the restrictive assumption of additivity, that is the independence of each commodity from all others. The directly additive utility function was found to be more realistic that the indirect one mentioned above.

Houthakker, H.S. "The Permanent Income Hypothesis: A Review Article." <u>American Economic Review</u> 48 (No. 3, June 1958): 396-404.

(VII)

The official review of Friedman's <u>Theory of the Consumption Function</u> in the <u>American Economic Review</u>. The theoretical basis of the permanent income hypothesis is attacked on four grounds: it assumes that the availability of liquid assets has no effect on consumption ("The man who has a lucky day at the races does not buy his friends a drink, and the poor fellow whose wallet is stolen does not postpone the purchase of a new overcoat."); that time effects are symmetrical; that uncertainty doesn't matter; and that there are no imperfections in the capital market restricting borrowing. The empirical justifications of the theory are not discussed in depth, though a new test is devised which the theory flunks.

Houthakker, H.S. "Revealed Preference and the Utility Function." <u>Economica</u> 17(1950): 159-179.

(III)

Houthakker shows that Samuelson's revealed preference approach to the theory of consumer's choice does not fully solve the problem of integrability. When more than two goods are involved, well-behaved indifference surface consisting of equally preferable bundles of goods can be generated. By generalizing Samuelson's fundamental hypothesis, nonintegrable cases are ruled out. Semi-transitivity is required to ensure that continuous, nonintersecting indifference surfaces can be formed. In other words, if bundle of goods A is preferred to B which is preferred to C, and so on to Z, then Z can never be shown preferable to A.

Houthakker, H.S., and Taylor, Lester D. Consumer Demand in the United States. Cambridge, Massachusetts: Harvard University Press, 1970.

(III)

This study derives demand equations for 82 commodities using time-series data and an additive system of demand functions derived from a quadratic utility function. A dynamic form was used, with habit formation predominant. Good fit and reasonably accurate projections were obtained.

Hoyt, Homer. Where the Rich and the Poor People Live, Technical Bulletin/55. Washington, D.C.: Urban Land Institute, 1966.

(III,V,VI)

The author deals with areas occupied by high income families in the largest metropolitan cities and in selected medium and smaller metropolitan areas of the United States. With information based on an analysis of statistics from the 1960 Census, he delineates, in map form, locations of residents at both ends of the income scale.

Hoyt's analysis of high income residential areas is an extension of his sector theory of residential neighborhoods. The sector theory of development is based on the fact that high-income or fashionable residential areas generally move outward in the same direction from the center of cities over a period of years. This directional trend holds even when development takes place in suburban areas outside corporate city limits.

Knowing the directional growth of the highest income areas is important to land developers, real estate owners, investors, appraisers and lending institutions. It is logical that the upper income areas set a pattern for urban growth, development and activity. Conversely, areas with a predominance of lower-income families show where programs for economic stimulation are likely to be needed or are apt to take place. By maps and tables the author shows that certain census tracts contain a higher proportion of high-income families than others and where these families are concentrated or distributed in metropolitan areas.

(Adapted from the Foreword)

'Hunt, Eleanor. "Infant Mortality and Poverty Areas." Welfare in Review 5 (August 1967): 1-13.

(XI)

A report summarizing national infant mortality levels at different ages in infancy and perinatal period. Taking advantage of a new Bureau of Census poverty index for neighborhoods of Standard Metropolitan Statistical Areas (SMSA), the report compares infant mortality within Chicago and Washington, D.C. In both comparisons, poverty areas within the SMSA were found to have higher mortality rates and lower birth weights than other areas. The new Census Bureau statistical information is viewed as a breakthrough for health indicators and will help to target future programs and planning efforts aimed at alleviating poverty.

Hurwicz, Leonid, and Uzawa, Hirofumi. "On the Integrability of Demand Functions." In Preferences, Utility and Demand, edited by John S. Chipman, et al. New York: Harcourt Brace Jovanovich, Inc., 1971.

(III)

"This paper deals with the properties of demand functions derived from utility maximization." The most common approach, developed by Hicks and Samuelson, asserts that utility maximization subject to a budget constraint "implies the symmetry and negative semidefiniteness of the substitution term matrix" derived by Slutsky and Hicks from direct demand functions (quantities taken as functions of prices and incomes). The paper takes the converse of this and shows that "a single-valued differentiable demand function arises from the maximization of a utility function subject to a budget constraint if the Slutsky substitution matrix is symmetric and negative semidefinite." In addition, it is shown that under certain assumptions, the utility function is monotone, its indifference surfaces are strictly convex to the origin and it is upper semicontinuous. Under an additional assumption, it is shown the "utility function is continuous not merely upper semicontinuous."

Inkles, Alex. "Personality and Social Structure." Sociology Today, edited by Robert K. Merton, Leonard Broom and Leonard S. Cottrell, Jr. New York: Basic Books, Inc., 1959.

(XI)

A "state-of-the-art" paper. Its major thesis is that adequate sociological analysis--the attempt to understand the structure and functioning of social systems--should include knowledge of the distinctive personality characteristics of participants in the system plus some general theory of the nature of human personality. An understanding of delinquency, for example, requires sociological measurement of objective characteristics--physical decay in the residential area, rates of alcoholism and crime, disruptions of family life, etc.--plus psychodynamic analysis of the response propensities toward delinquent acts in the personalities of those exposed to these special conditions. The combination of the social and the psychodynamic elements of the situation explains why only a few in the impoverished area ever became involved in delinquency. Inkles argues, therefore, that sociological analysis must deal with the personal component--the motivated actor in the situation of social action. A full understanding of any social situation, and its probable consequences should assume, Inkles suggests, a knowledge not only of the main facts about the social structure--the gathering of which is presumably the special province of sociological study--but also the main facts about the personalities operating in that structure.

Inman, Robert Paul. Four Essays on Fiscal Federalism. Cambridge, Massachusetts: Unpublished doctoral dissertation, Harvard University, 1971.

(VI)

An empirical analysis of forty-one major United States cities finds that with the exception of population density, community income, and the taxing decisions of neighboring local governments, various city and metropolitan area characteristics have little impact on either the level of total taxation or the mix of total taxation among the various tax instruments. When making taxation decisions, city officials are sensitive to the pressures of higher costs or tax-base competitions but are reasonably protected from political or other economic pressures.

Institute for Social Research. A Panel Study of Income Dynamics: Study Design, Procedures, Available Data. Survey Research Center, University of Michigan, 1972.

(IX)

This volume presents the documentation for the panel study of income dynamics: Five Thousand American Families--Patterns of Economic Progress. It is a manual, describing in full detail the data collected during the study. The sample design, sample weights, interview and field procedures as well as annual response rates are described. The five questionnaires administered are also presented.

Ireland, Lola M.; Moles, Oliver C.; and O'Shea, Robert M. "Ethnicity, Poverty, and Selected Attitudes: A Test of the 'Culture of Poverty' Hypothesis." Social Forces 47 (June 1969): 405-413.

(II,XI)

In order to test whether there is indeed a homogeneous "culture of poverty," poor residents of three different ethnic groups (Spanish-speaking, Negro and Anglo-Americans) were tested to determine whether they would differ significantly in their response to eight attitudinal areas.

Each ethnic group was divided into two levels of poverty based on receipt or non-receipt of public assistance. 1964 California data on the characteristics of recipients of public assistance funds were used. All respondents were poor, based on income levels, skill levels, and assets.

The eight attitudinal areas tested were:

1) feelings of dependency;
2) dependent behavior;
3) the precedence of "family of orientation" over "family of procreation";
4) valuing child autonomy;
5) responsibility of parents for the behavior of their children;
6) fatalism;
7) alienation; and
8) value of securing or holding a job.

In 14 out of 16 instances ethnic groups differed significantly from each other in attitudes. Thus, the hypothesis that poverty is a monolithic culture was rejected.

Isard, Walter, and Cumberland, John, eds. Regional Economic Planning. Paris: The European Productivity Agency of the Organization for European Economic Cooperation, 1961.

(V,VI)

A collection of papers presented at the Conference on Regional Economic Development which took place in Bellagio, Italy in June 1960. The following broad areas are discussed: the history and status of regional and national economic planning within each of the participating countries; certain structural problems common to all regions in their efforts to achieve industrial expansion, agricultural improvement, and orderly urban development; and the various techniques of regional and national economic analysis which were used at the time and their role in programming development. More specific issues that are considered include the following: applicability of analytical techniques in underdeveloped as compared with developed areas, priorities of infrastructure versus industrial plant, planning for positive rates of growth in all regions, urban problems, import-export planning, the role of public as compared with private investment, interrelations between agricultural transformation and industrial development, benefit-cost analysis, comparative cost analysis, industrial complex analysis and regional input-output analysis.

Isenberg, Robert. "Quality of Rural Education in the U.S." In Quality of Rural Living. Washington, D.C.: National Academy of Sciences, 1971.

(XI)

Author observes that advances have been made in the area of rural education primarily as a result of the tendency toward consolidation of schools. Merging of school districts has made possible greater diversity in school curriculum and created a greater wealth of educational resources. However, the pace of progress in rural areas has been slow because of resistance to educational improvements by rural people.

Author suggests several important program modifications: (1) school programs should be made more relevant to rural community life; (2) greater attention should be given to comprehensive planning; (3) personnel recruitment practices must be more aggressive; (4) schools should learn to capitalize on existing advantages of small size.

*Jencks, Christopher. Inequality: A Reassessment of the Effects of Family and Schooling in America. New York: Harper Colophon Books, 1972.

(II,V,XI)

The author explores the potential of the educational system in terms of its ability to affect the issue of inequality. The approach taken emphasizes individual rather than group inequality.

It is found that none of the evidence reviewed suggests that school reform can be expected to bring about social changes outside of the school, including reforms which make educational opportunity more equal. All considered, the child is more influenced by what happens at home than by what happens in school, and the effects of schooling are noted to be transient once an individual leaves school. It is suggested that income equalization is a more effective way of reducing social inequality than equalization of educational opportunity. The following conclusions are noted:

- educational opportunity, in terms of resources and choice of attendence, is far from equal;
- equalization of economic status would reduce inequality in test scores by 6% or less, and equally unimpressive results would be found for equalizing amount of schooling (5-15%), quality of elementary schools (3%), quality of high schools (1%), or from the elimination of racial and socio-economic inequality (10-20%);
- the most important determinant of educational attainment is family background, with cognitive skill ranking second;
- occupational status is strongly related to educational attainment, but enormous status differences still exist between people with the same level of educational attainment;
- job satisfaction is only tangentially related to educational attainment, occupational status, or earnings; and
- reformers would find greater results from the reduction of inequality within institutions, than between institutions.

Jensen, Arthur R. "Learning Ability, Intelligence, and Educability." In Psychological Factors in Poverty, edited by Vernon L. Allen. Chicago: Markham Publishing Co., 1970.

(XI)

The author "presents his research on the relations among educability, intelligence, and social class. Educability is a term used to refer to the benefit an individual can derive from formal in-instruction in school. There seem to be greater social-class differences in educability than in intelligence, which is less responsive to family and other environmental influences than is school performance. Jensen reports consistently finding the same intriguing result in several of his studies: intelligence test scores predict ability on simple learning tasks quite well for middle- and upper-class subjects, but not for lower-class subjects. Thus, lower-class children having IQ scores 20 points lower than middle-class children did equally well on direct serial learning tasks.

On the basis of extensive empirical data, Jensen proposes a simple conceptual model for explaining social-class differences in the relation between learning and intelligence test scores. Two levels or types of learning are simple stimulus-response association and more complex learning that involves verbal mediation between stimulus and response. It is assumed that social-class differences in ability exist in these two types of learning. The hypothesized relation among basic learning ability, intelligence, trainability, and educability contains many suggestions for leverage points that could be used to enhance the educability or scholastic performance of disadvantaged children. This model will no doubt stimulate additional research.

Finally, Jensen argues that we have tended to underestimate the role of hereditary and biological factors in determining intelligence and educability. He takes issue with the assumption that motivational factors are of primary importance in accounting for inferior classroom performance of the disadvantaged. Environmental factors have been considered by most psychologists to be the primary source of individual differences in educability and intelligence. Jensen would arge that we look closely at the facts of inheritance of mental ability in order to place the extreme environmental view in proper perspective.

(Partially taken from editor's introduction)

*Jerome, Norge W. "Food Consumption Patterns in Relation to Life Styles of In-Migrant Negro Families." _Institute for Research on Poverty Discussion Papers_ (15-68). Madison: University of Wisconsin-Madison, 1964.

(IV, V, VI)

Analysis of in-migrant Negro consumption patterns based on interviews with members of 23 households. Measurements were made of one week's food consumption which permitted comparisons of the cost, variety and nutritive quality of the diet. The 23 households were divided into 3 sociocultural groups according to family background, marital status, migration pattern, home ownership, dependency on public funds for family services, church membership and affiliation, leisure and reading habits. Socio-cultural "status" appears to function as an important factor in determining food selection and expenditure patterns among Negroes interviewed.

Johnson, Harry G. "The Macro-Economics of Income Distribution." In _Income Redistribution and Social Policy_, edited by Alan Peacock. Great Britain: Aldin Press, 1954.

(II)

A theoretical analysis of the effect of income redistribution on aggregate consumption and economic activity. Holding a host of variables such as prices and interest rates constant and ignoring market prices and volume of investment changes, Johnson explores the total impact of income redistribution on aggregate consumption resulting in a further change in income and consumption. The normal conclusion that income transfers from the wealthy to the poor increases aggregate consumption was found to depend on the assumptions that consumer choice is independent and that production is a homogeneous activity. When consumer choice is interdependent, the initial impact of a redistribution of income from rich to poor may lower total consumption because of the reactions of the rich to a reduction in consumption. The assumption that the marginal propensity to consume of the wealthy is lower than the poor is inadequate due to the interdependence theory. The total impact of the redistribution of income, taking into account the heterogeneity of the production of goods, may be the opposite of what would have occurred if aggregate income were held constant.

Johnson, Lyndon Baines. "Special Message to the Congress Proposing a Nationwide War on the Sources of Poverty, March 16, 1964." In Public Papers of the President of the United States 1963-64, Book I. Washington, D.C.: U.S. Government Printing Office, 1965.

(II)

This is the speech that President Lyndon Baines Johnson gave before Congress to announce his submission of the Economic Opportunity Act of 1964. It sets down the foundation of thought on which the poverty programs of the latter sixties were based. The view of poverty portrayed in this speech is primarily relative. Poverty is defined as the inability to share in the nation's abundance, and the denial of opportunity to improve one's lot. Johnson focuses on the vicious circle of poverty as the prime target when he describes poverty as the denial of a decent education, life in a "hostile and squalid environment," a broken home, ill health, and racial discrimination, which together lead to an attitude of hopelessness in the young and perpetuation of the cycle. The war on poverty was to be a war against denial of opportunity.

Johnson, Thomas, and Hebein, Frederick J. "Investments in Human Capital and Growth in Personal Income 1956-1966." American Economic Review 64 (1974): 604-615.

(II,IX)

There have been many estimates of the rate of return to investments in human capital. However, most of these studies base their estimate on a single cross-section of individuals or make separate estimates for a series of cross-sections. The purpose of this paper is to use the human capital model to estimate the rate of growth in personal income by combining a series of cross-sections in a single regression. One advantage of this method is that it is able to differentiate between the effects of external economic growth and depreciation in human capital. A cross-section with ages 18 through 64 is taken (from Current Population Reports) for six different years in the interval 1956-1966 in terms of income earned during the survey year and schooling completed. The determination of external growth as a separate factor yields a more reasonable rate of depreciation for human capital (years of schooling in this study) than had been estimated before. "Depreciation is greatest for high school graduates and for those with a few years of college...The greater depreciation encountered by these individuals suggests that their skills may be more sensitive, relative to individuals at other schooling levels, to capital innovation." Furthermore, the portion of earnings accounted for by schooling and on-the-job training is found to be larger for college graduates than for high school graduates.

Joint Economic Committee. "Report on the January 1964 Economic Report of the President." In The Economics of Poverty, edited by Burton A. Weisbrod. Englewood Cliffs: Prentice-Hall, Inc., 1965.

(II)

A review of the goals of the poverty program and the governmental policies needed to achieve them. The minority position takes issue with the $3,000 poverty level used in the 1964 Council of Economic Advisors (CEA) report. The minority argues that the CEA level does not account for assets and temporary income fluctuations and so overestimates the number of poor. The real problem of the poverty that remains is seen as providing a challenge "to provide the poor with job opportunities in an environment of balanced and sustained economic growth without inflation and to raise the productivity of the poor who already have jobs."

Joint Economic Committee, Congress of the United States. Tax Changes for Shortrun Stabilization. Hearings Before the Subcommittee on Fiscal Policy: 89th Congress, 2nd Session. Statement by H. M. Somers, "Sales Taxation and the Economist," 100-106.

(VII)

This testimony attempts to show that sales taxes are not necessarily regressive and do have a useful purpose as adjuncts to the income tax. Sales taxes are believed to be regressive because past measurements of their incidence used sales taxes without exemptions measured against current income. If a broadened measure of financial well being is used, and the sales tax exempts food, then it will be progressive. Five possible broadened measures of financial well-being are proposed: 1) income plus assets, 2) income plus the imputed value of the home, 3) consumption, 4) permanent income, and 5) income plus the value of assets amortized over the owners lifetime.

Kadushin, Charles. "Social Class and the Experience of Ill Health." In Class Status and Power, edited by Reinhard Bendix and Seymour Martin Lipset. New York: The Free Press, 1966.

(XI)

A review of studies since Malthus examining the relationship between the prevalence of illness and social class. This association seems to be decreasing and probably no longer exists. As standards of living in countries advance, as medicine controls communicable disease, as public sanitation improves, those gross factors which intervene between social class and exposure to disease diminish. However, it seems that the lower classes still "feel" more sick.

Kahn, Gerald, and Perkins, Ellen J. "Families Receiving AFDC: What Do They Have to Live On?" Welfare in Review (October 1964): 7-15.

(XII)

This article presents information on the income of families receiving Aid to Families with Dependent Children (AFDC) and compares their financial circumstance with that of other groups below the poverty level. It discusses the degree of unmet need among AFDC families and attributes this primarily to the low levels of state cost standards for living requirements. The degree of unmet need is even more extensive in those states which apply maximum requirements and percentage reductions to further lower the effective amount of their payment standards. Inadequate fiscal ability and lack of public understanding of the broken family account for this policy. The report concludes that a considerable increase in public assistance is needed if the children of those families are to escape poverty.

(Partially taken from Poverty and Human Resources Abstracts)

Kahn, Tom. The Economics of Inequality. New York. 1964.

(II)

Using the official poverty line as a criteria for poverty, Kahn examines the relative economic position of Blacks from the 1940's to the mid-sixties. From 1940 to 1953, Blacks made the most economic gains due to a movement out of agriculture into the goods-producing industries, where they took up unskilled and semi-skilled jobs. However, after that time, their relative economic position declined. In particular, Kahn observed (1) a widening dollar gap between Blacks and whites; (2) a relative income gap that remained virtually constant; (3) a widening employment gap; (4) the decline of the goods-producing industries where Blacks had previously made the greatest gains; (5) the growing percentage of Black workers in most of the declining job categories. Kahn attributes the economic inequality of Blacks primarily to the combination of generations of racial discrimination, and recent technological advances that eliminated thousands of jobs. He points to the failure of private manpower programs to help Blacks and criticizes private enterprise for causing a production lag in the economy. Finally, he calls on government to improve the economic position of Blacks.

Kain, John F. Ghetto Labor Markets and Income Maintenance. Cambridge, Massachusetts: Harvard University Program on Regional and Urban Economics, Discussion Paper No. 37, 1968.

(V,VI,X)

The urban hard-core unemployed are concentrated in the ghetto, while new blue collar job opportunities are increasingly located in the suburbs. Bringing factories to the ghetto would only increase its isolation. The geographical distance can be bridged by cheap transportation, and the social distance that prevents word-of-mouth and other informal sources of job information from being effective could be bridged by more formal employment services. Wage subsidies could be instituted which would encourage metropolitan area industries to hire the hard-core unemployed. But if conditions in the northern cities improve, the South will send forth another wave of rural immigrants. Hence, the long-run solution is the economic development of the South. The negative income tax would encourage this and also break down the social hegemony of the wealthy whites. The latter, however, would share in the benefits of general prosperity.

Kain, John. National Priorities for Regional Development. Cambridge, Massachusetts: Harvard University Program on Regional and Urban Economics, Discussion Paper No. 61, 1970.

(V,VI)

Despite a narrowing of regional economic differences over the past century, Southern poverty remains the nation's major regional problem. In 1968, the per capita income of the "core" South was 66%, and of the "border" South 68%, of that of the North and West. For the same year AFDC payments averaged $8.45 per recipient per month in Mississippi compared to $44.70 in Illinois. Interregional migration of labor and capital is the principal mechanism which has enabled some regions to grow more rapidly than others, and shifts in population have been closely related to the regional location of jobs. The latter are postulated to be closely related to regional location of capital.

Family Assistance Programs would be an important beginning to the restoration of regional economic balance. It is estimated that the aggregate transfer of income to the South would have been nearly $1 billion in 1969. In addition, capital subsidies to underdeveloped regions would play an important role in the development of the public infrastructure needed to support modern industrialization and urban economies.

Kain, John. Urban Form and the Costs of Urban Services. Cambridge: Harvard University, Program on Regional and Urban Economics, No. 6, 1967.

(V)

This monograph reports the results of a survey which focused on the question of how the costs of urban services vary with, or are affected by, various aspects of urban form such as density, contiguity, or compactness. Because there is no uniform definition of urban services, the author defines the term to cover the full cost of services provided urban residents both by the various levels of government and by public utilities and private concerns. Research and prevailing beliefs about the effect of urban form (spatial layout) on the costs of urban services are found to have been greatly influenced by personal and public ideology. While most urban planners seem to believe that urban costs are strongly affected by urban form, the study suggests that development standards may be more important than differences either in residential density or urban form. Increased institutional costs probably more than offset the savings in urban service costs for high density structures of more than two or three stories.

Kain, John, and Persky, Joseph. The North's Stake in Southern Rural Poverty. Cambridge, Massachusetts: Harvard Program on Regional and Urban Economics, Discussion Paper No. 18, 1967.

(V,VI)

Starting with the premise that the problems of urban poverty in the North and those of southern rural poverty are intertwined, Kain proceeds to argue why the urban North should be concerned with conditions of rural poverty in the South. After a discussion of the extent of poverty in the southern rural areas, the system of migration from the rural South to the metropolitan North is examined. The depressed economy of the rural South, the baby boom and the reduction of agricultural jobs are reasons given to explain the flight of the southern rural poor to northern urban areas.

Lower education level is presented as the main promoter of continued poverty for southern out-migrants. Strengthening of the educational system, equalization of employment opportunities, and expansion of southern metropolitan areas are recommendations which Kain presents for solving the South's poverty and migratory problems.

Kain, John, and Quigley, John. Housing Markets and Racial Discrimination: A Microeconomic Analysis. New York: National Bureau of Economic Research, November 1973.

(III)

"The demand for housing and the behavior of the urban housing market are better understood if housing is viewed as bundles of heterogeneous housing attributes, rather than as a single valued commodity." Kain and Quigley, recognizing major market imperfections, such as housing-market segregation, proceed to test this assertion on the housing market in St. Louis, Missouri. Their study, which uses a number of econometric models to evaluate housing stock tracts, indicates that Blacks suffer from housing discrimination due to prohibitive search costs, treatment by sellers and agents, and in general, fear. This in turn results in the non-market production of various attributes, and the geographic characteristics of others, which leave the Blacks without housing bundles of their liking. An active policy of "open-housing" enforcement and integrating suburban areas are recommended as strategies for increasing the housing supply alternatives facing Blacks and the economic growth of urban areas.

Kain, John, and Schafer, Robert. Effects of Income Maintenance on Urban Fiscal Problems. Cambridge, Massachusetts: Harvard University, Program on Regional and Urban Economics, Discussion Paper No. 83. 1974.

(V)

The purpose of this article is to analyze the distribution of benefit payments and of probable tax payments of three income maintenance plans between the suburbs and central cities in the 65 Standard Metropolitan Statistical Areas with one-half million or more persons in 1970. For the Family Assistance Plan and two other plans with higher benefit levels, the additional transfer payments above the current level of public assistance are computed that would accrue to the residents of each central city and suburban ring, and federal tax payments and net transfers to each area under each plan are estimated. For each city, the savings in local tax dollars that would result from the federal assumption of the welfare burden is estimated.

Analysis indicates that a national income maintenance plan would transfer income from well-to-do central city and suburban residences to poor households living in the same city, in smaller metropolitan areas, and outside of metropolitan areas. Because of the concentrations of poor in older central cities and the heavy expenditure by many local governments for welfare, the poorest central cities would receive larger benefits under a federal income maintenance program. The incomes of their poor households would be increased substantially and they would be relieved of a heavy burden of taxation.

*Kain, John F., and Schafer, Robert. Regional Impacts of the Family Assistance Plan. Cambridge, Massachusetts: Harvard University Program on Regional and Urban Economics, 1971.

(V)

This paper evaluates the impact of the Family Assistance Plan (FAP) on regional growth and development. Under the current AFDC system, average payments in the six richest states were over twice as high in real terms as payments in the six poorest southern states. FAP would equalize benefits and would make a small, but important contribution to reducing regional variations in the incidence of poverty. It would add three and one half billion dollars to personal income in the poorest part of the South. The authors speculate that FAP would have only a modest impact on migration between the South and the non-South. It would reduce somewhat the Black migration from the South to northern metropolitan areas, however, it has a substantially larger effect on discouraging the outmigration of southern whites.

Kaitz, Hyman. "Analyzing the Length of Spells of Unemployment." Monthly Labor Review 93 (No. 11, 1970): 11-20.

(IX,X)

This study analyzes both the frequency and the duration of spells of unemployment. Most spells of unemployment last five weeks or less, but such spells may occur several times in one year. In tight labor markets, short-term unemployment figures are the most active--reflecting the entry and exit of marginal workers, e.g., housewives and the young. In recession, the fast increase in the long-term unemployment rates partially reflects the fact that many short spells are being combined into one longer one.

Kakwani, N.C. "A Note on the Efficient Estimation of the New Measures of Income Inequality." Econometrica 42 (May 1974).

(II)

Maximum likelihood estimators of the Elteto and Frigyes (annotated elsewhere) three new measures of inequality are derived. These estimators can be derived only if one assumes that the income distribution is log-normal. These are, however, more efficient than the Elteto-Frigyes estimators.

Kaldor, Nicholas. "Alternative Theories of Distribution." Review of Economic Studies (1956).

(II)

A review of alternative theories of the income distribution, including Ricardo, Marx, neo-classicals, and Keynesian. Ricardo suggested that the shape of the income distribution resulted from the interaction of the marginal principle and the surplus principle. The marginal principle (later adopted by the neo-classicals) was used to explain rent: Ricardo argued that rent was determined by the difference between product on the marginal and the average land. The surplus principle was used to explain the division of the remaining income between labor and capital: wages were equal to subsistence wages and capital received the remaining income in the form of profits. Marx abandoned the Ricardian distinction between rent and profit and used Ricardo's surplus principle alone to explain the division of income between labor and capital. The neo-classical school (current) explains the distribution of income largely via the "marginal productivity" theory--that is, individuals are recompensed on the basis of the contribution made by the factor of production they contribute. The distinction between capital and labor is largely blurred--both are treated as simple factors of production.

Kaldor, Nicholas. An Expenditure Tax. London: Unwin University Books, 1955.

(VII)

The case for basing the dominant national tax on the expenditures rather than the incomes of individuals and business is made in this book. An expenditure tax would solve several of the problems associated with income taxes. It would provide a better measure of individual ability to pay and therefore be more equitable: individuals with large holdings of assets and small incomes would not escape taxation while those individuals with fluctuating incomes would not be punished for this fluctuation as they now are by progressive income tax rates. Saving would be encouraged because there would no longer be any 'double counting'. (Savings are taxed first when they are earned and again when they earn interest.) Only when savings were used for purchases would they be taxed. An expenditure tax would also not distort the risk-taking behavior of individuals the way income taxes can. Such a tax would also be a very powerful tool of fiscal policy, since it would affect individual spending decisions more directly than does an income tax.

The book concludes with several chapters on the practicality of such a tax. The administration of this kind of tax is shown to be possible and a model tax is discussed.

Kaluzhy, Richard. "A Comparison of Household Migration Determinants by Poverty Level and Race." Institute for Research on Poverty, University of Wisconsin. Working Paper 254 - 75. January 1975.

(VI)

The study examines and compares the determinants of migration for a sample of households during the periods 1968-69 and 1969-70. Household demographic and economic characteristics are defined in the context of a linear probability function. A measure of the expected gain from migration is developed to reflect the relative attractiveness of the area of origin.

The model explains the migration of white households more completely than that of non-white households. The effects of expected gain are positive and significant in both groups. When households are grouped by poverty level, the model explains the behavior of those below the 1.25 level most completely and is least successful for households at levels of 4.0 or more. The poor are highly sensitive to the expected gain measure.

Comparisons between groups suggest (1) that the migration determinants vary substantially by poverty level, and (2) that the behavior of the poor is not well reflected by the behavior of racial groups.

(From the article)

Katz, Irwin. "A New Approach to the Study of School Motivation in Minority Group Children." In Psychological Factors in Poverty, edited by Allen L. Vernon. Chicago: Markham Publishing Co., 1970.

(IX,XI)

Katz ascribes academic difficulty among lower-class Negro students to motivational problems. Motivation is conceptualized as the internalization of standards of excellence and covert self-evaluation of performance. Katz describes research designed to study self-evaluation of high and low achievers subsequent to their performance on a simple taks. Low-achieving boys were more self-critical than high-achieving boys, although the objective performance of the two groups did not differ. In a sense, these low-achieving boys were imposing failure on themselves by using more stringent critical standards for their own performance.

(Partially taken from editor's introduction)

Katzner, Donald W. Static Demand Theory. London: The Macmillan Company, 1970.

(III)

The purpose of demand theory is to explain consumer market behavior. Thus answers must be provided for at least two distinct but related questions. (1) Given various market parameters such as price, income, etc., what commodities will the consumer purchase and in what quantities? (2) How are these decisions affected by changes in the original parameters?

A convenient mathematical device for summarizing information about a consumer's behavior and analyzing these questions is the demand function. Therefore, "the purpose of demand theory is to explain the general properties of such functions."

This book presents a static analysis of demand theory, taking each time period separately. Katzner discusses the following topics: the similarity between utility functions and preference orderings; the maximization of utility functions; the properties of homogenous separable utility functions; the analysis of demand problems in the face of uncertainty; and some applications of demand theory to economic questions outside its realm.

(Partially taken from the book)

Kelly, Laurence A. Family Allowances and the Tax System. Ontario: Industrial Relations Center, Queen's University, 1971.

(IV)

An examination of "the relationship between family allowances and the tax system in Canada--what it has been in the past, what it is now, and what it will be under the new tax and family allowance legislation--and, on the basis of this, to assess the new family allowance plan and its implications."

The author notes that the program has been greatly criticized for paying allowances to all children; legislation which gears the program more toward the poor is explained. Kelly voices his reservations about the Family Income Security Plan and about the lack of coordination between this system and new tax legislation.

*Kelly, Terence. "Labor Supply and the Poverty Problem." In Perspectives on Poverty, edited by Dennis Dugan and William Leahy. New York: Praeger Publishers, 1973.

(II,X)

A theoretical and empirical study of the distribution and dynamics of poverty, based on data from the 1960-1969 Current Population Survey. Kelly tests the effect of changes in aggregate demand on employment and income for various sub-groups of the population: non-white males, non-white females, white males and white females. Families were followed over successive two-year periods to determine "escape rates"--i.e., the rate at which families move out of the Social Security Administration's poverty group. Kelly's results suggest that non-white escape rates are less responsive to changes in aggregate economic growth than are white rates.

Kelso, Louis O., and Hetter, Patricia. Two Factor Theory: The Economies of Reality. New York: Vintage Books, 1968.

(II)

The thesis of this book is that everyone wants to be affluent, that this desire is legitimate, and that general affluence is achievable in an economy physically endowed with, or having access by trade to, the natural resources, the manpower, and the knowledge necessary to produce it. By positing that there are two factors which can be used to produce wealth, man's labor and capital instruments, Kelso and Hetter advance a theory of "universal capitalism" which can be used to build an economic system in which all citizens own or have effective opportunity to own viable holdings of productive capital, and in which this opportunity stands as an essential personal and legal right.

Kershaw, Joseph. "Who Are the Poor?" Government Against Poverty. Chicago: Markham Publishing Co., 1970.

(II,VI)

Describes and assesses the first few years of the U.S. effort initiated by the Economic Opportunity act of 1964 to eliminate poverty. The Office of Economic Opportunity (OEO) definition of poverty had to serve several purposes: (1) to provide a statistical measurement of the progress of the war against poverty; (2) to be simple enough to be operational; and (3) to make rural/non-rural distinctions. There are several deficiencies inherent in this definition: (1) it is based on the assumption that poor people spend one-third of their income on food; (2) it distinguishes between farm/non-farm rather than rural/non-rural, although the latter would be more appropriate; (3) it assumes that the poor can and/or will spend wisely. Other poverty definitions are possible, such as the use of a certain fraction of the median income as the poverty line, or the examination of social characteristics (see Oscar Lewis, Michael Harrington).

Keyserling, Leon H. "Poverty and Its Cure." In Issues of the Sixties, edited by L. Freedman. 2nd ed. Belmont, California: Wadsworth Publishing Co., 1965.

(II)

A summary description of the author's perception of poverty--an immediate, massive problem with realizable solutions. The social context and roots of poverty are examined, but the author emphasizes that the one universal characteristic of all the poor is that they do not receive enough income in money and other forms to rise above poverty. Personal income is the best practical measurement of whether people are poor. The distinctions between poverty, deprivation, and modest-but-adequate categories are misleading. The average income within each group is far below the upper ceiling. The author considers the relative poverty concentration within various population groups and the possible role of the Government and changes in the federal budget to alleviate the poverty problem.

Keyserling, Leon H. Progress or Poverty. Washington, D.C.: Conference on Economic Progress, 1964.

(II)

The United States is confronted with the challenge of progress or poverty instead of the often held view of progress and poverty. Poverty is defined as having "too little income"; thus, only programs which will increase the poor's income can reduce poverty. A discussion follows which deals with what income levels define poverty (in 1962 dollars) and the relative progress made in lowering the number of families in poverty.

Seven "marks of poverty" are presented which are both causes and characteristics of the poor: inadequate shooling, deficient health services, crime and juvenile delinquency, inadequate social security and welfare programs, indecent housing conditions, civil strife, and high unemployment. Further delineations are made between personal characteristics and economic characteristics of the poor.

The remainder of the study focuses on these seven marks and makes specific recommendations of how the country and the War on Poverty can provide solutions to eliminate them. Included in the discussion are present trends and the extent of the problems.

Kilpatrick, Robert. "The Income Elasticity of the Poverty Line." Review of Economics and Statistics (1973): 327-332.

(II)

A statistical analysis of the extent to which society's judgment about the height of the poverty threshold changes as the average income of the society increases. Survey responses to Gallup poll questions on the minimum income needed to "get along" in the community were regressed against growth in per capita income. Kilpatrick's results suggest that as a society becomes richer, the real income level it uses to define poverty also increase, although less than proportionately. This conclusion suggests that the public at least does not hold an absolute standard of poverty.

King, Willford Isbell. The Wealth and Income of the People of the United States. New York: MacMillan, 1915.

(II)

One of the first comprehensive statistical accounts of the distribution of wealth and income in the United States. An attempt to provide a factual/statistical description of the rapid economic growth that occurred in this country during the latter half of the nineteenth century. A variety of innovative approaches to measure national income were used. Poverty is defined solely in terms of income.

Kinman, Judith L., and Lee, Everett S. "Migration and Crime." *International Migration Digest* 3 (1966): 7-14.

(VI,XI)

The issue of whether migration is highly correlated with crime rates is addressed using data from the Pennsylvania State Prison System records. For whites, the crime rates are higher among migrants than among non-migrants; for Blacks, the reverse is found to be true. White migrants from the South are found to have the highest crime rates of white migrants, while Black migrants from the South have the lowest crime rate for Black migrants. Evidence indicates that migrants, on the whole, are positively selected from their points of origin. The study suggests that high rates of crime should not be attributed to the migrant and his personal disorganization. Rather, the high rates of crime in the Pennsylvania cities must be attributed to the native born, and to the socio-economic situation which they must face in the poor areas.

Klebaner, Benjamin. "Poverty and Its Relief in American Thought, 1815-61." *Social Service Review* 38 (1964).

(II)

Investigates the American literature on pauperism focusing on the explanations offered for poverty and proposals for dealing with the problem, including the merits of the poor law versus private almsgiving. A distinction was made between the honest, industrious, but unfortunate poor, and the idle avaricious poor. The economic view, e.g. of Mathew Carey, stressed the role of factors such as unemployment in causing poverty. Proposed remedies dealt primarily with provision of work but also included temperance, character improvement by religious education, and savings banks.

Klein, Lawrence R. "Estimating Patterns of Savings Behavior from Sample Survey Data." *Econometrica* 19 (No. 4, October 1951): 438-454.

(VII)

A pioneering cross-sectional estimate of savings based on economic and demographic data. The savings rate was assumed to be a linear combination of income per capita and the ratio of liquid assets to income. Both variables were found to be significant, the first positive, the second negative. (Saving increases with income but decreases with the amount of assets already owned.) An analysis of the residuals showed that when income decreased, savings increased if the change was believed to be permanent, decreased if it was thought to be temporary. A decrease in income was found to increase the influence of the liquid asset term: the presence of liquid assets permitted dissavings.

Klein, L.R., and Rutin, H. "A Constant-Utility Index of the Cost of Living." The Review of Economic Studies 15(No. 2, 1947-48): 84-87.

(III)

The authors construct a cost-of-living index which depends only upon observable prices and the properties of demand functions. This index has both an upper and a lower bound to its interval of estimated value, in contrast to indices of the Paasche or Laspeyre type which have but one limit. The index assumes preferences remain constant over the period in question.

Klein, William A. "Familial Relationships and Economic Well-Being: Family Unit Rules for a Negative Income Tax." In Institute for Research on Poverty Reprint Series, 1971.

(II,IV)

Payments under a negative income tax program would be made to families rather than to individuals on the presumption that (1) income within the family is shared and (2) living together achieves certain savings in living costs. However, with separations, common-law marriages, working children and single adults in the household, people married in the legal sense may not meet the above criteria. This paper develops and defines a set of administrative rules for determining family size for negative income tax purposes. The rules allow a family to decide whether to include a child (and his income) for tax purposes, but the parent of one's child, married or not, must be included if the couple is living together. Thus, unmarried couples with permanent relationships will be treated as married.

*Klin, Deborah P. "Exploring the Adequacy of Employment." Monthly Labor Review (October 1973).

(X)

Describes available labor force indicators of employment quality and points out the need for employment statistics which measure social welfare. The Current Population Survey by the Census Bureau and Bureau of Labor Statistics "payroll" figures present data on economic aspects of inadequacy of employment for the "working poor" (including statistics on quantity of work and earnings from work). A further criterion for judging adequacy of earnings is the federal minimum wage level.

Greater problems present themselves in measuring underemployment ("manpower underutilization"). Assessment of this aspect of employment (quality) is hindered by difficulties in arriving at a suitably objective standard of measurement.

*Knox, Paul L. "Social Indicators and the Concept of Level of Living." Sociological Review (May 1974).

(XI)

An outline of the relevance of the level-of-living concept to the construction of meaningful measures of social conditions. Seeks to limit the definition of "social indicators" to those measures which can be related to a sociological model of some kind. Defines level of living as overall composition of housing, health, education, social status, employment, leisure, social security and social stability, together with those aspects of demographic and environmental structure and social institutions which influence the extent to which those needs and desires can be met. Measurement would be facilitated if all variables were normative in character (variables for which a move in a particular direction can be "good" or "bad" depending on its behavior along a quantified scale), but many variables (such as those relating to the provision of social services) are non-normative.

Koffsky, Nathan. "Farm and Urban Purchasing Power." Studies in Income and Wealth 7 (1949).

(VI)

An analysis comparing the purchasing power of urban and farm families. A direct comparison of income has little meaning since the two types of families face different price structures. Therefore, differences in the "cost of living" must be taken into account when measuring purchasing power. Prices can be compared in terms of what it would cost in an urban area to purchase the goods consumed by a farm family or vice versa. This is still of limited usefulness. Since rural needs are different from urban needs, the same quantity of the same goods will yield different levels of utility or satisfaction in the different areas.

Despite this weakness the author concludes that a price adjusted income comparison is more useful than no comparison. Using data compiled by the Bureau of Labor Statistics and the Bureau of Agricultural Economics, he finds that the ratio of factory earnings to farm earnings adjusted for price is 1.28 in 1941 and .97 in 1945, and the adjusted ratio of farm earnings to factory earnings is .72 in 1941 and .95 in 1945.

Kohen, Andres I.; Parnes, Herbert S.; and Shea, John R. "Income Instability Among Young and Middle-Aged Men." Washington, D.C.: U.S. Government Printing Office, 1973.

(IX)

This study analyzes changes in total family income and in annual earnings among male household heads who were 45 to 59 and among those 16 to 24 in 1966. For the middle-aged man, the period of study is calendar year 1965 and 1966; for the young men, it is 1966-1968. One focus of the study is the extent to which extending the accounting period affects the measurement of inequality of income distribution where the latter is measured by the Gini coefficient. A second focus is an investigation, via regression analysis, of the sources of instability in income and earnings. Throughout the study attention is directed to differences in income stability by race and base-year income class as well as age.

Kolko, Gabriel. "The Distribution of Wealth." In Wealth and Power in America. New York: Praeger, 1962.

(II)

Although income is unequally distributed, wealth is even more concentrated, and the high-income earners also tend to be wealthy. Since World War II the top income tenth has owned an average of two-thirds of all liquid assets. Only 8% of the population owns stock, and a mere 2% of them control 58% of total stocks. The concentration of stock ownership has remained roughly the same since 1929. Only the brokers gain from small-scale speculation in stocks. Pension funds may ultimately benefit workers, but their disposition is in the hands of large banks. Thus, "people's capitalism" is a myth. Negative net worth characterizes the two lowest fifths of the income distribution.

Kolko, Gabriel. Wealth and Power in America. New York: Praeger Publishers, 1962.

(II)

"The basic distribution of income and wealth in the United States is essentially the same now as it was in 1939, or even 1910." While real wages have risen, the percentages of the population which share the nation's wealth have not. The economic gains which have been made by the low-income groups have been greatly exaggerated and well over one-third of the nation's households still subsist on incomes too meager to provide the minimum standards of health and decency. "The gains of relatively full employment and a normally ascending real income have been largely offset by the rise of new causes of poverty and by the perpetuation of an important segment of the traditional causes."

According to 1958 figures from the Internal Revenue Service, individuals with personal incomes of between $0 and $4,000 contributed $6.037 billion in taxes. Yet for the same year the federal government spent only $4.059 billion on what by the most generous definition could be called "welfare" (including expenditures for public assistance, public health, education, public housing, and "other welfare"), and only a fraction of this went to individuals with under $4,000 personal income. Welfare spending has not changed the nature of income inequality, and statistics demonstrate that "in America, the legendary land of economic opportunity where any man can work his way to the top, there is only slight income mobility outside the natural age cycle of rising, then falling income."

Kondor, Yaakov. "An Old-New Measure of Income Inequality." Econometrica 39 (November 1971).

(II)

This paper is a comment on the article by Elteto and Frigyes that proposed a set of new income inequality measures. These inequality indices are the ratios of mean incomes ($u = m/m_1$ $w = m_2/m$ $v = m_2/m_1$ where m = mean income of the total distribution, m_2 is the mean income of the group above the overall mean and m_1 is the mean income of the group below); and it is noted that no single index in itself is a plausible measure of inequality since, for example, a given ratio contains no information about the relative frequencies of the groups whose means are considered. Taken together, the three ratios of Elteto and Frigyes do contain information about the total distribution; however, it is found that all of this essential content is actually present in the relative mean deviation of the distribution. It is noted that this latter measure was investigated by Pietra and others in the early part of the century but was neglected for a long time only to be rediscovered again in recent years. Today it is often referred to as the "maximum equalization percentage," since it is the percentage of total income which would have to be transferred from the group above the overall income mean to the group below in order to achieve perfect equality. "In a certain sense,...the interesting contribution of Elteto and Frigyes was another modern rediscovery of that time-honored measure of income inequality, the relative mean deviation."

Kosa, John. "The Nature of Poverty." In Poverty and Health. Cambridge, Massachusetts: Harvard University Press, 1969.

(II)

The poor are those who lack the means of subsistence and the privileges of life. This definition is useful: it describes the poor's unilateral exclusion from material and psychological possessions, and it is also the criterion by which anyone can assess and describe the distribution of wealth. Perceptions of poverty and reactions to it vary according to community attitudes. Historically, feudal societies regarded institutionalized poverty as part of the natural order. Its existence was either taken for granted or treated in a manner that did not affect the existing social order. However, in the 20th century, poverty is no longer taken for granted; the fact that it is a man-made condition is stressed. The poor of today are a residual group which, for geographic, social or psychological reasons, has been unable to take advantage of an open-class mobile society. Three major poverty spokesmen--Michael Harrington, Hubert Humphrey and S.M. Miller--have different typologies describing the poor. This article distinguishes on the basis of different deprivation processes between chronic and acute poverty.

(Partially taken from Poverty and Human Resources Abstracts)

Kosa, John; Antonovsky, Aaron; and Zola, Irving K. Chapter 10 in Poverty and Health. Cambridge, Massachusetts: Harvard University Press, 1969.

(XI)

Discusses the history of neighborhood health centers and the development of their role as providers of medical services to the poor in urban and rural areas. Particular attention is given to intention and scope of programs initiated in Boston, Los Angeles, and Cincinnati in the early 1900's. These and other early programs were hindered by such basic problems as an inability to attract sufficient number of public health physicians and a lack of systematic integration with existing health care institutions.

Recently, interest in neighborhood health centers has resurged in cities and rural areas throughout the country. Questions regarding their location, size, strategy, and clientele are being reconsidered, and new arrangements are being implemented in an attempt to overcome past mistakes.

Kosters, Marvin H. "Income and Substitution Effects in a Family Labor Supply Model." Ph.D. dissertation, University of Chicago, 1966.

(II)

"A model was developed in this study to investigate in a family context income and substitution effects of wage rate changes on the quantity of labor supplied to the market by individual family members. Regression analysis using cross-sectional data from the 1960 census was used in an attempt to estimate the income and substitution effects. Only two dimensions for which measures were readily available, hours of work per week and per year, were analyzed. For another dimension, labor force participation, results from three earlier studies are examined and reinterpreted."

"A change in the wage rate carries with it a substitution effect. The income effect on the quantity of leisure demanded of an increase in the wage rate is positive if leisure is not an inferior good. The substitution effect on leisure demanded is negative since the opportunity cost of leisure time (its price in terms of market goods given up) has increased."

"Although the estimates presented provide some evidence on the effect of a relative price distortion such as the personal income tax at the labor-leisure margin, the consumption-savings distortion or possible distortions in the occupational wage structure affecting the allocation of labor among different kinds of employment were neglected in this study."

Kosters, Marvin, and Welch, Finis. The Effects of Minimum Wages on the Distribution of Changes in Aggregate Employment. Prepared for the Office of Economic Opportunity, RM-6273-OEO. Santa Monica, California: Rand, 1970.

(II)

Using employment data for the period 1954-1968 from the Bureau of Labor Statistics and data on the level of the minimum wage and the extent of coverage of the legislation, the authors have analyzed the distribution of fluctuations in aggregate employment in the U.S. economy between whites and nonwhites, between males and females, and between teenagers and adults.

The relative income position of nonwhites has shown marked improvement over the past decade. Part of this improvement, however, may be attributable to the sustained economic expansion of the early 1960's and thus may be subject to rapid erosion as the expansion slows or is reversed. Nonwhites (except for adult females) are disproportionately affected by employment fluctuations. A short term change in aggregate employment, for example, has twice the impact on adult nonwhite males that it has on similar white males.

The impact of short term employment changes falls most heavily on teenagers (three and one-half times their proportionate share). Teenage males are more sharply affected than females, and nonwhites more than whites. Increases in the effective minimum wage have made teenagers more vulnerable than before to short-term changes, and have decreased their share of normal employment. These effects, moreover, are disproportionately concentrated on nonwhite teenagers.

The analysis indicates that a slackening in the pace of economic growth will adversely affect nonwhites, particularly teenagers.

(Taken from Monograph)

Kottis, Athena P. "Effects of Income Maintenance on the Economics of Communities: A Theoretical Exploration." Urban Affairs Quarterly 8 (June 1973): 495-589.

(II)

A consideration of the short run impacts of a negative income tax/income maintenance tax plan similar to President Nixon's proposed family assistance program. The short run effects of the plan on consumption, labor supply, labor demand, unemployment, wages, prices, housing, and aggregate income and output are analyzed. The most important impacts are rent and price increases for low and moderate income housing due to increased demand, higher wages in low wage industries because of an increase in demand and a decrease in supply for labor, and an overall increase in consumption and aggregate income. The impact of any community depends on the parameters and financing of the plan and the size, industry mix, location and income distribution of the community.

Kottis, A., and Kottis, G. "Average Propensity to Spend Inside the Ghetto Areas: A Comment." Journal of Regional Science 13 (April 1973): 123-126.

(III, IV)

In response to a case study which unexpectedly found the average propensity to spend within the community of four ghetto areas to be relatively low compared to that of other surrounding non-ghetto areas, the two authors build up an argument why these results should have been expected. Using a very simple hypothesized population model, Kottis and Kottis show how the expenditure behavior of the higher income and more mobile of inner city residents outweighs the average propensity to spend of those with low incomes who are less mobile. The higher local prices provide an incentive for those more educated and mobile to spend a large part of their budget outside the community. The absence of major department and retail stores in the ghetto areas, and the relatively shorter distance from ghetto areas to the Central Business District are cited as other reasons one should expect a lower average propensity to spend within the ghetto communities.

Kraft, G., et al. "On the Definition of a Depressed Area." In _Essays in Regional Economics_, edited by J. Kain. Cambridge, Massachusetts: Harvard University Press, 1971.

(V,VI,X)

This article addresses the problem of defining a "depressed area" to determine eligibility for participation in economic development or rehabilitation programs. The problems of area designation can be classified under two headings: 1) determining the welfare criteria or objectives implicit or explicit in the legislation establishing a redevelopment effort; and 2) attempting to specify these criteria in an empirical way." Three "discriminant functions" are developed measuring 1) the percent of the families with income under $2000, 2) the percent of unemployed, and 3) the percent of unemployed plus the number and percent of families with incomes under $2000. These functions are developed using 15 variables grouped into 4 areas: 1) physical, 2) income related, 3) education, and 4) labor market imperfections. The lowest 300 counties were selected from each discrimination. Ten counties appeared in all three groups. Eleven counties appeared in both the unemployment and the low income groups, 35 counties appeared in both the unemployment and the joint groups. Clearly, persistence of low income and unemployment do not necessarily coincide. Since both criteria must underlie any sensible rationalization of area redevelopment as a public policy, these observed differences in persistency characteristics of the two criteria could have important implications.

Kravis, Irving B. _The Structure of Income_. Philadelphia: University of Pennsylvania, 1962.

(II)

This study of United States income and saving is based on the 1950 Bureau of Labor Statistics' consumers survey. At that time, the United States had twice the per capita income of several of the highest income countries, while intertemporal U.S. comparisons are even more impressive. Incomes in the South were 12% lower than incomes in the North, with half of this differential accounted for by differing racial composition. Negro-white differences are diminished, but not eliminated, when comparisons are made within occupational groups. Property income differences also help account for the white/non-white gap, which showed no signs of closing. The income rankings of 11 occupational groups studied were consistent across all 6 classes of cities. After tax income rises with age until the 45-54 bracket and declines thereafter. Education grants entry into higher paying occupations. Female family heads are more likely to be unemployed than male heads (40% vs. 10%) and tend to be concentrated in unskilled service and clerical work. The share of wages in national income has risen over the century, with both entrepreneurial and property shares declining.

Inequality in income declined in the two decades after 1929, especially the share of the top 5%. The United States stands midway among the nations of the world in its degree of inequality, although the less developed countries account for most of the very unequal end of the scale.

Krosney, Herbert. Beyond Welfare: Poverty in the Supercity. New York: Holt, Rinehart and Winston, 1969.

(V)

Krosney argues that if welfare programs are designed to perpetuate poverty, then anti-poverty programs aimed at really changing the status quo will encounter severe opposition. The Kennedy and Johnson administrations' New York City youth programs, HARYOU, ACT, and Mobilization for Youth were not torn apart simply by different levels of government each seeking the credit. Efforts to advance the Black, white and Puerto Rican lower class met with real opposition from the Black, white, Jewish and Italian middle classes.

These programs wasted much effort and money creating an unrealistic "employability" when what was needed was unskilled and semi-skilled jobs, not experience or training. A negative income tax is seen as a way to avoid a new blossoming bureaucracy and the perverse work and family incentives of AFDC.

Kulash, Damian, and Silverman, William. Discrimination in Mass Transit. The Urban Institute, 1974 (URI No. 64000).

(V)

Community groups in many cities claim that racial minorities of lower income people of particular sections of the city are discriminated against in the provision of mass transit. This study explores the conceptual issues which arise in evaluating allegations of inequality, and identifies deficiencies in the techniques that courts, community groups, and transit authorities have used to determine whether services are distributed equally.

(Author abstract)

Kuznets, Simon. "On the Valuation of Social Income." Economica 15(1948): 1-16.

(III)

Social income should be defined to include consumers' outlay on all finished products (private sector) at market prices (final to consumer), plus services to individuals provided by public agencies -- at cost to the government, plus net business capital formation at market prices, plus net capital formation by government at market prices. Capital formation is included even though enterprises, not individuals *qua* individuals, are making the saving decisions. Competition is assumed to modify price ratios of capital goods and final products to adjust them to technical changes, thus making capital good prices reflect their welfare contribution.

Laber, Gene. "Human Capital in Southern Migration." <u>Journal of Human Resources</u> 8 (Spring 1973).

(VI)

This paper assesses the effects of interregional migration on the human-capital stock of the South. Data from the one percent sample maintained by the Social Security Administration are used to estimate the earnings level of in-and-out migrants for the period 1960-66, during which the South lost just under one percent of its labor force. When earnings of migrants are converted to human-capital values, the South is estimated to have gained human capital through migration. The gain, however, depends critically on earnings levels of migrants, and the paper demonstrates that the gain turns into a loss if migrants are assumed to receive earnings prevailing for non-migrants in the region.

(Taken from the article)

*Lamale, Helen. "Changes in Concepts of Income Adequacy Over the Last Century." <u>American Economic Review</u> (May 1968).

(II)

A historical review of poverty definitions. Prior to 1850, there was apparently little thinking on the concept of income inadequacy; poorhouses were used to care for all kinds of dependents. Between 1860 and 1900 social scientists subscribed to a "subsistence" concept of poverty. By 1900 analysts were defining subsistence as the cost of adequate food, housing, and clothing to maintain a minimum standard of health and decency. During the first decade of the century, much data began to be collected on income expenditures, savings and living conditions. Later, the idea that income adequacy must deal with real income and distinguish between long- and short-term needs was advanced. The concept of conformity with prevailing standards in selecting goods and services for inclusion in budgets is revealed by postwar budget studies. General concepts of income adequacy are not being challenged; what is usually challenged is the ability to express these concepts in quantitative measures and, therefore, the accuracy of estimates of needs which are based upon them.

Lamale, Helen. Levels of Living Among the Poor. Bureau of Labor Statistics Report No. 238-12, August, 1965.

(II,VII)

Supports a relative appraisal of poverty. Presents some historical statistics on consumer income and expenditures to give perspective to the discussion of current levels and distributions of income, spending, and saving. The report examines the following: (1) measurement by value of consumption; (2) levels of living as indicated by food expenditures; (3) percent spent for the basics (food, shelter, and clothing); (4) discretionary spending; and (5) use of credit as insurance. No real appraisal of the adequacy of the levels of living of the poor can be made without consideration of the existing wide variations in prices and living costs. Analysis of family spending and saving for welfare purposes is primarily microeconomic research.

(Partially taken from Poverty and Human Resources Abstracts)

Lamale, Helen C. "Poverty: The Word and the Reality." Monthly Labor Review (July 1965).

(II,IV,VI)

To define the poor as those "lacking the means of subsistence" requires "an explicit definition of 'means' and 'subsistence' and an approval of the relation between them in a specific situation." Standards of living, family size, and regional adjustments are discussed as factors relevant to a determination of "subsistence". To underscore the difficulty in specifying a minimum living standard, for example, it is noted that the average, annual, price-adjusted expenditures for comparable New York working families has increased by 125 percent in the period from 1919 to 1960. Problems in measuring a family's "means" arise from the fact that income alone does not specify all the resources which might be available from community services, public and private assistance agencies, supplemental wage benefits, insurance plans, and the use of credit. To demonstrate the importance of non-income contributions, figures are presented to show the percentage amount by which expenditures and consumption exceed income for non-farm families in the $3000 to $4000 income range. It is thought that any resolution of the poverty problem would have to come in the form of a series of answers to a variety of specific situations.

Lamale, Helen H., and Stotz, Margaret S. "The Interim City Worker's Family Budget." Monthly Labor Review 83 (August 1960): 785-808.

(II, III)

A description of "interim revisions" of the City Worker's Family Budget as formulated by the Bureau of Labor Statistics. The interim budget (1959), as with previous ones, relates to a family of 4 persons, consisting of an employed husband aged 38, with a wife not employed outside the home, and 2 children, a girl aged 8 and a boy aged 13, who live in a rented dwelling in a large city or its suburbs. The budget provides "the goods and services necessary for a healthful, self-respecting mode of living," allowing normal participation in the life of the community in accordance with current American standards. Former budgets needed revision because of average family increases in purchasing power and changes in consumers' market buying habits and what is acceptable as a "modest but adequate" level of living. The revised budget contains a new list of goods and services based on the actual choices of families. Because the revisions did not include a reappraisal and revision of previously used concepts, definitions and general procedures, it is considered an "interim revision." The purpose and methods used in the interim revision, the quantities of goods and services in the budget, and its cost in 20 large cities in autumn 1959 are discussed.

Lampman, Robert J. "Approaches to the Reduction of Poverty." American Economic Review 55 (September 1965): 521-29.

(II)

The article delineates the extent of poverty in the United States and describes its slow reduction over time. External circumstances, personal limitations and discrimination are given as causes of poverty which must be attacked by public policy.

The author begins his definition of poverty with the Council of Economic Advisors' income cut-off of $3,000 for families and $1,500 for unrelated individuals and modifies it with variations of $500 per person, setting in addition a lower mark for farm families. He also calculates the "poverty income gap"--the amount required to eliminate poverty--to be $12 billion or 2% of GNP.

*Lampman, Robert J. <u>Ends and Means of Reducing Poverty</u>. Chicago: Markham Publishing Co., 1971.

(II)

The book begins by reviewing antipoverty policies and social science thought, then develops a poverty reduction goal and discusses the economic and demographic considerations that must underlie any redistributive scheme. Finally various new strategies to fight poverty and improvements on existing strategies are reviewed.

The historical review points up the sharp distinction in historical British policy between the able-bodied poor who got no assistance but were forced to work, and those unable to work, for whom provisions were made. A redistributive goal may be defined in terms of the functional distribution of income (the wage/profit split), the size distribution of income (the share of the total going to the top and bottom groups), or simply as poverty reduction based on the needs of families. Whether calculated as three times the minimum food budget or as the price of a complete market basket of essentials, poverty lines are assumed to be relative and different for each society. Nonmoney income, irregular income, price level changes and the tax structure are mentioned as complicating factors.

*Lampman, Robert J. "Population Change and Poverty, 1947-75." In <u>Poverty Amid Affluence</u>, edited by Leo Fishman. New Haven: Yale University Press, 1966.

(II,IX)

A discussion of some essential characteristics of poverty in the United States. For the purpose of guiding remedial anti-poverty measures, Lampman identifies the poor's relationship to the labor market, their handicapping characteristics, their geographic location, and various processes by which people move out of and back into poverty. Several ways in which the total population's susceptibility to poverty changes as the composition of the population changes are also noted. Using several methods, Lampman makes projections of the number of families who will be in poverty in 1975. The results are not encouraging to anyone who might think poverty is going to disappear in a short time.

(Also, Lampman, Robert J. "Approaches to the Reduction of Poverty." <u>American Economic Review</u> 55: 521-29.

Lampman, Robert. Transfer and Redistribution as Social Process. Institute for Research on Poverty reprint #49, University of Wisconsin, 1970.

(II)

The scope of public and private transfers in the United States is examined with special attention to consequences for redistribution. The total amount of transfers for the fiscal year 1967 was 132 billion which was composed of a variety of private components such as employer financed insurance and individual insurance, philanthropies, and inter-family transfers; however, the dominant portion (100 billion) resulted from taxes and government related efforts. A study of such taxes and government expenditures undertaken by Gillespie indicates that these measures are "mildly redistributive toward the poor" where families were categorized solely on the basis of income bracket. Such analysis may be misleading insofar as "income bracket" ignores such things as family size and relative needs. To remedy this, data for the broad range of transfer processes is presented to display the differences for the poor and nonpoor as designated by the Social Security Administration poverty lines. Redistributive effects are similarly examined with respect to categories based on Morgan's "welfare ratio", an income over need index. It is found for example that property tax, which is always found to be regressive against a money income base, is strictly proportional against a welfare ratio base. In the overall process, the 1967 pre-transfer poor received a net gain of $37.5 billion which was more than their original income of 30 billion. The poverty income gap is another possible measure of redistribution. In 1964, the 28 percent pretransfer poor received 23 billion which left 18 percent in poverty with an $18 billion post-transfer poverty gap. In conclusion it is noted that an ideal transfer system would be one which achieved an appropriate balance among the three emphases in transfer programs: the income tax emphasis (concerned with income inequality), the minimum income emphasis (concerned with adequacy benefits), and the social fault emphasis (concerned with placement of loss).

Lampman, Robert J. "What Does It Do for the Poor?--A New Test for National Policy." The Public Interest 34 (Winter 1974): 66-82.

(II,V)

The measurements of poverty which are employed in public policy have not been well articulated. "Health care poverty," "education poverty," and "political poverty" have never been defined in a way which is comparable to the income poverty definition. As a result, many of the problems of poverty programs have occurred because of vaguely articulated goals--for example, in housing and child care--

new in-kind benefits for the poor were established, benefit standards per recipient were set which sometimes surpassed that spent by non-poor families, and then the programs were underfunded so that only a few of the poor could receive these benefits. Additionally, program design has created "dependency traps" in which the effective tax rate per dollar of non-welfare income earned by a recipient can be as high as 150%, discouraging economic independence.

During the past three decades, the number of people in income poverty (as defined by the government) has declined because of increased public social welfare expenditures which have carried disproportionate benefits to the poor. However, despite these increased expenditures, income distribution has not shifted over time and the problems of the poor have not been relieved. If we are to construct programs which will deal with the problems of poverty effectively, then we must first arrive at a clear definition of what we are dealing with, we must set goals to affect our intentions, and we must not change or elevate these goals in midstream to the detriment of our programs.

Lancaster, Kevin. "A New Approach to Consumer Theory." Journal of Political Economy 74(1966).

(III)

An extension of consumer theory, in which consumption is characterized as an activity in which goods are inputs and in which the output is a collection of characteristics. Traditionally, of course, goods and not the characteristics of goods were viewed as the direct objects of utility. This characterization provides a richer view of the relationship among goods. In particular, common characteristics of specific commodities under study can be identified, and probed much more easily than was possible under the earlier monolithic good formulation. Outlines of this general theory are presented, and specific applications to problems of consumer choice, the labor-leisure problem, assets, and general equilibrium analyses are sketched. The Lancaster model, by characterizing goods as bundles of separable attributes, provided an important foundation for subsequent developments on "hedonic price" indices.

Lancaster, Kevin. "The Theory of Household Behavior: Some Foundations." Annals of Economic and Social Measurement 4(1975): 5-21.

(III)

This paper examines the common practice of considering the household to act as if it were a single individual. Because a household is the closest-knit of groups, joint consumption and externalities are of great importance. If the household is an aggregate of independent consumers, the concavity properties of its demand function will be weaker than those for the individual, but will come closer to the individual properties as the size of the household decreases. The efficiency properties (observed as numbers of goods purchased relative to the number of distinct characteristics) will diverge from those of the individual as family size increases. The existence of joint consumption effects within the household will not affect the concavity properties of demand but will reduce the divergence in efficiency properties between the household and the individual. A dictatorial household will behave as a single individual.

Langner, Thomas. "Comparison of Experience and Behavior of Lower and Higher Status Groups: Findings and Hypotheses." In *Mental Health of the Poor*, edited by Frank Riessman et al. New York: The Free Press of Glencoe, 1964.

(XI)

Summarizes, in tabular form, behavioral and experiential differences relating to stress between higher and lower socio-economic strata. Demonstrates an inverse relationship between social class and mental illness; findings based primarily on data from "The Midtown Manhattan Study."

Lansing, John B. and Morgan, James N., "Consumer Finances Over the Life Cycle." In *Consumer Behavior and The Life Cycle*, edited by L.H. Clark. New York: 1955.

(VII)

A detailed examination of how income and assets change over the course of the life cycle. Income was found to increase after marriage until the birth of the first child, then to decline somewhat (because of the influence of working wives) and then rise again as the children get older. It peaks in late middle age after the children are adults. Automobiles are purchased early in the life cycle, while home ownership has an aggregate pattern similar to income. Purchases of homes are largest for families with growing children, but home ownership doesn't peak until children are grown. Spending on durables was found to reach its highest point for families with young children, then to decline until a period of major replacements some 20-25 years later. The heavy purchases of consumer durables early in life were found to strain liquid assets and most families resort to credit. Net worth did not show major increases until after children began to grow.

Lansing, John B., and Morgan, James N. "The Effect of Geographical Mobility on Income." Journal of Human Resources 2 (Fall 1967).

(VI)

When people move from one area to another they typically do so in order to raise their incomes. Economists would like to be able to estimate by how much migrants' incomes do in fact increase as a result of their mobility. Comparison of the incomes of migrants with nonmigrants in a cross section of the population, however, shows that the incomes of migrants tend to be lower, not higher, than those of nonmigrants. This paper reports an analysis of this apparent paradox using data collected by the Survey Research Center.

The difference in incomes between migrants and nonmigrants is traced to the disadvantages of those who move to economically advantaged areas compared to people who always have lived in those areas. The proper comparison is between those who were brought up in poor areas but left, with otherwise similar people who stayed. Holding constant number of years of education is not sufficient to remove the differences in earnings between people of different geographic backgrounds. It is suggested that the reason may be that there are important differences from place to place in quality of education which are not removed by taking into account the number of years of schooling.

(Journal of Human Resources)

Lansing, John B., and Sonquist, John. "A Cohort Analysis of Changes in the Distribution of Wealth." Studies in Income and Wealth 33 (1969).

(VII)

The technique of cohort analysis is used to measure changes in wealth between 1953 and 1962. Cohorts were defined by the age of the head of the spending unit, race, and educational achievement. These qualities showed little drift over time. The data on wealth was supplied by the Survey Research Center's Surveys of Consumer Finances. The results provided the first long-run data on changes in asset holdings over time. The principal results were:

1) The technique was practical, despite severe demands on the data and data collection technique.

2) Changes in net worth behaved as expected: net worth increased more rapidly for cohorts with middle ages, and with higher educational achievement; these correspond to the cohorts with greatest incomes.

3) Little of the increase in net worth was due to inheritances.

4) There were trends toward earlier ownership of housing and multiple ownership of automobile.

Lassiter, Roy L. "The Association of Income and Education for Males by Region, Race and Age." The Southern Economic Journal 32 (1965): 15-22.

(VI,IX)

A study of the effect of education on earnings for different races and in different regions. A low but positive relationship was found for all groups. Southern whites were found to receive higher rates of return to investment in education than others, and more of the variation in income was "explained" by education for this group than for others. The lower rates of return found for nonwhites may explain their lower educational attainment.

Laughton, Katherine B.; Buck, Carol W.; and Hobbs, G.E. "Socio-economic Status and Illness." Milbank Memorial Fund Quarterly 36 (1958): 46-57.

(XI)

A report of a re-examination of the relationship between social class and illness as observed in previous morbidity studies. Data were drawn from medical records of 105 urban families enrolled in a comprehensive care program in Essex County, Ontario. Morbidity was studied in three socio-economic groups distinguished by the median rental of the Census tracts in which they resided; it should be noted that socio-economic comparisons relate to a population which excludes the bottom of the economic scale. Participants were observed for two years.

The findings demonstrate (1) insignificant differences among the three groups in total illness or in psychiatric or psychosomatic illness; (2) notable differences in accidents, which were least common in the middle group and most common in the lowest group; (3) an increase in chronic illness with decreasing status, though not statistically significant; and (4) a significant gradient for total illness among children under two years old.

Laurence, P.S. "Chronic Illness and Socio-Economic Status." In Patients, Physicians, and Illness, edited by E. Gartly Jaco. New York: Free Press, 1958.

(XI)

Presents conclusions of a 1943 restudy of Sydenstricker's 1921-1924 illness survey in Hagerstown, Maryland. The report correlates data on chronic disease in individuals and families with socio-economic status at the time of each survey and with the interim gross change in status. In addition to confirming the frequently held assumption that the prevalence of chronic disease increases from the "well-to-do" to the "very poor," analysis reveals that chronic disease significantly affects reduction of status.

Lawrence, Joseph J., and Maxwell, Milton A. "Drinking and Socio-Economic Status." In Society, Culture and Drinking Patterns, edited by David J. Pittman and Charles R. Snyder. New York: John Wiley & Sons, Inc., 1962.

(XI)

A study of drinking attitudes and behavior by socio-economic status, which is scaled according to education, occupation and family income. Four status levels, from highest to lowest, are recognized.

Comparability of the study with the widely-accepted characterization of class styles of drinking by John Dollard is limited. The authors found little variation by class among men in percentages of drinkers and abstainers; however, only 20% of Status IV women drink, whereas approximately 60% or more of women in the other three levels drink. This observation is inconsistent with Dollard's description of unrestrained and considerable drinking by both men and women in the lower classes.

The study also investigated tolerance toward drunkenness in men and women by the respondent's status level, related behaviors such as time and place of drinking, and most-used beverage.

Leacock, Eleanor. "Distortions of Working-Class Reality in American Social Science." Science and Society 31 (Winter 1967): 1-21.

(II,XI)

Current definitions of the "culture of poverty" are seen as distortions of working class characteristics and as following from sociocentric interpretations of a limited range of attitudes and behavior taken out of context. This distorted image amounts to an attack on the working class that undermines an understanding of its political responsibilities and serves as a rationale for the status quo. The failure to follow through the implications of higher hospitalization rates for mental illness among low-income groups is cited as one example of partial analysis that exaggerates the occurrence of pathology among the poor. The main emphasis is on educational differentials for middle class and lower class children. Examples of the way school failures among low-income children are attributed to their cultural backgrounds are given, as well as materials from contemporary literature documenting the alternative hypothesis that children from poor and Negro backgrounds not only receive an inferior schooling in demographic terms, but are also consistently undermined in the classroom. The sociopsychological characterization of a "culture of poverty" contributes to the failure of social scientists to deal seriously with the real problems and potentials of workers in the political life and future of the United States.

(Sociological Abstracts)

Lee, Beatrice S., ed. Rankings of the States. Washington, D.C.: National Education Association, 1973.

(V)

This report consists of tables that rank states according to 129 separate data items that provide information for understanding, explaining, interpreting, and evaluating various aspects of state school systems. Although the latest available figures are used, some are estimates, and others are based on sampling studies. National totals are shown in most tables inclusive of those for Washington, D.C. Items covered in the tables are population; enrollment and attendance; teachers; educational attainment; general financial resources; governmental revenue, expenditures, and debt; school revenue and expenditures; and miscellaneous items.

(Taken from Research in Education Document Resumes)

Leibenstein, Harvey. "Socio-economic Fertility Theories and Their Relevance to Population Policy." International Labour Review 109 (May-June 1974): 443-457.

(IX,XI)

Fertility decline is the result not only of direct economic changes but also of numerous socio-cultural factors that are part of the economic development process. While the influences of family relationships and behavioral norms of society tend to support practices encouraging high birth rates, economic considerations may serve as inhibiting influences. Economic development is accompanied by changes which create gradually rising consumption standards which limit a population's ability to maintain a previous birth rate; most notable of these changes are migration from rural to urban settings and an increase in educational level. Social class mobility is the most significant social consequence of these changes and affects behavior expectations; consumption standards of housing, education, transportation, and entertainment, for example, are directly related to status. Maintaining a certain standard of living competes with resources available for raising children. The assessment of family planning programs and population policy must consider the many complex issues.

Lerner, A.P. "A Note on the Theory of Price Index Numbers." Review of Economic Studies 3(1935/1936): 50-56.

(III)

In 1935, Dr. H. Staehle developed a method of determining limits to price index numbers comparing the different incomes required to yield equal satisfaction in two situations. The situations differed in their price systems and nothing else. In previous index number theory, it had been assumed, in advance, that the two incomes relating to the two situations yielded equal satisfaction. This assumption was essential to the theory, but it rendered superfluous the complicated method of computing limits to the cost of living index, since the index number could be computed directly from the ratio of the money values of the two incomes. Staehle's method of comparing the incomes needed to buy three different bundles of goods in the two situations allowed him to drop this very restrictive assumption.

Using the framework developed by Staehle, Lerner examined how individuals with different incomes reacted differently to price differentials over time and space. Instead of comparing the cost of specific bundles of goods, comparison can be made between "expenditure curves" (how different incomes will be spent at a given price structure). Considering two countries, for any given income in country A, the upper limits of the equivalent income in country B is given by the cost in B of the bundle consumed in A, and the lower limit is the cost in B of a bundle that could be bought in A with the given income. With expenditure curves for two countries, such equivalents can be found for all levels of income.

Leverson, Irving. Poverty and Public Policy. Croton-on-Hudson, New York: Hudson Institute, Inc., 1975.

(II)

Poverty and inequality in the United States are examined in a broad perspective with the purpose of developing a specific set of policy recommendations. The question of how the poverty line might vary over time is explored in some detail. An income elasticity of the poverty line is used to quantify the way in which this line, expressed in constant dollars, responds to changes in median real income. The Social Security Administration poverty levels have an elasticity of zero, for example, since they are only adjusted for price changes and thus show no variation when expressed in constant dollars. A study by Kilpatrick using Gallup polls indicates that public opinion of minimum necessary income implies an elasticity of .6 in these terms. It is found that this figure is consistent with the view that sees the increase in the poverty threshold as a way of distributing the benefits from general sources of growth such as advances in knowledge and economies to scale (as distinct from specific sources such as changes in capital and labor whose benefits accrue to individuals). A study by Denison is cited in which these general sources of growth were estimated to account for 64 percent of the total, a result which is in agreement with the .6 elasticity figure. A projection is made on the basis of the zero elasticity SSA threshold giving the result that the poverty income gap would be effectively zero by 1985 assuming a 3% growth rate; however, with an elasticity of .6, the absolute deficit would be slightly higher in 1985 though it would decline from about 2 percent to one percent of national income. An attempt is made to construct the general form of a poverty measure that would weigh deficits with respect to a given poverty line in order to account for the marginal utility of masses and the unequal contributions of a variety of components of "social well-being."

Levin, Betsy, et al. Public School Finance: Present Disparities and Fiscal Alternatives, Vols. I and II. Washington, D.C.: January 1972.

(V)

This is a study "which confines itself to pointing out problems in current fiscal structure and to developing alternative mechanisms of financing education." Currently, there are wide disparities in school revenue distribution. Cities generally have lower property tax rates for schools than do the suburbs, and rural districts have the lowest property rate in any given state. The authors analyze various methods of federal and state intervention in financing education and conclude that increased state funding reduces disparity in educational financing within the state.

Levine, Robert. "Evaluating the War on Poverty." In On Fighting Poverty: Perspectives From Experience, edited by J. Sundquist. New York: Basic Books, Inc., 1969.

(II)

Review article on the evaluation being done concerning the War on Poverty. Necessary criteria and measurement methods include (1) definition of success and preparation to measure it in terms of dollars and cents; (2) study of individual programs, especially the most recent ones; and (3) preparation of criteria to compare cross-effects of various programs. Poverty is defined in terms of command over economic resources which can be measured in various ways, e.g. poverty line or the income gap. Total numbers of people below the poverty line can be used as indicators of War on Poverty Program success, so long as decreased numbers are taken not as the objective of the anti-poverty program, but as a simple indicator of the more complicated real objectives. To study success of individual programs two sets of criteria must be used. Their proximate effects as well as their anti-poverty effectiveness must be considered. Studied in this case are manpower, individual improvement (e.g. compensatory education), community improvement and income maintenance. Evaluation of relationships among War on Poverty programs can be done at three levels within the four program categories. These include the relationship among programs in four categories, the relationship of categories to one another, and the relationship of major thrusts.

(Partially taken from Poverty and Human Resources Abstracts)

Levinson, Perry. "The Next Generation: A Study of Children in AFDC Families." Welfare in Review 7 (March-April 1969): 1-9.

(IX,XI)

Using data from a series of large scale surveys of a medium sized southern city, Perry compares the behavioral and educational problems of children from similar socio-economic classes whose parents are and are not on public aid. 16,322 high school students were divided by socio-economic class into groups whose parents received aid, had been refused aid, and had never applied for aid (aid is almost always AFDC). The children whose families are on AFDC had significantly more behavioral and educational problems than those whose parents never applied for aid. Those whose parents had applied for aid and had been refused had as many problems as those whose parents had been accepted. The longer a family received public aid, the higher the probability that its children would have problems. Problems included such things as juvenile delinquency, trouble in school, premarital pregnancy, and dropping out of school.

Levitan, Sar A. "The Poor: Dimensions and Programs." In <u>Programs in Aid of the Poor for the 1970's</u>. Baltimore: Johns Hopkins, 1973.

(II)

Discusses income distribution and efforts to measure poverty. Describes Social Security Administration's "stagnant" poverty level which is based on the assumption that three times the estimated cost of a minimum diet equals the total cost-of-living for a low-income family. The author suggests use of a flexible poverty index which adjusts for productivity increases and rising living standards as well as price increases.

Identifies four major groups of poor: the elderly, the working poor, children in poor families. The problems and needs of these different groups vary. Therefore, special purpose anti-poverty programs are required. Levitan identifies four strategies to aid the poor: cash support; direct provision of necessities such as food, clothing, shelter, medical care; preventive and compensatory efforts for children and youth; and attempts to restructure existing institutions to adapt to those institutions.

(Partially taken from <u>Poverty and Human Resources Abstracts</u>)

*Levitan, Sar A., and Taggart, Robert. <u>Employment and Earning Inadequacy: A New Social Indicator</u>. Baltimore, Maryland: Johns Hopkins Press, 1975.

(X)

Cumulative changes in labor market behavior and the economy have created the need for a new employment measure which considers the adequacy of jobs as well as their availability. Toward this end Levitan and Taggart propose an "Employment and Earning Inadequacy Index (EEI)". The measure is derived by using a more refined subemployment count that excludes households with more than adequate income and then divides that figure by the total number of labor force participants and discouraged workers. Through the use of cross-sectional and longitudinal analysis, an attempt is made to determine how the components and the total of the new index vary by race, sex, family status, and area of residence, and how they fluctuate over the business cycle. Technical and conceptual problems include the exclusion of the elderly and college age students, the choice of adequacy standard and time frames chosen. Official publication and tabulation are two essential elements of EEI.

*Levitan, Sar A., and Taggart, Robert. "Employment Earnings Adequacy: A Measure of Worker Welfare." Monthly Labor Review (October 1973): 19-27.

(X)

"This article explores a new procedure which links together the existing measures of labor force activity into a single index of worker welfare. Building on previous subemployment concepts and pulling together a range of separate labor market statistics, it measures the number of persons who experience difficulties in competing for gainful employment paying an adequate wage." The authors list five criteria which they feel a successful welfare indicator should meet and then proceed to demonstrate how their proposed measure satisfies these criteria. "In brief, the new index should be bounded top and bottom by a concept of adequacy, excluding those who are too well-off to be considered in need simply because they experience employment problems, but including those with problems and genuine needs not accounted for by current unemployment and employment statistics." "The Employment and Earnings Inadequacy Index (EEI) is derived by a three-stage process: first, the 'subemployed' are counted using a measure which seeks to overcome some of the shortcomings of previous indexes. Second, all subemployed in households with incomes above the upper bounds defining adequacy are excluded. Third, the remainder is divided by the number of actual and discouraged labor force participants to derive a single index." Applying the proposed index to the data collected in the extended household Current Population Survey yields an EEI index of 11.5 percent compared to a 6.1 percent unemployment rate. The following preliminary conclusions were made:

1) Low earnings are at least as much a problem as unemployment.
2) Many of the unemployed do not have severe needs.
3) The compounding of frequent unemployment and low wages is a significant problem.
4) Persons with inadequate employment and earnings have serious unmet needs.

(Partially taken from article)

Lewis, H.G. "Economics of Time and Labor Supply." American Economic Review 65 (May 1975): 29-36.

(II)

This short review article begins by mentioning the recent wealth of research on the subject of the supply of labor. It then concentrates on the question of the effects of a negative income tax. It summarizes the results of the New Jersey-Pennsylvania Negative Income Tax Experiment and then proceeds to mention some of the problems associated with extrapolating from a small temporary experiment to a nation-wide permanent program. One danger, analyzed in depth, is that a temporary program will result in intertemporal changes in labor supply. People will shift their working hours from the negative tax period to the no-tax period that follows. This effect causes the empirical results of a test program to overstate the work disincentive effects of a permanent program.

Lewis, H. G. "Hours of Work and Hours of Leisure." In Industrial Relations Research Association, Papers and Proceedings of the Ninth Annual Meeting. Cleveland, Ohio: 1956.

(VIII)

The advent of the shorter work week marks both a declining trend in the fraction of workers' lifetimes devoted to labor market activities and an increasing fraction devoted to leisure. "Each worker, facing a given market price of leisure in terms of wage goods (real wage rate per hour) and a given real property income, is viewed as allocating his total income between leisure and wage goods in such a way as to maximize his utility.... The substitution effect of a rise in the real wage rate is a reduced consumption of leisure per head (increased hours of work per head); the income effect of a rise in the real wage rate or in real property income is an increased rate of consumption of leisure per head (reduced supply of hours per head) if leisure is a normal commodity."

Given this outline of the labor-leisure choice function, the author describes the effects of legislation, union activities, income tax, and changes in individual choice patterns of the distribution of leisure between young and old age and between concentrated or distributed leisure consumption, on leisure consumption. Accounting for the ways in which the work week has been shortened, the relative cost and taste factors that underlie the division of workers' leisure over their lifetimes has tended to remain quite stable over time. Unless there is a radical shift in social habits, therefore, it is safe to predict that trends in labor-leisure consumption for the next fifty years will mirror the changes which occurred over the last fifty.

*Lewis, Oscar. "The Culture of Poverty." In On Understanding Poverty, edited by Daniel P. Moynihan. New York: Basic Books, Inc., 1968.

(II,XI)

An anthropological view of poverty as a sub-culture where there is economic deprivation and disorganization, and simultaneously positive rewards necessary for the poor to carry on. In this view, the culture of poverty is an adaptation of and reaction to the position and the social stratification of the poor.

In developing this theory, Lewis discusses the subculture in relation to the larger society, the nature of slum communities, the nature of family, and the attitudes of individuals in poverty. The culture of poverty, while endemic to free-enterprise capitalism, is different from being merely poor.

Lewis, Oscar. Five Families. New York: Basic Books, Inc., 1959.

(II,XI)

Oscar Lewis used a new technique which he calls ethnographic realism to describe and understand the culture of the poor. His study consists of a detailed observation of a typical day in the life of five Mexican families. While never actually defining poverty at the start nor drawing any conclusions about what poverty is from his study, Lewis does compare the five families to reflect national and class cultural values. For the families that are in the "lower class" of Mexican society, the following traits appear to be predominant:

1) marriages tend to be of the common-law type
2) males play a dominant and authoritarian role, although it is a weaker role in lower classes
3) deserted children remain with the mother or her family which contributes to a "matrifocality" in family life
4) the standard of living is very low even in terms of Mexican standards. The diagnostic items Lewis uses to measure standard of living and to determine socioeconomic level are use of tableware for eating, gas stoves, tv sets, and wristwatches.

Lidman, Russell. "Cost and Distributional Implications of a Credit Income Tax Plan." <u>Public Policy</u> 20 (Spring 1972): 311-334.

(II)

A credit income tax plan (CIT), similar in design to the one suggested by Senator McGovern in 1972, is analyzed in terms of costs and benefits. The specific proposal considered here is assumed to replace the current income tax and welfare programs; it awards a $1000 tax-free credit to all persons regardless of age and levies a constant 33.3 percent tax rate. This means that it is possible for a family to have a negative net tax liability in which case the family receives money from the government. Because of the $1000 per person credit, the average net tax always amounts to less than 33.3 percent of taxable income. The 33.3 percent marginal rate avoids possible work disincentives of the high tax rates associated with income maintenance programs. The tax base assumed here is the whole of the adjusted gross income. (There are no deductions on exemptions, though the $1000 credits are not taxable.) At 1972 income levels, this is estimated to give a tax base of $914 billion which is almost double the normal tax base of $478 billion for that year. This expanded base is considered necessary to make the plan workable at the quoted tax rate and credit subsidy; yet it accounts for a major difficulty in implementing the plan, namely, the resistance to cancelling exemptions for such things as social security benefits, home mortgage payments, state land interest,etc. With the expanded tax base, the CIT plan provides a revenue of about $92 billion as compared with the estimated 97.4 billion income tax revenue in 1972. This deficit is somewhat balanced by a 4.5 billion savings by states in welfare payments. The families who benefit are not only those who receive net transfers but also some families above the tax breakeven point who gain through a tax relief effect. It is estimated that about 150 million people would benefit with the $74.3 billion transfer and tax relief cost borne by the remaining 60 million people. One of the problems with the plan as stated is that it exhibits a strong bias in favor of large families; 54 percent of the benefits go to families with five or more members who make up only 39 percent of the population. A possible remedy would be to vary the size of the tax credit according to the age of the individual with children receiving less than adults.

Little, I.M.D. A Critique of Welfare Economics. Oxford: Oxford University Press, 1958.

(III)

Little finds that the concept of consumer's surplus is a valid criterion for evaluating the economic worthiness of large, indivisible projects only under extremely restrictive conditions. Samuelson reached the same conclusion by less convincing means, stressing the alternative method of direct sampling of preferences. Since this is a criterion designed to be applied to particular projects, direct sampling is too costly to be a viable alternative.

Little advocates the use of two indices for making welfare judgments. One for individual welfare, comprising private savings plus private consumption, using a market price index as a deflator, and the other comprising public goods, using an index of costs as a deflator.

*Liu, Ben-Chieh. "Differentiated Net Migration Rates and the Quality of Life." Midwest Research Institute.

(VI,XI)

"The objective of this paper is to explore the relationships between the variations in net migration rates among states and the levels of quality of life measures in those states." A production model of the quality of life is constructed using the following nine component indicators: individual status, individual equality, living conditions, economic status, technological development, agricultural production, health and welfare provisions, educational development, and state and local government. "A linear additive model with more than 100 variables was utilized to construct the indexes for the component indicators." Empirical results indicated that net migration rates between 1960 and 1970 responded positively to the quality of life index. "Statistically significant coefficients were obtained for all migrants and nonwhite migrants. For every 1.0 percent improvement in the qualify of life, the net migration rate of all races would be 24.1% higher; for nonwhites, 17.5% higher."

*Liu, Ben-Chieh. "Quality of Life: Concept, Measure and Results." American Journal of Economics and Sociology 34 (1975): 1-15.

(XI)

Article describes indicators which adequately reflect the overall "health" of the nation or its Qualify of Life (QOL). The QOL is assessed by nine indicators: individual status, individual equality, living conditions, agriculture, technology, economic status, education, health and welfare, and state and local governments. These indicators were compiled from more than 100 variables for 50 states. Each state is given a QOL index and ranked. QOL is not necessarily a function of income and wealth for many states. Liu suggests that the QOL in the states, rather than variations in income and unemployment, were the decisive factors in differential migration rates.

Liviatan, Nissan, and Patinkin, Don. "On the Economic Theory of Price Indexes." Economic Development and Cultural Change (1961): 502-536.

(III)

A discussion of the theory of "true" price and quantity indexes and their use in determining cost of living allowances. Laspeyre's indexes are found to provide a valid limit for cost-of-living allowances, but according to the article, Paasche's index does not, as is commonly believed, provide a lower limit for such allowances. The authors conclude with a discussion of cost-of-living allowances dropping the assumption of fixed incomes. If incomes change as well as prices, cost-of-living allowances cannot be meaningfully defined.

Long, L.H. "Poverty Status and Receipt of Welfare Among Migrants and Non-Migrants in Large Cities." American Sociological Review 39 (1974): 46-56.

(VI)

This article discusses the widely held belief that southern blacks are attracted to northern cities by higher welfare payments. According to this reasoning, high welfare costs and other urban problems actually have rural origins. Long reviews the existing literature on the subject and presents some new findings developed from data in the 1970 Census concerning the migration, receipt of public assistance and poverty status of black and white families in New York, Philadelphia, Chicago, Detroit, Los Angeles, and Washington, D.C. He concludes that "the evidence from recent empirical research indicates that black migrants to the North become more economically successful and are less likely to engage in criminal behavior than blacks born in the North. The present study has added to this body of findings by showing that in the six cities with largest black populations, black migrants were less likely to be below the poverty level or on welfare than blacks native to their city of residence in 1970." Several explanations are offered for these findings that so clearly contradict the common attitudes about the motivation of black migrants.

Long, Larry H, and Hansen, Kristin. "Trends in Return Migration to the South." Demography (forthcoming November, 1975).

(VI)

The rate of return migration to the South rose by nearly 19 percent between the late 1950's and the late 1960's and was an important factor in changing the South's overall migration pattern. But an increase in the rate of return migration was somewhat less important in changing Southern migration than (1) decline in the rate of outmigration of native Southerners and (2) increase in the rate of which non-Southern-born persons move to the South. The probability of former migrants returning to the South was over four times greater for whites than for blacks in the 1955-60 period and 3¼ times greater in the 1965-70 period. Since 1970 the rate of return migration has apparently continued to rise at a faster rate for blacks, but the black rate of return migration is still below the white rate.

(Taken from the article.)

Lourie, Norman V. "Poverty." In Social Work and Social Problems, edited by Nathan E. Cohen. New York: National Association of Social Workers, 1964.

(II,XI)

A comprehensive discussion of poverty and its relation to society and social work. Poverty is defined by the author as "long-term inaccessibility to material resources that are adequate to provide a minimum standard of living consistent with the productive capacity and social requirements of the community." The incidence of poverty, its causes and consequences, and its etiological characteristics are considered.

Scrutiny of the conflicts and inconsistencies embodied in society's value system reveal that certain value orientations work toward alleviating poverty, while others do not. Prevailing attitudes toward achievement and success, activity and work, and group or individual superiority, for instance, are among those values which might serve to perpetuate poverty. The author criticizes the modern structure and practices of some social welfare agencies, which emphasize exclusion and restrictiveness in providing aid to only those "deserving poor," an historically prominent attitude. More acceptable to social workers and more appropriate for guiding policy are those more humanitarian values, such as the right of self-determination and preservation of integrity and self-respect.

Lourie delineates other obstacles interfering with attainment of social work's primary goal--the eradication of poverty--in comparing current practices and "the ideal," and cites priorities for the profession in moving closer to that goal.

*Lowry, Ira S. Migration and Metropolitan Growth: Two Analytical Models. Los Angeles: University of California, 1966.

(VI)

Two models for measurement of migration for metropolitan areas in the United States are presented; the first deals with specific directional flows of migrants and illuminates the behavioral factors involved, and the second is a potential forecasting model for measurement of population change in particular metropolitan areas due to migration. The data used are cross-sectional from 1950-1960 and from large metropolitan areas. The principal methods of analysis are multiple linear correlation and regression. Evidence presented suggests that the total volume of out-migration from a given place depends on the size and structural properties of the resident population rather than on the absolute or relative level of economic opportunity in this place. Prosperous as well as depressed areas have substantial annual out-migration, and migrant flows are heavily weighted with young adults and young children. Migrants tend to migrate to nearby destinations with attractive labor markets. The net effect of migration is to increase the prosperity of prosperous areas and to decrease the economic prospects of less prosperous areas. The latter type of area tends to become concentrated with older, less mobile, and unproductive individuals. Over time, net migration is directly related to the growth of unemployment and inversely related to the natural increase of the labor-force.

Luft, Harold. Poverty and Health: An Empirical Investigation of the Economic Interactions. Thesis presented to the Department of Economics, Harvard University, 1973.

(XI)

Studies effects of poor health on income, and effects of income on poor health. The effects of poor health on income account for a substantial portion of poverty in the U.S.; at least 30% of the disabled who are poor, are poor because of their health, possibly due to loss of wealth resulting from medical bills and loss of income-generating capacity. Days of work lost result in loss of income, and individuals who are frequently sick often end up with low-paying jobs in the long run. In a five-way cross-tabulation of age, race, sex, education and income, the probability of disability is negatively related to income. The income effect may be attributed to occupational differences related to income levels. The lines of causation from poverty to poor health may be traced as (1) difference in education, (2) unavailability of medical treatment, (3) low nutritional levels, and (4) crowded, less sanitary housing.

Lumer, Hyman. Poverty: Its Roots and Its Future. New York: International Publishers, 1965.

(II)

Lumer attributes poverty in the United States to the workings of monopoly capitalism and sees a remedy in socialism.

In the course of discussing the extent of U.S. poverty, he adopts the CEA definition ($3,000 a year for families, $1,000 for individuals) and mentions a higher standard of $4,000 for families and $2,000 for individuals used in Leon Keyserling's Poverty & Deprivation in the U.S. (1962).

Lydall, Harold. The Structure of Earnings. Oxford: Clarendon Press, 1968.

(II)

The first systematic, rigorous observations of the size distribution of income were made by Vilfredo Pareto in the 19th century. Pareto's measurements were only on upper income people; on the basis of this data, he concluded that the distribution of income was a rectangular hyperbola with an asymptote at the subsistence level of income (now called the Pareto distribution). Later measurements revealed that this distribution applied only to the upper tail of the population--the top 20%, and that the full distribution was more or less log-normal. Two types of theories have been used to account for the log-normality of the distribution: the stochastic process theory, and the ability theory. Under certain assumptions, a Markhov process (assumes current income is related to past income with a random error term) yields a log-normal distribution. A log-normal distribution would also result if ability were normally distributed, income depended on ability, and labor markets were segmented.

Lydall, Harold, and Lansing, John B. "A Comparison of Personal Income and Wealth in the United States and Great Britain." American Economic Review 49 (No. 1, March 1959): 43-67.

(II)

The development of similar comprehensive surveys of consumers in the U.S. and Great Britain permits a comparison of both the income and wealth distribution of the two countries. A comparison by decile of total income shows that the United States and Great Britain have similar income distributions except for the lowest income groups. The United States has a much greater percentage of very poor families.

The data for the two countries can be divided into similar categories by assuming that one pound is equivalent to nine dollars. (This reflects the differences in national wealth in 1954, the year the surveys were taken.) The lowest income division is much larger in the United States, primarily because many more farmers and unskilled laborers fall into this category.

The distribution of wealth in the two countries is very different. The United States has a much broader and more equal distribution of wealth than does Great Britain. This is primarily due to the much larger amount of home and car ownership in the United States, especially among farmers, and skilled and unskilled laborers. A much higher percentage of American wealth is held in the form of real assets and these are distributed much more equally than they are in Great Britain. Liquid Assets are distributed similarly in the two countries.

Mabry, Bevars D. "An Analysis of Work and Other Constraints on the Choice of Activities." Western Economic Journal 8 (September 1970): 213-225.

(VIII)

An extension of the usual analysis of the work-leisure choice which considers the constraints placed on any activity by income, time, and energy. The consideration of stamina (human energy) as a constraint is the major innovation in this analysis. When this constraint is binding, increases in time or money will have no impact on the amount of work that can be done. This situation is characteristic of a peasant society, and implies that labor saving goods or better nutrition will be more effective in increasing productivity than money grants. Mabry also uses this theory to analyze primary and secondary employment, industrial relations, and the economic habits of the affluent.

Mabry, Bevars D. "Income-Leisure Analysis and the Salaried Professional." Industrial Relations 8 (February 1969): 162-173.

(VIII)

The normal income-leisure analysis of microeconomics cannot handle the case of professionals who earn a fixed yearly salary regardless of their hours of work. It cannot explain why these individuals tend to work longer hours than is average. Three explanations within the income-leisure framework are proposed. The first postulates that income and leisure are perfect substitutes over a broad range of hours: professionals enjoy their work and work long hours because they do not value leisure higher than work. The second postulates that the utility of leisure becomes negative when it exceeds some small amount: the professional feels guilty or incomplete when not working. The third postulates that though increased work will not raise the professional's current salary--it will increase his future salary. A long-run, sloping, budget curve can then be drawn (with more long-run income for more work) and the analysis successfully completed. A limited sampling of college faculty showed this third hypothesis to be plausible.

Macarov, David. "Drawing the Poverty Line." In Incentives to Work. San Francisco: Jossey-Bass, Inc., 1970.

(II)

This chapter (from a book concerned with public policy regarding the poor) reviews poverty definitions which have been proposed in the past. The typology includes three approaches to defining poverty--relative, normative, and absolute. A relative definition compares two or more situations. It may statistically compare one fraction of the income distribution among the population with another, or it may compare lifestyles, using consumption patterns as criteria. The problem with the lifestyle comparison is that it allows a person with sufficient income who spends it on items not contributing to improved lifestyle to be defined as poor, while a person with insufficient income who somehow maintains appearances may be defined as non-poor. Another type of relative definition may be determined by the reference group used as comparison. Both absolute costs and expectations affect this definition; thus, in an economy which is raising the standard of living of the population as a whole, but which is raising that of the poor at a lesser rate, relative poverty will actually have increased. A similar definition of poverty is that based on self-image. The normative approach to poverty defines it as a necessary, existing condition, or, paradoxically, as a condition which does not exist at all. This definition denies a poverty situation the status of a problem, by positing it as expected, e.g., as inevitable, as a social "boundary-maintaining" mechanism, as social deviance (purposeful, reprehensible behavior), or as pathology. The "incentive mystique"--the idea that poverty is necessary to insure that work gets done--is based on the normative approach. Absolute definitions of poverty (usually used for policy determination) are based upon a necessary or desirable standard, but the methods of arriving at the standard are subjective. Orshansky's standards for the Social Security Administration (SSA) are the best available, but they do not account for all the possible variables (regional differences, higher prices paid by the poor, etc.). Nor are absolute definitions capable of expressing differences within categories, e.g., between a family earning $2,950--just under the SSA poverty line--and a family with no income.

MacDonald, Dwight. "Our Invisible Poor." The New Yorker, 19 January 1963.

(II,IX)

A discussion of poverty that reviews effort to gauge the true extent of this problem in the United States and examines some of the possible responses of government. As in Harrington's Other America, poverty standards are defined to be those "minimum levels of health, housing, food and education that our present stage of scientific knowledge specifies as necessary for life as it is now lived in the U.S." Though relative criteria are implicit here, insofar as the norms of life in the United States are used in establishing these minimum levels, this relative dimension of poverty is not seen to demand a massive redistribution of income. "Inequality of wealth is not necessarily a major social problem per se...Envy and emulation are the motives--and not very good ones--for the equalization of wealth." It is acknowledged that, in the past, economic growth has been the most effective measure in dealing with poverty; and, even today, the majority of the poor would certainly benefit from reduced unemployment. Nevertheless, a substantial segment of the poor (those not in the labor force, for example, the aged, disabled, and some women who head families) would not benefit from this growth and would still require direct government aid. It is hoped that this aid could assume the character of an obligation of government "to be taken as much for granted as free public schools have always been in our history."

MacDonald, John S., and MacDonald, L.D. "Chain Migration, Ethnic Neighborhood Formation, and Social Networks." Milbank Memorial Fund Quarterly 52 (1964): 82-97.

(VI)

"Push-pull" models of migratory activity are economically crude and are not useful by themselves in explaining migration. Migration is differentiated into "chain-migration" (friends-relatives as sources of information and aid to potential migrants) and "impersonally organized migration" (wage increase, employment, etc., as impetus for migration). The question of why people of similar cultural backgrounds tend to form ethnic neighborhoods in urban areas is addressed by looking at migratory patterns of Southern Italians into northern American urban areas. Three factors are isolated and discussed: assistance from earlier migrants who have settled, serial migration of breadwinners, and delayed family migration.

Maclachlan, Gretchen. The Other Twenty Percent: A Statistical Analysis of Poverty in the South. Atlanta: Southern Regional Council, Inc., 1974.

(IV, V, VI)

This report presents a statistical analysis of southern poverty derived mainly from the 1970 census. Its major findings are: (1) poverty among Southern Blacks remains more intense than among whites; (2) rural poverty rates are uniformly higher than urban rates; (3) the percentage of poor families headed by females is higher than the percentage headed by males--particularly among poor Black families; (4) the South's poverty bears heavily on children; (5) most southern poor work but earn too little to raise themselves above poverty levels; (6) the industrial structure of the South is more concentrated in low-wage industry than the rest of the country; (7) only a small percentage of southern poor receive public assistance, and those who do, receive assistance far below the federally-established poverty line; (8) Social Security participation among the South's elderly Blacks is well below national averages; and (9) Southerners have received less formal education than the nation's population as a whole. It is emphasized that the current inflation is likely to exacerbate these problems. Inflation in the South has been growing at a higher rate than elsewhere. Furthermore, items that have had the most rapid price increases such as food, housing, and transportation make up a relatively larger share of poor people's budgets. Although detailed policy recommendations are beyond the scope of this report, the author presents some broad guidelines.

McCall, John J. "An Analysis of Poverty: A Suggested Methodology." The Journal of Business 43 (1970): 31-43.

(II,IX)

"This paper presents two elementary models of the incidence, persistence and control of poverty. The first model is basically probabilistic and relies greatly on the theory of Markov processes to describe movements into and out of poverty. The second model is normative and evaluates alternative policies for alleviating poverty." Using two longitudinal data sources, the probabilistic model estimates the numbers of those who stay in or move out of poverty. The models "can be used to solve semi-Markov decision problems when the decision maker maximizes discounted net benefits over an infinite horizon and has a fixed amount to spend per period... (I)f the war on poverty is limited to a finite period, and *k* dollars can be spent over this time, then these funds can be allocated to maximize the present value of discounted net gains."

(Annotation taken partially from article)

McCall, John J. Income Mobility, Racial Discrimination, and Economic Growth. Lexington, Massachusetts: Lexington Books, 1973.

(II)

The objective of this book is to develop a methodology which will increase the understanding of poverty and racial discrimination and lead to the design of practical policies for the alleviation and control of these problems. Poverty is defined in economic terms and economic growth is cast as the most prominent control variable in the development of a theory of income mobility for low-income individuals. This theory is tested using a Markovian analysis of Social Security data, and an extensive empirical analysis of the relationship between economic growth and poverty dynamics is conducted.

Economic growth is found to have a powerful influence on individuals who tend to move across income boundaries, and this more for non-whites than for whites especially at the lower end of the income distribution. Non-whites are benefitted by a buoyant economy, though if the pattern is symmetrical they will be equally harmed by a depressed economy. However, sustained economic growth is not sufficient for the elimination of low earnings for a significant proportion of the poor who do not move across income boundaries. For these people, alternative programs are needed, either in the form of income maintenance or programs which invest human capital through health or occupational training.

*McCall, John J. "A Markovian Model of Income Dynamics." Journal of the American Statistical Association 66 (September 1971): 439-447.

(IX)

Using the Social Security Administration's Continuous Work History Sample of covered employees for the 10 years between 1957-1966, McCall estimates a Markov model of income dynamics. Separate matrices were developed for race, sex and age. The principal questions were: (1) is transition from low to non-low income related to race, sex, age and growth to GNP; and (2) is the relationship between transition and GNP affected by race, sex, or age?

He found:

1) The probability of remaining in either the low or non-low income group was greater than zero.

2) Whites are more likely to remain in the non-low income group than non-whites.

3) Non-whites are more likely than whites to remain in the low income group.

4) Both men and women, whites and non-whites benefit from growth in GNP; but men benefit more than women, and non-white men more than white men.

5) Of those whose income status changed, labor force participation rates are related to growth more strongly for women than for men.

Although the poverty measure is crude (income level) and the data has liabilities which are particularly severe for the low income population, this is a comprehensive analysis of turnover.

*McKenzie, J.C. "Poverty: Food and Nutrition Indices." In The Concept of Poverty, edited by Peter Townsend. New York: American Elsevier Publishing Co., 1970.

(XI)

A summary of food and nutrition indices of poverty currently used in Great Britain. Evidence on nutritional status of individuals in Britain comes mainly from the National Food Survey. Information on the actual consumption of families (by food type) is coded by the energy and nutrient value of foods consumed; this data is then compared with the British Medical Association's assessment of minimum necessary requirements to provide an estimate of malnutrition in Britain by family type and social class. Problems with this nutrition index include: difficulties in obtaining reliable estimate of individual needs, and roughness of estimates of the energy and nutrient content of particular foods. McKenzie suggests that both nutritional indices and indices of clinical malnutrition be used as social indicator measures of poverty.

McKinley, Donald. Social Class and Family Life. New York: Free Press of Glencoe, 1974.

(XI)

Presents an analytic review of the literature concerning the associations between class status and family life, as well as McKinley's contributions through his own research.

Some of the author's thoughts and major areas of concern and interpretation as excerpted and/or paraphrased from his book, follow:

(1) Status is defined as the position one occupies in the reward system of a society of system of behavior. As members of a stratum...interact frequently, they begin to develop adjustive norms and feelings of commitment to these norms.

(2) The importance of achievement and mastery over the environment makes the occupation central in determining one's position in the social world.

(3) This central significance of the work role in determining one's contribution to and status in society leads to a focus on the father role. His role, through his occupation, is the most direct link between a rewarding or depriving society and the emotional organization within the family.

(4) Variation in class or status leads to variation in satisfaction. The variation in gratifications felt and frustrations experienced leads to two primary responses--aggression and compensating "achievement" ...and to several secondary responses--regression, anxiety, and submission. These emotional or behavioral responses affect the way a worker plays his familial roles.

MacNamee, Holly. "Adding Up the Problems of the Poor." Conference Board Record 6 (No. 5, 1969).

(II)

Today it is food, not goods and services, which denotes the status of the poor. Although it is generally agreed that the means of dealing with poverty must be varied, so far the government definition takes into account only one measurement, derived from a study made in 1955 by the Department of Agriculture to determine what goes into the food baskets of poor families and what percentage of their total income is spent for food. First, the cost of a bare minimum of nutritional necessities was figured. Then, assuming that one should not have to spend more than one-third of total income for food, the cost of that economy food plan was used to compute minimum income requirements. A household was classed as poor if its income was less than three times the cost of the minimum basic diet for its members. The average bill for such a basic diet is about $1,000 for a poor non-farm family of four. The drawback is that the survey was made 14 years ago, and we have been measuring poverty by that absolute standard ever since, rather than adjust our measurement to changing conditions. Poor families no longer spend one-third of their income for food. The figure is now closer to one-fourth. Another problem is that our poverty line is based entirely on food, and food expenditures do not always accurately reflect the cost of living. Last year, for example, all prices, except food prices, went up 3 percent. The poverty index did not change, therefore, though nearly everything was more expensive, and the one million people who fell below the line as a result are unrecorded. Thus, the statistical decrease in poverty does not reflect actual poverty. A revision of the definition and a cash transfer program of some sort are required for the needy.

(Partially taken from Poverty and Human Resources Abstracts)

Madden, J. Patrick; Pennock, Jean; and Jayer, Carol. "Equivalent Levels of Living: A New Approach to Scaling the Poverty Line to Different Family Characteristics and Place of Residence." In Rural Poverty in the United States, President's National Advisory Commission on Rural Poverty. Washington, D.C.: 1968.

(IV, V, VI)

A critical evaluation of the official poverty scale (the Social Security line), and a proposal for an alternative approach. In the proposed approach, equivalent living standards are equated with ability to afford equal levels of food expenditures (adjusted for costs of home-served food). Food expenditures were regressed on a set of locational, social, and economic variables, including family size and type. Required income was calculated on the basis of coefficients derived. Among the major findings were that the ratio of food expenditures to income varied by family size and type. Thus, the constant ratio used by the Social Security Administration to transform food needs to poverty budgets is not appropriate.

*Madison, Bernice. "Canadian Family Allowances and Their Major Social Implications." Journal of Marriage and the Family 26 (May 1964): 134-141.

(IV)

A description of the Canadian family allowances program. Its evolution since its inception in 1944 is presented, followed by a discussion of the impact of the program on Canadian children. Analysis of the program's major social implications probes uses of the allowance by parents and by child-placing agencies; the effect on school attendance and child labor; influence on birth rate, infant mortality rate, and size of families; and the impact on home conditions. Suggestions for further research are put forth.

Mahoney, Bette S., and Mahoney, W. Michael. "Policy Implications: A Skeptical View." In Work Incentives and Income Guarantees, edited by Joseph A. Pechman and P. Michael Timpane. Washington, D.C.: The Brookings Institution, 1975.

(II)

The appropriate marginal tax rate has always been considered a critical feature of a negative income tax program. Lower rates mean a greater number of people will be eligible and hence imply greater costs; yet lower rates are assumed to minimize disincentives for work. If the objective of the program is simply to raise the incomes of the poor, however, then this might not imply lower rates. "Lowering marginal tax rates might not produce sufficiently greater work effort to make transfer costs go down." Furthermore, the distinction is made between outright entry and withdrawal from the labor force and mere additions or reductions in effort. "It seems unlikely that many persons would wish to commit funds for the sole purpose of inducing more work effort from secondary workers." Equity considerations too might dictate higher tax rates. High tax rates concentrate expenditures on the very poor whereas low rates direct funds to the less poor and to many who are not poor and so may be viewed as an attempt to alter the shape of the income distribution beyond the poverty level. The New Jersey Experiment provided little information about high tax rates; this was due, in part, to the introduction of a background welfare program during the course of the study. However, it is suggested that investigations of AFDC and some state run working poor programs, some of which have 100 percent marginal tax rates, would produce relevant information if the resources expended were at all comparable to investment made in the negative income tax experiment.

Malthus, Thomas R. An Essay on the Principle of Population. London: Reeves and Turner, 1848.

(II)

While population is to an extent directly related to the increase of human wealth, it becomes, after a certain point, also directly related to an increase in human poverty. "It may be safely pronounced... that population, when unchecked, goes on doubling itself every twenty-five years, or increases in a geometrical ratio.... (However), it may be fairly pronounced... that, considering the average present state of the earth, the means of subsistence, under conditions the most favorable to human industry, could not possibly be made to increase faster than in an arithmetical ratio." Therefore, over time, if the increase of population is not checked by some means then it will most certainly overrun the ability of the earth to produce means of subsistence for it, and increasingly larger proportions of human society will find themselves unprovided for. It is necessary to maintain a balance in the level of population which is sufficiently high to produce the means of subsistence to insure its well-being, but not so high as to overrun the power of agricultural production to support it.

Mangalam, Joseph J. Human Migration: A Guide to Migration Literature in English, 1955-1962. Lexington: University of Kentucky Press, 1968.

(VI)

A very complete annotated listing of the major studies of migration published between 1955 and 1962, and an unannotated listing of lesser studies for the same period. The introduction reviews the strengths and weaknesses of the research up to 1962 and outlines new directions for study. A methodology is offered for the study of social phenomena such as migration. From this methodology, a definition of migration is generated, which includes both the interactional dimension and the decision-making process which are involved in migration. A general theoretical orientation is presented, which includes the social structure left, the social structure entered and the characteristics of the migrating population itself, and the effects of the interaction of these three over time. Further directions for study are suggested.

Marmor, Theodore. "Poverty and Welfare Policy: Some Preliminary Observations." Policy Studies Journal 1 (1972).

(II,IV)

This article distinguishes between "narrow" and "broad" views of poverty and the governmental policies to ameliorate it. According to the "narrow" view, the measure defining poverty is some level of income, adjusted by family size, below which subsistence is a serious problem. The author notes that, to date, programs for the poor have reached a minority of the poor, the result of categorical problems which make the reason for one's poverty--age, disability or loss of a breadwinner--a condition for receipt of public assistance. The author cites some of the relevant literature: (1) scholarly studies by Morris and Rein, J. Kershaw, G. Steiner, and R. Levine; (2) the President's Commission on Income Maintenance Programs initiated in 1968; (3) the "determinants" body of literature, which measures welfare policy by expenditures for public assistance policies and seeks to explain the variations in those "policies" by a variety of economic or political factors. According to the broader view of poverty and welfare policy, relative poverty occurs when income is very unequally distributed, and leads to an interest in income redistribution, more equitable taxes, and a means of reducing inequality which does not selectively mark out the poor as the recipients of government subsidy.

Marshall, Alfred. Principles of Economics. New York: The MacMillan Co., 1961.

(II)

The author, writing in 1890, deals with poverty in terms of its cyclical nature; as it causes suffering, it tends to deaden the abilities of the poor to overcome it. "Overworked and undertaught, weary and careworn, without quiet and without leisure, (the poor) have no chance of making the best of their mental facilities. Although...some of the evils which commonly go with poverty are not its necessary consequences; yet, broadly speaking, the 'destruction of the poor is their poverty.'"

Marshall, Ray. Labor in the South. Cambridge, Massachusetts: Harvard University Press, 1967.

(X)

This book presents an analysis of the growth of organized labor in the South. Many factors created unfavorable conditions for the growth of unions in the region. These included the ethnic homogeneity of white managers and workers, racism, the surplus labor in a low-income agricultural economy, the nature and composition of southern industry, the undemocratic political tradition and the idea that industrialists were benefactors (because rapid industrialization was seen as the surest cure for the region's economic problems). Nevertheless, union growth was spurred by other factors. The exceptionally low wages and bad working conditions caused workers to turn to unions, and many national unions tried to organize in the South in order to protect union conditions elsewhere. In spite of the hostile environment, some unions became relatively strong. In general, the long term fortunes of organized labor in the region have been influenced by the development of industry and its diversification, the relative decline of agriculture, the break up of company towns, the presence of branch plants under national personnel and collective bargaining policies, the growing national homogenization of the country through transport and communications, and the presence of the federal government in development projects and social legislation.

(Partially taken from the book)

Masters, Stanley. "Are Black Migrants From the South Worse Off than Blacks Already There?" Journal of Human Resources 7 (1972): 411-423.

(VI)

Among Blacks living in SMSA's (Standard Metropolitan Statistical Area) outside the South in 1960, those born in the South had higher incomes and less unemployment than those born in the North--with or without standardizing for differences in age, years of school and a number of other variables. Recent migrants, defined as those living in an SMSA in 1960 but not in 1955, did have lower incomes than those who were in SMSA's in both years, although the differential is larger for whites than for Blacks. The following explanations for these results are examined: 1) migrants may choose to move to the more prosperous SMSA's; 2) there may be differences in the relationship between schooling and natural ability for those born in different regions; 3) there may be differences in work effort and in 4) intelligence between migrants and succeeding generations. The first hypothesis is not substantiated; the second and third seem to have validity; and there is some support for the fourth, although the results are ambiguous.

(Taken partially from the article)

Marx, Karl, and Engels, Frederick. The German Ideology, edited by R. Pascal. New York: International Publishers, 1947.
Marx, Karl. The Grundrisse, edited and translated by David McLellan. New York: Harper and Row, 1971.

(II)

"The social structure and the State are continually evolving out of the life process of definite individuals, but of individuals, not as they may appear in their own or other people's imagination, but as they really are; i.e., as they are effective, produce materially, and are active under definite material limits, presuppositions and conditions independent of their will." For example, the division of labor is a basic ordering of productive forces that is seen as a manifestation of the forms of private property. "The various stages in the development in the division of labor are just so many different forms of ownership, i.e., the existing stages in the division of labor determine also the relations of individuals to one another, with reference to the material, instrument and product of labor." The division of labor embodies a contradiction between the interests of the individual and the community. This forms a prototype for the situation in which the activity of the individual is externally imposed, is not his own. In the past, this external imposition could have the character of a personal relationship (as vassal to lord) and it is only in modern times that the material forces of production are found to achieve an independent existence completely external to the individual and in opposition to him. This occurs as division of labor becomes more and more comprehensive and the total interdependence resulting gives products a pure exchange value which is given material form as money. Labor too undergoes a process of generalization and in the extensive fragmentation of the worker's activity becomes abstracted from particular tasks. The activity of individuals is no longer validated in the context of a relation to another person or even to the community but rather to the abstract, independent form of the factors of production. "The social relations of individuals have become transformed into the social connection of material things." "The individuals are subordinated to social production which exists externally to them as a kind of fate." Furthermore, the process of division of labor entails the "division of the conditions of labor, of tools and materials, and thus the splitting up of accumulated capital among different owners and thus also the division between capital and labor. Thus we have a totality of productive forces which have as it were taken on a material form, and are for the individuals no longer the forces of the individual, but of private property themselves." The worker sells his labor for its exchange value, a price determined for an abstract amount of "work" and not for its use value for the capitalist who buys it. "Thus it is clear that the worker cannot enrich himself as a result of this exchange, since (like Esau, who exchanged his birthright for a mess of pottage) he gives up his creative power for the ability to work, as an already existing quantity. Rather he is forced to become impoverished." Those who justify the arrangement of wages and profit do so on the basis that the worker has no claim to enjoy the benefits of profit. "They point out that, contrary to the capitalist, the worker benefits from a certain stability of income, which is more or less independent of the great adventures of capital. In just the same way Don Quixote consoled Sancho Panza: certainly he had to take all the blow, but he had no need to be courageous." The poverty of labor is then distinguished from mere want; it consists in being deprived of a share in the productive forces, deprived even in the activity of labor, from its true product. "With the division of labor in which all these contradictions are implicit...is given simultaneously the distribution, and indeed the unequal distribution, (both quantitative and qualitative), of labor and its products, hence property."

The resolution indicated here is that the community destroy the private property basis and subjugate the production apparatus, make it subservient to individuals. The very evolution of the factors of production to this present independent status is thought to make this a real possibility since only in this form can they be utilized by the community as a whole. Earlier less developed states of production had implicit in their structure a pre-eminence of one group over another. Thus earlier revolutions only resulted in some new faction gaining power at the expense of other groups. The belief expressed is that the detached, highly developed form of modern production would make possible regulation by the community as a whole. "In the real community, the individuals obtain their freedom in and through their association."

Mayer, Thomas. "The Propensity to Consume Permanent Income." American Economic Review 56 (December 1966): 1158-77.

(IV, VII)

A comparison of the average propensity to consume at different "permanent income" levels. The initial hypothesis, that the average propensity to consume is independent of the level of permanent income, is tested by simply comparing average propensities to consume of different occupations. Mean income of the occupational groups is used as the proxy measure for permanent income. Mayer explains that occupational mobility and occupation mean income fluctuation could cause this proxy measure to be inaccurate. The inclusion of broadly defined occupation classes (e.g., manual workers versus white collar workers) and the use of 34 budget studies spread over 50 years safeguards against this possibility. Using a regression model in some cases and a strict mathematical formula in others, Mayer finds that in only 2 out of 31 cases does the higher-paid occupation consume a larger percentage of its income than lower-paid occupations. He also proves that the marginal propensity to consume for permanent income is greater than for measured income.

Mazek, Warren F. "Unemployment and the Efficacy of Migration: The Case for Laborers." Journal of Regional Science 9 (1969): 101-107.

(VI, X)

Different levels of unemployment are often said to help explain migration, but little is known about the efficacy of migration in the short run in reducing 1) interregional differentials in unemployment, 2) aggregate unemployment, and 3) unemployment for subgroups of the labor force--occupation, race, etc. This lack of knowledge is due to the scarcity of data suitable for empirical testing and the problem of correctly specifying the statistical model. The typical approach has been to use a single equation least squares model in which migration is regressed upon some measure of employment opportunity. This approach neglects two types of reverse feedback of migration upon unemployment: 1) high unemployment causes people to migrate, but a net out-migration will reduce that unemployment; and 2) net out-migration will reduce consumer demand thus reducing the demand for labor in the area.

Mazek attempts to overcome the feedback problem by looking at migration for two subgroups of the labor force--white and non-white laborers--between 1955 and 1960. The size of these groups relative to the population as a whole is not large enough to significantly affect the demand for labor or the statistical level of unemployment. He finds that "migration appears to have been unemployment--equilibrating and seems to have reduced unemployment as much as possible. This conclusion implies that there was structural unemployment in that period for laborers, that structure was not geographical." But he emphasizes that his conclusions are only tentative since they are based on questionable data.

Meade, James, and Hitch, Charles. "How Should Income Be Distributed?" In Inequality and Poverty, edited by Edward C. Budd. New York: W.W. Norton and Company, Inc., 1967.

(II,IV)

The principle that, for a given individual, marginal utility decreases with increasing income is used here to differentiate three bases for income distribution: equal opportunity for satisfaction, equal satisfaction, and greatest total satisfaction. The authors dissociate themselves from any ethical judgment of desirability and are only concerned to demonstrate that, by assuming different tastes in a group of individuals, the three goals above each yield a different prescription for income distribution. Acknowledging the difficulty of measuring the relative degree of satisfaction individuals derive from a specific income because of dissimilar tastes, the authors point out that nevertheless, in the area of needs, there is the somewhat more objective measure of family size. Thus, all things being equal, the individual with the larger family will derive more satisfaction from an added increment of income than someone else at the same income but with a smaller family. If greatest total satisfaction is to be objective, then income should be distributed equally to each person rather than equally to each family unit.

"Medicaid: The Patchwork Crazy Quilt." Columbia Journal of Law and Social Problems 62 (April 1966): 62-90.

(V)

Examines experience with Medicaid program since its inception. Author observes that budgetary concerns generated by unexpectedly high level of expenditure on Medicaid have created a restrictive attitude toward eligibility and service provisions of the program. Restrictive tendencies produce long-term inefficiencies and are counter-productive to the Medicaid program's ultimate aim of providing medical assistance to all needy persons.

Explores reasons for state differentials in provision of medical assistance to the needy. Poorer states tend to cover only categorically-related persons, those for whom matching federal funds are available. Author concludes that incentive aspect of matching funds program would be made more effective if the federal government would extend contributions to non-categorically-related persons.

*Meier, Gerald. Leading Issues in Economic Development: Studies in International Poverty. London: Oxford University Press, 1970.

(XI)

A comparison of living standards in developed and underdeveloped countries. Meier suggests that per capita income is an inappropriate index of international differences. As an alternative, Meier compares countries using social as well as "real" indicators. Education, measured by literacy rate, school enrollment and newspaper circulation, and health, measured by life expectancy and calories per day, are the two social indicators used. Real indices include energy consumption, motor vehicle use, and cement production.

Meissner, Martin. "The Long Arm of the Job: A Study of Work and Leisure." Industrial Relations 10 (October 1971): 239-260.

(VIII

An exploration of the effects the work place has on the worker's leisure activity decision making. Meissner tests what he refers to as the "carry over" hypothesis, which suggests that employees choose leisure activities with characteristics similar to those of their jobs. After a brief discussion on the alternative explanation for the effects of work on leisure, the various propositions are simplified into three impact dimensions: discretion, expression, and social interaction. Using data taken from a survey of 206 industrial workers on Vancouver Island, job and technical constraints and social interaction at work are measured along with their relationship to leisure activities. Findings indicate a negative relationship between work constraints and measures of activity involvement, a positive relationship between social interaction at work and participation in voluntary organizations, and a positive correlation between social isolation on the job and social interaction away from work. As Meissner says it, "The long arm of the job reaches out into life away from work."

*Mencher, Samuel. "The Problem of Measuring Poverty." In Poverty, edited by Jack L. Roach and Janet K. Roach. Penguin Books Ltd., 1972.

(II,IV)

A review of critical problems and sources of controversy associated with the measurement of income distribution and the definition of poverty levels. It is noted, for example, that the size of the social unit used by income studies affects the resultant distribution such that the larger the size of the income unit, the smaller the estimate of inequality of incomes. Another problem arises in trend studies that attempt to measure shifts in the distribution of income over time. The tolerance for error in these measurements is comprised by the difficulties of maintaining constant over time the value of money, the definition of the income unit, and changing sources of income. Finding an appropriate definition for poverty is seen as an even more formidable task. Absolute poverty level definitions are often unrelated to the way people actually live at these income levels, and the composition of the poverty group as well as its total population vary as estimates of minimum budgets attempt to account for family characteristics like size, age, and sex of family head, and non-money income. The concept of poverty might be best defined in terms of national objectives rather than subsistence levels. "Thus where a minimal income may be argued to be sufficient for its immediate recipients, it may be highly inadequate as it affects the economic and social welfare of the nation as a whole."

Meyer, Charles W. A Base for the Negative Income Tax. Discussion Paper. Madison: Institute for Research on Poverty, University of Wisconsin, 1969.

(VII)

The Negative Income Tax is designed to provide income maintenance for needy families without destroying work incentives. To do this effectively, it must have a fairly high basic living allowance (the amount a family with no income will receive) and a fairly low marginal tax rate. This, in turn, implies an expensive program that will give some payments to families earning substantially above the poverty level. A broad definition of income would reduce these payments to high income families. The addition of interest and dividend payment, realized capital gains, imputed rent, sick pay, unemployment benefits, strike benefits, categorical assistance payments, and state and local taxes to the taxable income used as a base for the negative tax would reduce the number of high income people eligible, increase work incentives, retain flexibility in the welfare system, and reduce the regressive effects of state and local taxation. Work related costs, nondiscretionary payments, and special individual payments (disability) should be excluded in the interests of equity and work incentives.

The effects of including a number of measures of wealth in the measure of income were studied. Only the inclusion of an imputed value for homes or of a capital consumption (fraction of net worth) measure were judged to be useful.

Meyer, Charles W., and Saupe, William E. "Farm Operators Under the Negative Income Tax." American Journal of Agricultural Economics 52 (May 1970).

(II, VII)

Article explores some of the possible effects of the negative income tax on farmers. The degree to which farmers would benefit by the negative income tax depends on both the breakeven level of income and the extent to which income imputed to assets is added to money income--a necessary step since 21% of the self-employed with incomes below the poverty level have a net worth in excess of $25,000. Different definitions of income and changes in accounting procedures will be necessary to adequately determine the negative income tax supplement. Some possible effects of the negative income tax are that it may induce farm laborers not to work and may affect farmers' decisions on what crops to grow. Assured of some income regardless of effort, some farmers may grow more risky, but possibly greater income-producing crops. The overall effect on agriculture is difficult to predict.

Meyer, Jack A. "The Impact of Welfare Benefit Levels and Tax Rates on the Labor Supply of Poor Women." Review of Economics and Statistics 57 (May 1975): 236-238.

(VIII)

The article presents an analysis of the determinants of the hours worked by poor women, both white and Black. The author begins by noting that any analysis should include non-paid labor (housework) and the marginal tax effects of welfare benefits. He then constructs a simple model wherein hours worked is a function of the net market wage, of potential non-work income (including relief benefits), of the implicit wage for housework, and of certain human capital variables. This model was tested using data supplied by a Census survey in 1967. Hours worked were negatively related to potential income but not significantly affected by either market or household wages.

Michael, Robert, and Lazear, Edward. "The Shadow Price of a Child." Paper presented at the American Econometrics Association meetings, 1971.

(II)

A model is developed in which the "cost" of a child is calculated, by examining the opportunity cost associated with child bearing and raising. Opportunity cost includes not only foregone wages during the unemployed period of the parent, but an imputed cost associated with the "depreciation of human capital" which occurs as a result of parental non-use of market skills. The model assumes people make rational decisions to produce children, in which benefits from the child are contrasted with costs (including the forementioned imputed costs) of the child. The model draws heavily on earlier human capital work of Becker.

(Paper available from authors)

Michigan Department of Social Services. A Policy Analysis: The Incidence and Implications of Multiple Benefit Receipt Among Michigan AFDC Recipients. Lansing, Michigan: Michigan Department of Social Services, 1974.

(V)

This study of recipients of Aid to Families with Dependent Children (AFDC) addresses three areas of concern: (1) whether the existing program structure has created incentives adverse to work activity among welfare recipients; (2) whether receipt of multiple benefits has enabled some recipients to live on welfare in relative affluence; and (3) whether the existing system is inequitable among program recipients and between recipients and non-recipients. The study sample is comprised of the 204 welfare cases which were selected for the Michigan Quality Control sample for the month of January, 1974.

On the basis of information collected, the following conclusions are drawn:

- the one-income "AFDC only" case is atypical (15% of the study population);
- the typical case (3.2 persons) had an average of 2.6 benefit and income sources;
- the average value of all income and benefits was $392 per case for the month (AFDC, $267; others, $107);
- the most common non-AFDC benefit was Medicaid (63% of the study group, who received an average benefit valve of $113 for the month); and

- receipt of aid from several sources, though it was associated with higher total benefit value, did not quarantee income adequacy.

The implications of these findings for policy include:

- as has been Department of Social Services policy, evaluation of benefit adequacy should include at least the value of Medicaid and Food Stamp benefits received, and should include recognition of other benefits;
- the availability of multiple benefits means that possible income from benefits may be sufficiently adequate so the employment is not necessary for a satisfactory standard of living; and benefit loss rates when non-welfare income is earned can be high, making employment unprofitable; and
- it is important to examine available options for coordinating the various systems of public benefits.

Miller, Herman P. Income Distribution in the United States. Bureau of the Census (1960 monograph). Washington, D.C.: U.S. Government Printing Office, 1966.

(II)

An analysis of the changes in income distribution in the United States during the last three decades is presented in this article. Using the decennial census of population which provides information on age, sex, color and national origin, Miller examines the income differentials of families and unrelated individuals from 1929-1962. The major finding of his exploration is that there was a reduction in inequality in the distribution of income between 1940 and 1950 and no significant change in inequality during the following decades. Miller finds that this income distribution scheme also exists when families are broken down by age, sex, residence and occupational variations. Changes in economic conditions are the prime reason given for the observed fluctuations in income and occupational classifications, and computations of non-money items are cited as problems of the study.

(Also, New York Times Magazine, 11 November 1962: "'Is the Income Gap Closed?' 'No!'")

* Miller, Herman P. "Major Elements of a Research Program for the Study of Poverty." In The Concept of Poverty, Task Force on Economic Growth and Opportunity, Chamber of Commerce of the United States. Washington, D.C.: Library of Congress Catalogue No. 65-21323, 1965.

(II)

An attempt to delineate several areas of research that would be fruitful in improving our understanding of the meaning and causes of poverty. Poverty is not just an economic problem but an emotional, cultural, and political problem as well. In the past, there has been no objective definition of poverty--hence the wide range in the estimates of the number of American poor. There are different types of poverty which have different causes and require different solutions. Poverty is a Black problem, a rural problem, a southern, aged, unemployment problem. The official poverty line definition is not enough. There is evidence that many of the people labeled poor by that definition are relatively well off. We need to arrive at a more comprehensive definition of poverty, and then use that definition to study the poor and the programs used to help them.

*Miller, Herman P. "Measuring Subemployment in Poverty Areas of Large U.S. Cities." Monthly Labor Review 96 (October 1973): 10-18.

(X)

The labor force concept with its emphasis on unemployment "is extremely useful as an economic indicator; but it has serious defects as a social indicator, for which it is often used, because it takes no account of the adequacy of the income from employment." The concept of the subemployed used here includes persons 21 to 64 years old and those 16-21 not enrolled full time in school or training programs who are: (1) unemployed, (2) not looking for work because they feel no work is available, (3) working part time involuntarily, or (4) family heads or unrelated individuals earning less than the minimum wage or less than the SSA poverty line for families of their size. This definition is applied to data from the 1970 Census Employment Survey on the poorest neighborhoods in 12 American cities with 2 million inhabitants or more. Out of a 2.9 million labor force in the poverty areas, about 19 percent were subemployed which is almost two and one-half times the 8 percent unemployment figure for this group. "The average family income of the subemployed workers at $6,600 was about $3,200 less than that received by the families of workers who were not subemployed." The results offer further comparisons between the categories of the subemployed and are differentiated by sex and race. In most of the metropolitan poverty areas, the subemployment rate was about two and one-half times the unemployment figure, though Washington and Houston were higher due to very low unemployment rates.

*Miller, Herman. "New Definitions of the Poor." New York Times Magazine, 21 April 1963.

(II)

An attempt is made to reconcile the surprisingly high estimates of the number of poor families in the United States--a study by Keyserling estimates 41%--with the fact that per capita goods and services have doubled since the thirties. The large percentages of the "poor" who own luxury items such as TV sets, automobiles, and dishwashers are cited to confirm the distinction between standards of poverty in the United States and the bare-subsistence levels of the starving poor in China or India. "Standards of poverty are culturally determined...they vary from place to place and differ from time to time." Miller chooses to define the poor as the lower one-fifth of the income distribution (families with incomes less than $2,900 in 1960). He notes that a Bureau of Labor Statistics estimate of a "modest but adequate" budget for a family of four living in New York increased by 28% from 1947 to 1959 (from $4,000 to $5,200 in 1961 dollars). It is not considered unreasonable then that the concept of poverty should reflect this rising standard. "As incomes go up, needs go up also--evidently in such a way as to leave a large proportion of the population at substandard levels."

*Miller, Herman. Poverty American Style. Belmont, California: Wadsworth Publishing Company, 1966.

(II, III, IV)

Selections from a variety of sources that aim "to show the diversity of opinion that underlies all of the major issues that are involved in the analysis of poverty." In the section related to definitions, an article by George Gallup determines levels of poverty "by consensus." Polls that ask for a personal appraisal of the minimum amount of money needed by a family of four yield figures that vary by income bracket and region. The under-$3,000 income group estimated $73 a week, while the $7,000-$10,000 bracket estimated $99. Rose Friedman, in another selection, criticizes the $3,000 CEA poverty level and contends that it overestimates the total number of poor and distorts the composition of that group. The elderly are overrepresented by the failure of the definition to account for savings and assets. Large families are overrepresented and small families underrepresented since the definition is insensitive to family size. A selection by Miller dealing with a subsequent revision of the original CEA statistics, in fact, bears out some of these criticisms. For example, the elderly constitute a smaller portion of the new estimate which does however still put the total number of poor at about one-fifth of all persons living in the United States. Miller calculates that in 1963 this figure represents a "poverty gap" of 12 billion dollars--"the amount required to bring all families and individuals above the poverty line."

*Miller, Herman. Rich Man Poor Man. New York: Apollo, 1971.

(II,IX)

A comprehensive study of the present distribution of wealth and income in the United States that also analyzes historical trends in distribution and gives particular attention to the characteristics of special classes (the poor, the wealthy, Blacks, Puerto Ricans). Miller acknowledges the usefulness of a fixed level definition of poverty such as the Social Security Administration's minimum market basket; yet he views it as an essentially unrealistic measure of poverty in an expanding economy since it fails to capture needs that result from a rising standard of living. The poverty level defined as a fraction of median income is seen as one way to avoid this problem. Such a definition would imply that there was little change in the number of poor during the 1958-1959 period. This contrasts with the marked decrease a fixed level definition implies and illustrates the conclusion that, "use of a constant standard exaggerates the improvement that is made over time...If this definition remains in use long enough, poverty will be eliminated statistically but few people will believe it."

Miller, Herman P. "Statistics and Reality." The New Leader, 30 March 1964, pp. 15-18.

(II, IV, VI)

An examination of the statistics of poverty using the official poverty line definition of poverty (i.e., below $3,000 annual income for a family of two or more). Although a flat poverty line implies an absolute definition of poverty, the American concept of poverty is a totally relative one. By world standards, American poor are well-off, and the amount of goods and services considered necessary for minimum or adequate levels of living has been rising at an annual rate of one or two percent. Discusses effect of a uniform, flat poverty line versus a variable one that adjusts for family size, needs, and regional differences. A flat poverty line tends to overstate the number of poor and understate the number of children in poverty. The number of farm families are overstated because of the neglect of non-cash income. The ignoring of assets in determining income is probably not very important because low income people do not tend to have assets. In general, the use of a flat poverty line tends to overstate the number of poor, but the convenience of the simple standard may outweigh its inaccuracies.

Miller, S.M. "The American Lower Classes: A Typological Approach." In New Perspectives on Poverty, edited by A.B. Shostak and W. Gomberg. Englewood Cliffs, New Jersey: Prentice-Hall, 1965.

(II)

Much confusion exists in recent discussions of the underprivileged. Frequently those members of households where the breadwinner is not involved in a white collar occupation are classified as lower class and are considered homogeneous with a centrality of attitudinal and behavioral patterns. Even where skilled and semiskilled regular workers are distinguished from unskilled, irregular workers, criteria of classification are conflicting. Concern with status, culture, or social disorganization understresses the importance of economic pressures; concern with class or economic deprivation discounts the importance of social and psychological problems. One way to recognize the variations among the poor is to use both class and status variables.

Some unskilled workers with stable jobs are not a pressing economic problem. Low-income poor are not basically welfare poor. Hard core families are smaller in number. Economic criterion thus has several components: level of income, stability of income, source of income. It can be expressed in terms of economic security and insecurity.

Style of life criterion referring to behavior and attitudes in family relationships and consumption patterns is difficult to formulate. The notion of family stability or instability is at best suggestive of the degree of effectiveness of different styles of life in handling the same environment.

These two approaches can be joined by cross-tabling the two dimensions of the two variables of economic security and familial stability. Each resulting type has many variations. The emphasis is on flux, rather than the permanence of a position in the pattern.

(Poverty and Human Resources Abstracts)

Miller, S.M., and Bloomberg, Warner Jr. "Shall the Poor Always Be Impoverished?" In Power, Poverty, and Urban Policy, Vol. 2, edited by Warner Bloomberg, Jr., and Henry J. Schmant. Beverly Hills, California: Sage Publications, Inc., 1968.

(II,IX,XI)

This chapter provides an argument for a multidimensional approach to poverty. Six dimensions of inequality are discussed: money income, assets, basic services, education and social mobility, political participation, and social status and self-respect. The multidimensional approach makes possible broader conceptions of poverty. It leads us to modify our understanding of what causes deprivation and to strike out in new directions as we extend well-being to the entire population. Such an approach is essential for developing policies and programs which can eliminate poverty. If we omit some dimensions of poverty from our models, human beings are left out of programs intended to bring our entire population into the social mainstream. When only an income measure for poverty is considered, for example, the effectiveness of any program is measured by the dollars devoted to it rather than by the distribution of our citizenry along the continua of opportunities and rewards. A multidimensional approach to inequality sees the problem in programs of opportunity structures of the community rather than success characteristics of individuals. Programs designed to ameliorate the lot of the disadvantaged frequently leave unchanged those characteristics of our society that produce inequalities.

(Poverty and Human Resources Abstract--edited by USR&E)

Miller, S.M., and Mishler, Elliott G. "Social Class, Mental Illness and American Psychiatry: An Expository Review." In Mental Health of the Poor, edited by Frank Riessman, Jerome Cohen, and Arthur Pearl. London: Collier-MacMillan Limited, 1964.

(XI)

A review by Miller and Mishler of Social Class and Mental Illness by August B. Hollingshead and Frederick C. Redlick. Miller and Mishler describe this book as a pioneering study. It has three major hypotheses: the social class structure is related to the treated prevalence of mental illness, the specific types of diagnosed psychiatric disorders and the types of treatment administered by psychiatrists to patients. The lowest class (defined by area of residence, occupation and education) contributes many more mentally ill patients than its proportion of the population warrants. The authors concur with Hollingshead and Redlick that psychiatrists should be trained to recognize and deal squarely with the differences between themselves and patients from other classes and that new modes of therapy be developed to reach the "difficult" patient (whose difficulty seems to reflect the difference between his and his therapist's class positions more than his psychological disturbance).

Miller, S.M.; Rein, Martin; Roby, Pamela; and Gross, Bertram M. "Poverty, Inequality, and Conflict." The Annals of the American Academy of Political and Social Science 373 (1967): 16-52.

(II)

Growing concern with poverty has ushered in the much more controversial issue of inequality within the affluent society. In America, relative deprivation is a more important aspect of "poverty" than poor physical conditions. Income alone is an inadequate indicator of level of living. This paper proposes six dimensions for the measurement of well-being: income, assets, basic services, social mobility and education, political position, and status and satisfaction. Questions of "who does and should get what" within each of these dimensions are issues arousing acrimonious debate. Social indicators are suggested which would create greater awareness of the extent of inequalities and make discussions of inequalities more useful. These indicators will not tell us what choices to make in inequality reduction, but they can prevent us from complacently ignoring the fact that choices are being made.

(Author abstract)

*Miller, S.M., and Riessman, Frank. Social Class and Social Policy. New York: Basic Books, Inc., 1968.

(II VII,XI)

This book examines the economic, political, social and psychological deprivations of the poor. Poverty is defined in relative terms, since, as society advances, the standards of poverty rise. The situation of poverty means that a family is falling behind others in access to the resources of society. Economic well-being is not solely related to annual monetary income; it also includes liquid reserves, pension reserves, durable goods, and housing. Command over resources include services, especially education, medical care, neighborhood amenities, and transportation. Political inclusion has four dimensions: (1) legal protection; (2) the exercise of the vote; (3) bureaucratic protection; and (4) political participation. The poor in America are a varied group, but in the urban centers the group is evolving into a Negro poor. Class and race issues give the poor a greater political potential than is usually true of low-income depressed populations. The poor are the new working class, a stratification term which emphasizes economic issues and raises the possibility of political action. Education, mental health, poverty, and community action are discussed as political problems. Programs have emphasized the pathology of the poor, ignoring their strengths; actually, it is the needs of the poor which have brought about improvements. The positive characteristics of the poor should be stressed.

(Partially taken from Poverty and Human Resources Abstract)

Miller, S.M., and Riessman, Frank. "The Working Class Subculture: A New View." Social Problems 9 (Summer 1961): 86-97.

(II)

The emphasis is on cognitive and structural factors (rather than on affectual and motivational factors) which provide a view of the working class. The working class is defined as regular, stable members of the non-agricultural labor force in manual operations. A distinction is made between this class and the lower class which has irregular employment and unskilled jobs in service occupations.

The analysis is aimed at developing "themes" in working-class life. The major themes discussed are:

1) striving for stability and security

2) traditionalism

3) intensity

4) person-centeredness

5) pragmatism and anti-intellectualism

6) appreciation of excitement.

Opposed to this is the lower-class life-style which is considered to be the inability to develop an adequate measure of coping with life so that some degree of security and stability is found. The unskilled, irregular, service-oriented worker lacks the disciplined, structured and traditional approach of the stable worker.

*Miller, S.M., and Roby, Pamela A. The Future of Inequality. New York: Basic Books, Inc., 1970.

(II,VII,XI)

Poverty is no longer a valid description of the disadvantaged in our society. Rather, the unequal distribution of material goods and the lack of full citizenship in the economy and in society are emphasized. New analyses of this multidimensional inequality are needed. A stratification approach, rather than measurement of income, can best identify the existing disenfranchisement and provide the basis for ameliorating programs. Six dimensions of well-being can be identified: (1) income; (2) basic services; (3) assets; (4) self-respect; (5) opportunities for education and social mobility; and (6) participation in decision-making. Direct annual money income inadequately reflects the flow of economic benefits to family. Assets, fringe benefits and stability of income are also involved. When factors are considered, especially in connection with the availability of basic services such as education and health, the differences between the poor and nonpoor are magnified. Discrimination continues to block education, income, and employment opportunities; the poor have no political leverage. A stratificational approach would be multidimensional, recognizing that poverty is a quality of life rather than a statistical economic position. Valid social indicators could measure the relative well-being of societal segments. Targets could be identified, subject to adjustment as advances occur in society as a whole. There would be potential for individual change with the existing structure and for the change of the structure itself. A radical restructuring is necessary if inequalities are to be decreased. A beneficial redistribution, however, will depend on effective and broad social policy.

(Poverty and Human Resources Abstracts)

*Miller, S.M., and Roby, Pamela. "Poverty: Changing Social Stratification." In <u>On Understanding Poverty</u>, edited by Daniel P. Moynihan. New York: Basic Books, Inc., 1968.

(II,XI)

The paper begins with the assertion that poverty, in an industrial society, should be defined in terms of relative position; that is the nature and size of the differences between the bottom 10%-20% and the rest of society. The poor are those who lag behind the rest of society in terms of one or more dimensions of life.

Alternative definitions of poverty are discussed including those which focus on: (1) class, with income as the determinant; (2) power and political strength affecting the command of resources; (3) education and social mobility; and (4) status, involving peer honor, styles of life, and self-respect.

Miller, Walter. "Lower Class Culture as a Penetrating Milieu of Gang Delinquency." <u>Journal of Social Issues</u> (March 1958).

(XI)

Author's primary thesis is that illegal behavior by lower class street corner gangs is buttressed by a persisting lower-class cultural tradition. Delinquency derives from "a positive effort to achieve status, conditions, or qualities valued within the actor's most significant cultural milieu."

Author perceives lower-class culture as a distinctive set of values and traditions rather than as a reverse function, or systematic pattern of deliberate violation, of middle-class norms. Lower-class values and norms represent behavioral adaptations to basic features of the lower-class way of life.

Among specific lower norms, or "focal concerns," which either explicitly support or implicitly demand commission of a range of illegal acts are: demonstrating toughness and an ability to outsmart others; demonstrating autonomy; and seeking excitement, risk, or change. Two additional concerns which affect patterning of focal concerns and motivate delinquent behavior among street corner gangs are a need for a sense of belonging and a dominant concern with status.

Millman, L., and Chilman, Catherine. Poor People at Work; An Annotated Bibliography. U.S. Department of HEW, Social and Rehabilitation Service, 1969.

(X)

An annotated bibliography of works which describe and evaluate public employment and training programs designed to bring poor non-professionals into the labor force.

Mincer, Jacob. "Labor Force Participation of Married Women." Aspects of Labor Economics. National Bureau of Economic Research. Princeton, New Jersey: Princeton University Press, 1962.

(II)

The article seeks to explain an apparent contradiction. If labor supply curves are generally backward bending (less labor as income from wages goes up), why has the labor force participation of unmarried women increased significantly since 1900 while income has risen significantly? At the same time, at any given time, the labor force participation of married women declines with increasing family income.

Mincer bases his explanation on the permanent income hypothesis of Milton Friedman. The labor force participation of married women is held to be negatively related to permanent family income and transitory family income, positively related to wages. The latter two relationships are roughly twice as strong as the first. This theory successfully explains most of the cross-sectional data already gathered. It offers a partial but not perfect explanation of the paradox mentioned above. Above all, it provides a useful, simple theory with which to analyze the effects of changing economic conditions on the labor force participation of married women.

Mincer, Jacob. "Labor Participation Rates." In The International Encyclopedia of the Social Science. New York: MacMillan Co. and the Free Press, 1968.

(II)

The labor force participation rate is defined as the fraction of a population that is in the labor force. The trends in participation rates among different age classes are discussed and explained. The participation rate for adult males has stayed constant over the last 60 years because the increase in income over that period has caused a decrease in hours worked, not in participation. The participation for both young and old males has declined sharply because of the increased income earned over the life cycle, new benefit provisions (social security and private pensions) and involuntary retirements for the old and the increased value of schooling as human investment for the young. Married women's participation rate has increased as a result of a shift from housework to work in the labor market.

Mincer, Jacob. Schooling, Experience and Earnings. National Bureau of Economic Research. New York: Columbia University Press, 1974.

(II,IX)

This book presents a detailed model of the human capital approach to the distribution of income. According to this approach, differences in human capital investment (schooling and post-school experience) are the major determinants of the differences in earnings among individuals. A complete model of human capital investment is proposed and explained. This model is then used to explain the actual income distribution of the United States. Some 50 to 70 percent of the variation in lifetime earnings among individuals is found to be explicable in terms of differences in experience, schooling, and the choice of hours of work. This very powerful conclusion makes this theory one of the most important in accounting for the income distribution of the United States.

Mirer, Thad W. "Aspects of the Variability of Family Income." Institute for Research on Poverty Discussion Papers. Madison, Wisconsin: University of Wisconsin, 1973.

(VII, IX)

This study explores the variability of family income, viewed as a random residual around a permanent income growth path. It is found that the poor are subject to more variability than families with higher incomes, and that this may be considered a welfare loss. Variability causes families to save more than they would otherwise, thus indefinitely postponing consumption opportunities. In a test of the effects of income experience on persons' attitudes toward the economic environment, it was found that the higher the degree of income uncertainty, the lower the sense of efficacy and trust; but, ambition is spurred.

Mix, Charles V.S., and Dickey, John W. "Rural Public Transportation in Virginia." Transportation Research Record 519. Washington, D.C.: Transportation Research Board, 1974.

(V)

Travel in most rural areas is now confined to one mode--the private automobile. Those who cannot own or operate cars either do not travel or must arrange, sometimes paying high prices, for others to take them where they need to go. Some very basic needs are not being met due to lack of travel opportunities in many rural areas; without transportation, health facilities, welfare programs such as food stamps and job training, educational, recreational, and religious facilities can not be used. Obtaining groceries and medication is difficult and may be more costly.

For these reasons, Mix and Dickey argue that public transportation should be made available to those in rural areas. This paper analyzes the rural transportation problem in Virginia and suggests how public transit systems can be developed and operated in rural areas of the state. A number of projects are reviewed that are in operation or are proposed for rural areas in other states. The study concludes that, although scattered, sufficient resources are available in Virginia for the planning and development of rural public transportation systems.

(Partially taken from the article)

Modigliani, Franco. "Fluctuations in the Income-Savings Ratio: A Problem in Economic Forecasting." Studies in Income and Wealth 2 (1949): 371-444.

(VII)

This paper introduces the cyclical/secular theory of the consumption theory. According to this theory, consumption depends both on current income and/or the highest previous ("peak") income. When income rises steadily, year to year, the consumption rate stays constant. When income falls below that of a previous year, consumption increases sharply. The general form of this relationship is $C_t = a + bY_t - C(Y_t - Y_t^*)$ where C_t- is consumption in year t; Y_t is income in year t; and Y_t^* is the previous peak income. a was found to be close to 0, b to be .902 and C to be .125. These figures gave a good approximation of the actual consumption data, given income. This theory was later developed by the relative income school of consumption theorists. Leontief, in his comment on this paper, made one of the first suggestions that a long-term moving average of income be used as part of a consumption function.

*Modligliani, Franco, and Ando, Albert. "The 'Permanent Income' and 'Life Cycle' Hypothesis of Saving Behavior." In MIT Department of Economics and Social Science, Publications in Social Science, Series 1, No. 52. Reprinted from Proceedings on Conference on Consumption and Saving, University of Pennsylvania, 1959.

(VII)

This paper tests two common aspects of the Friedman "permanent income" and Modigliani-Brumberg "life-cycle" hypothesis regarding savings/consumption behavior. The propositions in question are: (1) that consumption is basically determined not merely by current income but rather by a longer run measure of resources available to the household; (2) that the ratio of "permanent consumption" to "permanent income" ("total life resources" for Modigliani-Brumberg) is uncorrelated with permanent income. An analysis of the Bureau of Labor Statistics-Wharton Study of Consumer Expenditures, Incomes and Savings seemed to confirm the first proposition, while the second proposition was not fully supported by the authors' tests. The self-employed, salaried professionals and those with more than twelve years of schooling deviate from the predictions of these models.

*Modigliani, Franco, and Blumberg, R.E. "Utility Analysis and the Consumption Function: An Interpretation of Cross Section Data." In Post-Keynesian Economics, edited by K.K. Kurihara. New Brunswick: 1954.

(VII)

The authors address the paradox of the consumption function: that while cross-sectional data indicate a higher savings proportion at higher income levels, time series data show that as national income increases, the proportion saved remains the same. The authors claim that the proportion of income saved is independent of the level of income and that systematic deviations of the savings ratio from the normal level are largely accounted for by fluctuations of income around the normal level. Savings are proportional to income fluctuations and the provisions a household would want to (and can afford to) make are proportional to earning capacity. The authors' analysis of budget data supports this claim.

Mohktar, Metwally M., and Jensen, Rodney C. "A Note on the Measurement of Regional Income Dispersion." Economic Development and Cultural Change 22 (1973-74): 134-136.

(VI)

Jeffrey Williamson's use of the coefficient of variation to measure regional income dispersion is criticized and a more meaningful approach suggested. The coefficient of variation measures dispersion of regional mean income relative to the national mean income. This fails to consider the dispersion of income nationally or within each region. It is possible for the coefficient to decrease over time, suggesting a decrease in regional mean income dispersion, while the dispersion of actual incomes is increasing.

If data on individual regional mean incomes were available, application of analysis of variance would be a more meaningful approach. (Unfortunately, such data is difficult or impossible to obtain.)

The authors present a hypothetical example in which the coefficient of variation between two sets of regional mean incomes is the same--suggesting the same regional dispersion of incomes in both cases. When the F statistic (analysis of variance) is computed for each case, the hypothesis that there is no difference in regional incomes is rejected at the .05 level of significance in one case and accepted in the other.

Mohring, Herbert. "Alternative Welfare Gain and Loss Measures." Western Economic Journal 9(1971): 349-368.

(III)

For purposes of evaluating economic welfare loss and gain caused by price changes, Mohring finds that the compensating variation measure is superior to the consumer surplus. Given bundles of goods A and B, such a measure assigns greater value to A than to B if and only if the consumer prefers A, and this regardless of the order in which price changes take place, all under Pareto optimal conditions. Using information from the consumer's demand schedule for a commodity whose price has changed, the compensating variation can be calculated as the income adjustment required to give the same utility under the new price as prevailed under actual money income at the old price.

Mohring, Herbert. "Optimization and Scale Economies in Urban Bus Transportation." American Economic Review 62 (1972): 591-604.

(V)

Mohring analyzes the Twin City bus system to determine what changes are required to make it economically optimal. He includes in his cost curves the value of the time spent travelling to the riders as well as the more conventional operating costs. A bus system is subject to increasing returns to scale, and so requires a subsidy to operate efficiently. He concludes that busses should run as much as twice as often, with fares at 40 percent at peak periods and 75 percent at other times.

Moles, Oliver. "Up From Poverty; Intergenerational Movement Out of Low Income Occupations." Welfare in Review 8 (May-June 1970).

(IX)

The findings presented in this article are based on a secondary analysis of the data collected by the Michigan Survey Research Center. The objective of the analysis was to examine the relationship of occupational status and a variety of factors, such as previous job experience, education, demographic characteristics, and so on. The study has found evidence of significant upward mobility. First job experiences were found to be the most significant in measuring occupational status, with educational attainment affecting occupational status through first job experiences. Farm population improved its occupational status by migrating to the cities, and whites moved up more than their Negro counterparts.

*Mooney, Joseph D. "Urban Poverty and Labor Force Participation." American Economic Review 57 (March 1967): 104-119.

(X)

The direction and magnitude of the relation between the overall state of the economy, as indicated by the unemployment rate, and the labor force participation rates of the urban poor are estimated here using regression techniques. Poverty tracts in the 52 largest Standard Metropolitan Statistical Areas (SMSA's) are identified as those tracts which had a median family income less than two-thirds of the median family income for the entire SMSA. These poverty tracts are further classified by percentage of white/non-white racial composition. The negative correlation of labor force participation to unemployment rate was found to be substantially larger for the predominantly non-white groups than for white groups.

The most significant relationship existed for non-white married women with husband present. Some possible explanations for racial differential are suggested. For example, many of the urban white poor are over 65 and out of the labor force. The negative regression coefficients of the unemployment rate for the poverty populations, especially the non-white groups, are larger in almost every case than the same coefficients for the population as a whole. "It seems clear that the low income worker is more likely to be a discouraged worker than an additional worker especially if 'she' is a non-white married woman with husband present."

*Moore, Geoffrey H., and Stewart, Maxine. "New Developments in Labor Statistics." Monthly Labor Review (March 1972).

(IX, X)

The authors report on Bureau of Labor Statistics (BLS) efforts to improve the quality of labor and price statistics in line with the recommendations of the President's Commission on Federal Statistics; these efforts involve work in the areas of prices, wages, employment, construction, productivity and occupational health safety.

In the area of price statistics there is a major ongoing effort to revise the Consumer Price Index (CPI); principal features of this revision include placing the Consumer Expenditure Survey on a quarterly rather than an annual basis, increasing the number of areas included to 200, and using decennial census data to sample families. In addition, the Bureau is undertaking conceptual studies to develop a "cost-of-living oriented index" to supplement the CPI; this new index would attempt to measure the effect of both voluntary and forced substitution of commodities in the market-basket, to distribute the cost of durable goods over time, and to incorporate the benefits of government services in the index. New proposals are currently under consideration to develop city price indices using the same market-basket as the CPI; while the existing city CPI's show changes in prices over time, the new indices would permit price level comparisons between cities. The new proposals would, in addition, provide data on actual expenditure levels by income group and family type for individual areas. Additional efforts directed towards improving price statistics include the construction of a General Price Index (GPI) which will permit identification of the sources of divergence between the CPI, Wholesale Price Index (WPI), and the Gross National Product (GNP) Implicit Price Deflator and more extensive use of transactions prices in the construction of Import and Export Price Indices and the Wholesale Price Index.

In the area of wage statistics, the Bureau is planning to construct a general wage index which will command more general acceptability than Average Hourly Earnings, currently the most widely used measure of the price of labor. When completed, this index will cover all employees and all forms of compensation and will remove distortions resulting from overtime and shifts in industrial activity between sectors and regions. An intermediate step, the construction of an Hourly Earnings Index for non-farm production and non-supervisory employees, has already been taken and efforts are also underway to distinguish between union and non-union wages.

In the area of labor force statistics, four new sources are being made available; these include the employment status of Vietnam War veterans, measures of the duration of employment, expanded data on job vacancies by area, industry and occupation, and current non-farm employment by occupation and industry. Finally, the authors describe BLS efforts to expand statistical reporting in the areas of construction, productivity and occupational safety and health. Longer range plans include putting the CPI on a monthly basis, the construction of an Occupational Wage Index, and some further refinements in methods of seasonal adjustment for employment and unemployment statistics.

More, Sir Thomas. Utopia. Harvard Classics. New York: P.F. Collier and Son Company, 1516.

(II)

This fantastic account of a perfect commonwealth is credited to a philosopher-seaman, Raphael Hythloday, who sailed "not as the mariner Palinure, but as the expert and prudent prince Ulysses." Hythloday is portrayed as an outspoken, uncompromising man who could never suffer the dissembling and accommodation that would be required of a counselor to kings, a role for which his vast, well-measured experience particularly suited him. More appropriately therefore has Hythloday describe the idealistic order of the island Utopia while he himself listens on, intrigued but skeptical. Even with the name "Utopia" the author jests with a pun on the reality, the possibility of this ideal; yet it would be a mistake to discount the tale as merely a whimsical fantasy. If More smiles at the quixotic optimism of Utopia, it is not in condescension or ridicule; the smile is wistful. It is a little reconciliation between a perception of man that was not at all naive and a fervent idealism that was not so faint-hearted that it could be put off in cynical resignation. It should be remembered that, as a counselor to kings, Sir Thomas More did not resemble the flexible More of this narrative but proved to be, like Raphael Hythloday, a man prepared to stand on principle.

Utopia admits no private property because, "No equal and just distribution of things can be made, nor shall perfect wealth ever be among men, unless this propriety (private property) be exiled and banished." The abundance that the Utopians enjoy is possible on a six hour workday because very few men or women are exempt from work, and no one is occupied with what are considered vain or superfluous jobs (fashioning elaborate garments or moneylending, for example). Everyone has a trade of some sort and also works periodically for a two year term on a farm since the population rotates between city and county. The more offensive jobs are done by bondmen who are primarily those found guilty of serious crimes. The fifty-four cities on the island share equally and engage in little foreign trade. "Seeing they be all thereof partners equally, therefore can no man there be poor or needy."

Produce of all kind is brought to common markets; and, "Every householder fetcheth whatsoever he and his have need of, and carrieth it away with him without money, without exchange, without any gage or pledge." No one takes more than he needs because the only motivations for such action would be "a fear of lack," a fear which has no basis given the island's abundant common stores, and pride "which counteth it a glorious thing to pass and excel other in the superfluous and vain ostentation of things...the which kind of vice among the Utopians can have no place." That, in fact, there are many vices given little place among the Utopians is not however just a convenient assumption that allows the island's admirably sane institutions to function smoothly. The prudent, "virtuous" lives of the Utopians are considered a primary effect of those institutions. The customs and patterns of life are not thought to actually perfect the citizens but rather to encourage and foster their true, "natural" inclinations toward happiness. It is believed that these inclinations result in virtuous action except when men are deceived by "a false opinion of pleasure." (This might seem to be merely a re-labeling of the "pleasurable," but the labeling is less important than the belief which it entails.) Among the more light-hearted efforts at socialization is the practice of fashioning chains and chamber pots out of gold so that people will have little regard for the metal. Many lectures are offered as a possible way for Utopians to spend their leisure time; and care is taken that there be no "occasion of vice or wickedness, no lurking corners, no places of wicked counsels." And of course, there is no money. "So easily might men get their living, if that same worthy princess, lady money, did not alone stop up the way between us and our living.... Poverty itself, which only seemed to lack money, if money were gone, it also would decrease and vanish away."

Morgan, James. "The Anatomy of Income Distribution." The Review of Economics and Statistics 44(1962): 270-283.

(II,III)

The article shows how conceptual differences in the definition of income inequality affect the Gini Index of concentration. Income per "equivalent adult" shows greater inequality than family income. Single person families show great inequality while farm families show little. Short-run fluctuations in income are not significant. After age 25, older age-groups show greater inequality, with the overall index corresponding roughly to inequality at age 45. This is attributed primarily to the differential impact of less than a full year's work, and also to differential advancement. Exclusion of extra earners substantially increases measured inequality.

The educated show greater increases in income than the uneducated. Age and education do not appear to make such a difference for minorities. Taxes have little effect on inequality.

Morgan, James N. Five Thousand American Families--Patterns of Economic Progress, Vol. I. Survey Research Center, Institute for Social Research, University of Michigan, 1974.

(IV,IX)

This volume presents the findings of an authorative study of the determinants of the level of family economic wellbeing and its changes over time. The methodology employed for the study was a longitudinal survey of 5,000 families, with data collected annually on economic status, its components and determinants. The purpose of the study was to gain further insights into the dynamics of income and the causes of poverty in order to permit the formulation of more effective policies.

The survey collected data on environmental variables (local unemployment rates, urbanization), sex and racial characteristics, education, family size and composition, wage rates, and labor force participation, attitudinal and behavioral characteristics. Each of these was analyzed in terms of its relationship to the level of income, and to the trends in income levels.

According to the study, the main determinants of the level of income are the unchanging characteristics of individuals: age, sex, education, race and family background. Family composition is the only significant variable in the analysis of economic wellbeing. Behavioral and attitudinal variables do not seem to matter at all; in other words, the poor cannot control their own fate.

Morgan, James. "Measuring the Economic Status of the Aged." *International Economic Review* 6 (January 1965): 3-18.

(IV)

The problems and improvements in quantitative assessment of the economic status of the elderly is discussed. Morgan explains the difficulties of arriving at an accurate figure for the number of poor elderly. Income of older people tends to be overstated when an extended family measure is used and tends to be understated because of lower taxes, smaller families and lower food and clothing requirements. To resolve these inequities, Morgan suggests looking at income distributions, single and nuclear units and a refined gross disposable income measure instead of average income, extended family units and a faulty disposable income measure. Included in this new gross disposable income rate are the savings which the elderly accrue from growing their own food, repairing their homes, investment returns and transfer monies. Morgan claims that gross disposable income is as good an estimate of income as can be made, but family size and type must be compensated for. Other problem areas discussed are assessing housing assets, measuring the insurance worth, and evaluating leisure time value of the elderly.

Morgan, James N. "The Supply of Effort, the Measurement of Well Being, and the Dynamics of Improvement." *American Economic Review* 57 (No. 2, May 1968): 31-40.

(II,VIII,IX)

Current estimates of income and unemployment are much too narrow, according to this article. Unemployment does not take into account all those who wish to work more hours, who are sick, who are temporarily unemployed. Income measurements do not take into account many transfer payments (incoming non-money transfers, out-going taxes, charity, alimony). They do not take into account non-money income from unpaid work. The number of hours worked to gain this income also varies widely. The author proposes a new, much broadened measure of well-offness. This measure is the product of two components, the first measuring a family's control of economic resources, the second the amount of leisure it has. The first is the sum of money and non-money income less taxes divided by some measure of the needs of the family. The second is the sum of twenty-four hours minus twelve hours time needed for survival minus the time spent on both non free and paid work for each family member, the whole quantity divided by the number of adults in the family.

*Morgan, James N.; David, Martin H.; Cohen, Wilbur J.; and Brazer, Harvey E. Income and Welfare in the United States. New York: McGraw-Hill, 1962.

(II, IX, XI)

This book presents the results of a national research program conducted by the Survey Research Center of the University of Michigan's Institute for Social Research. Based on intensive interviews, it studies the distribution and redistribution of family income throughout the United States, combining demographic, economic, sociological, and psychological factors to provide a detailed explanation of what determines the economic position of the family. Data from the interviews are combined in a multivariate analysis that displays the role of each datum in relation to other relevant data. On the subject of poverty, the study gives detailed descriptive and inferential statistical analyses on poverty definition and measurement, turnover among the poor, the causes of poverty, earning power of the poor, and transmission of poverty between generations. Although not specifically on the study of poverty, the study discusses the many determinants of family income, including wealth and assets.

Morgan, James N., and Smith, James D. "Measures of Economic Well-offness and Their Correlates." American Economic Review 59 (May 1969).

(II,VII,VIII)

Several measures of economic well-being are reviewed here such as the ratio of income to needs and its various ramifications suggested by Orshansky and others, to account for different family circumstances. An attempt is made to construct a broader measure of "well-offness" by incorporating a determinant of leisure time and a more refined definition of income. "Real income" is determined for a national cross-section of 3000 families and a group of 2000 low-income families by including as income imputed rent, returns from do-it-yourself activities, as well as food, clothing and housing received from employment. Also, the costs of getting an income are deducted such as federal income taxes, union dues, and child care costs when all adult members are working. The ratio of real income to USDA food needs standard is multiplied by hours of leisure time. This procedure assumes that leisure and income are interchangeable. The correlation of this "well-offness" index with other indicators of economic status such as real income and income to needs ratio is then measured, as well as a correlation of these indicators with a variety of economic behavior such as risk avoidance, and economizing, and attitudes such as trust in others and planning. Many of these correlations are in the expected directions; however, "these static correlations prove little about the dynamic relations we seek." "In the case of economizing, the direction may even be different--economizing leading to better economic status which then allows less economizing."

Moriarty, B.M. "Socio-economic Status and Residential Locational Choice." Environment and Behavior 6 (1974): 448-469.

(XI)

This article analyzes two possible explanations for the different distribution of socio-economic groups within a city. "The economic competition hypothesis proposes that the different distribution is caused by differences in the budget costs and incomes of the different groups. The social choice hypothesis proposes that the distribution is caused by differences in the values, needs and desires of the different groups." Moriarty develops two indexes to test these hypotheses. One, for the economic competition hypothesis, is an index of the potential accessibility of an area to all employment in a home seekers occupational category. The other, for the social choice hypothesis, measures the area's proximity to "compatible" friends and neighbors. He concludes that the home seeker considers both an area's employment and social accessibility when making locational decisions, although the data support the social choice hypothesis more than the economic competition hypothesis.

*Morrill, Richard L., and Wohlenberg, Ernest H. The Geography of Poverty in the United States. New York: McGraw-Hill, 1970.

(VI, XI)

A comprehensive study of the regional distribution of poverty in the United States. The authors first describe the distribution of poverty in America and then attempt to explain why poverty is concentrated in particular areas. A stepwise regression analysis of 1960 Census data is used to determine whether environmental and spatial factors and economic, social, and dynamic factors can explain the variance in poverty incidence across regions. The authors concluded that "both social characteristics which families bring to possible jobs, notably education and race; the occupations and industries and jobs, if any, which the economy offers; and a spatial characteristic, relative location in the economy" account for the regionalization of poverty in this country. To set the stage for policies to eliminate poverty, the authors developed the following typology of poverty areas (listed in approximate order of severity):

- The Agricultural South
- The Small Appalachian Coalfields
- The Inland Hills and Mountains (East and West South Central U.S.)
- The Agricultural Interior (North Central U.S.)
- The Urban South
- The Metropolitan North (Northeast U.S.)
- The Non-metropolitan Periphery (West U.S.)

The poverty of the non-metropolitan areas of the country is basically regional or spatial in character and hence should be treated primarily by moving the poor out of these areas to areas of greater economic opportunities, or moving the opportunities to the non-metropolitan areas (i.e., encouraging rural industrialization). On the other hand, urban poverty, which is basically economic and social in nature, requires changes primarily in discrimination practices, education, and labor organizations.

*Morrison, Peter A. "Migration from Disturbed Areas: Its Meaning for Regional Policy." Prepared for the Economic Development Administration, the Ford Foundation, and the National Institutes of Health, October 1973.

(VI)

The complex relationships among migration, distressed areas and the problems of the poor are analyzed; and several directions for research are suggested. It was found that there are many people who would like to migrate but do not. Decisions to move or not to move and where to move are often based on considerable ignorance of alternatives. Migrants depend largely on friends or relatives for information, thus limiting their destination choices. Nevertheless, the choice is usually economically rewarding and personally satisfying for the migrants.

From the point of view of the localities that migrants enter and leave, Morrison concluded that migration is an adjustment mechanism transferring workers from surplus labor areas to scarce labor areas; but he pointed out that it also had a direct effect on regional growth. Migration to a growth area will tend to stimulate further investment and employment growth, while migration from a stagnant or declining area could have a reverse multiplier effect. Often, the most productive residents are the ones who move away from stagnant areas leaving behind a labor pool of diminishing productive potential. This makes such localities increasingly less attractive to new industry.

Morrison, Peter A. et al. <u>Review of Federal Programs to Alleviate Rural Deprivation</u>. Santa Monica, California: Rand, 1974.

(VI)

This study reviews federal programs in aid of the rural poor in the areas of human resources development, medical services, and legal aid. The programs are qualitatively evaluated in terms of their own goals. The legal services programs, for example, were deemed successful because they rendered substantial benefits to the rural poor. The authors note the difficulty of comparing program costs and benefits with those of other alternatives for enlarging people's access to income.

Moser, Sir Claus. "Social Indicators--Systems, Methods and Problems." <u>Review of Income and Wealth</u> 19 (1973): 133-141.

(II,XI)

"Professor Moser regards the purpose of social indicators as being to aid the policy maker by summarizing the state and changing conditions of society, pinpointing the outstanding existing and emerging social problems and monitoring the effects of social policies and programmes. Thus social indicators will frequently, though not necessarily, be normative and they will often, though again not necessarily, be concerned with outputs rather than inputs. Although many writers regard social indicators as being combinations of series, the problems of construction are substantial. Central to the idea of a social indicator, however, is that it should represent or summarize a broader concept than itself and that it should belong to a structure or system of series. Although there are no social theories about society in general on which a structure of indicators can at present be based, there are a number of middle range theories relating to specific fields or sectors, such as occupational mobility, education, migration, mental health, etc., around which quantitative relationships and models can gradually be built to give insight into social changes and perhaps eventually into the manipulation of policy instruments for the improvement of social conditions."

(Taken from article)

Moynihan. Daniel P. The Politics of A Guaranteed Income. New York: Random House, 1973.

(II)

Moynihan offers the participant-historian's account of the proposal and eventual failure of the Family Assistance Plan to become law. Initially, the author discusses the concept of dependency, including how the poor are perceived, and the political implications and social consequences of past social welfare legislation. Deducing that welfare programs such as Aid to Families with Dependent Children (AFDC) have failed utterly to reduce dependency, Moynihan argues in favor of a plan of income redistribution. A negative income tax plan provides for this type of economic realignment down the social scale--it ensures a guaranteed income while avoiding work disincentives. This book documents the story of the plan from its inception to its ultimate rejection by the 91st Congress, disclosing the myriad political factors at play.

Muellbauer, John. "Household Composition, Engel Curves and Welfare Comparisons between Households: A Duality Approach." European Economic Review 5 (No. 2, 1974).

(IV)

This paper is about household composition effects in consumer theory. These are important for the specification and estimation of Engel curves and demand functions. The models examined here have important applications in the areas of the measurement of cost-of-living indices, the study of poverty and inequality and in certain aspects of social policy. The models are based on the approach of Barten (1964). Taste differences between households are parameterized in a way which has been called simple good augmenting or simple repackaging in the literature on quality change. In this theory, changes in household composition play an analogous role to price changes. "True household equivalent scales" are developed which are analogous to true cost-of-living indices and permit welfare comparisons across households.

(Journal of Economic Literature)

Muellbauer, J. "Household Production Theory, Quality and the 'Hedonic Technique'." American Economic Review 64(No. 6, 1974).

(III)

In the hedonic technique of correcting prices for quality change, there are two variants of a regression of the prices of the varieties of a good on their characteristics. This paper investigates alternative consumer theoretic rationalizations of each and analyzes three groups of models: (a) household production models, (b) separability restrictions on preferences, and (c) supply generated models. The latter item (c) lacks a welfare interpretation, while "a" and "b" (especially "a") suffer from severe problems, particularly of aggregation, in finding decent approximations to theoretically sound price indices. Strong restrictions are required to overcome these problems; definite empirical restrictions are implied.

(Journal of Economic Literature)

*Muellbauer, John. "Inequality Measures, Prices and Household Composition." Review of Economic Studies (October 1974): 493-503.

(II,IV)

Comparisons of inequality across countries and over periods of time require correction for the effects of relative price changes and for differences in household composition. In this study two alternate general welfare functions, one specified in terms of individual incomes, the other in terms of individual utilities, are examined for possible measures of inequality. For example, on a two dimensional model of the income formulation, the line of equal income intersects the fixed income sum diagonal and the relevant welfare level social indifference curve. The ratio of the equal income share that would achieve the given welfare level to the equal share (average) of the fixed income sum is taken as one measure of equality. Subsequent sections modify the income variables in these welfare functions to account for price changes. An adjustment is made for family composition differences by means of adult equivalent scales for different types of household members; these parameters further modify the price-adjusted income variables. Some applications of these inequality indexes are presented using data from the Family Expenditure Survey in the United Kingdom for the years 1964 and 1970.

Muellbauer, John. "Prices and Inequality: The United Kingdom Experience." <u>Economic Journal</u> (March 1974).

(II, III)

It appears that the inegalitarian bias in relative consumer price changes in the United Kingdom, which has been a feature now for more than twenty years, has recently accelerated. Before 1970 the price increases in housing were the main element in this bias. However, recently food price increases, especially after the middle of 1972, have taken on a dominant role. Not only does this have the consequence that money measures of inequality are likely to be seriously misleading but that a single consumer price index is no longer adequate for understanding and formulating social policy.

(Taken from the article)

Mueller, Eva. "Public Attitudes Toward Fiscal Programs." <u>The Quarterly Journal of Economics</u> 77 (1963): 310-316.

(V)

This survey, based on nationwide cross-section data, measures public attitudes toward the amounts spent on fourteen government programs. Most felt existing programs should be expanded with aid to the aged and the needy, to education, slum clearance and health leading the list. There was no single program so popular that a majority would be willing to pay higher taxes for it. There were no significant differences in response by different income groups, although being reportedly unemployed or a farmer did affect attitudes towards unemployment benefits and support for agriculture. People with more education were more willing to pay taxes. Party affiliation did not affect attitudes toward taxes, but Democrats were more willing to support social welfare programs than were Republicans.

*Mugge, Robert H., and Eppley, David. "Urban-Rural Contrasts in Public Welfare." <u>The Quality of Rural Living</u>. Washington, D.C.: National Academy of Sciences, 1971.

(V, VI)

Express urban-rural differentials in public welfare. Presents data on payment and recipient rates, social services and staffing of welfare offices, living arrangements of recipients, duration of assistance cases, migration rates, and characteristics and circumstances of AFDC families. In all of these areas, urban residents appear to hold a more advantageous position in regard to the level of the assistance provided them and to their general living conditions.

Author asserts that these differentials are losing their importance in American life due to penetration of the cosmopolitan influence in non-metropolitan areas; urban and rural values, attitudes, and knowledge are converging.

Further significant differences in welfare programs are a result of variation among state attitudes toward welfare and welfare programs, not differentials between urban/rural recipients of assistance themselves.

*Murray, Janet. "Family Life Cycle Analysis in Research on Consumer Behavior." In The Life Cycle and Consumer Behavior, edited by L. H. Clark. New York: 1955.

(IV,VII)

A series of suggestions for research on the relationship between the life cycle and consumer behavior. This had not been studied in detail at the time of the article but it was known to have important effects. One important point is noted: different age groups have different patterns of resources and saving and these patterns show differential shifts over time. Any study of income, consumption, or savings must therefore carefully consider the demographics of its sample.

*Murray, Janet. "Potential Income from Assets." Social Security Bulletin 27(No. 12, 1964): 3-11.

(VII)

This study of the incomes of the U.S. aged prorated assets over the expected life of the holder. This figure, added to money income, is potential income. Median incomes were increased 10% when prorated assets excluded the owned home and increased more than 30% when equity in the owned home was included. More than three-fourths of those with income of less than $3,000 did not have asset holdings great enough to place their potential income in a higher $1,000 interval than that in which their actual income fell. The inequalities in the distributions of income are greater for potential than for actual income. The aged poor are most affected by the inclusion of asset income.

Muth, Richard F. "Migration, Chicken or Egg." <u>Southern Economic Journal</u> 37 (1971): 295-306.

(VI)

There is a strong association between in-migration and the growth of employment in U.S. cities. The most common explanation for this is that "the differential rates of migration are induced by differential growth in job opportunities and employment." Based on data covering U.S. cities in the 1950's, Muth finds this to be true, but he finds that its effect is smaller than the effect of the opposite process--growth in employment is induced by migration. Since there is an interaction between the two effects, "exogenous increases in either migration or employment growth lead to multiple increases in both." Income differentials have a substantial effect on migration and thus on employment growth.

Myers, Jerome K. <u>Family and Class Dynamics in Mental Illness</u>. New York: John Wiley and Sons, Inc., 1959.

(XI)

"Among the seriously debilitating illnesses in American today the mental disorders rank high.... This book deals with one particular aspect of the social environment, namely, social class, in its relation to the development and manifestation of mental health in the individual." In dealing with this relationship, both internal family dynamics and external social and community pressures are studied as they bear on the individual's personality development.

The conclusions of this study, added to the findings of an earlier study, are that:

- social class is significantly related to the prevalence of treated psychiatric disorders, the types of treated psychiatric disorders, and the type of therapy administered;
- the lower social classes have significantly higher proportions of psychiatric patients in their populations;
- the lower social classes have lower rates of neurosis but higher rates of psychosis; and
- the lower classes tend to receive custodial and organic treatments for psychiatric disorders, while the higher classes tend to receive psychotherapeutic treatment.

*Nagatani, Ke. "Life Cycle Saving: Theory and Fact." American Economic Review 62(1972): 344-353.

(VII)

Nagatani explains the statistical contradictions to the Modigliani-Brumberg life cycle hypothesis in terms of uncertainty and risk aversion. Although consumers would like to maintain a steady rate of consumption based on their "permanent income," they are uncertain as to what their future earnings will be. Because of the risk attached to borrowing, consumers borrow less against expected future income than they would in a riskless environment. As real income increases, consumers adjust their consumption upward.

Nakayama, Toshiko, and Bahr, Richard C. "New CPI by Size of City Shows Larger Increases in Big Areas." Monthly Labor Review 96 (March 1973).

(III,V,VI)

"In 1972, as in 1971, prices tended to rise more (in percentage terms) in large urban population centers than in smaller cities and towns." The consumer price index for all items rose 3.8 percent for the year 1972 in urban areas with populations of 3.5 million or more. This compares with a 3.1 percent overall rise for cities with a population of 2,500 to 50,000 and a 3.4 percent rise for the U.S. as a whole. This update of the BLS consumer price index report presents a table that gives the index for subgroups of goods and services in five different population-size groups for equivalent three-month periods in 1971 and 1972. "Apparel" and "Upkeep" were the only items that did not rise more in the larger areas. The 1972 increases were generally the same as the 1971 increases, though in 1972 there was a sharper rise for food in all groups except the 50,000-250,000 category. It is noted that the 1971 results were influenced by the August to November price-rent freeze of Phase I.

Nakayama, Toshiko and Warsky, Diane. "Measuring Regional Price Changes in Urban Areas." Monthly Labor Review 96 (1973): 24-38.

(VI)

Since 1973, the Bureau of Labor Statistics has been publishing a set of consumer prices indexes which measure price changes in urban areas grouped by regions. The indexes are calculated from price data collected in 54 of the 56 (Anchorage and Honolulu not included) metropolitan and nonmetropolitan areas of the U.S. for the national Consumer Price Index. The areas are grouped into four regions--Northeast, North Central, South and West. The indexes are published quarterly for all items and for the following subgroups: food, housing, apparel and upkeep, transportation, and health and recreation. These indexes cannot be used to compare price levels in different regions. They can only compare price changes in the different regions over a given time period.

The indexes indicated that regional influences are significant factors in price behavior. Between 1967 and 1973 prices rose most sharply in Northeastern urban areas (36%). Prices rose 32.1% in the South, 30.9% in the North Central states and 28.7% in the West. Data comparing price rises in cities by size of population suggests that regional influences are more significant than population size in explaining price behavior in the food, housing, and health and recreation subgroups.

*National Academy of Sciences. The Quality of Rural Living. Washington, D.C.: 1971.

(V)

A collection of papers and discussions which assess the quality of various aspects of rural life including education, health, housing, nutrition, employment, and public welfare. Presents commentary and makes recommendations on needed research, needed changes in education and in government policies and programs.

*National Advisory Commission on Rural Poverty. The People Left Behind. Washington, D.C.: Government Printing Office, September 1967.

(V,VI,XI)

A comprehensive study and appraisal of the current economic situations and trends in American rural life as they relate to the existence of income and community problems of rural areas, including problems of low income; the status of rural labor, including farm labor, unemployment and underemployment and retraining in usable skills; rural economic development and expanding opportunities; sources of additional rural employment; availability of land and other resources; adequacy of food, nutrition, housing, health and cultural opportunities for rural families; the condition of children and youth in rural areas and their status in an expanding national economy; the impact of population and demographic changes, including rural migration; adequacy of rural community facilities services; exploration of new and better means of eliminating the causes which perpetuate rural unemployment and underemployment, low income and poor facilities; and other related matters.

Evaluates the means by which existing programs' policies and activities relating to the economic status and community welfare of rural people may be coordinated or better directed or redirected to achieve the elimination of underemployment and low income of rural people and to obtain higher levels of community facilities and services.

Develops recommendations for action by local, state or federal governments or private enterprise as to the most efficient and promising means of providing opportunities for the rural population to share in America's abundance.

(Taken from the report--the stated "Task of the Commission")

National Advisory Commission on Rural Poverty. Rural Poverty. Washington, D.C.: U.S. Government Printing Office, 1967.

(IV, V)

Witnesses testified to the extent and causes of rural poverty in the South and suggested ways of restoring prosperity to the region. Deteriorating land, mechanization of agriculture, and lack of access to borrowed funds at reasonable rates all contribute to poverty in the area. The existence of a minimum wage makes employers unwilling to hire. A high birth rate leads to a high dependency ratio. Poverty is invisible in the countryside, particularly the plight of the aged rural poor, and government money flows only into the cities. Local politicians are blamed for stymying federal efforts. Education, training, economic development, credit unions, cooperatives, health, legal and social services, improved transportation and better farm techniques are called for. As many as 80% of these poor in some countries are Black. Indians complain of paternalism from government officials.

National Bureau of Economic Research. The Measurement and Interpretation of Job Vacancies: A Conference Report. New York: Columbia University Press, 1966.

(X)

The demand for labor as reflected in the concept of Job Vacancies was the subject of a Conference held under the auspices of the National Bureau of Economic Research in 1966. The papers presented in that conference are gathered together in this book. They fall under four headings: theoretical discussions of the measurement of current demand for labor, the collection and use of job vacancy data in foreign countries, job vacancy surveys in the U.S., and alternative approaches to measuring job vacancies. A paper by John T.

Dunlop is included under the first heading. In it, the notion of internal labor markets is developed and the concept of job vacancies is examined in light of these internal markets (an internal labor market is one in which promotion is internal and outsiders enter at only a couple of 'entry-level' positions). Other papers examine the status of state employment services and their collection of job vacancy data, and present theoretical models of the labor market in which job vacancy data is used. The second and third headings are self-explanatory; the fourth includes papers on the use of help-wanted ads, employment service listings, and temporary help services as measurement devices to estimate job vacancies.

National Center for Social Statistics. Aid to Families with Dependent Children: Standards for Basic Needs, July 1974. Washington, D.C.: Department of Health, Education, and Welfare, 1975.

(XII)

In administering public assistance programs, each state employs various criteria and methodologies in establishing its own level-of-living or "need" standard to be used in determining eligibility and amount of money payment. Requirements for need are defined in terms of number, kind, and cost of specified consumption items. Though generally states consider food, clothing, shelter, and utilities "basic," and most include personal care items, household supplies, and medical supplies, budgeting of other items and cost standards vary widely among states. Actual money payment to recipients may be all or a percentage of the need or "full" standard. Document contains data comparing state need and payment levels for AFDC 2- and 4-member groups.

National Industrial Conference Board. Family Budgets of American Wage-Earners, A Critical Analysis. National Industrial Conference Board, Report No. 41. New York: The Century Company, 1921.

(II,III,VII)

Factors which must be taken into account in measuring either poverty or the minimum demands for "decent" living for a family are: housing, including fuel, light, and household equipment; diet; clothing; and cash for incidental expenses. The expense and necessity for these will vary from area to area depending upon the climate and customs of individuals in each locality. Local studies which were done in America and Britain between the 1890's and 1921 are critiqued and commented on, and the factors contributing to the standard of living increase in American cities between 1914 and 1921 are discussed.

Nesbitt, Timothy. "Indexing the Economy: A Brief Primer." In The Economic Crisis Reader, edited by David Mermelstein. New York: Vintage Books, 1975.

(III)

The accelerating inflation of the early seventies has created an increasing interest in linking all wages, prices and monetary values to a standard measure of inflation such as the Consumer Price Index. Previous experience with this type of indexing suggests that it will be harmful to workers. Unions that have demanded automatic cost of living escalators have often seen them as a trade of long term safety for the long term status quo, thus not a real gain. In Brazil, indexing, implemented in 1964, brought inflation down from 90% to 15% by 1973, but wage increases had dropped even further. The net effect of indexing will obviously depend on the particular arrangements established by law or contract. These arrangements will depend on political and institutional factors.

Indexing will also give more power to large corporations and conglomerates. With indexing, price hikes are not only passed on but become part of the law. The Brazilian index rose from 15% to 35% within a few months in 1974 due to oil price increases. Prices charged by the largest corporations, which are not the product of free market forces now, will become a direct means of controlling other aspects of the economy.

"New Program Initiated to Help Seattle's Medically Indigent." Hospitals 45 (March 16, 1971): 123-124.

(V)

Announces initiation of comprehensive health care program by the Seattle Model Cities Program. Aims to provide care to people whose incomes are too high for Medicaid, but who have no health insurance and who cannot afford continuing medical care. Project operated in cooperation with Blue Cross, Blue Shield, and Group Health Cooperative of Puget Sound. Administered by health professionals and community representatives. Federal grants totalling $889,000 for first year operation.

Newman, Dorothy K. "The Decentralization of Jobs." Monthly Labor Review (May 1967).

(VI,X)

A discussion of the movement of businesses, industries, and institutions out of the central cities to the suburbs, and the detrimental effect that this decentralization was having on the center-city poor. Many of the jobs created by new industry, retail and wholesale trade, and business, professional, and technical services are within the capability of the center-city dwellers but are inaccessible due to distance. Generally lacking automobiles, the urban poor tend to rely on public transportation to get to work. But public transportation is often inadequate for commuting long distance out of the city, especially during rush hour, and too expensive for most urban poor.

Newman, Dorothy K., and Wachtel, Dawn Day. The American Energy Consumer. The Washington Center for Metropolitan Studies. Ballinger, 1974.

(V,VI)

The Washington Center for Metropolitan Studies (WCMS) conducted a study for the Ford Foundation Energy Policy Project to investigate the relationship between energy use and various socio-economic factors. The study was based on two national surveys and considers not only energy used by families in their homes, but also the energy used directly for private transportation. The household survey examined the relationship between household income and energy use and found that energy expenditures accounted for a higher proportion of the household budget of the poor (15%) than of the affluent (4%).

The two surveys which form the basis for this study were performed in 1973. The first was a national sample of 1,455 households; families answered questions about their dwellings, heating systems, energy-using appliances, and vehicles. These data were correlated with socio-economic status, living and transportation habits. The second survey was directed at electric and gas utility companies serving the sample households. With permission of the surveyed families, WCMS asked the utilities how much electricity and natural gas the households used and how much they had paid for it during the preceding twelve months.

Nickson, J.W., Jr., and Karp, H.B. "Deprivation, Incentives and Mental Illness." The American Journal of Economics and Sociology 33 (April 1974): 113-125.

(XI)

An application of motivator-hygiene theory to motivational patterns and economic variables among the black, working poor. The motivator-hygiene theory hypothesizes that man has two separate and independent needs systems that do not interact. Motivator factors deal with psychological growth--achievement and recognition, etc.--and they provide man with satisfaction. Hygiene factors deal with salary, status, company policy, etc., and they keep man from states of dissatisfaction. It is possible to have job satisfaction (if the proper motivator factors are present) and dissatisfaction (if poor hygiene factors exist) at the same time. In a study of the employment turnover by black, working poor, Nickson and Karp found the lack of motivation to be more important than hygiene factors. They explained that hygiene--salary, status and working conditions--is somewhat constant on the job market of the poor so that it is easier to respond to motivator deprivation. The implications for public policy are significant. Various schemes to provide additional income to the poor (i.e., guaranteed income) will be only partially successful since they do not directly affect the working poor's motivation, the deprivation of which is significant.

Niven, Betty. "Current Issues Explored, A Response to Issue Number II." Journal of Housing (May 1974): 220-222.

(V)

A paper which takes issue with the theory that the "best" basis for allocation of funds for housing is poverty. The first argument is that there can be no single criterion for the allocation of housing resources and secondly, that poverty, while the most critical single factor, is not an absolute but a relative factor. If only one across-the-board number such as the poverty index is used to identify the areas of greatest need, then the extent and nature of housing problems in different places will not be accounted for. The author proposes that an allocation system be developed which would combine the proportion of households which spend 25% of their income on shelter "with the number of units lacking private plumbing, with the number of homeowners with incomes under $4,000--with adjustments to be made based on distribution of existing subsidized housing as a percent of all households with incomes under $5,000."

Nokes, Gregory. "Census Says South's Blacks Do Better Than Northerners." Austin Statesman, 10 May 1973, p. 40.

(V,VI)

This article from the Austin Statesman reports on a Census Bureau study's findings that southern-born Blacks do "better economically in northern cities than northern-born Blacks. Southern-born Blacks in the North are less likely to go on welfare, more likely to hold their jobs, and less likely to engage in criminal behavior than northern-born Blacks." In contrast, southern-born whites do not fare as well economically as white urban natives.

Nygien, Maie. "Rural Housing in the U.S.: Essential Steps Required to Upgrade It." The Quality of Rural Living. Washington, D.C.: 1971.

(V)

Describes inadequacies in rural housing and discusses various government programs established to help families purchase homes or improve their housing conditions. Author observes that progress has been limited in rural housing improvement because of lack of effectiveness of existing programs. Program constraints include insufficient funds, restrictions on loan programs, and inefficient methods of housing production.

Oakland, W.H.; Sparrow, F.T.; and Settler, H.L. "More on Ghetto Multipliers." Journal of Regional Science 13 (1973): 127-128.

(VI)

Several studies have observed higher prices in ghetto retail outlets. This could be accounted for by the relative immobility of ghetto residents. Immobility would force residents to shop within the community creating a high propensity to consume in the ghetto and a low price elasticity of demand. This would predict higher ghetto prices and a high expenditure multiplier. (The multiplier is higher the higher the propensity of ghetto residents to consume within the ghetto--especially if retail outlets are owned by the residents themselves.) On the other hand, Kottis and Kottis argued that, for whatever reason the price differential existed, its presence would encourage residents to shop out of the area causing a low propensity to consume. They maintained that one reason consumers shopped out of the ghetto was that many retailers avoided the ghetto because of low demand caused by low incomes. In a previous study of consumption in Hough, the authors found that the propensity to consume in the ghetto was very low, but in this article they conclude that raising ghetto income would not raise the propensity to consume by attracting more retail outlets. This, they argue, is because ghetto areas are depressed not only because of demand deficiencies, but also because of defects on the supply side of the market. Such areas typically lack the risk capital that is necessary to expand their markets.

Office of Research, Equal Employment Opportunity Commission. Employment Profiles of Minorities and Women in the SMSA's of 17 Large Cities, 1971. Washington, D.C.: U.S. Government Printing Office, 1971.

(X)

Report encompasses employment data concerning minorities and females in the labor forces of 17 selected Standard Metropolitan Statistical Areas (SMSA's) as well as data which dwells on the quality of life of those groups. In every SMSA minorities were underrepresented in the higher paying, more prestigious jobs and overrepresented in the lower paying, menial jobs. Minorities were the "have nots" when selected economic factors were considered. They had the lowest median income, the highest percentage of families receiving incomes below the poverty level, and the greatest percentage of families who were receiving public assistance income Females were found primarily in white-collar jobs. However, most of them were classified as office and clerical workers, with just a comparative few holding upper echelon postitions. The employment patterns presented in the report prove that much needs to be done to eliminate discrimination in our industrial scene.

*Offner, Paul. "Labor Force Participation in the Ghetto." Journal of Human Resources 7 (Fall 1972).

(X)

It is generally recognized that one factor contributing to ghetto employment problems is the poor location of the ghettos relative to job locations. This study, based on 1960 Census tract data for New York City, was an effort to find out how important the location factor is. The major findings are: (1) labor supply is depressed in the ghetto for the prime age groups (about 3 percent for males, 6 percent for females) rather than for teenagers and older people, as might have been expected; (2) after controlling for their demographic, social, and economic characteristics, prime age people in the ghetto have depressed participation rates at least partly as a result of the shortage of jobs there.

(Taken from Journal of Human Resources)

Olsen, Edgar R. "A Normative Theory of Transfers." Public Choice 6 (Spring 1969): 39-58.

(II)

This article provides a new theoretical framework to answer the questions posed by the problem of transfers. Current economic theory does not adequately cover the problem of the optimal distribution of taxes and subsidies for society as a whole. By integrating transfer payments into the ordinary theory of efficient resource allocation, Olsen derives several of the standard results of social welfare theory. At the same time he gives these results the legitimacy of a formal postulate based proof.

*Ornati, Oscar. "Health and Poverty." In Poverty Amid Affluence. New York: The Twentieth Century Fund, 1966.

(XI)

Writer points out a statistical relationship between low income and poor health. Includes data to demonstrate that the poor are especially susceptible to certain diseases stemming from poor housing and/or lack of immunization, are more vulnerable to accidents characteristic of hazardous occupations and are more likely to suffer from mental disability.

Statistical findings indicate an inverse correlation between low-income and non-use of preventive medical care. The author attributes this correlation to the fact that the poor generally fail to identify minor symptoms of disease and have a more limited knowledge of hygiene.

In addition, the author advances the theory that the conditions of poverty (poor nutrition, ignorance, overcrowding) lead to inherent physical weakness and susceptability to disease among the poor themselves. He presents data on infant mortality, diseases of children, physical characteristics of the poor, as well as observations on maternal care in poor families to support this hypothesis.

Reveals inverse relation between mental illness and poverty based on high rate of institutionalization of people from slum areas. Two theories may explain this tendency: the "drift" theory (downward social drift of psychotics) and the residue theory (the inability of the mentally ill to improve their social status).

(Poverty and Health in the United States)

Ornati, Oscar. Poverty Amid Affluence. New York: The Twentieth Century Fund, 1966.

(II,X)

The New School for Social Research poverty study found that today's low-income Americans include disproportionate numbers from certain demographic groups. We are developing a poverty of underdog or pariah classes versus the mass poverty of the Depression. The groups with a great likelihood of being poor are frequently unemployed, underemployed or ill-paid. The most serious aspect of unemployment is the growing amount of structural unemployment resulting from factory mechanization and geographic shifts in industry. The under-endowment in human capital of the contemporary poor--their low levels of skill, education and health--is one of the most important aspects of their poverty. Americans have traditionally considered poverty as an aspect of the employment problem. But being entirely outside the economy, many of the abject poor do not benefit either by the nation's growing productivity nor by unemployment compensation or old age insurance. They must be trained to enable them to join the labor force.

From the pioneering work of Rowntree on downwards, social scientists drawing "poverty lines have set more than one minimum budget. The New School study explicitly recognized this by developing a three-level "band" concept based on some sixty workers' budgets developed over the years. The three cut-offs, called "minimum comfort," "minimum adequacy," and "minimum subsistence" have tended both to rise and widen over time. Workers' budgets reflect both what society thinks men ought to spend and what they do spend, given a particular standard of living.

*Ornati, Oscar. "Poverty in Cities." In Issues in Urban Economics, edited by H.S. Perloff and L. Winco, Jr., 1968.

(V,VI)

Author discusses application of urban poverty statistics to formulation of anti-poverty policies. Discusses use of a "poverty band" concept of a poverty line in defining and measuring poverty for policy purposes. The poverty band concept allows for measurement of internal variation (density and quality of poverty) among the band of poor and adds the dimension of relative intensity of poverty to a numerical counting of the poor.

Explores use of poverty composition and incidence data as they relate to poverty differentials within the poverty band and to intra-city and urban/rural spatial distribution of poverty. According to the author, these differences "relate crucially to the 'causes' of poverty." It is important, therefore, to study them when targetting policy efforts.

Author also discusses usefulness of typologies of economic and social activity (i.e., employment profile, mobility/migration patterns) and of urban development models (such as Community Action Program) to a study of poverty in a spatial context.

Orr, Daniel, and Ramm, Wolphard. "Rawls; Justice and Classical Liberalism: Ethics and Welfare Economics." Economic Inquiry 12 (September 1974): 377-379.

(II)

This article reviews many of Rawls' concepts on the principle of social justice. Starting with a brief overview of his book, The Theory of Justice, the two authors develop a dichotomy between equality and liberty. Rawls contends both variables should be used to determine the effectiveness of social welfare programs. Toward this purpose, Rawls suggests a taxonomy of representative individuals be constructed which ranks liberty enjoyed, opportunity open, income level, power and "other bases of self-respect." Around this taxonomy, social policy should be molded. The drawbacks of this procedure, they contend, are that it uses the income measure as a predictor of an individual's life prospect, that policy action may actually hurt the poor, that it is very ascriptive in nature, and that the group representative must be a typical case chosen in the original position. Orr and Ramm urge those in the economic field, who best understand the programmatic approach to social problems, to clarify the dangers of Rawls' approach.

Orshansky, Mollie. "Benefits and Costs of Children's Allowances." In Children's Allowances and the Economic Welfare of Children, edited by E. M. Burns. New York: Citizen's Committee for Children of New York, Inc., 1968.

(IV)

A presentation of some of the fiscal considerations related to implementation of a children's allowance program. Areas in need of further appraisal include proposals for conditions of payment and income distribution among families. The author discussed estimates of program costs and effectiveness in raising people above the poverty line at differing levels of cost.

Orshansky, Mollie. "Budget for an Elderly Couple: Interim Revision by the Bureau of Labor Statistics." Social Security Bulletin 23 (December 1960): 26-37.

(III,IV)

Article reproduces the summary cost figures and discusses Bureau of Labor Statistics newly revised budget for an elderly couple. Orshansky raises a number of questions about the uses of the elderly couple's budget as a reference for public assistance payments. Whose circumstances does the budget represent? The standard was devised for a retired couple yet only half of all persons aged 65 and over are currently married and living with a spouse, and many of them are not retired. Orshansky also found that the living arrangements for which the budget costs were designed as a measuring rod were characteristic of only a small minority. How can this budget for two be broken down into a budget for one? How can the budget be updated for shifts in consumer values and ideas of what is necessary? For these and numerous other special circumstances, Orshansky suggests that special adjustment factors be devised.

Orshansky, Mollie. "Counting the Poor: Another Look at the Poverty Profile." Social Security Bulletin 28 (1965): 3-29.

(II,IV,VI)

The article describes the Social Security Administration's definition of the poverty line. Food expenditure standards were set using Department of Agriculture food plans, which provide some variety as well as sufficient nutrition. Family size as well as age and sex of members was considered. Different cut-off points were established for farm vs. non-farm families and aged (head over 65) families, for a total of 248 separate income points. Since food consumption has been shown to be roughly a third of poor families' total expenditures, the food budget was tripled to get the total budget. Supposed "economies of scale" to large families turn out merely to reflect lowered dietary standards. Farm families were assumed to need 40% less cash because of home grown food and owned housing.

The effect of switching from the flat Council of Economic Advisers (CEA) cut-off of $3,000 to this definition is to substitude large, non-farm families for rural and aged families while keeping the total number of poor roughly the same. The article goes on the describe the characteristics of the poor in terms of children, age, work and occupation.

Orshansky, Mollie. "Equivalent Levels of Living: Farm and City." Studies in Income and Wealth 15 (1952): 175-200.

(III,V,VI,

Comparing costs of living on farms and in cities presents numerous problems; "... the different nonmoney incomes the two groups receive and the differences in their family situations have made it difficult to know at what points to equate the two income distributions for comparisons of family expenditures and levels of living. It is increasingly apparent that a real answer can come only by recognizing that farm and city families use different kinds of goods and services, and that a comparison can best be made in terms of two sets of items or budgets which, though different in content, are equivalent in satisfaction."

Orshansky explores the use of the income elasticity of purchases to investigate differences in living costs for farm and urban families, a method suggested by BLS studies. Though the method has technical problems, it successfully (1) yields a set of quantities for the farm family for many categories of consumption that can be priced and compared in terms of cost with a corresponding budget for the city family; and (2) indicates the categories of consumption that lend themselves to a comparison of urban-farm levels of living and those where the difference in the family situation make comparisons inappropriate.

The author defines the quantity-income elasticity method, its assumptions and implications, and inherent technical problems in its application. She discusses the farm family clothing budget and an urban food budget taking into account such variables as regional differences, price weights, grouping items, quantity elasticity, and price elasticity.

*Orshansky, Mollie. "How Poverty is Measured." Monthly Labor Review 92 (1969): 37-41.

(II,IV,VI)

The Social Security Administration (SSA) first defined poverty in terms of the policy issue: with how many people and with which ones is policy to be concerned. Currently, two poverty thresholds are defined, corresponding to what the SSA refers to as the poor and the near-poor. These thresholds are set separately for 124 different kinds of families, based on the sex of the household's head, the number of children under 18, the number of adults, and whether the household lives on a farm. The threshold defines the minimum money income that could support an average family of given composition at the lowest level consistent with the standards of living prevailing in the United States. It is based on the amount needed by families of different size and type to purchase a nutritionally adequate diet, assuming that no more than one-third of the family income is used for food. The two thresholds are distinguished by differences in the food plan postulated as providing an adequate diet. The SSA's poverty index has been criticized because it refers only to current income and ignores assets and other money income. It specifies no list of goods and services other than food. However, there are no data on assets or on the income flow of families and how it affects consumption. Questions have also been raised as to why the SSA does not recognize regional or other differences in the poverty line except for farm versus nonfarm families. One reason is the lack of evidence that, at the poverty line or near it, the cost of living varies greatly from one area to another. The two basic problems are how to adjust the poverty line to conform to changes in productivity and how to measure the impact of price change on consumers living at or below the margin.

(Poverty and Human Resources Abstracts)

*Orshansky, Mollie. "Measuring Poverty." In The Social Welfare Forum, 1965. Proceedings of the National Conference on Social Welfare. New York: Columbia University Press, 1965.

(II,IV,VI)

This article points out the shortcomings of the Council of Economic Advisers' original poverty definition, and discusses the refinements made by the Social Security Administration in its poverty index. The article goes on to discuss characteristic family types and sizes among the poor and their relation to poverty and its remedies. The new Social Security Administration index sets poverty thresholds for 124 different types of families according to sex of the head, the total number of adults and children under 18, and whether or not they live on a farm. The Poverty Criteria were computed at two levels, that of the USDA's Low-Cost Food Plan and the more restricted Economy Plan. The Office of Economic Opportunity chose to use the lower of the two.

*Orshansky, Mollie. "Recounting the Poor." Social Security Bulletin 29 (1966): 20-37.

(II-XII)

A study of trends in the numbers of poor people between 1959 and 1964, as defined by the Social Security Administration's poverty index. The poor declined in number over the period and the poverty gap shrank by one quarter. Poverty became even more concentrated among families with aged, young, female or nonwhite heads. The farm population continues as another pocket of poverty, and the number of children and other members of large families living in poverty was increasing.

Orshansky, Mollie. "Who's Who Among the Poor: A Demographic View." Social Security Bulletin 28 (1965): 3-32.

(II,III,IV,VI,VII,X)

The article classifies those designated as "poor" by the SSA index according to race, age, and employment status. This index was derived from USDA low-cost food plans with the cost of such plans tripled to allow for other necessities. Distinctions by sex, family size, age, farm-nonfarm provided different ceilings for families with different needs.

The article goes on to point out the large number of aged and of children among the poor. The absence of significant assets, the large and unstable families and shared households are also characteristic of poverty. Intermittant employment and unemployment were found prevalent. Non-white persons were found poorer than others.

Orshansky, Mollie. "Who Was Poor in 1966?" In Children's Allowances and the Economic Welfare of Children, edited by E.M. Burns. New York: Citizen's Committee for Children of New York, Inc., 1968.

(III, IV, VI)

In 1966 over one-half of poor families consisted of a woman with children, the aged, and the households of the disabled.

This paper compares differential changes in poverty between 1959 and 1966, using the poverty index of the Social Security Administration which defines minimum income per household of specified size, composition, and farm-nonfarm status. The author presents an overview of poverty issues as they relate to geography, the employed, the aged, women, and children of financially disadvantaged parents.

Numerous tables depict relevant aspects of poverty in 1965 and in 1966 and the cost-effectiveness of specified children's allowance programs in 1965.

Ozawa, Martha N. "Family Allowances and a National Minimum of Economic Security." Child Welfare 50 (1971): 313-321.

(II)

"A family allowance program is one proposal for achieving a national minimum of economic well-being. This is an examination of the background, goals and problems of such a program."

Any income maintenance program should aid the satisfaction of these objectives: reduction of the income deficit of the poor; preservation of incentives to work; preservation of dignity; incremental approach; and achievement of positive effects on the poor. Family allowance programs should therefore be paired with the following recommendations toward a coordinated, non-overlapping system for the provision of public assistance: minimum wages should be high enough to support two adults; for the unemployed, social insurance and family assistance should play major parts in income maintenance; income-conditioned pensions should be set up for the blind, aged, and disabled; noncategorical public assistance programs should be established to take care of the residual poor not covered by other programs; and noncontributory, income-conditioned income maintenance programs should include incentives to work.

In 1965, of the 27.4 million non-elderly persons in poverty, 23.3 million were children and adults living in families with children under the age of 18. Family allowances would affect 85% of the non-elderly poor, and 79% of all the poor. However, the major disadvantage of such a program is high cost. Leakages to the non-poor would be higher than those for a negative income tax program, and family allowances are an economically less efficient means of gaining anti-poverty goals than the negative income tax.

Paaswell, R.D., and Reckman, W.W. "Location of the Carless." Transportation Research Record 516. Washington, D.C.: Transportation Research Board, 1974: 11-20.

(V)

This paper identifies the "carless" and shows where they are and what transportation alternatives exist for them. More than 65 percent of the country's population are carless. Data from Buffalo, New York, serve to indicate the relations among carlessness, median income, race, age, and accessibility of public transport. For the study area, the public transport system, which has a development consistent with the traditional pattern of urban growth, no longer adequately serves the needs of those who rely on it most. Examination of the extent of carlessness in the suburbs shows that the problem of mobility among suburban households may be more severe than that in the inner city.

(Author abstract)

Page, S.A.B., and Trollope, Sandra. "An International Survey of Indexing and Its Effects." National Institute Economic Review 70 (November 1974): 46-60.

(II,III)

Price index linking (automatic cost-of-living adjustments) has been introduced to mitigate the uncertainty and redistribution associated with inflation. This article discusses indexation in 21 countries, introduced to varying degrees in three sectors: wages, pensions and other transfer payments, and investment (interest or capital values). The direct effects of index linking are often hard to discern since it is usually implemented simultaneously with other policies. The available information suggests that it has only a minor influence on the inflation rate. Its redistributional effect "seems to have been to improve the return to capital in relation to that of labor." Its application to wages has been most often for automatic interim adjustments in long term contracts. Where labor has been strong enough to force frequent renegotiations (i.e., yearly), indexation has not benefited labor. The authors argue that renegotiation is more efficient in both the capital and labor markets unless inflation is very rapid, so that renegotiation has to be so frequent that its cost outweighs its advantages over indexation. Indexation, they conclude, is most suitable to a situation where there is agreement that "the existing distribution of income should be retained and that market or welfare influences that might tend to change it should be restricted to fixed intervals. Without such agreement, indexation may prevent a redistribution considered desirable and thus necessitate additional government action."

*Palley, Howard A., and Palley, Marian Lief. "Social Policy Analysis: the Use of Social Indicators." Welfare in Review 9 (March-April 1971): 8-13.

(XI)

Article describes the potential use of social indicators and provides a case study using social indicators to examine a social policy. Social indicators can improve public policy-making by giving social problems more visibility and by making possible better evaluation of what public programs are accomplishing. In a case study of social inequities between Negroes and white persons, Palley and Palley used four social indicators--racial differentials in economic opportunities, educational attainment, health services, and level of police protection--to determine whether they might serve as adequate predictors of racial disorders in U.S. cities. The results of this study indicate that these four social indicators alone are not adequate to predict the probability of a disorder in a Negro ghetto. The authors conclude with several suggestions for improving their study.

Palm, David. "The Limitation and Uses of Data on Job Vacancies." Nebraska Journal of Economics and Business (Summer 1974): 49-64.

(X)

An overview of the problems and uses of job vacancy information. After a brief discussion on the inadequacy of employment and unemployment data, Palm explains how the job vacancy measure could be used to identify structural barriers to the labor market, indicate general economic activity, alleviate poverty by providing more job information to low-income people, and aid in developing a comprehensive manpower policy. A job vacancy index of which unoccupied, immediately available and external positions are accounted for, also exhibits some limitations. Palm finds difficulties in finding a measure to represent the universe, developing consistent terminology for occupation classifications and covering all firms. An empirical study showed that at the national level job vacancies are related to turnover but not changes in employment. On the state level the reverse was true.

Palmer, Gladys. Labor Mobility in Six Cities. New York: Social Science Research Council, 1954.

(V,VI,X)

A study of job changes in six United States cities between 1940 and 1949. Women are found to enter and leave the labor force more frequently than men. Younger workers changed jobs most frequently and mobility decreases steadily with age. Migrants to the city hold more jobs over a given time period than long-time residents. Voluntary job shifts, usually for higher wages or position, out-numbered lay-offs and firings, especially in tight labor markets. Those over 45 reported a higher rate of involuntary shifts. A labor force adapts more readily to changes in industrial demand than to changes in occupational structure. Workers skilled in a particular occupation can transfer their skills to new occupations to a limited extent.

Intergenerational mobility is assumed to be a function of son's access to education.

Not all members of the work force are equally mobile: every industry has a stable core of workers surrounded by a more mobile group.

*Parnes, Herbert; Adams, Avril; Andrisani, Paul; Kohen, Andrew; and Nestel, Gilbert. The Pre-Retirement Years: Five Years in the Work Lives of Middle-Aged Men. Columbus, Ohio: Center for Human Resources Research, Ohio State University, December 1974.

(IX)

An examination of the labor market experience and behavior of middle-aged men, based on the National Longitudinal Surveys of 1966, 1967, 1969, and 1971. Topics covered include: a study of mid-career education and its contribution to earnings; middle-aged job changers; extent and causes of occupation mobility; a study of early retirement, and the effect of individual attitudes on performance. Kohen's study of occupational mobility concludes that upward mobility is positively related to human capital (i.e., education and training), personal motivation, marriage and change in firms. Age seems to be a weak deterrent to upward mobility, at least within the age range studied (45-59). Race was not significantly related to mobility. On balance, Kohen finds, contrary to earlier hypothesis, that there is a substantial amount of occupational change among middle-aged men.

Parnes, H.S., and Spitz, R.S. "A Conceptual Framework for Studying Labor Mobility." Monthly Labor Review 92 (1969): 55-58.

(X)

"Conventional labor market theory tends to conceive of labor as a more or less homogenous and fluid factor continuously flowing in the direction of economic advantage." To test this hypothesis, five thousand employed men in each of two age groups (16-24 and 45-59) were asked the questions, "Suppose someone in this area offered you a job in the same line of work you're in now. How much would the new job have to pay for you to be willing to take it?" A similar question was asked concerning a job in a different area. It was found that several factors other than pure economic gain were important in the worker's decisions. These included labor market characteristics such as the number and characteristics of alternate job opportunities and employer hiring specifications; job satisfaction: relevant characteristics of the job; tenure; and characteristics of the worker such as values, abilities, personality characteristics, and knowledge of the labor market. It was concluded that the conventional conception of mobility is "doubtless valid and adequate for many purposes, but it neglects the rich variety of behavior that actually exists in the labor market."

Parr, John. "Outmigration and the Depressed Area Problem." Land Economics 42 (1966): 149-159.

(VI)

Despite the dramatic post-war rise in prosperity levels in the Western countries, many depressed areas, usually in rural regions, have remained. These areas are characterized by high unemployment and underemployment, a narrow range of economic activities, declining basic industries, unskilled or unadaptable labor forces and decayed or inefficient infrastructures. There are two broad approaches to solving these problems. One involves encouraging rural industrial development and the other involves the migration of labor out of high unemployment areas.

This article concentrates on the migration approach. The author concludes that outmigration is often a good policy, particularly when a depressed area is in a country that is experiencing general growth and prosperity, although it cannot solve the problem of general depression. Outmigration can also have negative effects. It could deplete the area of certain types of skilled labor, increase per capita taxation, cause a top heavy age structure and a shortage of capital, and reduce aggregate demand in the area. All of these effects could reduce the demand for labor thus increasing unemployment, leaving the region less able to revive itself.

In terms of policy, Parr concludes that "In those situations where outmigration may be of benefit to depressed areas public agencies can perform a valuable service in selecting, planning and facilitating the movement away from depressed areas."

Parsons, Talcott. "Equality--Inequality in Modern Society, or Social Stratification Revisited." In Social Stratification: Research - Theory for the 1970's, edited by Edward Laumann. New York: Bobbs-Merrill Co., 1970.

(II)

An updating of Parsons' conception of social stratification, with particular attention given to the bases of inequality. Inequality can be justified in terms of its contribution to social functioning. Recently, however, the traditional arguments on the functional need for inequality have been attenuated; hence, a new interest in and commitment to equality has arisen. Parsons then suggests several mechanisms through which the demands of equality and inequality can be balanced.

Pasamanick, Benjamin; Roberts, Dean W.; Lemkau, Paul W.; and Krueger, Dean B. "A Survey of Mental Disease in an Urban Population: Prevalence by Race and Income." In Mental Health of the Poor, edited by Frank Riessman et al. New York: The Free Press of Glencoe, 1964.

(XI)

Presents some results of the study begun in 1952 by "The Commission on Chronic Illness" to examine prevalence of chronic illness and needs for care in an urban setting--in this case, Baltimore. A detailed explanation of survey methodology precedes a discussion of partial findings of the Commission. These show the distribution of mental disorder--limited here to psychosis, psychoneuroses, and psychophysiologic, autonomic, and visceral disorders--in persons classified by sex, impairment severity, age, race, and economic status.

*Passow, A. Harry, ed. Education in Depressed Areas. New York: Teachers College Press, 1963.

(XI)

A collection of 15 essays presented and discussed at a two-week Work Conference on Curriculum and Teaching in Depressed Urban Areas. The essays explore: the unique characteristics and roles of the school in the urban setting and in urban development; the nature of existing and required instructional procedures; the characteristics of personnel and material resources; and other aspects of the problems faced by schools in depressed urban areas. Guides for suggestive solutions are presented, but the practical how-to-do-it-in-a-classroom questions still remain.

Patten, Thomas H., Jr., and Clark, Gerald E., Jr. "Literacy Training and Job Placement of Hard-Core Unemployed Negroes in Detroit." Journal of Human Resources (Winter 1968).

(X)

In 1965 a study was conducted to test the relative effectiveness of the use of the initial teaching alphabet and traditional orthographic approaches to reading among 53 hard-core, functionally illiterate, unemployed persons (largely Negroes) in Detroit. Differences in the appropriateness of the two mediums were found. In the spring of 1966 a follow-up study was conducted to determine the job placement and general social adjustment of the participants. Only six of them had obtained jobs, and many of the remainder were continuing in literacy training programs. The findings of the follow-up study generally corroborate research on extended joblessness conducted in other cities and at different times. The achievement of literacy and job placement remain distant goals for the hard-core unemployed. More empirical research regarding specific programs and the sociocultural barriers to adult learning among urban poor minority group members remains to be done despite the growing number of sophisticated studies of human resources in recent years.

(From the abstract)

Pavlick, Anthony L., and Coltrane, Robert I. Quality of Rural and Urban Housing in the Appalachian Region. Washington, D.C.: United States Department of Agriculture, Economic Research Service, 1964.

(V)

A paper analyzing housing conditions in the Appalachian Region. That the Appalachian Region has suffered depressed conditions for some years is clear. Income data comparisons for one of the depressed years are illustrative. In 1959, per capita income in Appalachia was $1,451, while in the surrounding area per capita income was $1,617 and for the United States was $1,850. Per capita income in the Region was highest in Pennsylvania at $1,715, lowest in Kentucky at $842, and intermediate in the other state areas, according to U.S. Census of Population: 1960. These data support the belief that housing in Appalachia is generally inferior to that in the surrounding area and in the United States generally; and, that within the region housing in some parts is inferior to housing in other parts. Housing condition (sound, deteriorating, and dilapidated) and plumbing facilities were used as evaluation criteria.

Part of the general disparity in Appalachia housing results from the Region's relatively high percentage of rural housing compared to the United States average. Further, in each housing category analyzed--urban, rural nonfarm, and farm--Appalachian housing is of below-average quality.

(Taken from the study)

Peacock, Alan T., ed. Income Redistribution and Social Policy. London: Jonathan Cape, 1954.

(II)

"The main purpose of this set of studies is to investigate the nature and magnitude of the redistribution of income brought about by social policies and to examine some of the likely consequences brought about by this distribution." The concept of redistribution describes a situation in which the state alters the distribution of income in a given community by fiscal and non-fiscal means, among them a minimum wage, price controls, rent controls, and taxation. Redistribution occurs, in fact, whenever the state enters the field of economic regulation or public finance, even if redistribution is not the intended consequence.

The essays which are included cover two areas. The first is the application of economic analysis to the phenomenon of income redistribution through public finance; the second is the measurement of the extent of, and in some cases a consideration of the effects of, income redistribution through social policy in different countries.

Pechman, Joseph A., and Timpane, P. Michael, eds. Work Incentives and Income Guarantees. Washington, D.C.: The Brookings Institution, 1975.

(II)

The results of an experiment in negative income tax involving some 1,300 poor or near poor families are reviewed and analyzed. The principal objective of the experiment was to determine the effects of such a system on the work incentives of recipients. However, information was also sought concerning the effects on lifestyle and consumption patterns. The study was conducted at three urban sites in New Jersey and one in Pennsylvania and was restricted to male-headed families. The experiment ran for three years at each site and examined eight combinations of guarantees and tax rates (guaranteed cash payments of 50 to 125 percent of poverty line and tax rates of 30 to 70 percent of family income). The major finding was that there resulted only a small (5 to 6 percent) reduction in average hours worked by the male heads of families who received payments. The results for working wives, who had a low participation rate to begin with, was greater (one-third to one-half of previous work effort). One of the problems noted was that the background of the New Jersey welfare system changed during the course of the experiment from a situation in which there was no substantial aid to male-headed families to one with rather generous benefits for such families. This increased the attrition rate in the less generous tax-benefit categories and confused the distinction between test groups and control groups. It is suggested that, under the circumstances, the results provide more information about differences between various tax rate-guarantee plans than about the response to any particular rate. There are also problems in distinguishing short-term and long-term effects. It is unlikely that a program of such short duration would be able to display all the early retirement effects and consequences of less inhibition in quitting or changing jobs that a permanent negative tax might entail. It is thought, therefore, that the experiment probably led to an understatement of the labor supply response by male heads of families.

Peitchinis, Stephen G. "Programs in Aid of the Poor." Canadian Welfare 49 (1973): 5-11.

(II,X)

A discussion of governmental aid to four classes of low-income persons: the aged or disabled, mothers with dependent children, the working poor and the unemployed. The first group is aided without question. There is a debate whether female household heads are employable. Social justice bids us help the working poor, especially victims of automation, but what about the worker who chooses leisure over higher income? Retraining as well as cash aid is recommended for the unemployed.

Poverty is defined as "a persistent inadequacy of the goods and services necessary for life," a consumption standard which includes free or subsidized services (e.g., health, housing, education) to which the poor have access, as well as money income.

Pender, David R. Strategic Hamlets in America: An Approach to the Problems of the Urban and Rural Poor. Columbia, South Carolina: Vogue Press, Inc., 1969.

(V,VI,VII)

"Strategic Hamlets in America presents a provocative alternative to the conventional recommendations about what should be done to help the poor in the nation. Rather than assuming that more governmental aid to urban ghettos will somehow trickle down to rehabilitate the poor, Professor Pender breaks fresh ground by documenting that the cities, as centers of urban culture, are not conducive toward meeting the special needs of the poor. The new approach developed in this essay recommends that many of the poor would be in a better position to break the poverty cycle if they were able to create their own Implanted Communities outside of existing urban complexes with a sufficient industrial and agricultural base to make these communities in large part self-sufficient. The author recognizes that his alternative is not a panacea for all of those who find themselves chained by poverty, but the idea of the Strategic Hamlet offers a chance to those who have recently migrated to the city from a rural background. The essay not only builds a case to support the creation of the Implanted Communities, but also outlines a plan for implementing their establishment."

(Taken from the essay)

Pennock, Jean L., and Armstrong, Helen. "Income and Consumption as Measures of Economic Status." Family Economics Review (June 1966).

(VII)

An analysis of the income and expenditure patterns of North Central farmers in 1960-61 showed that many of the families with incomes of less than $2000 consumed more than that amount. 17% of the families had incomes of less than $2000, but only 9% had consumption of less than that amount. 58% of those whose income (including the imputed value of home grown food) fell below $2000 consumed more than that amount. Thus consumption was felt to be a better measure of economic well-being since income frequently measured temporary effects. If consumption rather than income is used, a greater percentage of single individuals would fall into the less than $2000 category and a much smaller percentage of 2 or more person families. Very few three or more person families consumed less than $2000, according to the Census expenditure survey figures used.

Perlman, Robert. Consumers and Social Services. Wiley & Sons, 1975.

(V)

Assesses effectiveness of social service delivery and discusses interface between service user and provider. Views the service user as a consumer rather than as a client. Explores orientation consumers bring to their use of the social services and measures degree of provider success in fulfilling consumer expectations.

Outlines effectiveness of the Roxbury Multi-Service Center to illustrate the dynamics of social service delivery in an urban area. Measures accessibility, comprehensiveness, and degree of coordination of that program.

Phelps, E.S. "Anticipated Inflation and Economic Welfare." *Journal of Political Economy* 73(February 1965): 1-17.

(III)

This article presents a discussion of the welfare effect of anticipated inflation. It had been previously argued that an anticipated inflation would unambiguously hurt economic welfare by forcing people to hold real assets when they would normally prefer to hold liquid assets -- money. Later Robert Mundell argued that the welfare effect of an anticipated inflation was *not* unambiguously bad. While the increase in liquidity preference will cause the nominal rate of interest to rise, it will not rise as much as the cost-of-living (inflation). The real rate of interest will therefore drop. The welfare effect would depend on the desirability of the changes in investment and growth induced by the change in the real rate of interest. In this article, Phelps argues that unconstrained government policy can counteract both the liquidity preference and interest rate effects of inflation. The government can use monetary policy to bring about an inflation with high savings and a low real rate of interest or fiscal policy to bring about an inflation with low savings and a high real rate of interest. If the government can pay interest on money holdings it can prevent the drop in liquidity preference normally associated with inflation. If the government is constrained in its implementation of monetary policy, attaining the optimum level of economic welfare may *require* a rising or a falling price trend brought about by fiscal policy.

Philips, Louis. "A Dynamic Version of the Linear Expenditure Model." *The Review of Economics and Statistics* 54 (1972): 450-458.

(VII)

Philips extends the linear expenditure system of Samuelson and Geary by basing estimates of the "minimum quantities required" term on past consumption data. Habit formation, stock adjustment and depreciation were also taken into account. The restrictive assumption that utilities are independent and additive remains. The Geary utility function is $u = E_i B_i \log (q_i - j_i)$ $(i = 1, z \ldots n)$ where the q's are quantity flows and the B's and j's are parameters such that $0 < B_i < 1$ and $E_i B_i = 1$, the function being defined only for $(q_1 - j_i) > 0$. The j_i's are interpreted as "minimum required quantities which the consumer purchases "without regard to prices."

Phillips, D.F. "Reaching Out to Rural Communities." <u>Hospitals</u> 46 (June 1, 1972): 53-57.

(V)

Outlines need for greater commitment to providing health services in rural areas. Explores hospital's role in providing extended services to rural communities through outreach programs and linkages with other community agencies. Calls for increased involvement of university medical schools in rural health care and for wider use of paramedical personnel. Discusses viability of health maintenance organizations in a rural setting.

Pigou, A.C. <u>The Economics of Welfare</u>. London: MacMillan and Co., Ltd., 1920.

(II)

A comprehensive classic work in economics. Pigou says (in Chapters Seven and Eight) that any redistribution of income towards the poor, unless it reduces national income, is advantageous and will result in an increase in economic welfare. In making this argument, Pigou depends on the then-popular model in which marginal utilities declined with income, and all individuals had similar tastes. The latter assumption is defended by the argument that tastes are largely endogenous: "in the long run differences in temperament and taste between rich and poor are overcome by the very fact of a shifting of income between them." Pigou also takes issue with the Malthusian notion that gains from redistribution will be neutralized by population growth among the poor.

Podoluk, Jenny R. "Some Comparisons of the Canadian--U.S. Income Distributions." <u>Review of Income and Wealth</u> 16 (1970): 279-302.

(II)

"This paper compares the income distribution of Canada and the United States as well as other characteristics of the population such as the labour force and income trends in the two countries in the post-war years. In both countries family income distributions show similar degrees of inequality and similar movements in real incomes through time. However, an examination of Canadian data suggests that differences do exist in underlying patterns. For example, there are greater earnings differentials between skilled and unskilled workers in Canada than in the United States while on the other hand in the United States greater differences exist between family incomes with heads in different age groups than is the case in Canada.'

(Taken from article)

Pollack, Robert, and Wales, Terence J. "Estimation of the Linear Expenditure System." Econometrica 37(1969): 611-628.

(III)

The authors estimate coefficients for Stone's linear expenditure system. Demand for each good is a function of the price vector and total income, and each of these functions is homogeneous of degree zero. The implied Slutsky substitution matrix is symmetric and negative semidefinite. The implicit assumption of independence among the goods is made relatively plausible here by the fact that only very broad categories of expenditure -- goods, clothing, shelter and miscellaneous -- are considered. Good correlations are obtained.

Poverty Amid Plenty: The American Paradox. Report of the President's Commission on Income Maintenance Programs. Washington, D.C.: U.S. Government Printing Office, 1969.

(II,V)

General description of poverty and composition of the poor in the United states--location, mobility, numbers, etc. Current anti-poverty programs are inadequate because: (1) they provide no support for the employed poor; (2) intra-state variations have potential for arbitrariness and discrimination; (3) unemployment insurance payments are below poverty line for families in most states; (4) eligibility requirements for AFDC and Old Age Assistance are restrictive; and (5) social security insurance benefits are earnings-related. Two basic problems of the Social Security Administration poverty index are that it is basically a food budget multiplied by three (to reflect the assumption that food represents one-third of a low-income family's expenses), and that many necessary items are not budgeted. A federally-financed universal supplemental income program is recommended, to make cash payments to all members of the population with income needs. Other alternatives are examined in some detail.

Powell, Alan H.; Hoa, Tran Van; and Wilson, R.H. "A Multi-Sectional Analysis of Consumer Demand in the Post-War Period." The Southern Economic Journal 35(1968): 109-120.

(III)

An empirical estimate of consumer demand functions for broad classes of goods based on the hypothesis of separability of utility functions. As a first approximation, it is plausible to assume that marginal rates of substitution between any two commodities are independent of the consumption levels of all other commodities, at least when "commodities" are such broad categories as "food" or "housing". The results obtained were only nominally significant.

Powell, Douglas H., and Driscoll, Paul F. "Middle-Class Professionals Face Unemployment." Transaction: Social Sciences and Modern Society 10 (January/February 1973): 18-26.

(VIII,XI)

"Clinical" study, based on open-ended interviews, to determine the attitudinal reaction of middle-class professionals to prolonged unemployment. Respondents consisted of laid-off scientists and engineers in Massachusetts. A series of 30 group discussions was conducted with 25 men, and individual interviews with 50 more. Mean age of the sample was 41, education 16 years, length of unemployment 9.5 months.

The difficulties and responses of the men were similar, and tended to pass through 4 distinct stages:

(1) Relaxation & Relief from the anxiety of job insecurity. Most treated the initial period as a vacation and felt more "between jobs" than "out of work". Optimism was high (about one month)

(2) Concerted Effort, usually systematic and well-organized, to find work. Optimism still high, even after several rejections; support and assistance from friends mutually reinforcing with person's own active efforts. (about three months)

(3) Vacillation and Doubt after above efforts fail. Job-seeking becomes sporadic, anxiety and identity problems increase. Anger, depression and panic ensue; personal relations become strained. (one and one-half months)

(4) Malaise and Cynicism grow, and efforts to find a job cease (except in ways designed to protect self-esteem, such as answering blind ads). Become generally inactive--"just sitting around the house," sense of powerlessness, pessimism and cynicism. Tend to resist apparent opportunities for fear of failure--become "present-oriented."

The authors note the similarity of Stage 4 attitudes to those often considered typical of poor and minority workers, who deal with unemployment more frequently.

*Prais, S. J. "The Estimation of Equivalent Adult Scales From Family Budgets." Economic Journal 63 (1953): 791-810.

(III,IV)

A method is devised to determine the effects on household consumption patterns resulting from the addition to the household of a person in a particular age-sex group. One approach to this problem in the past has been to compare Engel curves of different size households for some standard commodity and calculate the amount of income it would be necessary to give to the smaller household in order to raise its consumption of the standard commodity to the level of the larger household. This method bases the whole estimate on behavior related to only a single commodity and has no provision to account for the varied consumption patterns of different types of individuals. On the other hand, studies which simply take the regression of consumption on different types of persons ignore the effect of income level and can be expected to provide accurate results only if the elasticity of income of a commodity is zero. The present article proposes to avoid these difficulties by constructing an explicit consumption function in which expenditure for a given commodity is per person with different age-sex type individuals having different scaling coefficients. The income variable is also per weighted individual; but the different age-sex scale coefficients in this case are the same for all commodities, since the variable is a measure of living standard, and the scaling factors here are really an average, over all commodities, of the expenditure scales. Data from a 1937-1938 British working class survey was used in an iterative procedure to estimate the value of these coefficients for eight age-sex types with respect to seven categories of foodstuffs. The results indicate, for example, that the proportion of food consumption to be attributed to females is about 15% less than that attributed to males. The effect of the addition of an extra person depends specifically on the appropriate individual scale factors and commodity income elasticity.

*Prais, S., and Houthakker, H. The Analysis of Family Budgets. Cambridge: Cambridge University Press, 1971.

(IV,VII)

An in-depth look at the analysis of consumer behavior. Prais and Houthakker concentrate on such aspects of consumer behavior as the relationship between expenditure on individual commodities and total income, quality variation in the consumption pattern, household composition and unit consumer scales, economies of scale in consumption and social, occupational and regional factors in expenditure patterns. The two authors develop a single model of family budget inquiry, which relates expenditure per effective unit--consumer on various commodities to the standard of living of the household as measured by the level of income per effective unit consumer. The advantages to this equation include the ability to draw distinction between luxuries and necessities in terms of change in expenditure on the commodity consequent upon an increase in household composition and economies of scale from their income effects. Prais finds that no function has been discovered that is uniformly suitable for all commodities, but improvement on the linear function used by Allen and Bowley is possible.

The President's Commission on Income Maintenance Programs. Background Papers. Washington D.C.: U.S. Government Printing Office, 1970.

(VII)

These papers examine the need for income maintenance programs and analyze the effectiveness of existing welfare programs. As a society advances economically, poverty becomes increasingly defined in relative terms. Income is the basic measure of poverty, but differences in wealth, by providing security for freedom of action, may also actually improve the efficiency with which a consumer can deal in the marketplace. An income-net worth poverty definition would exclude many aged households whose assets are in illiquid real estate, unavailable as a reserve for living expenses. The distribution of benefits from public services should also be measured. Measures of social rank and political power have also been suggested. The administrative poverty line should be used to define the target population, not to evaluate welfare. It is not true that crossing the poverty line is a better move than, say, moving from 45% to 40% below it. A poverty line may be set by estimating total needs or estimating food needs only and multiplying by a factor based on the proportion spent on food. A poverty line may also be set at some fixed proportion on the income scale, or as less than some proportion of the median income. Education and training programs are based on the assumption that lack of economic opportunity, not undesirable behavior, is the cause of poverty. A poverty line should include an allowance for social participation and should leave the family free to choose its consumption pattern.

*Projector, Dorothy. Survey of Changes in Family Finances. Washington: Federal Reserve Technical Papers, 1968.

(VII)

This study investigates the relationship of saving to age, using survey data from 1963 and 1964 to test the saving/consumption theories of Modigliani, Thore, Crockett and Watts, among others. Savings increase with age to a peak after middle age when dependents are few but income is still high. After retirement, capital is often drawn down. The Modigliani-Brumberg life-cycle hypothesis--that the function of saving is to smooth out consumption over one's lifetime--is not confirmed by the data, although in later life as uncertainties diminish, some redistribution of resources is observed. Data on the relationship of wealth to consumption are erratic.

The importance of homes and automobiles in the composition of assets declines after age 54 in favor of investment assets.

*Projector, Dorothy S., and Weiss, Gertrude S. "Income-Net Worth Measures of Economic Welfare." Social Security Bulletin 32(1969): 14-17.

(VII)

Studies of the economic position of consumers have combined net worth with income by converting a family's wealth into a life annuity and adding this to current income from sources other than net worth. This article questions the usefulness of such a procedure either as a tax basis or an index of need. Consider two families, identical except that one saves while the other does not. Both pay the same income taxes, but under a wealth tax system the thrifty one pays more. A better system would tax income from all sources: e.g., capital gains and implicit rents as well as money income. When assets are used as a criterion for public assistance, those who risk having to go on welfare have no incentive to save: such savings serve only to delay the start of welfare payments.

The annuity method finds a sixty-year-old with a $10,000 net worth to be substantially better off than a forty-year-old with equal net worth. Yet the sixty-year-old's earning power has peaked while the forty-year-old's wealth can be expected to increase.

*Projector, Dorothy S., and Weiss, Gertrude S. Survey of Financial Characteristics of Consumers. Washington: Federal Reserve Technical Paper, 1966.

(VII)

A survey of the size, distribution, and composition of wealth in the United States, with emphasis on the holdings of the wealthy. Savings rather than inheritance was the major source of wealth for most individuals. Both wealth and current saving vary positively with current income. Liquid assets, homes and automobiles are widely held while holdings of financial assets are highly concentrated in the upper income/wealth groups.

Of those falling below the Social Security Administration's economy level poverty line, 28% reported no assets while 2% had a negative net worth. Another 21% had some wealth but less than $10,000, and 12% had between $10,000 and $12,000 in assets. Only 6% had more than $25,000 in assets. The aged poor had more wealth on average than younger heads of poor families. Only 7% of the poor had sufficient home equities that the addition of a 4% implicit return would raise them above the poverty line. When net liquid and investment assets are considered as being used up over five years to supplement income in addition to home equity, 9% of families and 19% of individuals are raised above the poverty line.

*Projector, Dorothy; Weiss, Gertrude; and Thorenson, Erling. "Composition of Income as Shown by the Survey of Financial Characteristics of Consumers." In Six Papers on the Size Distribution of Wealth and Income, edited by Lee Soltow. New York: National Bureau of Economic Research, 1969.

(VII)

Data from the Survey of Financial Characteristics of Consumers (1963) is used to analyze the composition of income in the aggregate, by income level, age, family size, employment status, and education of family head. Wages are the major component of income, providing 75% of total income for the population as a whole. The share of wages in total income is highest for the young and those with low-income. Business income contributes 12% to total income for the population as a whole; with its share increasing with age and income. The share of property income also increases with age and income. Pensions, which contribute only 5% to total income for the population as a whole, represent 30% of the income of the population over age 65.

Pryor, Frederick L. "Simulation of the Impact of Social and Economic Institutions on the Size Distribution of Income and Wealth." American Economic Review 63 (1973): 50-72.

(II,IX)

A computer simulation is used to explore the equilibrium distributions of income and wealth that result from various patterns of intergenerational grants. Rules of inheritance (primogeniture, equal division), rules of mate selection (equal choice or choice weighted by proximity on an income scale), differential fertility rates of income classes, and different methods of governmental redistribution are some of the socioeconomic parameters investigated in terms of their consequences for distribution. Most of the combinations used were found to converge to a stable distribution in less than thirty generations, often much less depending, among other things, on the initial configuration of wealth. The simulation is made more comprehensive when income is specified by means of a random variable representing differential abilities and when the amount of wealth transferred from one generation to the next is considered as a linear or non-linear function of income. As an example, it is found that if intergenerational wealth transfer is a linear function of income, then the trend toward equal distribution occurs more rapidly than with the more realistic assumption that, below some income level, no wealth will be transferred at all. In the latter case, only high income individuals would transfer wealth to their children. The specification of this transfer function affects not only the speed of convergence to some equilibrium configuration but also the resulting inequality (as measured by Gini coefficients). A general conclusion is that past analysis of income and wealth distribution has left unspecified too many critical variables that determine intergenerational transfers.

Rabianski, Joseph. "Real Earnings and Human Migration." Journal of Human Resources 6 (Spring 1971).

(VI)

The theory of human migration based on the concept of individual costs and returns from relocation has succeeded in identifying the more important factors affecting an individual's decision to move. However, while the theoretical models indicate the importance of a real earnings variable, empirical models have only considered some form of a nominal earnings variable. This article, then, outlines the analytical framework of a costs and returns approach to migration, utilizes a real earnings concept as an integral part of such a theory, subjects the resulting model to empirical test by means of regression analysis, and compares the real wage model with a nominal wage mode. To accomplish this and conform as closely as possible to the theory, it was necessary to develop a method for deriving an interregional nominal earnings deflator from existing data to obtain real wages.

(Taken from Journal of Human Resources)

Rainwater, Lee. "Poverty, Living Standards and Family Well-Being." Studies in Public Welfare. U.S. Joint Economic Committee, Paper No. 12, Part II, 1973.

(XI)

Contends that low-relative incomes produce the culture of poverty. The paper specifically addresses the argument that poor economic situation is a major factor in causing family instability and disruption.

Policy implications of this argument call for programs that change the distribution of income to equalize personal well-being. Specific suggestions include a tax-credit form of guaranteed income and a guaranteed employment strategy.

* Rainwater, Lee. "The Problem of Lower-Class Culture and Poverty-War Strategy." In On Understanding Poverty, edited by Daniel P. Moynihan. New York: Basic Books, Inc., 1968.

(II,XI)

An examination of lower class attitudes towards sex, marriage, children, and family using data from the Pruitt-Igoe housing project as an example. A discussion of a "lower class sub-culture," as a social heredity, leads to the conclusion that it is a valid precept based on a distinctive pattern of existential and evaluative elements shared by a particular group. Rainwater proceeds to a review of policy implications which emphasize opportunity within the existing system to change the shape of the distribution of families by income; that is, income or resource equalization.

Rainwater, Lee. What Money Buys: Inequality and the Social Meanings of Income. New York: Basic Books, 1974.

(II, IX, XI)

A comprehensive integration of existing data and research conducted by the author on the topic of the social and psychological implications of the possession or lack of financial resources. The author utilizes a wide range of public opinion studies including a survey of 600 families in the Boston metropolitan area in order to determine the role of money in achievement of individuals' and society's assessment of self-worth.

The author states that poverty is a "specification of larger issues in the social psychology of materialism" and elaborates upon this by saying that:

> "Poverty can arise only in a materialistic society--defining the latter as one in which members achieve and act out membership in their society and its institutions through the use of objects and services that they pay for...a society in which goods and services are essential to achieving and acting out membership and in which these goods and services are not in such sufficient supply that one can have them simply for the asking...
>
> "In order to better understand the meanings of inequality we must learn to chart the connections between the individual's sense of place and purpose...and his access to, and command over, the resources represented by goods and services provided through private and public markets."

Rainwater stresses his belief that poverty defined in an economic sense, i.e., unavailability of resources, has implications which deeply affect self-worth, attitudes and behavior, and concludes that solution of many social problems cannot occur until individuals have adequate resources:

> "The vital connection between deviance--particularly destructive forms of deviance that affect other people in more than a symbolic way--and a poverty of resources to achieve validation in the mainstream of society, emphasize the fact that reducing the prevalence of such deviance can come about only through changes that in fact provide the necessary resources to young persons as they grow up and achieve adulthood."

Rainwater stresses the importance of having a job--and the sense of security about future income that a job provides--as being critical to an individual's sense of well-being, given the values of contemporary America.

The remainder of the book contains a detailed discussion of the interaction between the economic and social psychological definitions of poverty by reviewing empirical evidence on such topics as the changing societal images of a "minimum standard of living" and the reasons for such changes, differing images of what it means to be "rich" as well as "poor," of the relationship of status and income, of an equitable distribution of resources in our society, and the public conceptions of current public policies in the fields of poverty and welfare.

Rainwater's basic conclusion is consistent with that expressed in several of his previous works, namely that "poverty policies must be addressed to changing the income distribution in such a way that the relative gap between the mainstream and the bottom becomes smaller and smaller."

Rawls, John. <u>A Theory of Justice</u>. Cambridge, Massachusetts: Harvard University Press, 1971.

(II)

A philosophical treatise in which fundamental laws of justice are expounded. Rawls develops principles of justice and equality which free and rational people would accept in an initial position of equality. In this hypothetical situation, the state of nature in social contract theory, no one is aware of his position in the hierarchy, either in terms of assets or personal attributes. Rules of justice are those which would be selected in this hypothetical case.

Part 1 sets forth Rawls' theory of justice, as well as his criticisms of alternative theories, particularly utilitarianism. In Part 2, Rawls applies his theory to the institutions of society. Finally, the theory is connected to a doctrine of morality.

Raynaud, Edgar. "The Time Concept in the Evaluation of Rural Under-Employment and Leisure Time Activities." <u>Social Science Information</u> 8 (June 1969): 59-86.

(VIII)

Underemployment in developing nations has often been equated with attitudes on leisure. This correlation has been considered as both a cultural and economic function of the society living in that country. Raynaud explores this relationship as it relates to the goals of furthering development. The analysis of recent studies made on underemployment and leisure is the method used by Raynaud. Initial findings indicate that future surveys must objectively look at both work and leisure time behavior and that any attempt to assess values and attitudes should be done with a "subjective appreciation." Another major conclusion Raynaud derives from his examination of the academic studies on developing countries is that, as a country becomes more industrialized, the dichotomy between work and leisure becomes clearer. That is, in pre-industrial societies the social cleavage between means of production and the mass of workers is not dominant; whereas in industrial societies this cleavage is more profound, resulting in the exclusion of workers from investment decision-making and the confinement of workers to work and play within their own circles.

Rea, S.A. "Incentive Effects of Alternative Negative Income Tax Plans." Journal of Public Economics 3 (August 1974): 237-249.

(II)

Labor supply functions are estimated for those age 25 and over from the March 1967 U.S. Current Population Survey. The supply response to seven different negative income tax plans is simulated, with particular attention paid to those initially earning more than the breakeven income. A $2,400 guarantee for a family of four is estimated to reduce the recipients' hours supplied by 12 percent. If the tax rate increases to 67 percent, the hours reduction rises to 17 percent. Research is done at the Institute for the Quantitative Analysis of Social and Economic Policy, Toronto.

(Author abstract)

Reckord, Gordon E. "The Geography of Poverty in the United States." In Problems and Trends in American Geography, edited by Saul B. Cohen. New York: Basic Books, Inc., 1967.

(II,V,VI)

"The purpose of this brief exploration of the geography of poverty in America is to highlight the nature of its distribution, or maldistribution, to explore the causes of that distribution in interrelationship with other phenomena, and to indicate what steps are being taken to eliminate poverty where it exists." Reckford considers specific poverty groups: migrant workers; the urban poor; and the dispersed non-urban poor, which are further declassified by size and location and by characteristics relating to physical geographical similarities and causes not directly associated with resource availability.

The author explains the geographer's categorization of welfare programs: there are those which attempt to modify the environment in order to improve regional efficiency, and those which aim to improve individual efficiency of group members within a regional context. The Appalachian Regional Development Act of 1964 is among those programs mentioned which are designed to modify the infrastructure of regions, while many other plans attempt to help the disadvantaged whose poverty is unrelated to their natural environment.

Reeb, Donald J., and Kirk, James T., Jr., eds. Housing the Poor. New York: Praeger Publishers, 1973.

(V)

A compendium of sixteen articles related to housing the poor. "The Housing Needs of the Poor: A Reinterpretation," by Irving Silver and Lawrence Smith, discusses whether a "housing solution" independent of an income solution is either possible or preferred. An important segment of their conclusion is that although the number of substandard dwellings is a reasonable approximation for the extent of the housing aspect of the poverty problem, it is not a definitive measure. The basis for this conclusion is that there is not a one-to-one correlation between the number of persons requiring housing assistance and the number of persons occupying substandard housing.

James R. Prescott in "The Regional Allocation of Public Housing Expenditure" measures the performance of the public housing program. These measures are derived and related to estimates of direct benefits provided by public housing. One of the principal conclusions is that given budgetary constraints, it is likely that "the reliance on decentralized responsibility for project initiation results in excessive expenditures in the larger urban communities and the northeastern states of the nation."

Reed, Ray. "Displaced Farm Workers Lose Industrial Jobs in Rural South." New York Times, 22 January 1975.

(VI,X)

The industrial push of the late 1960's brought many factories to southern rural communities. "These plants were mainly light industry--electronics assembly, small motors, watches and clocks, garment sewing rooms"--and they were brought in to provide jobs for thousands of displaced agricultural workers. In 1975, these plants have been hard hit by the recession. The Bureau of Labor Statistics estimates that 168,000 manufacturing jobs were lost in eight southeastern states between November 1963 and November 1974. In addition, many southerners who had migrated to northern cities are returning because of unemployment in the North. They not only find that there are no jobs in their hometowns, but that they can no longer go back to the land.

Rees, John. Equality. New York: Praeger Publishers, 1971.

(II)

A study of political and economic equality, in which historical conceptions of the definition and role of equality are surveyed and criticized. Two principles of equality can be distinguished: "absolute" equality which requires that all people be treated in the same way in all respects; and "conditional equality" which requires equal treatment unless reason exists for discrimination. Absolute equality violates ordinary notions of justice, and is overly rigid. Conditional equality, first proposed by Aristotle, is preferred, despite the difficulties associated with determining the factors which constitute reasonable bases for discrimination.

Reid, Margaret. "Distribution of Non-Money Income." In Studies on Income and Wealth 13 (1951): 124-185.

(VII)

A thorough discussion of non-money income and how it is measured. Non-money income is composed of many things: earnings in kind, home produced goods, home produced services, the services produced by durable goods, gifts, private relief in kind, public relief in kind, and public goods. Many of these are not considered in surveys measuring the size of this form of income. These surveys do show that non-money income is concentrated among farm families and more evenly distributed than normal income.

The choice of economic unit, the method of computing the imputed value, the price chosen as the market equivalent, and the choice of costs associated with the good's net value, will all have an impact on the size of imputed value. The conclusion of the discussion was that, in general, it is not a good idea to lump money and non-money income together because the two are, in very fundamental ways, different things.

Reid, Margaret W. "The Effect of Income Concept upon Expenditure Curves of Poor Families." Studies in Income and Wealth 15 (1952).

(VII)

Income is a particularly bad proxy for welfare among farm families, who tend to have variable incomes. Consumption had a larger correlation with the number of cows on the farm than it did with general net income in one study of Wisconsin farm families. A number of problems peculiar to estimating the income of farmers and methods to deal with these problems are discussed. Problems include the distinction between current expenses and capital outlays, changes in farm inventions, and dynamic incomes. Consumption was found to be a poor substitute for income because the occasional purchase of consumer durables makes it randomly variable and because it will show a spendthrift family to be better off than a miserly one even if everything except tastes are the same. This last objection also holds for the use of net worth as a measure of welfare. The separation of permanent and transitory components of income through the use of correlation analysis is also suggested in the paper.

*Reid, Margaret. Statement Before the Subcommittee on the War on Poverty Program of the Committee on Education and Labor, House of Representatives, Eighty-eighth Congress, Second Session. Washington: U.S. Government Printing Office, 1964.

(VII)

Reid criticizes both the provisions of the Economic Opportunity Act and the Council of Economic Advisors' definition of poverty. Manpower training, the main thrust of the bill, will do little to aid the abject poor who need welfare payments and casework. Any definition of poverty based on a single year's money income will not capture a family's level of living, for many poor families spend more than they earn. Thus, the Council's estimates of the extent of poverty are inflated by the number of those suffering temporary reductions of income but who are in fact maintaining their previous levels of consumption.

Reid, Roy. "Rural Areas' Population Gains Now Outgrowing Urban Regions." New York Times, 18 May 1975, p. 1.

(VI)

Census Bureau surveys since 1970 suggest that nonmetropolitan areas are now growing faster than metropolitan areas. This trend is accounted for by several factors including decentralization of manufacturing, earlier retirement, development of rural recreation areas, the growth of colleges and universities in nonmetropolitan areas, the levelling off of farm population loss, the environmental movement, long distance commuting facilitated by improved transportation, and the antimaterialistic, antisuburban "youth revolution." Despite the dramatic reversal of the rural-urban migratory trends, demographers are reluctant to conclude that the reversal is indicative of a long-term trend. Higher transportation costs will undoubtedly slow down or reverse the urban-rural migration. The industrial development implications of the trend are ambiguous. Industry attracted to rural areas has been characterized by low wages and stagnation. In fact, the rate of industrial decentralization has slowed down since before 1970.

*Rein, Martin. "Problems in the Definition and Measurement of Poverty." In Poverty in America, edited by Louis A. Ferman, Joyce L. Kornbluh, and Alan Haber. Ann Arbor: University of Michigan Press, 1965.

(II)

A detailed discussion of the problems inherent in a definition and measurement of poverty that is based on the costs of subsistence. Some attempt is made to place the analysis in an historical context, although no systematic historical review is attempted. Rein tries to demonstrate that the subsistence level definition of poverty is circular, arbitrary, and relative. Since it must be based on actual levels and patterns of living as well as nutritional requirements, a subsistence definition requires that we know in advance the relevant income group which distinguished the poor from the non-poor. Numerous procedures in the subsistence level definition are challenged. Other definitions of poverty related to inequality (income distribution) and externality (social consequences of poverty) are examined.

Reiner, Janet S. "Typologies of Poverty Populations." In The Meaning and Measurement of Poverty, edited by Morton Baratz and William Grigsby. Pennsylvania: Institute for Environmental Studies, University of Pennsylvania, 1968.

(II,XI)

A survey article of alternative definitions of poverty. Reiner distinguishes between two types of poverty definitions: social class oriented definitions and cultural definitions. Poverty definitions are classed as social class oriented if they focus on the objective attributes of an individual's economic position as measures of poverty. The cultural approach, on the other hand, identifies the poor by referring to their values--including life styles and attitudes--rather than their attributes. Reiner notes that while the cultural definitions offer a richer picture of poverty, they are somewhat more difficult to use for measurement purposes than the social class definition.

Reinhardt, Paul G. "Economies of Scale in Consumption." Rivista Internazionale di Scienze Economiche e Commerciali 21 (May 1974).

(IV)

Quantity discounts (reductions in the unit price of a good as the purchase size increases) are examined, particularly in the case of goods such as groceries which have a relatively large packaging overhead. If the packaging cost is essentially constant for the manufacturer regardless of package size, then, under the assumption of fixed unit prices, the large package buyer subsidizes the small package buyer. If packaging overhead is simply added to the price of the contents, then there is an effective quantity discount. A production model patterned after Becker is developed; and it is shown that a household which maximizes output, under the condition of quantity discounts, will consume in a manner that uses resources more efficiently than the constant unit price situation. Though manufacturers might be indifferent to these two pricing alternatives since they are compensated in either case, it is suggested that market pressures from those households which gain from quantity discounts would force the issue. Manufacturers not offering quantity discounts would lose their large quantity buyers and would be forced to raise prices since they would have no buyers to subsidize the fixed unit prices they offered to small quantity consumers. Data collected by the Chicago Consumer Panel on the prices paid for grocery items by high and low income families divided into groups of small, medium, and large purchasers are presented to show that this prediction is borne out. "Quantity discounts allocate most efficiently among consumers the vast resources society decides to channel into packaging. Judged in terms of the wastes that would be created if fixed unit prices prevented this allocation, quantity discounts are seen to perform a substantial allocative role in our society."

Reynolds, Lloyd George. The Structure of Labor Markets: Wages and Labor Mobility in Theory and Practice. Westport, Connecticut: Greenwood Press, 1951.

(VI,X)

The first seven chapters of this book consist of a detailed case study of labor mobility and wages in a medium-sized New England town. The study was restricted to manual workers and it involved interviewing workers, managers, personnel directors, and others. Workers were found to exhibit a pattern of mobility consistent with the hypothesis that they stayed in the same firm, occasionally shifting jobs, as long as the conditions in their job remained above some minimum level. Should conditions not remain above that level, the worker would quit and search for jobs in the same locality, relying primarily on word-of-mouth and friends. He would accept the first open job he came across that seemed to meet his minimum conditions and test it out for a few months. Should it turn out to be unacceptable he would quit and resume searching. Otherwise, he would stay. Included in the book are detailed examinations of the characteristics of labor demand and labor recruitment, worker attitudes, and interindustry and interoccupational shifts by workers. The determinants of plant wage levels were also examined in great detail.

Ribich, Thomas I. Education and Poverty. Brookings Institution, 1968.

(IX,XI)

A cost-benefit analysis of investment in education as an anti-poverty weapon. The author holds that there is a natural tendency toward under-investment in education due to existing capital market barriers. These forces apply a fortiori to the poor. Some degree of government subsidization is necessary to compensate for these inhibiting factors. Subsidization policy should be based on favorable cost-benefit ratios.

Explores payoff justifications for anti-poverty programs in the area of education such as compensatory education, job retraining and drop-out prevention programs. A quantitative analysis reveals generally low cost benefit ratios attached to these programs.

Notes that justification for these limited financial gains may be seen in perceived social and non-pecuniary by-products of education such as reducing dependency, providing equal opportunity, and developing individual character and intellect. Preferential weighting of such anticipated social benefits may alter cost-benefit calculations.

*Rice, G. Randolph. "Poverty and Industrial Growth Patterns: Some Cross-State Evidence." Journal of Regional Science 13 (December 1973): 377-384.

(VI)

Tests the hypothesis which states that regional growth patterns are dependent upon the extent of poverty in the region. The author argues that poverty hinders state growth patterns; this contention reverses the direction of the causal sequence proposed by many studies. The empirical results show that "studies which treat economic growth as a causal variable in the fight against poverty are neglecting the simultaneous bias inherent in such a cause-effect sequence." Secondly, poverty is an obstacle in a state's ability to follow national growth trends; and thirdly, "differential shifts, the indexes which characterize relative state advantages among the industrial sectors, result mainly from the historical, natural advantages that exist among states..."

Richardson, Harry W. Regional Economics: Location Theory, Urban Structure and Regional Change. New York: Praeger Publishers, 1969.

(VI)

Traditional economic theory abstracts from spatial aspects of the economy. For instance, international trade usually is implied to take place in a world economy without distance or transport costs. Furthermore, if classical economic assumptions are accepted (i.e., wage and price flexibility and factor mobility within a country), many regional problems will not arise since differences in prices, costs, wages, and incomes between regions cannot persist. These assumptions have excluded from economic analysis many important problems. For instance, "market forces do not lead inevitably to equality of regional per capita incomes or to the optimal spatial allocation of resources, and in some circumstances may operate in a disequilibrating manner."

This textbook develops economic theory to include spatial aspects. Three approaches are used to analyze the economic implications of the spatial dimension: 1) one approach "assumes that the location of population, industry, and resources is fixed, as well as channels of transportation, and conceives of space as a friction to the flow of commodities between fixed points." 2) The second approach is a "more generalized spatial analysis which includes the determination of the spatial structure itself." 3) And the third concentrates on the interrelationships between regions in the national economy. The book is divided into three sections covering location theory, urban economics and regional economics. Topics covered in the regional economics section include the concept of a region, interregional income theory, regional business cycles, factor mobility, regional growth, and policy objectives and strategies.

Richardson, Harry W. "Regional Growth." In Regional Economics: Location Theory, Urban Structure and Regional Change. New York: Praeger Publishers, 1969: 321-357.

(VI)

This chapter concentrates on adapting growth models developed for national economies to a regional context. Four models are discussed. The Harrod-Domar theory is a Keynesian demand-dominated theory. It suggests that "with balance of payments equilibrium, regions should grow faster the higher their propensities to save and the lower their capital-output ratios." This model is most relevant to explaining growth in lagging regions where effective demand is likely to be insufficient. The neoclassical model concentrates on the demand side. According to this model, the rate of growth of income is based on capital accumulation, the increase in the labor supply and technological progress. The third theory of regional growth is based on exports. An increase in the export base (all exportable goods and services of a region) "sets off a multiplier process where the multiplier is equal to the total regional output divided by the total exports." This model has severe explanatory and predictive limitations. According to the sector model, which is also of limited usefulness, growth depends on relative growth of the agricultural, manufacturing and service sectors in the region.

Another approach to regional growth which is less abstract and theoretical, but more adaptable and useful, is to examine the dynamics of the industrial structure of the region. Richardson concludes with a discussion of the question of long run convergence of per capita income. He finds that the "dominant factor behind differential changes in regional per capita income throughout the period 1880-1950 was changes in the relative importance of agricultural and manufacturing employment within each region."

Ries, Albert, and Watts, Harold W. "An Overview of the Labor Supply Results." In Work Incentives and Income Guarantees, edited by Joseph A. Pechman and P. Michael Timpane. Washington, D.C.: The Brookings Institution, 1975.

(II)

The labor supply results of the New Jersey graduated work incentive plan are reviewed here. The classical theory of labor-leisure choice was the basis for expectations that plans with higher tax rates would have larger substitution effects and would produce greater reductions in labor supply. Similarly, at a given tax rate, plans with the most generous payments were expected to cause the largest reduction in labor supply. The above theory does not take into account certain dynamic elements that were present in the experiment: wage rates were not exogenously given but rather could be influenced by the worker, the experiment was of finite duration, and there existed a background welfare system. In general, the estimated effects on labor supply were in accord with expectations. The major surprise was the absence of any negative effect on the labor supply of black households. For the group as a whole, the effects were "negative, usually significant, but not large." There was a large relative reduction in the labor force participation rate of white wives. If the cost of a negative income tax program is calculated on the assumption of no reduction in labor supply, then these results indicate that the estimated cost will be too low. "The added cost produced by the supply response is, however, a rather small portion of the total cost--not more than 10 percent and probably closer to 5 percent.

Riessman, Frank; Cohen, Jerome; and Pearl, Arthur, eds. Mental Health of the Poor. New York: The Free Press of Glencoe, 1964.

(XI)

Sixty contributors discuss "psychotherapeutic, social, and casework approaches, techniques, and goals appropriate for low income and blue collar workers." The issues which are covered include social class factors and mental illness, treatment, low-income behavior, new approaches to treatment, socio-therapy, new institutions, and drug addiction.

(Partially taken from Poverty in Canada and the United States)

Riew, J. "Migration and Public Policy." Journal of Regional Science 13 (1973): 65-76.

(V)

This paper argues that there are significant differences between individual and social calculations of the net economic benefit of migration. Aspects that are important to social economic welfare but usually escape individual consideration include the effect of migration on resource use in private housing, public and privately owned social overhead capital, and the costs of providing public services. For instance, migration causes congestion in cities and forces remaining residents in the sending areas to bear a heavier per capita burden for supporting the costs of essential services. Neither of these aspects would necessarily be considered by potential migrants. But it is not self-evident that the migration that actually does take place is beyond what is justified socially. Many factors pose barriers to mobility that prevent the economically optimal amount of migration from an individual point of view. These barriers include emotional attachment, financial constraints, lack of information and uncertainty. Riew concludes that public programs should be "aimed at improving earnings prospects where the potential migrants currently reside."

Riew, John. "Scale Economies in Public Schools." Review of Economics and Statistics 54 (1972): 100.

(V)

Riew defends criticism of his finding of economies of scale in public high schools by indicating the flaws in a study which had failed to confirm his findings. Riew (1966) had found that an increase of pupil enrollment from 200 to about 1,700 would lead to a total average savings of over 200 dollars per pupil in operating expenditures. Osbur's (1970) finding of negligible economies of scale in high school operation is attributed to his use of an expenditure function (which includes demand variables "tax levy," "assessed valuation per pupil," "median educational level of residents") instead of a cost function.

Ritchey, P.N. "Urban Poverty and Rural to Urban Migration." Rural Sociology 39 (1974): 12-27.

(VI)

There is the widespread view that rural-to-urban migrants are saturating the ghetto areas of large cities and disproportionately contributing to poverty in urban areas. In this paper, data from the 1967 Survey of Economic Opportunity are analyzed to explore two dimensions of the presumed relationship of rural-urban migration and the plight of cities: (1) the location of rural migrants in urban areas and (2) the extent of their contribution to urban poverty. This paper compares the location and poverty of rural-urban migrants with that of indigenous urbanites in nonmetropolitan and metropolitan areas by size--including the metropolitan ring and poor and nonpoor areas of central cities. White-Black differences are emphasized and the relationship of poverty and previous or prolonged urban experience among migrants is also examined. The findings indicate that urban poverty and the plight of cities are the consequences of broader structural features of our society--the handicaps of age, of being a female head of household, or of the status ascribed to Blacks--and not the product of rural-urban migration.

(From the article)

*Roach, Jack L. "Sociological Analysis and Poverty." American Journal of Sociology 71 (July 1965): 68-75.

(II)

The article reviews historical concepts of poverty and proposes a scheme in which the conditions and effects of material deprivation are given a more prominent role in the causal analysis of poverty.

In a footnote, Roach defines his use of the "poor" to mean that part of the population "which has been existing under sub-standard conditions of life for an extended period of time." By "conditions of life" he means physical needs such as food, clothing and shelter.

The article's main focus is two-fold: (1) the reasons for the lack of studies on the poor and the misconceptions of so many sociologists, as opposed to other students on the subject, who have studied the poor; and (2) the consequences of the material conditions of poverty for social behavior.

Roach, Jack L., and Gursslin, Orville R. "An Evaluation of the Concept 'Culture of Poverty'." Social Forces 45 (March 1967): 383-392.

(II,XI)

An examination of the concept of a culture of poverty and logical and empirical deficiencies in its use. There are a number of problems in the use of the concept of a culture of poverty, including:

1) differentiating between conceiving the culture of poverty as a natural evolvement from the main culture or as a reaction to it;
2) generalizing from related subcultures to the culture of poverty;
3) failure to indicate the purposes served by the concept;
4) inadequate designation of subcultural characteristics; and
5) lack of specification of independent and dependent variables, e.g. failure to distinguish between culture as description and culture as cause.

If sociologists are to continue to use the concept of a culture of poverty then attention must be paid to the type of population for which it is appropriate, for example, the long-term poor.

Rodomoski, Alexander L., and Mills, Anita U. "Family Income and Related Characteristics Among Low-Income Counties and States." Welfare Research Report #1. Washington, D.C.: Government Printing Office, 1964.

(IV,VI)

This 1960 poverty study emphasizes rural poverty. Nearly half of all the U.S. poor (incomes under $3,000) were rural; and in the poorest region in the country, the South, poverty was primarily a rural phenomenon. Non-whites were found to be especially likely to be poor, whether on southern farms or in northern cities. The poor were found to be sharing in economic growth, with the poorer states' and counties' incomes often rising faster than the national average.

Rogers, Tommy W. "Migration Attractiveness of Southern Metropolitan Areas." Social Science Quarterly 50 (1969): 325-336.

(VI)

An examination of the net migration rates of Southern Standard Metropolitan Statistical Areas (SMSA) from the standpoint of SMSA differences which appear to be associated with the size, rate, and direction of flow of migrants during the 1950-1960 decade. The Simon-Bealock technique for making causal inferences from correlational data is used. Migration was found to be caused by a composite of interrelated demographic and socio-economic factors, and not explanable by any single factor. The indicators of industrial status and socio-economic status and the variable of past migration were the strongest causal influences. Socio-economic variables clearly outweighed purely demographic factors. High migration rates were characteristic of areas of industrial expansion.

Rokeach, Milton, and Parker, Seymour. "Values as Social Indicators of Poverty and Race Relations in America." Annals of the American Academy of Political and Social Science (March 1970).

(XI)

Explores the usefulness of values, i.e., preferred end-states of existence or modes of behavior, as social indicators of underlying social problems. Using value choices of a national sample, an attempt was made to determine the extent and nature of cultural differences between groups differing in socio-economic status and race. The publication of The Negro Family (the "Moynihan Report") caused lively debate and invective about the issue of whether or not cultural differences exist between the poor and the rich and between Negro and white. The issue of whether those living in poverty, particularly the Negro poor, are characterized by a distinctive "culture of poverty" has policy ramifications for programs of poverty-amelioration and community development. The findings reported here lend support to the idea that considerable value differences distinguish the rich from the poor, but not Negroes from whites. (For the most part, differences found between the latter disappear when socio-economic position is controlled.)

Roosevelt, Franklin D. "The Second Inaugural Address. 'I See One-Third of a Nation Ill-Housed, Ill-Clad, Ill-Nourished.' 20 January 1937." In The Public Papers and Addresses of Franklin D. Roosevelt, 6 (1937): 1-6.

(II)

The purpose of this speech is to draw attention to the poor people in this country and to establish the goal of bettering their lot. Though Roosevelt's definition of "poor" people is very vague, we infer that he defines them as that part of the population with the bottom third standard of living. These are people denied adequate food, housing, clothing, education, recreation, and "the opportunity to better their lot." FDR's definition includes both the economic and the social aspects of poverty, the economic being the lack of income to obtain adequate food, clothing, housing, recreation; and the social being the inability to obtain adequate housing, education, and the opportunity to improve one's situation. This definition seems to be both absolute and relative--absolute in that he refers to people lacking "the necessities of life," and relative in that he refers to people having the lowest standard of living.

Rose, Arnold M. "Distance of Migration and Socio-Economic Status of Migrants." American Sociological Review 23 (1958): 420-443.

(VI,XI)

Data on immigrants to the Minneapolis area between March 15 and July 1, 1955 are used to test the following hypothesis: higher status persons, seeking better jobs or opportunities, must move a greater distance to find them, on the average, than persons seeking less desirable opportunities.

"These data indicate that the 'upper class' neighborhoods are being disproportionately filled with persons who have migrated a long distance, while the opposite is true for the 'poorer class' neighborhoods." The exception is for the poorest class of neighborhoods. Most of these contain disproportionate numbers of Negro residents, many of whom come all the way from the South.

(Annotation taken partially from Mangalam, J.J. Human Migration: A Guide to Migration Literature in English, 1955-1962. Lexington: University of Kentucky Press, 1968.)

Rosen, Shervin. "Comment on the Effects of Child-Care Programs on Women's Work Effort." Journal of Political Economy 82(1974): 5164-5169.

(II,X)

The theory of utility and demand is applied to the supply of labor with leisure treated as a consumption good. The indifference map may be computed directly from survey data or inferred from observation of actual work patterns. The observed infrequency of short-week workers may not imply a discontinuity in the supply function, but simply a lack of market offers of such jobs.

*Rosenthal, Gerald. "Identifying the Poor: Economic Measures of Poverty." In On Understanding Poverty, edited by Daniel Moynihan. New York: Basic Books, 1968.

(II,IV,VI,VII)

This article discusses the issues involved in developing poverty identification measures based on economic or consumption-related circumstances and the implications for policy of these poverty identification measures. Ideal measures for identifying the poor should provide a single, measurable characteristic or group of characteristics that the poor possess and the non-poor do not possess. It is agreed that any measure even approximating this criterion must be related to consumption opportunity. This poverty measure would be sensitive to changes within the groups described as poor, capable of distinguishing degrees of poverty among the poor, and able to allow comparison within and between groups over a period of time. The most elementary measures of poverty are those using a single level of income. Although these measures are objective, reproducible, and relatively unambiguous, they are deficient in indicating the degree to which individuals or groups face limitations in consumption opportunity. Another approach suggested is development of separate estimates of single levels of income for different subgroups of the population. These measures take into account such characteristics as family size, geographic location, and age and sex of head of the family. Specific budgets are determined for specific types of families so that a minimal level of consumption can be supported. Other measures are discussed which measure poverty in terms of relative economic levels. One suggestion is that the poverty income cut-off line should be approximately 50 percent of the median income. The cut-off point is shifted automatically as the economic level of society in the aggregate is improved, since such improvement is reflected in a rising median income. In discussing the specific problems of economic poverty identification measures, Rosenthal points out that the income/consumption relationship is not perfect and that income based measures only partly reflect consumption ability. They do not take into account the degree of relative deprivation associated with a given income (e.g. adequacy of public services) or the fact that the poor pay more in many instances than those in the same area who are not poor.

(Poverty and Human Resources Abstracts)

*Ross, Arthur. "The Negro in the American Economy." In Employment, Race, and Poverty. New York: Harcourt, Brace & World, Inc., 1967.

(X)

An overview of the Negro plight in the American economy from slavery to 1964. Statistical information on the Negro employment problem is explored to demonstrate its magnitude and indicate the need for and direction of change. Labor force participation figures for 1950 to 1964 indicate a decline for Black males and no substantial rise for Black females. Ross goes on to explain how the absence of part-time workers from the unemployment measure and the use of percentage rates instead of absolute numbers understate the degree of the Black employment problem. Statistics for 1964 show an improvement in the employment picture of Blacks. Ross contends this is because of the large margin of error in BLS reports.

Ross, John A. "Social Class and Medical Care." Journal of Health and Human Behavior 3 (1962): 35-40.

(XI)

An examination of the nationwide relationship between social class and medical care based on National Health Survey data for 1957-59. Family income and education of the household head determined class standing; frequency of visits and type of service are discussed.

Results of the study corroborate previous work revealing the direct correlation between class and medical care. Though the lower classes experience greater disability and morbidity, they consult medical personnel and seek preventative services less frequently than the middle and upper classes. This may be attributed to unequal purchasing power, differing interpretations of illness, varying theories of illness and orientations toward treatment, and differential knowledge and use of information. Other factors may reside in the medical practitioner, in economic conditions, or in ecological arrangements.

Rossi, Peter H. "A Critical Review of the Analysis of Nonlabor Force Responses." In Work Incentives and Income Guarantees, edited by Joseph A. Pechman and P. Michael Timpane. Washington, D.C.: The Brookings Institution, 1975.

(II)

Those reports on the New Jersey negative income experiment which deal with the behavior of participants aside from labor supply response are reviewed here. Some of the areas considered are consumption behavior, family composition changes, educational effort of adolescents, job turnover, and health care. For example, it was found that families in the experimental group were more likely to purchase a home during the study period; and renters increased the amount of rent they paid, presumably achieving better housing. Experimental families were also more likely to acquire durable goods, particularly large home appliances. "The findings concerning housing expenditures and durable purchases are among the firmest positive effects to be found in the entire set of papers coming from the experiment." By contrast, no significant experimental effects could be determined relating to family composition or family relationships. It was found, however, that the more generous the plan experienced, the less probability of job turnover; and occupations that had good expected job characteristics (earnings, status, job satisfaction) tended to retain their employees. "These findings taken together suggest that the generous plans act as wage subsidies, elevating the ability of poorer jobs to retain their employees." Some criticism is made that economists dominated the design phase of the experiment, and it is suggested that a true interdisciplinary approach involving psychologists and sociologists during later states of the experiment would have been better achieved by a collaborative effort rather than the method of independent analysis which was employed.

*Rossi, Peter H., and Zahava, D. Blum. "Class, Status, and Poverty." In On Understanding Poverty, edited by Daniel P. Moynihan. New York: Basic Books, Inc., 1968.

(II,XI)

The emphasis of the paper is on how the poor--those at the bottom of our American class system--are different from the rest of society, what the causes of poverty are, and how the causes are reproduced. Important variables include: labor force participation, occupational participation, family and interpersonal relations, community characteristics, relationships to the larger society, and value orientation. Three considerations that should comprise a theory of how class differences (social stratification) are generated are discussed: (1) socioeconomic status levels, (2) reaction to social class, and (3) maintenance and reinforcement of class differences. Factors of ethnicity, religion, and race are also briefly explored.

Rothenberg, Jerome. "Local Decentralization and the Theory of Optimal Government." In The Analysis of Public Output, edited by Julius Margolis. New York: National Bureau of Economic Research, 1970.

(V, VI)

A mathematical economic model of suburbanization analyzes potential diseconomies due to external effects. Externalities arise in the following way. When individuals move out of the city into the suburbs they do not thereby sever their relations with the central city. They continue to use urban public facilities and services for which they no longer pay to a greater extent than urban dwellers use suburban facilities. Therefore suburbanization is carried too far, because private incentives reflect social interests in a systematically distorted way. This leads to inefficient patterns of housing, transportation, and employment. Excess suburbanization leads to excess resource costs of conducting local government in the metropolitan area, and increases the real price of public goods for the city.

Rowntree, B. Seebohm, and Lavers, G.R. Poverty and the Welfare State. London: Longmans, Green and Co., 1951.

(II)

In this, the authors' third survey of York, England, the number of people in poverty is shown to have declined between 1900 and 1950. Various public assistance measures were found to have played a part in the reduction of poverty in York. The poverty line is stringently and biologically defined, and depends on the cost of the cheapest sources of calories and protein. Standards for minimal consumption of clothing, "household sundries," and fuel and light were estimated from interview data, ruling out the figures much higher than the rest and adopting the mean of those remaining as "normal."

Rubinow, I.M. "Poverty." In The Encyclopedia of the Social Sciences, edited by Edwin R.A. Seligman. New York: The MacMillan Company, 1930.

(II)

The article discusses poverty definitions, poverty in different countries, the history of poverty in modern times, and changing attitudes and policies toward poverty. Poverty may refer to economic inequality, economic dependency or economic insufficiency. Even the third is a relative measure, as sufficiency is determined by comparison with the rest of the society. The poverty line in real terms tends to rise as a society advances.

Rubinow, I.M. "Relief Budgets and Standards of Living." Jewish Social Service Quarterly 1 (1924).

(II,III)

A comparison of family budgets set by two Philadelphia social service agencies, one for relief purposes and the other for the purpose of setting minimum wages. The budgets were determined by surveying the expenses of average-sized Philadelphia families maintaining a "decent" standard of living. Costs included housing, fuel and light, food, clothing, carfare, cleaning supplies and services, health, furniture, taxes, education and reading, recreation, insurance, and miscellaneous. Both agencies sought to establish a comfortable but not excessive standard of living both for workers and relief recipients, however the relief agency was wary of establishing a standard that would discourage able family members from working. People in need of relief, i.e., poor people, were implicitly defined as those with incomes insufficient to provide them with a "decent" or "comfortable" standard of living.

*Rucker, George W. Six Years of Progress. Washington, D.C.: Rural Housing Alliance, 1974.

(V)

An analysis of the Farmers Home Administration's Section 502 home ownership loan program covering the six-year period 1969-1973. The purpose of the analysis is to attempt to measure the size and changes in the program, both nationally and by state against need. In the context of the report, need is defined as the "target constituency." Using a simple formula, it was found that FmHA began with a target constituency six years ago of 2.3 million families. On a national basis, in six years, it made enough initial loans to cover 21% of the target constituency. However, the great variations in performance among the states is not reflected in this national figure; and it is the performance of the state agencies which affect the population to be reached.

*Rural Housing Alliance and the Housing Assistance Council. Public Housing: Where It Is and Isn't--Summary. Washington, D.C.: 1972.

(V)

A summary of an analysis of public housing. The study measured the extent to which the program retains an urban bias and found what other geographical disparities are evident, using county-based data. In order to get an urban/rural classification system that would offer a range of measurement, counties were classified both as to their metropolitan status and as to their population density. The analysis found that based on population density the public housing program clearly remains an urban-focused one. Moreover, the distribution of public housing appears closely related to the density of population and the metropolitan status of the county; that is, the amount of public housing in the United States bears little relationship to the need for it, and this disparity is closely related to the degree of urbanization.

(Partially taken from the study)

Rural Poverty, Hearings Before the National Advisory Commission on Rural Poverty. Washington, D.C.: 1967.

(II,IV,V,VI,IX,X,XI)

On September 27, 1966, President Lyndon B. Johnson established the National Advisory Commission on Rural Poverty. To this group was assigned the responsibility of constructing a comprehensive study and appraisal of the current economic situation and trends in American rural life.

Public hearings were conducted in Tucson, Arizona; Memphis, Tennessee; and Washington, D.C. during the winter of 1967. The verbatim transcripts of these proceedings are presented in three volumes and include discussions and formal presentations of participants; taking part in these hearings were government officials on the local, regional, and federal levels; labor and community leaders; representatives of private industry and public interest groups; supervisors of training programs; employers; farm workers; university professors; and various interested parties.

Based on these public hearings and other extensive research, the Commission presented a final report to the President on September 27, 1967. This report describes poverty in rural America and recommends the most efficient and promising means of providing opportunities for the rural population to share in the country's economic abundance.

(Partially taken from the Foreword)

Rushing, William A. "Objective and Subjective Aspects of Deprivation in a Rural Poverty Class." Rural Sociology 33 (September 1968): 269-284.

(VI)

Although farm workers constitute a major proportion of persons at the bottom of the class structure, they have been almost ignored in sociological research. This investigation, based on samples of both farm workers and growers in Washington, describes several dimensions of objective and subjective deprivation in this class; objective factors include class background, occupational skills and social participation patterns, while subjective refers to perceptions of deprivations. Differences by ethnicity (Mexican-American vs. Anglo) and resident status (resident vs. migrant) are noted. Results show that on all dimensions of objective deprivations, workers are more deprived than Anglo and resident workers. Differences in perceived relative deprivation parallel differences in objective deprivation, indicating that such perceptions are realistic. However, they are unrealistic in that workers perceive themselves as less deprived than they objectively are, whereas growers perceive themselves as more deprived than they are.

(Revised author abstract)

Russel, R. Robert. "The Empirical Evaluation of Theoretically Plausible Demand Functions." Unpublished doctoral dissertation, Harvard University, 1964.

(III)

Russel integrates empirical research on consumer demand with the theoretical proposition that demand functions represent a maximization of utility. Four theoretically plausible demand functions were fitted both to cross-sectional and time-series data. All the methods were reliably convergent using cross-section data, but in with time-series data which include flexible prices the quadratic and generalized addilog estimates were erratic. Whether utility was directly taken from consumption or taken indirectly from total income and the price vector made little difference to goodness of fit.

Rutton, Vernon W.; Waldo, Arley D.; and Houck, James P., eds. Agricultural Policy in an Affluent Society. New York: W.W. Norton & Co., 1969.

(II, III)

A collection of essays on agricultural policy that focuses on the following issues: (1) the economic and political changes that are reshaping the concept and role of agricultural policy; (2) price and income policy for commercial agriculture; (3) food marketing policy; (4) bargaining power for farmers and farm workers; (5) overcoming rural poverty; and (6) agricultural trade, aid, and development policy. On the subject of rural poverty, an essay entitled "Rural Poverty" by W. Keith Bryant is the most relevant to poverty definition and measurement. Bryant uses a relative definition of poverty, adapted from definitions used by the Social Security Administration which are based on the income needed by individuals and families of various sizes to afford a low-cost diet and other necessities of life.

*Ryscavage, Paul M. "Employment Developments in Urban Poverty Neighborhoods." Monthly Labor Review (June 1969).

(X)

The article compares changes in the employment status of people in urban poverty neighborhoods with that of people in other urban neighborhoods during the period 1967 to 1968. Poverty neighborhoods were defined as the "poorest" one-fifth census tracts which were ranked according to 1960 census data on income, education, skills, housing, and proportion of broken families. The article examines population changes, employment rates, occupational status, subemployment and overemployment figures, and labor force participation rates.

In absolute terms, unemployment in urban poverty neighborhoods declined greater than unemployment in other urban neighborhoods (6.8 to 6.0 percent in poverty neighborhoods compared to 3.4 to 3.2 percent in non-poverty neighborhoods); but in relative terms, there was no difference in the decline between the two groups. Much of the decline in the poverty neighborhood jobless rate may be attributed to a decline in those neighborhoods' populations. The occupational distribution of poverty residents, which is skewed heavily toward the unskilled and service jobs, contributes significantly to the income gap between poverty and non-poverty groups. Although there was an improvement in occupational distribution relative to other urban residents, poverty residents, particularly non-whites, work fewer hours than non-poverty urban residents due to the high incidence of slack work, material shortages, and so on. This situation did not improve. Poverty residents' participation in the labor force declined slightly in 1968, while non-poverty residents' participation did not. This decline is attributed to discouragement, disability, voluntary idleness, and waiting to enter school or the Armed Forces. These issues are further examined by age, sex, and racial differentials.

Sackrey, Charles. The Political Economy of Urban Poverty. New York: W.W. Norton and Company, 1973.

(II,VI,X)

An analysis of the economic causes of poverty combined with "a discussion of the implications for political activity which are inherent in all such analyses." The author outlines a radical critique of liberal analyses of poverty. Liberal theories, he argues, maintain that poverty is the result of personal characteristics, but never asks how those characteristics are obtained. Such theories lead to policy that inevitably fail for two reasons: "(1) liberal theorists, thinking of poverty only in absolute terms, propose remedies which do nothing to fundamentally alter the distribution of income or wealth; and (2) the control of the political system by power elites ensures that the poor will receive only enough to keep them from generating a serious threat to the existing order."*

Sackrey develops suggestions for what radicals can do to achieve fundamental change. Nevertheless, he "concludes that the misery of the poor can be most feasibly mitigated in the short-run by a guaranteed annual income generous enough to free them from the necessity of taking degrading jobs--a program he acknowledges is more liberal than radical."**

(* and ** taken from a book review by Robert S. Smith in Review of Social Economy 31 (1973): 205-206.)

Salem, A.B.Z., and Mount, T.D. "A Convenient Descriptive Model of Income Distribution: The Gamma Density." Econometrica 42 (No. 6): 1115-1127.

(II)

A new mathematical distribution is proposed to approximate the income distribution of the United States. The two parameters of this Gamma distribution are measures of the inequality of the distribution and of its scale. The distribution is easy to estimate using maximum likelihood techniques on a sample of the existing data. The distribution was estimated for 1960 and 1969 and compared with the log-normal distribution, another candidate with easy to interpret parameters. The Gamma-distribution gave a much better fit for both years. Finally, a simple regression model was set up; it was shown that inequality decreases with decreasing unemployment and inflation and increasing real GNP.

*Sample, C. James. Patterns of Regional Economic Change: A Quantitative Analysis of U.S. Regional Growth and Development. Cambridge: Ballinger Publishing Co., 1974.

(VI,VIII)

Regression analysis and factor analysis are used to study patterns of regional economic change in four major geographical areas in the United States (Southeast, Northeast, Central, and West). These measures of economic change are examined to determine which of about 50 variables have the most influence on each measure. It was found that overall, the relative importance of national growth industries and residentiary industries and the stock and potential source of financial capital were the most important factors determining the level of per capita income in 1959 ("used as a measure of long-term structural economic development"). The rate of growth of residentiary employment, the net migration rate and the rate of increase in financial deposits were the most important factors determining the average annual rate of increase in total personal income between 1950 and 1966 ("used as a measure of short-term growth in the total volume of economic activity"). And "the mobility of labor and its migration to higher income areas within regional groupings" was found to be the most significant factor determining rates of growth of per capita income between 1950 and 1966 ("used as a measure of short-term change in the average level of economic welfare"). The study also tests the hypothesis that the expansion of regional exports is important in determining the rate of economic growth. The data suggests that this hypothesis is only true for less developed regions.

Samuelson, Paul A. "Constancy of the Marginal Utility of Income." Studies in Mathematical Economics and Econometrics, edited by Oscar Lange et al. Chicago: University of Chicago Press, 1947.

(III)

Samuelson examines the implications of the common assumption of the constancy of the marginal utility of income. This assumption implies unitary income elasticities of demand for every good, a conclusion contradicted by a vast amount of budgetary statistical data.

The Marshallian concept of consumer surplus, used to gauge the welfare effects of a price change, assumes constancy of the marginal utility of income. Without this assumption, it cannot be determined whether the compensating variation or the equivalent variation is the greater.

Samuelson, Paul A. "Evaluation of Real National Income." Oxford Economic Papers 2 (1950): 1-29.

(III)

Index number calculations may be used to indicate whether an individual is better or worse off due to a price change. For groups, however, an ethics free definition of changes in potential real income must be based on uniform shifts in the utility possibilities function of the group. Price and quantity calculations (index numbers) from aggregate data can never reveal such shifts.

Consider two different observed combinations of two commodities produced in two situations (situation 1 and situation 2). If the total value of the output in situation 2 at situation 2 prices is greater than the value of the output in situation 1 at the same prices ($\Sigma p_2 q_2 > \Sigma p_2 q_1$) then the observed conditions in situation 2 are superior to the observed conditions in situation 1. But the observed conditions may not coincide with the potential conditions in either or both of the situations--in other words, the production points calculated from the price-quantity data may not lie on the production possibilities function. We can therefore make no inferences from such data concerning the relative positions of the production possibilities functions of the two situations. Furthermore, shifts in the production possibilities function do not necessarily imply similar shifts in the utility possibilities function. A policy that causes uniform improvement in the utility possibilities function for society as a whole may cause such an adverse and ethically undesirable effect on some individuals that we would have to evaluate such a policy unfavorably.

Samuelson, Paul A. Foundations of Economic Analysis. Cambridge, Massachusetts: Harvard University Press, 1947.

(III)

Samuelson finds that for the purposes of assessing the relative costs and benefits of a particular project, the concept of consumer's surplus is less useful than the consumer's ordinal preference field. As renovated and altered, consumer's surplus survives as the economic theory of index numbers. This economic theory, developed by Wicksell, Konus, Leontief and others must be distinguished from the statistical theory associated with Edgeworth, Marshall and Irving Fisher. The essential problem of the economic theory -- determining merely from price and quantity data which of two situations is higher up on an individual's preference scale -- is shown to elude complete solution.

Samuelson, Paul A. "The Problem of Integrability in Utility Theory." Economica 17(1950): 355-385.

(III)

When the deductive theory of demand is extended to include more than two goods, that is, when indifference contours are no longer lines, but figures in 3- or n-space, the problem of integrability arises. Samuelson shows in the three good case that for certain kinds of preferences no "indifference bowl" (a three-dimensional indifference curve) can be drawn. By postulating semi-transitivity, (i.e., that if bundle of goods A is revealed preferable to B and B to C and so on through Z, the last of the sequence will never be revealed preferable to A), integrability is assured for the case of many goods and the economic theory of index numbers is put of firm footing once more. This proof is due to Houthakker.

Samuelson, P.H., and Swamy, S. "Invariant Economic Index Numbers and Canonical Duality: Survey and Synthesis." American Economic Review 64(1974): 566-593.

(III)

Although an ideal economic price and quantity index cannot be constructed for more than one good, interesting results can be obtained in the homothetic case of unitary income elasticities in which at all levels of living the calculated price change is the same. The economic price index is simply the ratio of the (minimum) costs of a given level of living in two price situations. However, to "deflate" monetary totals, the economic quantity index is called for. This measures for two presented quantity situations Q^o and Q^1, the ratio of the minimum expenditure needed, in the face of a reference price situation, to buy their respective levels of well-being. The authors treat the mathematical properties of homothetic indices and describe methods of approximating it.

Saupe, William E., and Weber, Bruce A. "Rural Family Income in Wisconsin." In Institute for Research on Poverty 187 (1973).

(II,III,V,VI)

A comparison of the income characteristics of farm and rural nonfarm families in Wisconsin. Total family income was about the same for farm and nonfarm families. Single-earner families earned much less than multiple-earner families among both farm and nonfarm families. About a third of wives in rural households earned money income in both farm and nonfarm families. Almost half of the farm families had an income recipient in addition to the head; spouses and other members contributed almost equally, together accounting for about 33 percent of total income. A "welfare index," calculated as total family income divided by a measure of subsistence income, was computed for each family. There was a pronounced inverse relationship between the percentage of income coming from farming and the level of well-being.

The inequality of income distribution was about the same for both farm and nonfarm families. The distribution of wages and nonfarm business income tended to increase inequality among farm families, while farm income decreased it. Social security benefits equalized the distribution of income for both groups.

Scharff, Ned. "'Go South, Young Man'--The Current of Migration Reverses." The Washington Star, 1 June 1975.

(VI)

Recent census statistics indicate drastic changes in national migratory trends. The south to north migration has been reversed, the movement from small towns and rural areas to big cities has ended and east to west migration has fallen off significantly. Urban to suburban migration is the only major trend that has remained unchanged. There are several reasons for these changes. Apparently, the United States has become "over-urbanized" to the extent that cities no longer "offer an attractive way of life to people;" racial problems have led to "white flight;" and changes in the relative economic structure of urban and rural areas have shifted jobs away from the cities. Improved transportation and communication have allowed many industries to move plants to less populated areas where they can take advantage of lower wages and avoid many other problems associated with cities. These trends are likely to cause increasing problems for urban areas. As middle-class and skilled workers as well as industry migrate to rural areas, the cities will be left with more poor, young and unskilled workers and less jobs to employ them.

Schiller, Bradley R. "Turnover Rate in Public Assistance Programs." Welfare in Review 8 (September-October 1970): 27-30.

(IX)

There are three distinct types of caseload turnover measures: coverage--the number of families receiving aid at a given time, recidivism--the probability that a family will receive aid more than once, and tenure--how long the average family will receive aid. A random nationwide sample of 11,623 cases was used to obtain figures for all three of these measures. Coverage was calculated by adding the number of cases opened during the year to the number of cases open at the beginning of the year and subtracting the number of families receiving aid more than once during the year. This measure gives figures some 50% larger than average yearly caseload figures. Surveys of recidivism have shown that some 35-40% of all public assistance families receive aid more than once. The long-run mean value of time spent on public assistance is 25 months. Both of these estimates may be low because they cannot include time in the future that may be spent receiving public aid.

Schorr, Alvin L. "The Family Cycle and Income Development." Social Security Bulletin (February 1966).

(II,IX)

An examination of the phases of poverty during the life of a family for the purpose of better understanding the poor, and planning and evaluating poverty programs. The four critical phases are (1) initial marriage and childbearing; (2) timing and direction of occupational choice; (3) financial squeeze which becomes hindrance rather than stimulus to improvement; and (4) family breakdown. The next phase is phase one for the next generation. The underlying theme is the vicious circle of poverty: that "most people who die poor were born poor."

Schultz, Theodore W. "The Economics of Poverty; Investing in Poor People." American Economic Review: Papers and Proceedings. (May 1965).

(II)

Economics has not as yet supplied an adequate theory of poverty despite the considerable interest in income distribution evidenced by nineteenth-century economists. In terms of current analysis, the poor are treated as anomalies, "pockets of people who by preferences or circumstances have not been cleansed by progress!" Two applications of demand theory are cited as contributing insights into the causes of poverty. The relationship between the growth of real household income on the one hand and the poverty line on the other can be interpreted as society's income elasticity of demand for welfare services for the poor; since real income has risen twice as fast as the poverty line since the mid-1930's this strongly suggests that the relevant elasticity is substantially below unity. At the same time rising per capita income has increased the demand for independent living arrangements particularly for the young and for the elderly; despite the fact that some of those households show up statistically as poor, economic theory suggests that their welfare position is in fact improved.

In attempting to explain observed changes in poverty, the author states that virtually all the rise in per capita income can be accounted for by increase in the earnings of labor. This increase in earnings can be explained by (1) a reduction in the "price" of claims on income from labor relative to the prices of other claims on income, (2) a consequential increase in the rate of investment in human capital, and (3) a consequential increase in earnings from labor. The author finds support for these hypotheses in recent work on returns to educational investment and the rapid growth of investment in labor force training and education relative to other forms of investment. Furthermore the maintenance of full employment, technological changes and reduction in job discrimination have all tended to increase the demand for the productive services of labor relative to other factors; since the growth in demand for labor has tended to favor skilled rather than unskilled labor, there has been a tendency for workers to acquire more valuable skills; where this tendency has been weakest (agriculture, blacks and the South), poverty has remained most persistent. The implications are seen to be a need for more investment in human capital if further declines in poverty are to be realized.

Schultz, T. Paul. The Distribution of Personal Income. Joint Economic Committee, U.S. Congress Subcommittee on Economics and Statistics. Washington, D.C.: December 1964.

(VII)

This detailed study of the distribution of income in the United States is divided into two sections. The first section contains an analytic treatment of the problem of deriving an income distribution. A part of that analysis is a detailed discussion of the problems of using annual money income as a measure of economic well-being. The problems discussed include:

1) The fact that economic well-being depends on lifetime income as opposed to current income. Consumption is proposed as a proxy for lifetime income, which requires detailed demographic information to calculate.

2) Transitory income changes appear in the annual data. The use of a longer period of measurement or of consumption will alleviate this problem.

3) Money income for different classes of individuals changes with the business cycle, but in different directions.

4) The amount of goods a unit of money will buy changes with location, income of the buyer, and time. This makes comparisons difficult.

5) Non-money income is an important resource for some classes of people.

6) The needs of a family are dependent on its size and composition.

The second section contains a description of all the major programs in the U.S. that measure personal income. The methods used in these programs are discussed and their scope and the reliability of their results are discussed and compared. The programs in question are run by the Office of Business Economics, the Census Bureau, the Bureau of Labor Statistics, the Department of Agriculture, the Internal Revenue Service, and the Federal Reserve System.

* Schultz, T. Paul. "Secular Trends and Cyclical Behavior of Income Distribution in the United States: 1944-1965." In Six Papers on the Size Distribution of Wealth and Income, edited by Lee Soltow. New York: National Bureau of Economic Research, 1969.

(II,IX)

An examination of the magnitude and causes of secular and cyclical changes in the size distribution of income in the United States. Equality in the income distribution, as measured by the Gini coefficient and the variance of incomes, did not change perceptibly over the 1944-65 period. Using data from the Current Population Survey, Schultz estimates the effect of changes in aggregate demand on income concentration: unemployment and output growth both increase concentration; inflation decreases concentration. Changes in the composition of the labor force, in particular the increased flow of low paid young people and married women into the labor force, have reduced the trend toward equality in the income distribution.

Schulz, James H., and Carrin, Guy. "The Role of Savings and Pension Systems In Maintaining Living Standards In Retirement." Journal of Human Resources (Summer 1972): 3.

(VII)

Over the years there has been a general recognition that serious economic problems have plagued and continue to plague the majority of aged persons in the U.S. and other countries. This article examines the personal savings rates required to provide an average worker with adequate retirement funds. The influence of (1) various definitions of adequacy, (2) inflation, and (3) economic growth on the magnitude of the retirement preparation task are examined. With this perspective, the current roles played by the social security system and private pensions are assessed.

(Journal of Human Resources)

Schumpeter, Joseph. Imperialism and Social Classes. New York: Augustus M. Kelley, Inc., 1951.

(II,XI)

A classic essay on the nature and origin of social classes. Schumpeter rejects the notion that class can be defined strictly in terms of economic status, or in terms of ownership of land or capital. Indeed, social class is as much a socio-psychological phenomenon as economic: "a class is aware of its identify as a whole...has its own peculiar life and characteristic spirit." It is interesting to note that Schumpeter believed that one could identify a class on the basis of the extent to which its members intermarried, a clearly social/cultural criteria. The forces which move people across classes (luck, ability, social change) as well as the forces which precipitate the rise or fall of whole classes are then considered.

Schutz, Robert R. "On the Measurement of Income Inequality." American Economic Review 41 (March 1951).

(II)

An alternative measure of inequality based on the Lorenz curve technique is presented here. The slope of the Lorenz curve is plotted as a function of ranked percentage income units. (The derivative of the Lorenz curve is graphed in incremental form here as a step function.) On this graph, the horizontal, slope-equal-to-one line represents equality and corresponds to the forty-five degree diagonal of the Lorenz curve. This method makes the difference of individual income unit groups that are over or under the equality line more apparent since it does not represent income in a cumulative fashion as does the Lorenz curve. A numerical inequality index based on this graph is given as the area under the curve with respect to the slope-equals-one horizontal. Either the area (absolute value) over or under the equality line can be used since the two will be equal. Such an index can be applied quite easily to situations involving negative incomes or to populations divided into ranked subgroups, both of which present difficulties for the Gini coefficient approach. In the case of a subdivided distribution, the "over" area of a particular subgroup will not necessarily equal the "under" area (since the subgroup as a whole will not necessarily have an income equal to the average for the total distribution); in this case, the area difference ("over" minus "under") of a particular subgroup can also be used as a comparative measure.

Schwartz, Aba, and Parsans, Donald O. "Time Series Changes in Personal Income Inequality in the United States from 1939 with Projections to 1985: A Comment." Journal of Political Economy 82 (September/October 1974): 1027-1032.

(II,IX)

A reply to the article by Chiswick and Mincer (1972) that attempted to explain income inequality in terms of a human capital approach. The original article related the variance in net earnings to the variances of number of years of schooling, number of years of experience on the job, number of weeks worked throughout the year, and rates of return on self-investment. The criticism made in this reply is that the "number of weeks worked" variable is used as though it were independent of the other human capital variables. As a matter of fact, "both rate of return on human capital stock and investment costs will be influenced by weeks worked per year...For a given productivity, clearly a reduction in weeks worked will reduce the annual rate of return expected on a given capital stock." Incorporating this relationship into the return rates for schooling and on the job training is considered a necessary complexity since the unmodified form suggests some implausible estimates of investment.

Schwartz, Richard. "Functional Alternatives to Inequality." American Sociological Review 20 (1955): 424-430.

(II)

An attack on the position that inequality serves a unique functional role in the survival of society. Schwartz studies two Israeli collectives and demonstrates that socialization of workers and transformation of jobs can replace wage differences as a means to efficiently allocate and motivate workers. His conclusion is that inequality cannot be viewed as either a necessary or an inevitable concomitant of economic development.

Schwarzweller, Harry K. "Education, Migration, and Economic Life Chances of Male Entrants to the Labor Force from a Low-Income Rural Area." Rural Sociology 29 (June 1964): 152-167.

(V,VI,XI)

This study focuses on a population of young men who were reared in a low-income rural situation. A follow-up study was undertaken, and the men were interviewed ten years after their enrollment in the eighth grade; many had migrated to industrial areas. The influence of education on occupational placement and economic life chances is explored. Expected relationships are found for non-migrants. For migrants, however, significant relationships between schooling and job sites, occupational status, or level of living are not observed. Migration appears to be an important contingent condition explaining the economic life chances and occupational placement of rural, high school "drop-outs." A number of questions which emerge from the analysis are discussed.

(Author abstract)

Schwarzweller, Harry K., and Brown, James S. "Social Class Origins, Rural-Urban Migration, and Economic Life Chances: A Case Study." Rural Sociology 32 (March 1967): 5-19.

(VI)

This paper explores the thesis that in a rural low-income area with a high rate of out-migration, the social class position of a family influences the pattern of out-migration, the structure of the migration process, and the economic life chances of individual migrants and families in the areas of destination. Data are from a restudy, after twenty years, of persons who had been living in three isolated mountain neighborhoods in eastern Kentucky. It was found that social class differences in the form or strategy of out-migration contributed to the maintenance and stability of the social class hierarchy within this migration system. A migrant's social class origin influenced not only when he left the mountains, where he moved, and with whom, but also his subsequent level of living in the urban area.

(Author abstract)

Schwarzweller, Harry K.; Brown, James S.; and Mangalam, J.J. Mountain Families in Transition. University Park: The Pennsylvania State University Press, 1971.

(VI)

A case study of Appalachian migration.

The book reveals to us the Beech Creek people, who live in three small adjoining neighborhoods located in the isolated, subsistence farming, mountain area of eastern Kentucky. We view their families and behavior patterns as they have adapted through migration to the increasing pressures of unsatisfactory economic and other circumstances that have been such a dismal and persistent feature of the Southern Appalachian region.

The major foci of the present inquiry are as follows: (1) to describe and document in a systematic manner the patterns of migration of people and families from Beech Creek neighborhoods to communities in southern Ohio and elsewhere; (2) to explore the utility of viewing this type of rural-to-urban migration as a sociological phenomenon, i.e., as a migration system in a sociological sense; (3) to acquire an understanding of the problems and processes of adjustment encountered by people who move from a low-income, rural area to an affluent, urban industrial one; (4) to ascertain the part played by family and kinship in the migration process and in the social adjustment of migrants during the transitional period.

(Adapted from the Preface)

Scott, Geraldine J. Preliminary Statistics of State School Systems 1969-1970. Washington, D.C.: National Center for Educational Statistics, 1973.

(V)

This report summarizes data from the regular biennial survey of state elementary and secondary school statistics for the 1969-70 academic year. Data are reported on a state-by-state basis. The first five tables of the report contain data on school administrative units, pupils, and staff. Data are presented on the number of school systems, the number of public schools, the school age population, enrollment, average daily membership, average daily attendance, length of school term, grade enrollments, postgraduates, high school graduates, and instructional staff. The remaining five tables present data on financing public elementary and secondary school systems. Data included in these tables include revenue and nonrevenue receipts for public schools, total expenditures, account balances on hand, current expenditures, capital outlay, interest on school debt, and expenditures per pupil.

Seashore, Stanley. "Job Satisfaction as an Indicator of the Quality of Employment." Social Indicator Research 1 (September 1974): 135-168.

(II,X)

It is suggested that the quality of employment should be assessed from the value perspectives of the employer and of society as well as the perspective of the worker. The prevailing conception of the nature of job satisfaction and the associated measurement methods provide useful but unnecessarily limited indicators of the quality of employment. An enlarged conception is offered with respect to the nature of job satisfaction, its causes, and its possible consequences. The implications of this conception for the utility of satisfaction measures as social indicators are examined with regard to three aspects: the psychology of job satisfaction, the sociology of job satisfaction, and the approach and technology of using subjective satisfaction measures in conjunction with other indicators. The view is expressed that direct measures of subjective job satisfaction are an essential component in any effort to make comparisons or monitor changes in the quality of employment, but that such measures, like other subjective and objective indicators, have ambiguous meaning if used alone.

(Taken from Social Science Research 1 (September 1974): 135.)

Seevers, Gary L., and Pulsipher, Allan G. "Environmental Resources and Energy Supplies." Future Land Use, edited by R.W. Burchell and D. Listokin. New Jersey: Center for Urban Policy Research, Rutgers University, 1975.

(V,VI)

This paper discusses problems that are arising from the interaction of attempts to meet increasing energy supply requirements and desires to maintain and improve the quality of the environment. The current controversy over "significant deterioration" of air quality is used to illustrate the damage which can result if efficient harmonization of energy and environmental policy is not achieved. In addition the potential economic and social costs associated with "significant deterioration" are considered.

The social and economic costs of non-deterioration regulations would likely be borne disproportionately by the poor, the aged and the disadvantaged. These regulations would tend to restrict growth and development in precisely those areas in which there are disproportionate numbers of the disadvantaged--large central cities and rural areas. In the former case, development would be limited because air quality is generally already worse than secondary standards; while in rural areas, "significant deterioration" regulations would preclude development. Therefore, most development would have to occur in the suburban fringe, with consequent limits on the access of the disadvantaged to participation in the jobs and energy supplies resulting from this development.

Seligman, Ben B. "American Poverty: Rural and Urban." Current History 55 (October 1968).

(II,V,VI)

A discussion of the urban and rural poor and a brief history of measures to combat poverty since 1964, when President Johnson declared the War on Poverty.

The Negro, elderly, and youth populations comprise large percentages of the urban poor, while rural poverty affects large numbers of inhabitants of Appalachia and of northern sections of Michigan, Wisconsin, and Minnesota; American Indians; Mexican Americans; and migrant workers. Seligman describes those unique living conditions, crises, and outlooks for each disadvantaged group before discussing the objectives of the War on Poverty and factors which have limited the effort's effectiveness. Legislators and the Office of Economic Opportunity (OEO), created specifically to command the attack on poverty, promised tax cuts, civil rights legislation, regional development, urban rehabilitation, youth programs, vocational training, and hospital insurance as strategic weapons. The financial and political obstacles affecting the newly-created programs invoke cynical commentary from the author, who then cites the work of Lampman and of Tobin on the negative income tax, a possible alternative to federal models whose impact has proved disappointing.

Seligman, Ben B. Permanent Poverty. Chicago: Quadrangle Books, 1968.

(II,IX,XI)

An examination of the problem of poverty in the United States, in 11 chapters, preceded by an Author's Preface. (1) The Roots of Poverty--traces the history of poverty in the modern era in the slums of the industrial cities. (2) The Numbers of Poor--deals with modern definitions of poverty as made by various authors and institutions. It appears that by several standards about 20% of U.S. families are to be considered poor. (3) The Shape of Negro Poverty--discusses American slavery, the modern Negro ghetto, and the situation of inequality of the U.S. Negro. (4) The Poverty of Aging--examines the problem of the elderly poor and the position of the agencies responsible for their care. (5) Poor Youth in an Affluent Society--points out that children from poor families have still little chance for improving their status through education. Federal programs, e.g. Head Start Programs, and the Job Corps, are examined as to their effectiveness and weaknesses. (6) Appalachia, Cutover, and other Minorities--deals with the rural poor of certain backward areas of the U.S., especially poverty on Indian reservations, among migratory agricultural workers, and in eastern Kentucky and Appalachia. Some federal programs, e.g. VISTA, are found to have been unexpectedly effective in raising the expectations of the poor and stirring up dissatisfaction. (7) The Toll of Technology--is concerned with the impact of technological change on the labor market and employment. It is suggested that not only must job-creating techniques be developed, but society must provide income maintenance for those unable to adjust quickly. (8) The Law of the Poor--discusses the legal problems of the poor, most of which go unresolved, since "the law, to all intents and purposes, reflects the attitude of the majority." The need for legal aid for the poor is stressed. (9) Poverty and National Power--deals with the "War on Poverty," the Organization for Economic Opportunity, and similar federal efforts. (10) Poverty and Local Power--considers local efforts to diminish poverty, e.g. the HARYOU Act, the illiteracy project of CORED, etc. (11) The End of Anti-Poverty--analyzes the political struggles involved in anti-poverty programs, leading to the abandonment of many efforts, a lack of concern, and complete retreat.

(Sociological Abstracts)

Seninger, Stephen F. "Alternative Methods of Identifying the Poor in Utah." Utah Economic and Business Review 32 (October 1972): 1-6.

(VI)

"This report deals with the measurement and geographic distribution of poverty in Utah.... The objective of this research is to determine a socio-economic profile of the poorer areas within Utah and as such is addressed to the following questions: (1) How do different measures of poverty interact with one-another? (2) What changes in the geographic or spatial distribution of poverty have occurred in Utah between 1960 and 1970?" Census data from 1960 and 1970 are used.

For a comprehensive profile of poverty, measures of housing, education, and occupation must be added to measures of income. In Utah there is a high correlation between income poverty and: residence in areas of low-rent, low proportion of owner-occupied housing; frequent lack of high school education; residence in areas with high proportions of individuals aged over 65, and high proportions of youths not living at home; high proportions of female-headed households; and low frequency of individual occupation in professional or managerial fields, and high frequency of service workers. The annual rate of change or spatial shift in population was lower for the lowest ranking income areas than for middle and higher areas. Two thirds of the urban tracts which were among the thirty least affluent areas of the state in 1960 were still in that category in 1970, and a similar pattern was noted for the thirty least affluent rural tracts.

*Sexton, Patricia. Education and Income. New York: Viking Press, 1961.

(V,IX,XI)

A study of the American public school system. Sexton explores school inequities, social class distinctions and the relationship between income and educational opportunity. Although the term "poverty" is never mentioned, the "lower class family" is defined as one which possesses either low-income, low-status occupations, poor housing or little education. Some exceptions to this definition such as professionals with low incomes and high education levels are cited. Sexton finds that family income is a good index to occupation and educational levels, as well as the "socio-economic classification of community areas" (housing conditions, public assistance, behavior and vital data) or social class. Based on the income and social class mobility data used in this study, the author argues that our public school system has refused to promote social mobility and has become a tool of social and economic class distinctions.

*Sheldon, Eleanor B., and Moore, Wilbert E. Indicators of Social Change: Concepts and Measurements. New York: Russell Sage Foundation, 1968.

(XI)

A wide-ranging analysis of the fact and extent of social change in the United States, with 16 contributing authors: sociologists, demographers, economists, political scientists, and social indicator specialists.

Presents both methodological discussions and findings on changes in the United States demographic base, social and economic structure, distribution of selected social benefits (leisure, health, education), and levels of mobility and social welfare.

Sheldon, Eleanor Bernert, and Parke, Robert. "Social Indicators." Science 188 (May 16, 1975): 693-699.

(XI)

"Social science researchers are developing concepts and measures of changes in society." Social scientists and policy-makers have recognized a need to quantify certain "non-economic dimensions of well-being" in an effort to evaluate and subsequently improve domestic social programs. Toward a Social Report, a statement of the need for social indicators issued in 1969 by the Department of Health, Education, and Welfare (HEW), is discussed, as well as recent origins of the work on social indicators and explication of distinguishable types of research to date. Sheldon and Parke document the significant literature in the area in their presentation of the uses of social indicators as tools for improving the data base and as components in social systems models. In conclusion, the authors quote O. D. Duncan for an apt statement on the expectation for work on social indicators:

> The value of improved measures of social change... is not that they necessarily resolve theoretical issues concerning social dynamics or settle pragmatic issues of social policy, but that they may permit those issues to be argued more productively.

*Sherwood, Mark K. "Family Budgets and Geographic Differences in Price Levels." Monthly Labor Review 98 (March 1975): 8-16.

(III, VI)

In order to measure interregional differences in the cost of living, the Bureau of Labor Statistics (BLS) estimates the cost of "standard budgets" in 30 metropolitan and 4 nonmetropolitan areas. They do not compare identical market baskets, but baskets that are weighted differently to reflect different consumption patterns across regions. The index numbers derived from these budgets can be used to compare regions only if we accept the strong underlying assumption that the different market baskets yield equivalent satisfaction. It is possible that different consumption patterns reflect interregional differences in real income and not differences in tastes and needs.

Sherwood constructs two alternative indices. One compares identical market baskets and the other takes into account climatic differences. These indices compare interarea price level differences. Removing the interarea differences tended to raise the index for poor areas and lower it for rich areas, thus reducing interregional inequality, although this effect was minor. The rank ordering of regions was the same for the BLS and Sherwood's indices. Removing interarea weight variations had "a considerable effect on the indices for food and transportation but a relatively small effect on overall consumption costs in the budgets."

Shiskin, Julius. "Updating the Consumer Price Index--An Overview." Monthly Labor Review (July 1974): 3-20.

(III)

The monthly Consumer Price Index (CPI) serves two major functions: "it is a yardstick for revising wages, salaries and other income payments to keep in step with rising prices; and it is an indicator of the rate of inflation in the economy." The incomes of nearly one half of the population are or soon will be pegged to the CPI (including dependents). In addition, the school lunch program, the poverty threshold, criteria for the distribution of manpower revenue-sharing funds, and many rental, royalty and child support agreements are now linked to the CPI. Shiskin estimates that a 1% rise in the index will cause at least a $1 billion increase in incomes under automatic escalators.

In the light of the important influence of the index, the BLS is in the process of revising the methods of its surveys to overcome some of the present limitations. New methods are being developed to take into account changing patterns of consumption, problems with measuring housing costs, and quality changes. Organized labor and other groups have argued that the one index understates price inflation of the goods consumed by particular groups. Recognizing that different groups consume different goods in different proportions, starting in 1977 the BLS will publish two CPI's: "an improved index for urban wage earners and clerical workers to meet the requirements of collective bargaining, and an index of all urban households." Despite these improvements, important limitations in the CPI as a measure of the cost of living will remain.

Shostak, Arthur. "An Overview of Current Administration Policy." In New Perspectives on Poverty, edited by Shostak and Gomberg. Englewood Cliffs, New Jersey: Prentice-Hall, Inc., 1965.

(II)

A description of the federal programs which were about to be initiated in 1964. The author recommends: (1) repeal of the Loyalty Oath and Disclaimer of Membership in Subversive Organizations for program candidates; (2) careful observation of local community agency personnel to insure proper administration; (3) reorganization to lessen bureaucratic conflict; and (4) coordination of the Anti-Poverty Act with related legislative programs. The elimination of poverty depends more on channelling money, goods, and services to the poor than on eliminating unemployment.

Shostak, Arthur, and Gomberg, William, eds. New Perspectives on Poverty. Englewood Cliffs, New Jersey: Prentice-Hall, Inc., 1965.

(II, V, VI, IX, XI)

The book consists of eighteen chapters, which are briefly reviewed: (1) "Reflections on Poverty in America," by H. Caudill--traces much of contemporary poverty to four historical sources: the frontier, waste entailed in settlement, slavery, and the great immigration waves, and suggests two programs of reform; (2) "The Poor Who Live Among Us," by L.E. Dirks--concerns people who now live in poverty, using interviews; (3) S.M. Miller (annotated separately); (4) "The Strengths of the Poor," by Frank Riessman; (5) "Birth Control and Poverty," by A.B. Shostak--discusses excess fertility and suggests that it is not necessary; (6) "Bonus for Babies," by I. Sclanders--endorses the Canadian system of child subsidy;

(7) "Educational Reforms and Poverty," by A.B. Shostak--deals with the problems of educating underprivileged children; (8) "Barriers to Medical Care for the Urban Poor," by D. Rosenblatt--highlights the poor care which the poor take of themselves and their reliance on non-scientific attitudes and treatment; (9) "A Second Chance for Ninety Men in Norfolk," by J.S. Canan--describes and evaluates the first attempt to train hardcore poor under the 1962 Manpower Development and Training Act; (10) "The Job-Finding Machine: How to Crank It Up," by E.T. Chase--evaluates the U.S. Employment Service as "pitifully unequal to its mammouth responsibility" and cites the Swedish equivalent as more effective; (11) "The Poverty of Welfare in America," by A.B. Shostak--critically reviews welfare services and makes recommendations for reform; (12) "Urban Renewal--for Whom?," by S. Lynd--raises disturbing questions about the nation's housing problem: why urban revewal has done so little for the poor, why public housing projects have failed so miserably, and why we don't resolve finally that land and housing are public utilities. It is noted that desire and power, not resources, are what is lacking; (13) "The War On Poverty," by G. Myrdal--is an overview of the country's needs and some promising reform measures re the federal Anti-Poverty Campaign; (14) "An Overview of Current administration Policy," by A.B. Shostak (annotated separately); (15) "For A Guaranteed Income," by M.D. Reagan--challenges the Administration's confidence in eventual full employment and offers a counter-proposal of family subsidy; (16) "Some Proposals for Government Policy in an Automating Society," by Herbert J. Gans--presents a list of 17 proposals for coping with poverty and unemployment; (17) "Keeping the Poor in Their Place: Notes on the Importance of Being One-Up," by A. Walinsky (annotated separately)--contends that the middle-class majority does not want to significantly improve the lot of the poor because of basic status insecurities; and (18) "The Lower Classes and the Negroes: Implications for Intellectuals," by H. Rodman--explores the role whites can play in civil rights and the role intellectuals can play in the War on Poverty. An Appendix by N. and H. Harrison describes the "Design for Living" course and queries whether it can work.

(Partially taken from
Sociological Abstracts)

Shryock, Henry S., Jr. Population Mobility Within the U.S. Chicago: Community and Family Study Center, University of Chicago, 1964.

(VI)

Population mobility is analyzed using 1940 and 1950 census records and the Current Population Survey from the 1940's to the early 1960's. Issues include concepts and definitions, historical patterns, geographic variation, spatial mobility vs. type of residence, and individual characteristics and motives of migrants. Mobility within the country was found to be mostly short-distance, with less than one-sixth of the migrant population moving across state lines. The proportion of recent movers in an area was found to be correlated with the propensity of the population of that area to move. After 1950, non-metropolitan areas were found to have higher migration rates than metropolitan areas; and within large urban areas, the fringes had higher rates than the central cities. The largest central cities contained relatively fewer recent movers than even the farm areas.

Simon, Arthur. Faces of Poverty. St. Louis, Missouri: Concordia Publishing House, 1966.

(VI)

A look at urban poverty in America. Simon, using three examples--a white couple, a black female-headed family and an elderly man--describes the plight of the urban poor. Along the way, Simon dispels many current myths surrounding the poor. Among these are that the poor are lazy, unclean, mobile and that those on relief have it too good. In a section entitled "Politics and Poverty" he describes the powerlessness and voicelessness of the urban poor. The book concludes with a section on the church and how it has lost touch with poverty. Simon cites more employment opportunities for the poor and a more personal feeling for the poor by society as solutions to the poverty problem.

Simpson, Richard. "Parental Influence, Anticipatory Socialization and Social Mobility." American Sociological Review (August 1962): 517-522.

(IX)

Using data from questionnaires administered in two southern city high schools, the author explores the relative impact of parental and peer group influences on occupational mobility aspirations. His findings support the hypothesis that for both middle class and working class boys, the extent of anticipatory socialization into middle class values depends in large part on their associations and friendships with middle class peers. He concludes, however, that parental advice has a stronger effect in influencing mobility aspirations.

Singell, Larry D. "Barriers to Earning Income." _The Quarterly Review of Economics and Business_ 8 (No. 2, 1968): 35-44.

(IX,X,XI)

Three explanations for poverty are offered: the overall state of the economy; the level of aggregate demand; and correlates with poverty status, especially for households headed by non-aged white males. Poverty resulting from low productivity may be exacerbated by low geographical and occupational mobility. These, in turn, may be explained by age, insufficient access to education and family restrictions for females. Several groups suffer from economic discrimination. Non-white median family income was half that of whites and the gap was widening. Non-whites were less likely to escape from poverty. Leaving the labor market was tantamount to entering poverty for most of those over 65. Women were at a substantial disadvantage in the labor market, with many occupations completely closed off.

Sjaastad, Larry A. "The Costs and Returns of Human Migration." _Journal of Political Economy_ 70 (1962): 80-93.

(VI)

Classical migration theory predicts that migration will equalize the per capita income of different regions. Although there has been a long term trend in this direction, the equalization has been very incomplete. This contradiction is often thought to be caused by barriers to mobility. Sjaastad argues "that disaggregation of both the migrant and parent population by at least age and occupation may be required to confirm (or deny) the alleged failure of migration to achieve a reasonably equal income distribution over space." This suggests that migration cannot be viewed in isolation. Migration, training and experience should be seen as investments in human capital. Human capital investments other than migration, such as training and experience, could explain the observed immobility in the face of large differentials in current earnings. "In addition, only the estimation of the direct as well as associated costs of migration together with returns can reveal the extent of the misallocation created by the frequently alleged barriers to mobility."

The author also emphasizes that net migration rates are more relevant "for studying the returns to migration as well as the impact of migration upon earnings differentials." Typically, areas with a net out-migration have a gross in-migration several times larger. This in-migration must be explained even though the out-migration is greater.

*Sjaastad, Larry. "The Relationship Between Migration and Income in the United States." Regional Science Association Paper and Proceedings 6 (1960): 37-64.

(VI)

Viewing migration as an investment in human capital, Sjaastad examines the relationship between measured income differentials and labor mobility. In the first part of Sjaastad's study, he uses a simple least squares regression analysis to investigate the relationship between migration and other economic variables. By looking at the in- and out-migration patterns of California, income differences do not appear to be equalizing. Distance and climate tend to have more impact on in- and out-migration than income. In the second part of his study, non-equalizing income differentials are assumed and the focus is shifted onto the population change in several states due solely to migration. Kuznets and Thomas' migration estimates are run through a multiple regression model, and the expected signs of the coefficients of the variables (farm population, rate of change in income, and education) consistently turned out to be incorrect. Rapidly increasing income was shown to scare away the migrant. Sjaastad recommends improving the channels of information and artificially increasing the incentive the market offers as a national migration policy.

*Smeeding, Timothy. "Cost of Living Differentials at Low-Income Levels." Institute for Research on Poverty Discussion Papers 190 (1974).

(III,V,VI)

Intercity nationwide cost-of-living differences are estimated at low (poverty and below) income levels using the Bureau of Labor Statistics' Urban Family Budgets for three higher living standards. In addition, intra-area big city/small city cost-of-living differences are extrapolated in the same way. The results support the conclusion that even the most extreme nationwide cost anomalies are not so large as to substantiate regionally differentiated income maintenance benefits or poverty thresholds. Such a policy would probably create much more inequity than it corrected. The intra-area differentials are smaller than inter-regional cost discrepancies in every case. Finally, a caveat is posed for the current welfare maze. Substantial money benefit differences in public assistance programs between the states are for the most part real benefit differences which may have caused unwanted migration of low-income households to high benefit states.

Smith, David. The Geography of Well-Being in the United States. New York: McGraw-Hill, 1973.

(V,VI,XI)

Beginning with a description of the present research on regionalization and the classification of cities, Smith lays the "groundwork" for comparing social well-being in different parts of the United States. Smith then proceeds to design an index of social well-being for each of the states. His six indicators include income, wealth, and employment; environment; health; social disorganization; alienation; and participation. Using these he runs a series of correlations with socioeconomic variables and rating patterns. Nonwhites and the poorly educated ranked lower on the scale of social well-being.

*Smith, James D., and Franklin, Stephen D. "New Dimensions of Economic Inequality: The Concentration of Personal Wealth, 1922-1969." American Economic Review 64 (May 1974).

(II,VII)

Estimates of the concentration of personal wealth are presented for the years 1922 to 1969. The wealth of the richest 1.0 and .5 percent was calculated using the estate multiplier technique and data from the IRS estate tax returns. The results indicate that the distribution of wealth became significantly more equal in the 1930's and 1940's but that it has remained essentially unchanged since 1945. "The diminution has not been great, however, and it all occurred during periods when the market system was functioning under duress or was in administrative abeyance, specifically, the Great Depression and World War II." Lampman determined that the richest .5 percent owned 32.4 percent of the net wealth in early 1929 and 19.3 percent in 1949. The gradual upward trend since the 1950's suggested by Lampman is rejected by the authors who see the wealth share at the top essentially stable, with differences since 1945 attributable to data inadequacies, sampling errors, and short run market fluctuations. Estimates are given for the shares of specific assets held, and the only striking change noted is the decline in the concentration of corporate stockholdings. "The richest .5 percent of the population held 86 percent of the value of personally owned stock in 1953, but only 44 percent in 1969."

Smith, James D., and Morgan, James N. "Variability of Economic Well-Being and Its Determinants." American Economic Review 60 (May 1970): 286-299.

(IV,IX)

A group of 4500 families is ranked by income decile for the years 1967 and 1968, and the percentage shifts across decile ranks is calculated. The same procedure is followed for a ranking on the basis of the ratio of income to Social Security Administration (SSA) family need standard. The pattern of change is similar for both measures though the ratio standard indicates that a larger number of families altered their relative position. These short run variations are then correlated with changes in family size and employment pattern as well as a variety of motivational factors. For example, it is found that "Education, where it is significant, places last after the middle class virtues of aspiration, efficacy and planning ahead, and risk avoidance in enlarging the predicted value of change in family income." However, only about 11.5 percent of the income variance was accounted for by this analysis. A similar correlation was run on a subsample of the group that only included families in the lower three deciles of 1967 income. The short run variation in poor family income "is explained primarily by changes in labor force participation and by status variables such as age and education."

Smith, Vernon K. "Welfare Work Incentives: The Earnings Exemption and Its Impact upon AFDC Employment, Earnings, and Program Costs." Michigan Department of Social Services Studies in Welfare Policy #2, 1974.

(IX)

An analysis of the changes in employment and earning levels of AFDC recipients in two Michigan counties following the implementation of the 1967 Social Security Act Amendment. This amendment included an earnings exemption for the first $30 a month earned and a 67% implied tax rate on all additional earnings. This exemption replaced a system in which any earnings of an AFDC recipient resulted in an equal reduction in benefit payments--a 100% implicit tax on earnings. An analysis of 1184 welfare mothers in Michigan showed that the exemption caused a significant increase in employment and in the number of un-employed AFDC mothers becoming employed. The absolute percentage employed remained very low (it increased from 10 to 14%) because of the many problems AFDC mothers face in attempting to enter the work force. The five primary determinants of employability and earnings were found to be the expected market wage, child care costs, income from welfare (a 10% increase in welfare resulted in a 12% decrease in the probability of employment), the presence of a child under 3, and the health of the head of the household.

Smolensky, Eugene. "The Past and Present Poor." In The Concept of Poverty. U. S. Chamber of Commerce, Task Force on Economic Growth and Opportunity. Washington, D.C.: 1965.

(II,X)

A brief historical survey of poverty and income distribution in the United States in the 20th century. Author observes that definition of poverty changes over time and that changes in definition are reflected in the way poverty is measured. He presents two kinds of measures to describe the course of poverty: (1) the "minimum-decency" estimate, an absolute but periodically changing measure; and (2) a "distribution estimate" based on "proportion of income going to lowest income groups."

A paradox reveals itself in the historical view of changes in the meaning and measurement of poverty: "Higher rates of growth will lead to a more rapid rise in the definition of poverty, but only when that definition rises rapidly can poverty be reduced." To illuminate this point, author discusses effect of sustained full-employment level during periods of extraordinary economic growth (i.e., 1880-1910 and 1940-1945) on income distribution and incidence of poverty. The recent growth in unemployment is seen as a foreshadowing of a rise in income inequality.

Smolensky, Eugene; Stiefel, Leanna; Schmundt, Maria; and Plotnick, Robert. "Adding In-Kind Transfers to the Personal Income and Outlay Account: Implications for the Size Distribution of Income." Institute for Research on Poverty Discussion Papers 199 (1974).

(V)

The paper urges that the official government Personal Income and Outlay account be altered to record all government in-kind transfers to clearly identifiable beneficiaries (e.g., food stamps, public housing, education, manpower programs, etc.). Since the cost of these transfers to taxpayers was found to be a suitable approximation to their value to recipients, the transfers should be valued at cost.

Most of these transfers are not from the very rich to the very poor, but rather in and among the great numbers near the median income. The poor gain some in the process, but not enough to have any substantial impact on overall measures of inequality.

Snyder, Eleanor M. "Financing a Family." Eugenical News. New York: (December 1953).

(IV)

Observes effect of differences in family size and changes in family circumstance over time on level of family consumption. Concludes that:

1) "Cost of financing at a constant level of living varies over time for families of a given size." Author attributes this fact to shifting relation between income and price level and to changes in the economic milieu.

2) "For families of different sizes, the relative cost of equivalent levels of living varies from one period of time to another" due to changes occuring in equivalent market baskets.

3) "Relative cost of financing families of different sizes varies between income levels;" relative differences in equivalent living costs, by family size, increase as income increases.

4) "Relative cost of financing families of given size varies with age of parents."

Snyder, Eleanor M. "A Method of Identifying Chronic Low-Income Groups from Cross-Section Survey Data." Studies in Income and Wealth 25 (1958): 321-354.

(VII)

A discussion of the methods and concepts used in an estimate of the poor population based on a 1950 Bureau of Labor Statistics Survey. The estimate was based on a minimum budget line derived from the Bureau of Labor Statistics minimum family budget for city workers and a family equivalence scale developed by Dorothy Brady. All families with current income above this level were classified as non-poor. The remainder were checked against four standards of high consumption and dissavings in an effort to eliminate those families whose low incomes were due to temporary factors. Only those families whose home equipment and durable expenditures were less than 10% of their income, whose food and home expenditures were less than 100% of their income, and who had not bought either a car or house during the preceding year were considered poor.

19% of the population qualified as having low economic status; another 8% had low incomes but adequate economic status. An examination of the income-consumption patterns of these two groups showed that consumption equaled income for the low economic status group but was much greater than income for those in the low income, adequate economic status group. The paper concludes with a detailed discussion of the economic well-being of "doubled up" families. Comments on the paper generally praised it but objected to one or more of the standards of high consumption, particularly the two dealing with auto and home buying.

Sochet, Mary Allen. "Does Our Education Perpetuate Poverty?" Journal of Human Relations 13 (No. 4, 1965): 466-474.

(IX,XI)

The author uses findings of several community studies to argue that class disposition affects behavior and community acceptance. The education system, as it is now set up, does not sufficiently recognize these cultural differences, especially between the middle and lower classes; the system is middle class oriented and subordinates lower class values. This situation has a deleterious effect on the lower class child's self-respect as his pre-school identities are negated.

Because the poverty syndrome is directly related to education, or the lack of it, it is necessary that this wrong be rectified. A human touch and an understanding of different life styles are required. For teachers, this effort calls for more sociological training and a greater degree of community involvement. For the parents, this means greater participation in the schools.

Solomon, Arthur P. Housing the Urban Poor. Cambridge: The Massachusetts Institute of Technology Press, 1974.

(V)

An examination of the objectives and costs of programs and strategies for housing the urban poor. The study offers a systematic comparison of alternative strategies for meeting this objective. The performance of new construction, rehabilitation and programs for using existing housing are empirically contrasted. The major area of consideration is the magnitude of the benefits received by subsidized tenants and how these benefits are distributed. Based on analysis of the performance and costs of alternative strategies to deal with the problem of housing the urban poor, the author concludes that the national housing policy must be redirected toward a leased housing program.

*Solow, Robert. "Income Equality Since the War." In Inequality and Poverty, edited by Edward C. Budd. New York: W.W. Norton and Co., 1967.

(II,IX)

A brief essay on the trends in income inequality between 1939 and the late 1950's. Solow concludes that during this period, income has become somewhat more equally distributed. The largest gains in equalization occurred during the period before 1945, and reflect at least to some extent the large reduction in the unemployment rate during the period.

Soltow, Lee, ed. Six Papers on the Size Distribution of Wealth and Income. New York: National Bureau of Economic Research, 1969.

(VII)

A collection of six papers presented at the Conference on the Size Distribution of Income and Wealth held in 1967 at the University of Pennsylvania.

The first paper deals with trends in the wealth distribution in the 19th century. The second is a similar study for the period 1950-1962. The last four papers, by Schultz, Projector-Weiss-Thoresen, Epstein, and Reder all deal with income and are separately annotated.

Sorenson, Aage B. "The Structure of Intragenerational Mobility." Institute for Research on Poverty Discussion Papers (237-74), University of Wisconsin, Madison.

(IX)

Paper analyzes mobility rates for Black and white men using life history data on intragenerational mobility. Structural changes in society (more jobs, etc.) are reflected in the mobility of men. Sorenson defines this impact in a model for the rate of mobility. It appears that Blacks have profited somewhat less from the expansion of the economy in terms of opportunities for better jobs than have whites. In his analysis, Sorenson conceived of mobility as generated by an interplay between individual characteristics (such as choice) and structural characteristics (of the economy). More specifically, mobility is seen as the outcome of an individual's attempts to improve his occupational achievement in an occupational structure where opportunities for better jobs are finite.

*Spady, William G. "Educational Mobility and Access: Growth and Paradoxes." The American Journal of Sociology 73 (1967): 273-286.

(IX,XI)

The educational attainments of American males aged 25-64 are examined in relation to the educational backgrounds of their fathers. Although attainment levels improve for men in all status groups over time, the differences in reaching and completing college between men from high- and low-status origins appear to be increasing over time. The attainments of whites exceed those of non-whites for all status and age groups. Status differences are found to be increasingly important determinants of one's final level of educational attainment.

Spring, William. "Underemployment: The Measure We Refuse to Take." New Generation (Winter 1971).

(III,X)

A strong statement in favor of the adoption of a sub-employment index. The initial sub-employment index developed by the Department of Labor in 1966-67 is reviewed. This index included not only the unemployed, but those earning at or below the poverty level, discouraged and part-time workers seeking full-time employment. When this index was calculated for ghetto areas, the results were startling. In 1966, Harlem, for example, had sub-employment rates of 33%. The political difficulties encountered by the Secretary of Labor (then Williard Wirtz) in gaining acceptance and use of the sub-employment index are chronicled. Spring suggests that sub-employment indices are essential, since "unemployment statistics bear only a fractional relationship to the failure of the economy to provide support for its members."

*Spring, William; Harrison, Bennet; and Vietorisz, Thomas. "The Crisis of the Underemployed." New York Times Magazine, 5 November 1972, pp. 14-16.

(X)

One of the problems of the economies in America's large cities is that a large proportion of the residents work for wages which are below living standard. Spring, Harrison, and Vietorisz probe into this problem by investigating new employment measures and criticizing the traditional employment statistics. They cite the present monthly unemployment standard to be weak because it covers up the real employment problem in urban areas, that of "subemployment." The consequence of continuing to use these statistics is that present economic difficulties are understated, and this leads to false assumptions about the urban ghetto life style. Solutions include the use of the subemployment index, adequate income redistribution, public employment jobs, and a significant minimum wage bill.

Stack, Carol B., and Semmel, Herbert. "The Concept of Family in the Poor Black Community." <u>Studies in Public Welfare</u>, U.S. Joint Economic Committee, Paper No. 2, Part II. Washington, D.C.: U.S. Government Printing Office, 1973.

(IV)

Explores domestic sharing patterns among poor blacks and the effects of government programs on those patterns. According to the authors, household networks formed by poor black families promote strength and stability and maximize available resources.

The article examines the relative merits and disadvantages of the support enforcement programs in their effect on domestic network tendencies. Also presented is the argument that the definition of "family" under the current AFDC benefit schedule is a deterrent to these beneficial sharing tendencies; poor people are less likely to form extended domestic units when benefits per person decline with family size. The policy implications of this conclusion call for a benefit schedule which allows equal allowances per person on the grant.

Staehle, H. "A Development of the Economic Theory of Index Numbers." <u>The Review of Economic Studies</u> 2(1934-35): 163-88.

(III)

The purpose of cost-of-living comparisons is to determine the money incomes that will yield the same satisfaction in two or more situations. Allen and Haberler developed theories of cost-of-living index numbers showing that the Laspeyre and Paasche indexes constituted respectively valid upper and lower limits to the measure of the price differences. But their results, while formally correct, were not useful. They assumed, <u>in advance</u>, that the incomes corresponding to the situations yielded equal satisfaction. Thus, the "true" cost-of-living index was simply the ratio of the two incomes. The detailed computation of limits was irrelevant.

Konus developed a model that dropped this restrictive assumption, but only half completed the solution. Staehle developed Konus' model thereby obtaining valid limits to the price measures relating to the two situations.

While dropping the equivalent incomes assumption, Staehle's model retained the very serious assumption of identical tastes and milieu without which this method of limits is not meaningful.

*Stambler, Howard V. "New Statistical Barometers of Poverty." Occupational Outlook Quarterly (Spring 1969): 1-3.

(III,X)

A discussion of the Bureau of Labor Statistics' (BLS) efforts during the late sixties to provide new statistical measures of poverty using unemployment and subemployment data. The department's first program began in 1966 when broad estimates of unemployment in poverty areas of large cities were developed as a preliminary analysis for further study. This work led to intensive surveys in late 1966 of employment and unemployment in 9 city slums. "By separating the problems of the slums from those of the more affluent surrounding areas in the cities and by publishing findings on a city by city basis, many specific slum problems were diagnosed for the first time...." The data from 9 cities provided the information needed to measure the entire employment-hardship complex--the subemployment index, which combines unemployment data with data on underemployment, involuntary nonparticipation in the labor force, and inadequate earnings. The index revealed a "subemployment" rate of 34 percent in inner city ghettos, compared to an unemployment rate of 10 percent.

Following these surveys, the BLS began regular surveys of employment problems in six large cities. Also data is now being published on the labor force and unemployment in 20 major metropolitan areas and 14 of their central cities.

Stein, Robert L. "New Definitions for Employment and Unemployment." Employment and Earnings and Monthly Report of the Labor Force (February 1967): 1-7.

(X)

Improved methods for measuring employment and unemployment which went into effect as of the January, 1967 issue of the Current Population Survey (CPS) are reported. The CPS sample has been enlarged from 35,000 households in 357 sample areas to 52,500 households in 449 sample areas. The lower age limit for official statistics on employment and unemployment has been raised from 14 to 16. To be counted as unemployed, a person must have engaged in some job-seeking activity within the past four weeks, must be waiting to start a new job within 30 days, or must be waiting to be recalled from lay-off. The new definition of "unemployed" does not include inactive work seekers who have not searched in four weeks. The new definition of "unemployed" does include persons holding jobs but not at work. In addition to these changes, new questions have been added to the survey to clarify information reported and additional information about the composition of the employed, unemployed, and persons outside of the labor force is being compiled.

Stein, Robert L. "Reasons for Non-Participation in the Labor Force." Monthly Labor Review 90 (July 1967): 22-27.

(X)

"Nonparticipation in the labor force has become a major concern for manpower research and analysis. Among the important questions that need to be answered are the size and composition of the labor reserve--the groups of persons not seeking work at present, but who do move into and out of the labor force, either in response to seasonal changes or on a more irregular basis; the dimensions of the discouragement problem--its causes and the remedial steps that might help discouraged workers find their place in the job market; the number and characteristics of people who need or want work and would be able to take jobs if something were done to help them (health programs, child care, training, etc.). It is also essential to develop a method for measuring changes in these various groups over time."

The article reports the results of a 1966 survey whose specific purpose was to try out a group of sample questions for measuring some aspects of nonparticipation.

Steinberg, Alan. "The Case for a Wealth Tax." Social Policy 3(1973): 51-54.

(VII)

Steinberg advocates replacing the present tax structure with a wealth tax on the very rich and a modified sales tax. The income tax on corporations and professionals is passed on to consumers in the form of higher prices, making it in fact regressive. Income taxes leave great wealth intact while hindering new entries into the ranks of the wealthy. And they corrupt the integrity of society by rewarding cheating. The new wealth tax would equalize the distribution of wealth and power in society. The sales tax would fall only on non-necessities and thus be less regressive than present sales taxes.

Stigler, George. "Determinants of the Distribution of Labor Incomes." In Inequality and Poverty, edited by Edward C. Budd. New York: W.W. Norton, 1967.

(II,IX)

A standard exposition of the neoclassical model of the determinants of wage variance. Stigler begins with a model of the competitive wage structure, in which an equilibrium is reached "when the net advantages of all occupations open to the workers are equal." Observed wage differences arise in this model from cross-occupational differences in job-related expense, training costs, employment instability, living cost differences and psychic income associated with the job. In an extension of the model, Stigler further suggests that income differences arise from differences in individuals' abilities, luck, information, and discrimination. No attempt is made to quantify the relative contribution of these diverse factors.

Stocker, Frederick D., and Ellickson, John C. "How Fully Do Farmers Report Their Incomes?" National Tax Journal 12 (1959): 116-126.

(VI)

A comparison is made between 1955 IRS farm income statistics and farm income and expenditure statistics from various sources in the Department of Agriculture to determine how accurately farmers report their incomes. It is found that some personal expenditures of farmers are deducted as business expenses, but this practice appears to be no more widespread among farmers than among owners of other small unincorporated businesses. Some farmers undoubtedly understate their incomes, but the authors conclude that unreported receipts in farming amount to very little in the aggregate.

Stockwell, Edward G. "A Critical Examination of the Relationship Between Socio-economic Status and Mortality. American Journal of Public Health 53 (1963).

(XI)

Past studies noted a definite inverse relationship between mortality rates and socio-economic status. In more recent times this differential has been disputed, either for total mortality or for mortality from specific causes. If this relationship exists, there is still disagreement as to whether or not it is narrowing.

These determinations seem to vary from one area to another, and they may depend on the variables used in any particular study. To clarify this situation, a series of studies for purposes of comparison is needed. It is proposed that studies of the 1960 Census be utilized to start a series of ongoing reports of the relationship of socio-economic status to mortality in this country.

(Poverty and Health in the U.S.)

Stockwell, Edward G. "Infant Mortality and Socio-economic Status: A Changing Relationship." Milbank Memorial Fund Quarterly 40 (1962): 101-111.

(XI)

The decline in infant mortality has long been used as an index of level of living and an indication of social and economic well-being since man has been able to control environmental conditions related to infectious diseases and countries have undergone economic development. Numerous studies have related infant mortality to income level and social class, as well as other variables such as race, feeding practices, and physical condition of the mother.

Though infant mortality may still be used as a measure for ranking countries' overall levels of social and economic well-being, the present study indicates that, at least in Providence, infant mortality is no longer a sensitive index of socio-economic difference as it was in the past. "The erratic pattern that was observed when total infant mortality was related to SES was found to be a reflection of the fact that the majority of deaths under one year of age today occur during the first few hours or days of life, and are due to causes that are associated with biological rather than SES factors. On the other hand, for those few deaths that take place between the ages of one month and one year, where the major causes of death are farther removed from the physiological processes of gestation and birth, infant mortality continues to be inversely related to differences in SES."

Stone, R. "Economic and Demographic Accounts and the Distribution of Income." _Acta Oeconomica_ 11 (No. 2-3, 1973): 65-176.

(II)

An attempt to provide a basis for a model of the social economy. The model as a whole is concerned with two aspects of human endeavor: the attempt to find work of a kind suited to individual capacities and inclinations; and, at the same time, the need to produce goods and services which will satisfy the same group of individuals in their capacity as consumers. It is also concerned with the distribution of income which emerges from these two sets of preferences. Stone posits that the distribution of income results from job preferences and consumer preferences; and since these latter two factors can only be measured in an empirical sense (not predicted, nor easily changed), it follows that the distribution of income will be very difficult to change.

Stotz, Margaret. "The BLS Interim Budget for a Retired Couple." _Monthly Labor Review_ (November 1960).

(III,IV)

Retired couple's "modest but adequate" budget originally developed in '40's to parallel City Worker's Family Budget. Revised budget reflects increase in postwar standard of living as well as increase in standard itself. Budget constructed to provide for social and psychological needs, not just minimum subsistence.

The "budget family" consists of a husband and wife, 64 years-old-plus, living in a 2- to 3-room dwelling in an urban area. They are profiled as self-supporting and in good health.

Kinds and quantities of goods and services provided in the budget for this family derived according to scientific standards and prevailing consumption preferences as reflected in consumption data. Report presents specific methodologies for revising quantities and kinds of food; rent, heat and utilities; other goods and services. Actual pricing studies of these kinds and quantities of items conducted to set costs.

Straszheim, Mahlon. The Economics of the Urban Housing Market. New York: National Bureau of Economic Research, 1975.

(III)

An overview of the economics of the housing market and its function in urban and community development. After a review of the existing economic theories on housing, Straszheim examines the compartmentalization of the urban housing market in San Francisco. Using data from a large scale home interview treating housing as a multidimensional commodity and estimating prices of different housing services in different locations indicate that urban housing needs to be analyzed along a "disaggregated geographic" basis. Household demand functions are then estimated as well as the effects of racial discrimination on housing consumed by Black households. The results indicate that both the price of a particular housing attribute and the prices of several substitute and complementary housing attributes are very significant to the bundle of services decision. Other conclusions include that household choices pertaining to lot size and age of structure are sensitive to the spatial variation of relative prices of different characteristics, and household decisions collectively tend to influence the sale price of the house.

Straus, Murray A. "Deferred Gratification, Social Class, and the Achievement Syndrome." American Sociological Review 27 (June 1962): 326-336.

(IV,XI)

The theoretical and research literature on self-imposed postponement of gratifications or satisfactions is reviewed with emphasis on the relation of a "Deferred Gratification Pattern" (DPG) to social class and social mobility. Three hypotheses evolving from this review were tested on 338 male high school students. The hypothesis of a deferred gratification pattern received some support from the data; the hypothesis of positive correlation between socioeconomic status and DPG was not supported; the hypothesis of positive correlation between the DPG scales and achievement role-performance and role-orientation was supported. Findings were interpreted as supporting the theory that needed deferment is functional for social mobility in American society.

(Partially taken from American Sociological Review)

Straus, Robert. "The Problem of Conceptualizing Poverty." In <u>Poverty: New Interdisciplinary Perspectives</u>, edited by Weaver and Magid. San Francisco: Chandler Publishing Co., 1969.

(II)

A discussion of attitudes toward and conceptions of poverty, calling for a holistic, integrated approach. The historical origins of conceptions of poverty include the medieval notion that it was a mark of divine intervention, and the Darwinian notion that the poor are victims in a natural survival-of-the-fittest struggle. In current American thought, the value of rugged individualism opposes that of economic security for all citizens; humanitarian values conflict with the forces of prejudice and discrimination. A unifying study of poverty must recognize the fundamental interaction among components of behavior which are often viewed as self-contained systems. Poverty must be studied in relation to man as a biological organism, as a personality, as part of his physical environment and cultural milieu, as a social being, and in the dimension of time. Initial steps toward a more unified approach are now occurring, concomitant with more comprehensive governmental programs.

(Partially taken from <u>Poverty and Human Resources Abstracts</u>)

Streightoff, Frank Hatch. <u>The Standard of Living Among the Industrial People of America</u>. Boston: Houghton-Mifflin, 1911.

(II,III,VII)

Standard of living is a result of two forces: environment, comprising time, income, and class; and individuality. "The standard is properly counted ideally high in proportion as it achieves this end (healthy symmetrical development, physical, mental, and moral), and especially as its emphasis falls upon the intellectual and moral elements." The content of the lowest tolerable standard of living should include: food, clothing, and shelter sufficient to maintain economic efficiency, with provision against sickness and unemployment, and a family. A family with a normal standard of living should have a house which includes a room fit for the entertainment of company, and should be able to provide for education, books, pictures, wholesome recreation, and religion as a routine. In 1911 monetary values this would require an annual income of $825 for an average family in New York City. Generally, the extreme low limit of the annual living wage necessary to provide a tolerable standard of living is $650 for the cities of the East, North, and West, and $600 for the cities of the South.

Stuart, Bruce. "Equity and Medicaid." Journal of Human Resources 7 (Spring 1972).

(V)

This paper is concerned with the differential impact of the Medicaid program on state incomes in 1967-68. Benefits and costs of the program are calculated for each state and the results are evaluated in terms of the program planners. It was found that although the program favors the poor in all states with Title XIX plans, it does so at the expense of extreme horizontal inequity. The conclusion is that federal incentives for the development of comprehensive state Medicaid programs are inadequate to insure an equitable system for the distribution of program benefits and costs.

(Journal of Human Resources)

Studies in Public Welfare, U.S. Joint Economic Committee, Paper No. 12, Parts I and II. Washington, D.C.: U.S. Government Printing Office, 1973.

(XI)

A collection of papers which explore the inter-relatedness of government welfare programs and family instability among the poor.

An introductory paper by Robert Lerman presents a summary review of the separate essays in the report. The essays address issues relating to the causes and effects of broken families and female headship of families, the extent to which government programs promote disruption of families, the appropriate role of government programs in influencing family structure, the effectiveness of vigorous state support enforcement programs in discouraging desertion, and the equity and incentive effects of income transfer programs.

Sturdivant, Frederick D., and Cocanougher, A. Benton. "Low-Income Consumers in Non-Urban Marketplaces." Social Science Quarterly 55 (June 1974): 131-140.

(VI,VII)

Several studies in the 1960's and early 1970's have concluded that low-income consumers in urban settings participate in a retail market that is significantly different from the market system serving the rest of society. "Ghetto retailing systems were found to be more fragmented, less efficient, faced with serious cost problems, and too often characterized by questionable or illegal merchandising practices. Consumers, in addition to being poor, were often minority group members, relatively immobile shoppers (for physical and/or psychological reasons), heavily dependent on credit, ill-informed about their legal rights, and vulnerable to unethical merchandising practices."

In this article, the authors compare the urban retail market with the retail market for low-income consumers in two small towns of 5,000-10,000 population in Texas and California respectively. They found that while it cannot be said that small town poor are not victims of discriminatory merchandising practices, they are victimized in this way much less than low-income urban residents. Since, for the most part, smalltown low- and middle-income residents shop in the same marketplace, rural poor "enjoy an 'umbrella' effect largely unknown to the city poor where shopping is largely restricted to a separate marketplace."

Suchman, Edward A. "The 'Addictive' Disorders as Socioenvironmental Health Problems." In Handbook of Medical Sociology, edited by Howard E. Freeman et al. Englewood Cliffs, New Jersey: Prentice-Hall, Inc., 1972.

(XI)

In recent years, as medical advances have largely controlled infectious diseases, the social as well as the physical aspects of man's environment have warranted attention. An individual's social relationships, family, work, leisure activities, and eating, sleeping, and exercise habits all influence where and how he lives which, in turn, determine his physical and mental health. All of these factors are related to exposure and susceptibility to disease.

Suchman states:

> There is a complex interplay between socioenvironmental factors, social problems, health conditions, and public-health programs. Each may lead to the other in myriad ways. For example, poor housing (a physical condition) may lead to the growth of slums (a social problem), which in turn increases exposure to tuberculosis (a health condition), which then requires the development of a preventive and therapeutic measure (a public health program).

Certain addictive disorders are a result of socio-environmental forces; there is a direct relationship between addiction and poverty with its associated hopelessness and futility. A disproportionately large number of drug addicts, for example, are members of minority and lower class groups.

The author defines and describes alcoholism, narcotics addiction, and marijuana and comprehensively studies each in terms of its extent, distribution, and consequences, as well as social factors in its etiology and control. Suchman describes future prospects for the addictive disorders and suggests directions for treatment and rehabilitation programs and further research.

Surface, Bill. <u>The Hollow</u>. New York: Coward-McCann, Inc., 1971.

(V,VI)

As Surface reports the occurrences of five consecutive days, including the important "check day," in the lives of the inhabitants of eight small houses in a nameless eastern Kentucky hollow, the people's lives, beliefs and associations illustrate the dilemma of Appalachia. The isolated and deprived existence depicted might be considered a microcosm of all that the word "Appalachia" connotes. Lengthy, descriptive passages and realistic dialogue transport the reader as we share the author's experiences in a journey through the mountains. The memorable people he encountered become partially fictionalized as we view what has happened to them since $600 million in federal-state assistance has gone into the area since 1965. Surface asks, "Have these people been forgotten, or have a meaningful number of lives been upgraded?"

Sweet, James A. "The Employment of Wives and the Inequality of Family Income." Institute for Research on Poverty (120-72). Madison: The University of Wisconsin-Madison, 1971.

(II,X)

Article challenges Wilber Thompson's assertion that the existence of jobs for women acts to reduce inequality (of family income) in that working wives come more proportionately from the lower income groups. Using Gini measures computed on "husband's income," "family income," and "family income less wife's earnings" distributions, Sweet concludes that the employment of wives has only a very small effect on the inequality of family income in the United States. The disproportionate contribution of adults other than husband and wife rather than the greater proportion of Negro wives in the work force explains why family income is considerably less inequitably distributed between the races than is the income of married males.

"Symposium: Views on American Poverty." <u>Journal of Human Relations</u> 15 (No. 2, 1967): 146-168.

(II)

A presentation of three papers on American poverty from a social-psychological and philosophical point of view. Ben Kaplan's "The Culture of Poverty: The Moral Perspective" gives a brief descriptive profile of the culture of the poor, a culture lacking cohesiveness and generating nihilism. Alvin L. Bertrand's "Poverty as Relative

Deprivation: A Sociological View" discusses the problem of defining poverty, the reasons for our interest in poverty, and the statistical realities of poverty in America. To him, poverty is relative deprivation, which is a state of mind that comes from differential possession of things. Peggy Siegmund's "Poverty From Behind the Plow: The Rural Generation and Spread of American Poverty" believes that rural poverty, which is primarily agricultural, is the root of American poverty. She describes the characteristics of the small farmer, his plight, and the social consequences of his poverty. Although she has no definition of her own, she cites Michael Harrington's definition of poverty--"those who are denied the minimal levels of health, housing, food, and education that our present stage of scientific knowledge specifies as necessary for life as it is now lived in the United States," and "...those whose place in the society is such that they are internal exiles who, almost inevitably, develop attitudes of defeat and pessimism and who are therefore excluded from taking advantage of new opportunities."

Tabbarah, Riad M. "The Adequacy of Income: A Social Dimension in Economic Development." Journal of Developmental Studies 8 (April 1972): 57-75.

(II,IV,VI)

Income measures alone are generally found to be of limited usefulness to welfare studies so that some measure of need is often used in conjunction with income to account for such variables as family size and location. In this article, needs, as viewed by the families themselves, are also considered relevant and are incorporated into an index of income adequacy. This index is defined as the ratio of income to need for income where this need is a function of socio-economic status as well as parameters like family size and location that are typically considered in poverty studies. The dependency on socio-economic status is to be determined by revealed tastes and opinion polls. A definition of this kind is considered appropriate for a broader range of social phenomena such as pattern of savings and consumption or even studies of alienation. Moreover, the analysis of trends in economic growth measures in per capita income or the comparisons of international income averages can conceal the relative adequacy of these incomes as perceived by individuals.

*Taeuber, Karl E. "Duration-of-Residence Analysis of Internal Migration in the U.S." Milbank Memorial Fund Quarterly 39 (1961): 116-131.

(VI)

This paper discusses the migration information provided by responses to a question on duration of residence and presents the first national migration data derived from this approach. Most of the data were from Current Population Reports.

"The most distinctive feature of duration data, however, is the glimpse they give into migration as part of the life history of persons. An individual's changes of residence are not independent of previous changes of residence; neither are the migrations of a given year independent of the changing residential patterns of the nation." Responses to a single question on duration of current residence can provide only a small proportion of the data needed to proceed very far with the longitudinal analysis of migration. Information on place of previous residence, is necessary to permit duration analysis of specific migration streams. Even more information is necessary to provide more complete longitudinal data.

"Analysis of the basic duration data continually suggest the need for such additional information. Duration-of-residence analysis is but a preliminary step in the systematic study of migration within the context of the life cycle of the individual and the population redistributions of the nation."

(Annotation partially taken from Mangalam, J.J. Human Migration: A Guide to Migration Literature in English, 1955-1962. Lexington: University of Kentucky Press, 1968.)

*Taeuber, Karl E. "Toward a Social Report: A Review Article." Journal of Human Resources 5 (No. 3, 1970).

(XI)

Reviews Toward a Social Report, the Department of Health, Education, and Welfare's report discussing the development of a comprehensive set of social indicators. The HEW Report covers the following areas: health and illness; social mobility; physical environment; income and poverty; public order and safety; learning, science, and art; participation and alienation. Taeuber assesses various aspects of the Report and concludes that although the Report has shortcomings, social reporting is indeed an idea whose time has come. The strength of social reporting lies in its social perspective and its policy relevance, both of which, unfortunately, are lacking in the Report.

Taeuber, Karl E., and Taeuber, Alma F. "The Changing Character of Negro Migration." American Journal of Sociology 78 (1965): 429-441.

(VI)

Recently published data on migration during the 1955-60 period reveal that, contrary to the popular stereotype, Negro in-migrants to a number of large cities, despite the presence of a socioeconomically depressed group of non-metropolitan origin, were not of lower average socioeconomic status than the resident Negro population. Indeed, in educational attainment Negro in-migrants to northern cities were equal to or slightly higher than the resident white population. Comparisons with limited data for earlier periods suggest that, as the Negro population has changed from a disadvantaged rural population to a metropolitan one of increasing socioeconomic levels, its patterns of migration have changed to become very much like those of the white population.

(From the article)

Taeuber, Karl E., and Taeuber, Alma F. "White Migration and Socio-Economic Differences Between Cities and Suburbs." American Sociological Review 29 (1964): 718-729.

(VI)

Large cities are apparently becoming increasingly differentiated from their suburban rings in socio-economic status. It has been speculated that this results from an influx of low-status migrants to cities and an outflow of high-status persons from cities to suburbs. Analysis of census data on migration patterns between 1955 and 1960 for 12 large metropolitan areas indicates a different and more complex pattern. Nearly all streams of migrants are of higher average socio-economic status than non-migrants. Large cities contribute to their suburbs and to other metropolitan areas more high-status migrants than they receive, whereas suburban rings receive more high-status migrants than they lose. This circulation of persons of higher levels of educational attainment and occupational status has the net effect of diminishing the socio-economic level of central city populations and augmenting the socio-economic level of suburban populations.

(From the article)

Tarver, James. "Metropolitan Area Intercounty Migration Rates: A Test of Labor Market Theory." Industrial and Labor Relations Review 18 (1965): 213-223.

(VI)

This study proposes to determine whether geographic movement between counties from 1955 to 1960 follows those tendencies specified in labor market theory. It uses a multiple co-variance design to ascertain the significance of six independent covariables and two variables in explaining the migration rates of the 1960 residents of Standard Metropolitan Statistical Areas (SMSA's) and urbanized areas of the United States who moved between counties during the five years. Results show that census region of residence is the most prominent marginal factor and employment in manufacturing industries is the second most important marginal factor in explaining migration rates. Employment in white-collar occupations and the proportionate number of adults completing high school account for significant proportions of the variability in migration rates. Family income differentials have no appreciable influence on migration across county boundaries, after one adjusts for the effects of the other seven variables. Altogether, the independent variables account for 69 and 70 percent of the variations in 1955-1960 intercounty migration rates of the 212 SMSA's and 213 urbanized areas of the United States, respectively.

(From the article)

Tarver, James D. "Predicting Migration." Social Forces 39 (1961): 207-214.

(VI)

"Postulating that demographic, economic, and social variables are interdependent in explaining spatial mobility, this study accounts for 98 percent, 87 percent, and 95 percent, respectively, of the variations in the 1940-50 intercensal net migration rates of whites, nonwhites, and the total population of the 48 states and the District of Columbia. One of its contributions is the formulation of a technique which partitions the coefficients of multiple correlation, based on the three sets of structural variates, into their independent and interactive components."

The economic variable, employment in construction, was the dominant variable in explaining the variations in migration rates; however, for Blacks, demographic and social variables were more important than economic variables in explaining migration. For the total population, economic factors alone accounted for 77% of the variations in migration, demographic and social factors combined accounted for 80%, and taken together, the three factors accounted for 95% of the variations.

(Partially taken from article)

* Task Force on Economic Growth and Opportunity, Chamber of Commerce of the United States. The Concept of Poverty. Washington, D.C.: Library of Congress Catalogue No. 65-21323, 1965.

(II)

This report is the first of several published by the Task Force on Economic Growth and Opportunity as part of a large study of poverty. It examines: (a) the evolution of poverty in America, particularly the change in income distribution since 1929; (b) the concept or definition of poverty; (c) the measurement of poverty; (d) the evaluation of poverty programs; and (e) directions for further study. For each of the above issues, the Task Force concludes with one or more recommendations for action. Included in the report are papers on poverty written by Dunlop, Fuchs, Miller, and Smolensky. (These are annotated separately.) On the subject of poverty definition, the authors emphasize that poverty in the United states involves specific people, families, and groups, and is not a mass phenomenon as it may be in other countries. A distinction is made between the totally dependent and the potentially self-sufficient. On the issue of measurement, the authors compare the poverty line yardstick (i.e., identifying the poor as those falling within certain income levels at the bottom of the national standard) with the "market basket" yardstick (i.e., identifying the poor as those living below some minimum decency standard of living). Several reasons are given for the superiority of the "market basket" yardstick in meeting the needs of the American poor and suggestions are provided for further study and eventual implementation of the "market basket" standard.

Task Force on Urban Education Report. Schools of the Urban Crisis. Washington, D.C.: National Education Association, 1969.

(V)

This report focuses on urban education as it is offered to the American poor. Many schools in urban areas have reached a state of neglect and continue to deteriorate. Those schools specifically mentioned in the report are inferior to others because of older school buildings, greater number of pupils per teacher, smaller amount of money per pupil, fewer textbooks, fewer fully certified teachers, and teachers with less experience. Authority should be distributed so as to allow parents, citizens, and local school officials greater control over the educational decisions affecting their children. In addition, individualized approaches to learning should be developed, including programs which reflect the true history of minority Americans. Teachers should be given more responsibility for decision-making, schools should sponsor and pay for in-service training, incentive programs should be introduced, representatives of ethnic and racial minorities should be employed as professionals and executives, and resource persons in the community should be utilized. Funding should include more money obtained through taxes shared by federal, state and local governments. Uses of this income should include upgrading professional and staff salaries; providing for extensions of the programs now offered, including day care centers; health and nutritional programs; and money for research. A final recommendation is that an ideal inner city school be designed and operated as a model from which other school systems could learn.

(Poverty and Human Resources abstract)

Tawney, R.H. "Equality." In Inequality and Poverty, edited by Edward C. Budd. New York: W.W. Norton and Company, 1967.

(II)

The acknowledged inequality of natural capacities and gifts is considered here to be an inadequate premise for justifying the inequality of social and economic environment. It is argued that the common humanity of individuals should provide the motivation for efforts to promote equality of circumstances and opportunity in the same way that it justifies efforts to insure that men are equal before the law. Furthermore, this effort to give equal consideration to all people would insure that individual differences were best served; for "equal consideration" is not seen to imply identical treatment but rather an equivalent effort to provide for particular needs and skills. Tawney takes issue with the arbitrary distinctions created by birth and wealth that bias opportunity toward certain classes, and he disapproves of inheritance laws which allow such wealth to perpetuate itself. In the absence of "capricious inequalities" of circumstances and opportunities, "Differences of remuneration between different individuals might remain; contrasts between the civilization of different classes would vanish."

Taylor, Lester D., and Weiserbs, Daniel. "On the Estimation of Dynamic Demand Functions." Review of Economics and Statistics 54(1972): 549-465.

(III)

An application of utility theory to empirical demand analysis. The additive quadratic utility function of Houthakker and Taylor is compared with the Geary-Samuelson utility function employed by Stone which is a linear-expenditure system. Both methods use estimating equations showing expenditure on a commodity to be a function of income and a price vector. In the linear-expenditure form, the term representing the marginal utility of total consumption expenditure times the price of the ith good is replaced by its reciprocal. The additive quadratic model has the intrinsic defect of showing a sharp decline in the marginal utility of income at higher income levels and was rejected for empirical use in favor of the linear-expenditure system.

Theil, Henri. "A New Index Number Formula." Review of Economics and Statistics 55(1973).

(III)

An analysis of an earlier price and quantity index formulation of Theil and Tornquist. These index numbers are derived by calculating the log of the relative prices in the two periods (or relative quantities, for the quantity index) where the commodities priced are weighted by the arithmetic average expenditure share of the commodities in the two successive periods. These indexes have since been applied by Christensen and Jorganson (1970) and found to possess a number of attractive qualities: they are time-symmetric, and consistent in aggregation. The major problem with the index, its inability to deal with goods which disappear in one of the two time periods, is considered in the article. Theil suggests that if weights are based on a mix of geometric and arithmetic-mean expenditure shares, this problem is avoided. The new index number is then applied to data from the Netherlands. Differences in price indices thus obtained and the earlier arithmetic-mean index are slight.

Theil, Henri. "On the Geometry and the Numerical Approximation of Cost of Living and Real Income Indices." De Economist 116(1968): 677-689.

(III)

The economic theory of the "true" cost of living and real income index numbers is described and illustrated geometrically in the logarithmic price-income space. Special attention is paid to the real income index evaluated at the geometric means of the prices in the two periods and to the cost of living index evaluated at the utility level which is associated with these geometric mean prices and geometric mean income. It is shown that this particular pair of index numbers is the only pair which satisfies a certain simple set of axioms. It is also shown how these index numbers can be approximated on the basis of observable price-quantity data. The approximation is accurate up to the second order in price and income log-changes.

(Taken from the article)

Theil, Henri, and Friedman, Yoram. "Regional Per Capita Incomes and Income Inequalities: Point Estimates and Their Standard Errors." Journal of the American Statistical Association 68(September 1973).

(III)

A simple statistical model is developed to assess the implications of random measurement errors in reported per capita incomes and of the bias caused by the use of official exchange rates for (1) regional per capita incomes and (2) regional income inequality. It appears that regional per capita incomes can be estimated with a fair degree of accuracy, provided that the measurement errors of the reported per capita incomes of individual countries are not too highly positively correlated. The measurement of regional inequality is characterized by considerable uncertainty.

(Author abstract)

* Thernstrom, Stephan. "Poverty in Historical Perspective." In <u>On Understanding Poverty</u>, edited by Daniel Moynihan. New York: Basic Books, 1968.

(II,IX,XI)

The article investigates the notion that the nineteenth century poor had justified hopes of advancement, in contrast to the inhabitants of today's "ghettos of despair." He finds little social mobility in the past, and much continual migration. Blacks are noted worse off at all levels.

His definition of poverty is conditioned by the limitations of his historical data: "the poor are those who occupy the lowest level of the social pyramid, as measured by occupational rank and command over economic resources."

Thernstrom, Stephan, and Sennett, Richard. <u>Nineteenth Century Cities</u>. New Haven: Yale University Press, 1969.

(IX)

An interdisciplinary effort by several sociologists and historians to discuss social dimensions of urbanization. Papers included in the study treat a variety of U.S. and foreign cities and explore topics of family structure, political and social control, residential and ecological patterns, and urban patterns of class stratification. Questions of social mobility and class structure are treated in an attempt to demonstrate the dynamic character of social elements in the city.

Thomas, George. <u>Poverty in the Nonmetropolitan South: A Causal Analysis</u>. Lexington, Massachusetts: D.C. Heath and Co., 1972.

(II, V, IX, XI)

A study of the persistence and magnitude of poverty in the rural South. Five theories of the causes of poverty were analyzed: genetic, culture-of-poverty, lack of opportunity (i.e., discrimination), maldistribution, scarce resources (i.e., poverty is inevitable). Each of the theories has certain implications for the ability of families/individuals to escape from poverty. Genetic and scarce resource explanations consider poverty irreversible. Lack of opportunity, culture-of-poverty, and maldistribution explanations all believe poverty to be reversible, although the structure of programs needed to accomplish this of course vary widely. Empirical evidence is not conclusive on validating the alternative theories offered.

Thomas, George. "Regional Migration Patterns and Poverty Among the Aged in the South." Journal of Human Resources 8 (Winter 1973).

(VI)

Data from the 1967 portion of the 1966-67 Survey of Economic Opportunity have been aggregated for the South to illuminate current economic conditions among the region's elderly population. Race, age (65-74 and 75+), sex, and regional migration patterns were utilized to isolate the heaviest concentrations of the aged poor. Results indicate that poverty is concentrated among Blacks, females, those over age 75, and those born and still residing in rural areas. A comparison of the results with 1960 and preliminary 1970 Census data suggests that the region's indigenous aged population may be no better off now than in 1960. An apparent regional decline in poverty among the aged during the 1960's is probably attributable to the substantial in-migration of well-fixed white retirees.

(Journal of Human Resources)

Thompson, John H. "What About a Geography of Poverty?" Economic Geography 40 (October 1964): 283.

(VI)

An editorial urging the elucidation of the geography of poverty and suggesting directions that studies might take. Thompson suggests a research prescription which would involve, in part, (1) an identification and mapping of the household economic status; (2) a comparison of results with spatial characteristics of suspected causes of poverty; (3) proposal and testing of hypotheses which will explain the spatial patterns of poverty; (4) an evaluation of findings and an attempt to place them in a broad conceptual framework which will contribute to theory or illustrate ways they may be used for solving poverty problems.

Thompson, John H.; Sufrin, Sidney C.; Gould, Peter R.; and Buck, Marion A. "Toward a Geography of Economic Health: The Care of New York State." Annals of the Association of American Geographers 52 (March 1962): 1-20.

(VI, X)

A research paper which considers the meaning of economic health by comparing its various facets presenting a statistical interpretation of the data used and exploring the possibility of making "geographic reality" out of a grid of county statistical units. Using nine indicators of economic health, a distinction is made between level of economic health and trends in economic health. Factor analysis is then used to isolate three independent ways in which the counties of New York State vary according to their degree of economic health: (1) a general economic health dimension to which all nine indicators contribute approximately similar proportions; (2) an urban-rural dimension to which the indicators contribute widely different proportions; and (3) a dimension of economic-demographic growth which contrasts growth and unemployment. The procedures used in this analysis could be applied to any geographic area.

Thompson, Wilbur. "The National System of Cities as an Objective of Public Policy." Urban Studies 9 (1972): 99-116.

(VI)

This article analyzes the objective of containing the size of the largest cities and considers two alternatives to achieving that end: slowing in-migration and promoting out-migration. Greater city size probably benefits affluent more than poor households. As a city's public sector grows it is first strengthened, but this process is probably reversed for cities of more than 1,000,000. Actually, the rate of growth may be a more important determinant of welfare than the size of the city. On the other hand, small towns face depopulation caused by out-migration. This could lead to general deterioration or dependency as satellites. Transportation progress makes containment of cities nearly impossible. This suggests that land use may be a better policy focus. For instance, megalopolis could be a more efficient land form than low density urbanization. In general, migration should be judged by its effect on those left behind and those joined as well as on the migrants.

(Partially taken from the article)

*Thompson, Wilbur R. <u>A Preface to Urban Economics</u>. Baltimore: The John Hopkins Press, 1965.

(V, VI)

This book develops an economic theory of city-size and studies the growth, income and economic structure of American cities. The problems of poverty, transportation, urban decay and suburban sprawl are especially considered.

In the provisions of public services, the larger metropolis often suffers the disorganizing effects of too little monopoly. As a city grows in size more and more services must be publicly provided, first water supply, garbage collection and sewage disposal and eventually transportation and recreation. But the larger the population and spatial extent of the urban area, the greater the likelihood that this population will spill over the boundaries of the central city into independent suburban municipalities. Fragmented urban public services may labor under "internal diseconomies of scale" resulting from plants which are too small to exploit the optimum technology. More costly are the "external diseconomies of political fragmentation." Since no overall decision unit embraces all benefits and costs, a project which benefits one locale greatly at the small expense of another will not be undertaken.

Thurow, Lester. "Disequilibrium and the Marginal Productivity of Capital and Labor." <u>Review of Economics and Statistics</u> (February 1968).

(II)

Data from the period 1929-1965 are used to estimate the marginal productivity of capital and labor in the United States; these estimates are then compared with actual wages and profits during the period to determine whether or not the conventional marginal productivity theory of income is an accurate predictor. Thurow finds that, in every year between 1929 and 1965, profits exceeded the estimated marginal product of capital; conversely, actual wages during the period were consistently lower than the marginal product of labor. Moreover, the gaps between marginal products and returns are both large and variable. These empirical results suggest that the perfectly functioning equilibrium model which underlies marginal productivity theory is not in fact a good approximation to the real world. Monopoly power, labor immobility, risk and uncertainty, technical progress and economies to scale in production all help to explain the divergence of marginal productivity and returns to capital and labor.

*Thurow, Lester C. "Education and Economic Equality." Public Interest. (Summer, 1972)

(II)

The role assigned to education by the standard theory of the labor market is challenged here, and an alternate model of the labor market is presented. It is generally thought that the labor market matches labor demand with labor supply by varying wage scales. Workers market pre-existing skills and compete with one another on the basis of wages. In theory, the result is that each person is paid at the level of his marginal productivity. Education is critical because it creates the skills. An increase in skills for a given worker not only results in added income for that worker but also increases overall productivity and equalizes wages since a slightly lower premium would be paid to the increased number of high skill workers and a slightly higher premium would be paid to the reduced number of low skill workers. However, statistics are presented for the post-1950 period on overall productivity and percentile income shares which are contrary to the implications of this model, given the substantial gains in education level that have occurred. An alternate "job competition" labor market model is suggested in which skills are acquired primarily on the job, and the market merely matches trainable individuals with "training ladders." Education serves here not to confer skills but to certify trainability and thus becomes an important factor in determining a kind of rank of workers on the basis of estimated training costs. Jobs are distributed to individuals in order of their rank. An individual's income is determined by (a) his relative position in the labor queue and (b) the distribution of jobs in the economy. The overall wage-income distribution is determined by the underlying set of job opportunities; rank in the labor queue only affects an individual's position in that distribution. The available job-wage opportunities themselves are seen as the result of such things as the nature of technical progress, social pressures on wage determination, and the distribution of training costs between employers and employees. Because skills are acquired on the job in this view, demand for job skills creates its own supply. Traditionally, the emphasis of programs to equalize income has been to change the supplies of different types of workers and alter the labor characteristics that an individual brings to the market; it is suggested that, instead, efforts should be directed toward labor demand by attempting to influence the types of jobs available and the wage differentials themselves.

Thurow, Lester C. The Impact of Taxes on the American Economy. New York: Praeger Publishers, 1971.

(VII)

This study analyzes the effects of taxation on the American economy and suggests reforms to better achieve society's expressed intentions. The distributions of consumption, human capital, and physical wealth are examined as they exist and as they would be without taxation. Taxes are found to alter the structure of demand for goods and services, but to have little effect on the supply of labor and capital. Different taxes have different impact multipliers.

The correct tax base should be consumption plus wealth, not consumption plus increments to wealth as in an income tax. The stock of wealth, not just increments to it, create economic benefits. Existing death duties are incurred very infrequently, and property taxes affect only real estate. A wealth tax is, however, feasible and necessary.

*Thurow, L. "The Optimum Lifetime Distribution of Consumer Expenditure." American Economic Review 59(1969): 324-30.

(VII)

Thurow presents evidence that contradicts the Modigliani-Brumberg "life cycle of saving" hypothesis. In particular, he finds evidence that there is a strong relationship between consumption and income, with a peak in both activities between the ages 45 and 54. Thurow offers an explanation for this apparent contradiction by building a model based on imperfect credit markets. He conjectures that while consumers desire to consume according to their "permanent incomes," they are prevented from doing so early in their lives when their incomes are low because discounted future income cannot be fully transferred at the borrowing rate. Hence, during the early years, consumption is more influenced by current income than permanent income.

Thurow, Lester. "Toward a Definition of Economic Justice." _The Public Interest_(Spring 1973): 56-80.

(II)

"There is a difference between allowing individual preferences to affect the form of the social welfare function and making social welfare purely a function of individual utilities." Thus, an individual might seek to become extremely wealthy in the current economic game ("private personal preferences") while still believing that in a better system there would be no "extremely wealthy" prizes ("individual societal preferences"). In a world without innate preferences and without the possibility of interpersonal comparisons, the "utility function" approach is misconceived; however, a basis for economic equity can be specified "by an act of social judgment" founded on individual-societal preferences. "In a similar manner, the optimum distribution of economic resources is socially specifiable even though it is not derivable from any aggregation of private-personal preferences." It is noted that relative income seems to dominate absolute income in terms of making people satisfied or dissatisfied. "Psychologists would label the same phenomenon envy." Thus the social specification of equity is seen as a problem of relative income determinination. In the movement towards relative income equity, two guidelines are given: that economic benefits should be proportional to the individual's economic costs and that those who incur equal economic costs are to be treated equally. A principle of economic merit is derived from the consensus that individuals should be paid their marginal product. This is seen to impose another constraint on redistribution which is that rank-order equity should be maintained. It is suggested that the distribution of earnings (not income) for white adult males working full time is one that society would acknowledge as representing some measure of fairness. This distribution of economic prizes, which would reduce income dispersions by 40 percent if it were the national structure, is advanced as an interim goal. It is felt that such a redistribution could be accomplished primarily by restricting market rewards with lesser emphasis on tax and transfer policies.

Tiebout, Charles M. "Exports and Regional Economic Growth." Journal of Political Economy 64 (1956): 160-164.

(VI)

This article discusses the hypothesis that regional economic growth depends on the extent of the region's exports. This hypothesis separates a region's economic activities into export activity and residentiary activity. The ratio between these groups of activities determines how much growth in residentiary activities will be brought about by an increase in exports. Tiebout argues that for smaller regions, this may be substantially correct, but for large regions, the export base is merely one aspect of regional income determination. Other variables such as business investment, government expenditures, and volume of residentiary construction may be as important as the export base. Furthermore, the export base is partly determined by residentiary activities that affect factor costs of possible regional exports. If a region's mix of economic activities represents a suboptimal division of factors between export and residentiary outputs, "a decline in export activity may even be accompanied by rising regional income."

Till, Thomas. "The Extent of Industrialization in Southern Nonmetro Labor Markets in the 1960's." Journal of Regional Science 13 (1973): 453-461.

(V)

This article examined the controversial question of the extent of the growth of nonfarm jobs in the nonmetropolitan counties of the South during the 1960's. It found that such growth, especially in manufacturing, was sizeable (e.g., an increase of 61 percent--308,972 jobs--in manufacturing since 1959), not relatively insignificant compared with SMSA counties, and not primarily confined to SMSA fringe areas. Neither the hypothesis that factor markets and public services operate in a superior manner in rural areas near cities (though the test was weak) nor the hypothesis that the amount of growth is directly proportional to the size of the leading city were backed by the data from nonmetro areas. Furthermore, the attraction of abundant pools of low-wage labor was apparently a prime locational inducement.

(Taken from the article)

*Till, Thomas. "Industrialization and Poverty in Nonmetropolitan Labor Markets in the South." Center for the Study of Human Resources, University of Texas, October 1974.

(V, VI)

This paper presents an analysis of the implications of nonmetropolitan industrialization for the rural poor in the South. "Urban-rural and racial differences have persisted in the South despite the improvement in the relative economic position of the South as a region." This is because southern economic development has mainly benefited urban whites. Rural industrial development is an important approach to bringing rural southerners closer to the economic level of urban residents. Rural industrial growth reached its peak in the 1960's. Despite some gains, development was very uneven. Many areas, particularly areas with a high percentage of Blacks, were largely unaffected. Large towns, small cities and areas near interstate highways experienced the most growth. Development, when it did happen, occurred in two stages: (1) the growth of low wage, labor intensive, nonunionized industry accompanied by a slack labor market, and (2) the growth of high wage, more capital intensive, moderately unionized industry accompanied by a tighter labor market. Each stage is characterized by a reduction of poverty in the area. In areas that have reached the second stage, nonfarm income is a crucial and growing source of income for farm families as well as the regional population as a whole. Past experience suggests the need for several policies to help make rural industrial development a viable approach to poverty reduction: enforcement of anti-discrimination laws, manpower training, encouraging low-wage industry when there is no industry present, and discouraging unionization until the second stage of development is achieved.

Tilly, Charles. "Race and Migration to the American City." In <u>The Metropolitan Enigma</u>, edited by James Q. Wilson. Cambridge, Massachusetts: Harvard University Press, 1968.

(V, VI, XI)

The thrust is that migration is not a major public problem; rather it <u>points up</u> grave problems which already exist in American cities. Migrants are forced to migrate because of employment expectations or because of friends and relatives in the urban areas. They tend to be above average in education and occupational skills for the populations in their places of origin and, at least in the case of non-whites, above average in the urban areas where they settle. Especially for non-whites, evidence seems to contradict the picture of high delinquency and crime rates among migrants. Rather, problems of violence and crime seem to be what the migrants encounter as they arrive in urban areas, and seem to be more highly correlated with the failure of the urban areas to either assimilate or provide good education and employment opportunities for their long-term non-white residents. Both tables and evidence from governmental reports are presented to back up the arguments. Data on family structure of migrants is presented.

Tinbergen, Jan. "The Impact of Education of Income Distribution." Review of Income and Wealth 18 (1972): 255-265.

(II)

In this paper the author adds some further empirical tests of his theory of income distribution. This theory sees income distribution as the distribution of prices of production factors, especially labour, of different quality and prices as the effect of demand and supply factors. The quality of labour is represented only by the number of years of schooling. Its supply is described by the actual numbers of people having each of the possible years of schooling; this frequency distribution can be characterized by its average and by some measure of its dispersion or by one of its deciles (in particular the highest) expressed in terms of its median. The demand for the various qualities of labour can be supposed to be reflected by (i) total demand for commodities, but (ii) more accurately by the percentage of third-level educated people used in and weighted by the size of the four main sectors of production: agriculture, manufacturing, trade and transport, and other services. Extensive material collected and reworked by Professors B.R. Chiswick for the U.S.A. and Canada and T.P. Schultz and L.S. Burns with H.E. Frech III for the Netherlands is used in cross-section tests to explain variations in income distribution in the states of the U.S.A. and the provinces of Canada and the Netherlands. While further increase and smaller dispersion in years of schooling, according to some of the findings presented, would only moderately reduce the degree of inequality in the U.S.A. and Canada, more result seems to be possible according to other findings, including those for the Netherlands. In the latter category the second demand index mentioned above has been used.

(Taken from article)

Tipping, D.E. "Price Changes and Income Distributions." Applied Statistics 19(1970): 1-17.

(III)

Tipping priced market baskets typical of five income groups to determine the relative effects of inflation on each. Using British data between 1956 and 1966 he found that those at the lower end of the income scale have experienced greater price increases than those at the upper end, thus increasing the inequality of the distribution of real income. It also appears that differences in the rate of inflation between income classes becomes larger as national income increases.

Titmuss, Richard. Income Distribution and Social Change. London: George, Allen and Urwin, Ltd., 1962.

(II)

Surveys of the income distribution in Britain during the 1940's and 1950's indicated a trend towards equality. The intent of this study is to re-examine the picture of income distribution generally accepted during this period, particularly in relation to "substantial changes in social and demographic structure." The division of income and wealth among members of the same family and mechanisms such as pension funds and life insurance premiums that transform income into capital are just two examples of the processes considered. Definitions of poverty in which "daily subsistence is both the yardstick and the objective" demand reappraisal as well. "We cannot delineate the new frontiers of poverty unless we take account of the changing agents and characteristics of inequality." The intent is not to define poverty but to put it in a context of social change.

Titmuss, Richard. "Poverty versus Inequality." In Poverty, edited by Jack L. Roach and Janet K. Roach. Penguin, 1972.

(II)

The terms "poverty" and "inequality" are used here to characterize two different viewpoints of the poor. In the sense of "poverty," the poor are seen as a pathological culture of individuals deficient in skills and motivation. They are best approached through programs of relief and rehabilitation. This view of poverty has the appeal that, "if the culture of poverty is to blame, then logically the social and economic system is blameless." The article maintains that by devising separate laws for the poor and providing aid through extraordinary channels, one avoids the more crucial issue of "inequality" and the question of redistribution of resources. The latter course of action would divert resources to the poor through "normal," socially acceptable channels (tax deductions, social security, medical care). It is a more painful alternative in that it implies structural change and demands a reformulation of basic goals. However, the current income disproportions are considered unhealthy and are seen to pose a basic question: "In the past we have distributed resources according to success and failure in economic competition; in the future we must decide if it is morally right to continue on this basis."

Tobin, James. "Asset Holdings and Spending Decisions." American Economic Review 42 (May 1952): 109-123.

(VII)

A discussion of different hypotheses of how asset holdings affect spending decisions when income, prices and interest rates are held constant. Three microeconomic hypotheses are examined: they hold, respectively, that the determinant variables in the above situation are individual cash balances, liquid assets, and net worth. These three hypotheses lead to three similar macroeconomic hypotheses when aggregated. One general implication of all three is the Pigou effect: consumption is inversely related to the price level because of the latter's effect on wealth. The first and second hypotheses fail because households control the distribution of their own assets. Cash balances and liquid assets can be converted into other types of assets easily, and are not, therefore, independent variables. The third hypothesis fails because it assumes that the actual distribution of assets has no effect: a man with a $50,000 house will spend the same way as one with $50,000 in the bank. This is unrealistic. According to the paper, the best that can be done is to state that individuals choose between savings and consumption and between different types of assets on the basis of income, the prices of various assets and debts, total net worth, and the prices of nondurable goods and services.

Tobin, James. "Do We Want Children's Allowances?" The New Republic 157 (November 25, 1967): 16-18.

(IV)

Programs of public assistance to the poor are examined here in terms of two characteristic dimensions. These are, first of all, the program of guarantees, reflecting family size and composition, that the government pays to families with no resources of their own; and secondly, the provision for an "offsetting tax" that determines how the government's net payment to a family decreases as the family's own resources increase. Programs for children's allowances often simply designate a flat sum to be paid for each child; this ignores the possibility of economies of scale in the living costs of larger families. Even those plans which make adjustments for the diminishing cost of a second or third child still suffer from the more serious problem of completely ignoring childless adults. Furthermore, such programs represent substantial waste since they involve no mechanism to scale down government benefits for more affluent families. "There are 70 million persons under the age of 18 in the United States, of whom only approximately 17 million are in poor families." Thus a fixed tax-free outlay for each child would result in about 75% of the total benefits going to families not considered poor. Even subjecting the allowances to regular income tax has the result that aid to nonpoor families would constitute about 70 percent of the outlay. These deficiencies are avoided by an assistance program that employs a graduated scale of minimum need guarantees for individual adults, childless couples, and families of increasing size and in which the designated government payments are reduced by either the full amount or some fraction of the family's resources. In any case, "Though the label is appealing, 'children's allowances' are not a promising way of providing the new system of income supplementation that America urgently needs."

Tobin, James. "Life Cycle Saving and Balanced Growth." In Ten Economic Studies in the Tradition of Irving Fisher, edited by William Fellner et al. New York: John Wiley and Sons, Inc., 1967.

(VII)

This paper tries to show how the life cycle saving theory can complete and close aggregate growth models and help to determine the equilibrium interest rate and saving rate in steady balanced growth. It also engages in some speculation concerning the amount of capital accumulation which life cycle saving, unaided by saving for subsequent generations, can account for. This numerical speculation is based partly on a priori assumptions and partly on some observed characteristics of the contemporary United States population and economy.

(Taken from the article)

Tobin, James. "On Improving the Economic Status of the Negro." Daedalus (Fall 1965): 878-888.

(II, X)

An analytical essay on the economic status of the Negro and recommendations for its improvement. Tobin maintains that the "backwash theory" does not apply to Negroes. He claims that half of a race of 20 million people cannot be victims of specific disabilities that isolate them from economic impact. Recommendations toward the betterment of the economic status of Blacks includes increased governmental spending to promote a tight labor market and a negative income tax program that will provide incentives for work and adequate living allowances for those unable to work. Tobin cites inflation and the balance of payments deficits as two fears which the government must overcome for the success of these programs. Better education and manpower policy are also needed to supply more qualified workers.

*Tobin, James. "On Limiting the Domain of Inequality." The Journal of Law and Economics 13 (October 1970): 263-277.

(II)

Henry Simmons is acknowledged here for his differentiation of economic policy into two departments, one for equity which effects change through taxations of income and wealth and one for efficiency which endeavors to make markets work competitively. There are however certain commodities that provoke sentiment for "specific egalitarian" measures. "Can we somehow remove the necessities of life and health from the prizes that serve as incentives for economic activity, and instead let people strive and compete for non-essential luxuries and amenities?" In this context, the critical areas of food, housing, and medical care are examined as well as questions of equity involving voting rights, the draft, education, and the right to bear children. Commodity vouchers and ration tickets are analyzed as possible redistributive mechanisms. For example, an education voucher that could be used in private schools would shift some of the burden of those who elect private schools to the society at large; if those who opt out of the public school systems are in fact more affluent, then such an alternative might not be preferable to the present system in terms of redistribution. Food stamps are considered to be merely "inferior currency" since adequate income for food does not insure the objective of adequate nutrition. In general, positive and negative income tax are considered to be the best means of moderating the inequality generated by a competitive market. "A cash negative income tax would be, dollar for dollar, the most effective anti-poverty and pro-equality program that could be adopted at this time." It does make sense in some cases to adopt specific egalitarian distributions of commodities essential to life and citizenship when supplies are inelastic and the scarcity cannot be corrected by drawing on the resources of the general economy. "Difficult practical cases arise when, as in the case of medical care and housing, supply is inelastic in the short run but responsive to increased demand in the long run."

Tobin, James. "Relative Income, Absolute Income and Saving." In <u>Money, Trade, and Economic Growth: Essays in Honor of John Henry Williams</u>. New York: The MacMillan Co., 1951.

(VII)

Two hypotheses of consumption are compared. The absolute income hypothesis declares that families with identical amounts of income will spend the same percentage of that income. The relative income hypothesis declares that families in the same percentile of the local income distribution will spend the same percentage of their income. A number of empirical comparisons are made and the absolute income hypothesis does a better job. It cannot explain some empirical facts without additional theory. This is supplied by a liquid assets theory of saving: two families with identical incomes will not save the same proportion if they have different amounts of liquid assets. The family with the small amount of assets will instead save more due to a precautionary motive. The absolute income plus assets theory proves capable of explaining the empirical savings rate of different groups very well. However, both it and the relative income hypothesis have generally been replaced by the newer permanent income and life-cycle theories.

Townsend, Peter, ed. <u>The Concept of Poverty</u>. New York: American Elsevier Publishing Company, Inc., 1970.

(II)

A selection of papers presented to the 1963 International Committee on Poverty Research. Contributions address the conceptual problem of defining poverty as well as the difficulties of translating definitions into meaningful, operational terms. Also included are a number of papers concerned with the social characteristics of poverty and the relation of the poor to society as a whole. Relevant articles are annotated separately.

Townsend, Peter. "The Meaning of Poverty." *British Journal of Sociology* 13 (No. 3, 1962): 210-227.

(II)

The belief that poverty has been virtually eliminated in Great Britain is commonly held. This belief is examined by (1) taking traditional definitions of poverty and showing that when they are applied to budget data collected nationally by the Ministry of Labour a substantial percent of the population are around or below the poverty standard, and (2) showing that the traditional definitions are theoretically weaker than has been supposed and are, in any case, quite unsuited to the study of poverty in modern society. Two subsistence standards--one put forward by Seebohm Rowntree and the other used since 1948 by the National Assistance Board--are discussed and criticized in some detail. Particular attention is given to the difficulty of estimating the costs of meeting nutritional needs. The conclusion is that the vague concept of subsistence is an inadequate and misleading criterion of poverty. Instead, the general theory should be "that individuals and families whose resources, over time, fall seriously short of the resources commanded by the $\bar{X}$ individual or family in the community in which they live, whether that community is a local, national, or international one, are in poverty."

(*Sociological Abstracts*)

Townsend, Peter. "Measures and Explanations of Poverty in High Income and Low Income Countries: The Problems of Operationalizing the Concepts of Development, Class, and Poverty." In *The Concept of Poverty*, edited by Peter Townsend. New York: American Elsevier Publishing Company, Inc., 1970.

(II)

An appropriate definition of poverty must retain validity within the context of the large disparities in national living standards. The view presented here is that "needs which are unmet can be defined satisfactorily only in terms relative to the society in which they are found or expressed...Poverty must be regarded as a general form of relative deprivation, which is the effect of the maldistribution of resources." The basis for this maldistribution is seen to be the social structure as it is organized in classes, "stratified." Society is considered to be organized such that certain levels are protected and receive benefits at the expense of others. A system of "international social stratification" is found to parallel the class structure in individual societies. "Some societies are desperately poor, more because wealthier societies are continuing to follow policies of protecting their own special interests than because the poor societies lack technology and special skills which they need to learn."

Attempts are made to display this stratification in societies and classes using various parameters. One such study identifies a "total rank" by means of a composite rank in separate categories of income, assets, employment benefits, value of social services, and income in kind. The burden of responsibility for poverty is seen to rest on the structure of society, not on the individual.

Townsend, Peter. "Measuring Poverty." British Journal of Sociology (1954).

(II)

A historical survey of methods of measuring poverty in England, and recommendations for a new set of standards. Booth and Rowntree's pioneering work (late 19th century) defined two types of poverty: (1) primary poverty--families whose total earnings are insufficient to obtain the minimum necessaries for the maintenance of merely physical efficiency; and (2) secondary poverty--families whose total earnings would be sufficient for the maintenance of merely physical efficiency were it not that some portion is absorbed by the other useful or wasteful expenditure. The arbitrariness of "necessaries" poses problems. The main fault in the standards used has been their lack of relation to the budgets and customs of the working class. The following procedure is recommended: (1) collection of data on food consumption and expenditure as well as the income of working-class households; (2) comparison of these data with a scale of nutritive needs; and (3) the isolation, from all those securing minimum nutrition, of the 25% in the various household groups who achieve it on the smallest incomes, less one or two fixed involuntary overheads such as rent and compulsory insurances. The average total expenditure of these households, less the overheads, according to their different sizes, can be taken as the poverty line.

Townsend, Peter. "Poverty as Relative Deprivation: Resources and Style of Living." In Poverty, Inequality and Class Structure, edited by Dorothy Wedderburn. London: Cambridge University Press, 1974.

(II)

Poverty can be appropriately defined only in terms of relative deprivation. Individuals are poor if their resources are so seriously below those of the average individual that they are effectively excluded from "ordinary" living. Early definitions of poverty based on subsistence, including the Social Security definition, are criticized on technical grounds: the poverty index has not changed since 1959 despite changing needs; the food standards used are nutritionally acceptable only as temporary requirements; the use of actual propensities to consume food as a device to transform food costs into total subsistence budget amounts to extrapolating from behavior of families to the "needs" of those families. Townsend argues that a dynamic and relative concept of poverty is necessary because economic growth alters the availability of goods and changes life styles considered acceptable.

Triplett, Jack E. "Quality Bias in Price Indexes and New Methods of Quality Measurement." In Price Indexes and Quality Change, edited by Zvi Griliches. Cambridge, Massachusetts: Harvard University Press, 1971.

(III)

Most discussions of quality change measurement in index numbers have assumed that the Consumer Price Index (CPI) overstates inflation due to inaccurate quality adjustment. The argument is formulated as follows: (1) the quality of products improves over time; (2) quality adjustments are inadequate or non-existent; therefore, the quality of goods priced by the Bureau of Labor Statistics is improving so that direct comparison of prices overstates the magnitude of inflation. This conclusion does not follow from the premises. Despite the fact that the quality of products is improving, the substitution for which comparisons are made may involve a movement to lower quality varieties. Furthermore, even if direct comparisons involve quality improvement, the conclusion that the CPI is biased upward does not follow. First, "some substitutes are handled by deleting the price quotation from the index when the new variety is first observed, rather than by comparing directly." Second, quality variations lead to many measurement errors in the indexes. Because of these factors, at least for some products and during some time periods, inaccurate quality adjustment may cause the CPI to understate inflation.

Triplett suggests several new approaches to quality measurement that are likely to overcome some of these problems. He is particularly interested in research on "hedonic" measures of quality change.

United Nations. Attack on Mass Poverty and Unemployment. New York: United Nations Publication, 1972.

(X)

The United Nations Committee for Development Planning presents its views and recommendations on the problem of mass poverty, unemployment, and underemployment in developing countries. Discussion begins with a small piece on the difficulties in measuring poverty and unemployment in developing countries. Poverty is said to be a relative matter which changes from country to country; and employment, unemployment, and underemployment are difficult to quantify. Strategies for resolving mass poverty need to be focused at raising the productivity and income of the poor. This development planning should include an industrial shift toward labor-intensive items of mass consumption, an agricultural expansion, and the establishment of public land improvement and construction activities. The focus of these strategies should be at providing employment and productive activities for the masses of poor. Other support services, such as education and training, health, and international financing, must also be included in the attack.

United Nations. Compendium of Social Statistics: 1963. New York: United Nations, 1963.

(XI)

This is an international compendium comprising tables dealing with statistical indicators of the internationl level of living components. Organized into eight sections, the Compendium describes the major aspects of the social situation in the world by nation and regions indicating trends or changes in the levels of living over the decade ended 1960. Data was contributed and the Compendium was prepared under the auspices of the Inter-Agency Working Party on Statistics for Social Programmes by United Nations organizations, the International Labour Office, the Food and Agricultural Organization, and the World Health Organization.

(Taken from Social Indicators and Societal Monitoring)

United Nations. International Definition and Measurement of Levels of Living: An Interim Guide. New York: United Nations, 1961.

(XI)

A joint progress report of the UN, ILO, FAO, UNESCO, and WHO concerning action taken on suggestions the Committee of Experts made in 1954. Components and indicators appropriate for the international definition and measurement of levels of living are specified with a proposal for also gathering national background data on demography, labor, income, expenditure, communications, and transportation. The explicated components of level of living are: health, nutrition, education, employment conditions, housing, social security, clothing, recreation and human freedoms.

(Taken from Social Indicators and Social Monitoring)

United Nations Bureau of Social Affairs. Assistance to the Needy in Less Developed Areas. New York: U.N. Department of Social and Economic Affairs, 1956.

(II)

A survey of methods of administering assistance to the needy in nine poor countries. While U.S.-style anti-poverty programs are beyond the reach of these governments, assistance is commonly provided to widows, orphans, war victims, undernourished children, the handicapped and victims of calamaties. The aged are generally cared for by their families while the unemployed go uncompensated.

The term "needy" was taken to cover persons who as a result of temporary or permanent circumstances peculiar to them have not available, in one form or another, the means of subsistence to achieve the level of living prevailing among the majority of the people living in the same town or community.

U.N. Committee of Experts. Report on International Definition and Measurement of Standard and Levels of Living. New York: 1954.

(XI)

A discussion of the concept of "level of living" (distinguishes between level--actual conditions--of living and standard--values and aspirations--of living) and its measurement through the use of social indicators. This small volume, the result on a U.N. conference points out the problems involved in determining appropriate social indicators: (1) technical problems with measurement, such as unavailability or lack of standardization of data; (2) ideological problems such as using "non-material" as well as material indicators when cultural values on an international scale are involved; (3) validity of indicators such as life expectancy, since lengthening of life by modern medical techniques does not necessarily imply improvement of living in other respects; (4) imposition of value judgments in selecting indicators, and (5) problems in defining even simple material needs with universal validity, e.g., even required calorie intake depends upon age, sex, work, climate, etc.

U.S. Congress, Joint Economic Committee. Studies in Public Welfare, Paper No. 1, Public Income Transfer Programs: The Incidence of Multiple Benefits and the Issues Raised by Their Receipt, by James Storey. Washington, D.C.: U.S. Government Printing Office, 1972.

(II, IX)

The Studies in Public Welfare series represents perhaps the most recent effort at "comprehensive and nonpartisan review of all phases of the nation's system of welfare-related programs." In all, twenty papers were prepared between 1972 and 1974 under the auspices of the Congressional Joint Economic Committee, Subcommittee on Fiscal Policy, under the leadership of subcommittee Chairman Martha Griffiths.

Paper #1 in the series accepts an economic definition of poverty ("low income") and discusses the wide range of government programs designed to counteract poverty, focussing upon the dysfunctions which can occur when the same individuals are recipients of a large number of different income maintenance programs. The study notes that:

> The consequences of combined benefits, in some instances, may not be those that policymakers desired in establishing programs individually...The policy implications of the interactions of these programs deserve greater scrutiny. Chief among the issues raised are the following:
>
> - work incentives
> - family stability
> - administrative error
> - differential treatment based on personal characteristics
> - program inefficiency
> - administrative complexity

The paper considers both income-tested and non-income tested programs. Two criteria conclusions of the paper are: the extent of benefit overlaps and the seriousness of the issues they raise suggest that, should further investigations verify the tentative conclusions of this report, better coordination of legislative and administrative changes in these programs seems essential; much of the information needed to evaluate the performance of our public welfare system has yet to be collected.

Because of its focus, this paper is more useful in reviewing current welfare policy and planning welfare reform than it is for the purpose of elucidating the definition of poverty.

U.S. Congress, Joint Economic Committee. Studies in Public Welfare, Paper #6. How Public Welfare Benefits Are Distributed in Low Income Areas, by James Storey, Alair A. Townsend, and Irene Cox. Washington, D.C.: U.S. Government Printing Office, 1973.

(XII)

The Studies in Public Welfare series represents perhaps the most recent effort at "comprehensive and nonpartisan review of all phases of the nation's system of welfare-related programs." In all, twenty papers were prepared between 1972 and 1974 under the auspices of the Congressional Joint Economic Committee, Subcommittee on Fiscal Policy, under the leadership of subcommittee Chairman Martha Griffiths.

Paper #6 follows paper #1 in adopting an economic definition of poverty and discussing the government programs designed to eliminate or alleviate the problems caused by inadequate income. The paper is specifically directed towards answering the question "to what extent do public welfare programs provide an adequate level of living?" The authors review the results of a General Accounting Office study of six low-income areas and point out that it can be misleading to look at any single welfare program and its benefit levels in answering the question because:

- the typical beneficiary receives aid from more than one source;
- the level of cash assistance is a limited indicator of income adequacy when about half the assisted households also had private income and a very high proportion received noncash assistance; and
- the assistance unit as defined by most program rules is less useful as an economic unit than the household as defined by the Census when we find that from one-tenth to one-third of the sample households...contain more than one family.

In the six low income areas surveyed, six of every ten households was found to receive one or more benefits for some part of the year. The paper further expands upon many of the topics discussed in paper #1, including the overlapping between programs and the inequities in benefits resulting from households with differing family structures.

This paper is more useful in review of current policy and planning welfare reform than it is for the purpose of elucidating the definition of poverty.

U.S. Congress, Joint Economic Committee. Studies in Public Welfare, Paper #15, Welfare in the 70's: A National Study of Benefits Available in 100 Local Areas, by James Storey. Washington, D.C.: U.S. Government Printing Office, 1972.

(XII)

The Studies in Public Welfare series represents perhaps the most recent effort at "comprehensive and nonpartisan review of all phases of the nation's system of welfare-related programs." In all, twenty papers were prepared between 1972 and 1974 under the auspices of the Congressional Joint Economic Committee, Subcommittee on Fiscal Policy, under the leadership of subcommittee Chairman Martha Griffiths.

Paper #15 continues the discussion contained in Papers #1 and #6 of specific welfare benefits available to Americans in different states and with different personal and family characteristics. This paper seeks to shed further light on this question through analysis of data concerning welfare benefits in 100 local jurisdictions throughout the United States. The findings of the study are that: "Benefits from individual programs are often quite low, but that combined benefits (from several programs) can mount up to more than a low-wage worker can earn after taxes; and, the analysis shows that...financial incentives to work can be low...the data reveal sizable financial inducements for families to break up, or to never be formed legally..."

These and related findings are more useful in analysis of current programs and planning welfare reform than they are for the purpose of elucidating definitions of poverty.

U.S. Congress, Joint Economic Committee. Studies in Public Welfare, Paper #19, Public Employment and Wage Subsidies. Washington, D.C.: U.S. Government Printing Office, 1974.

(V)

The Studies in Public Welfare series represents perhaps the most recent effort at "comprehensive and nonpartisan review of all phases of the nation's system of welfare-related programs." In all, twenty papers were prepared between 1972 and 1974 under the auspices of the Congressional Joint Economic Committee, Subcommittee on Fiscal Policy, under the leadership of subcommittee Chairman Martha Griffiths.

Paper #19 is in fact a compendium of five papers entitled "JOIN: A Jobs and Income Program for American Families," "JOIN: A Labor Market Analysis," "Public Employment Programs: An Evaluative Study," "The WPA: Public Employment Experience in the New Deal," and "The Indirect Market Effects of Wage Subsidy and Public Employment Programs." The first two papers describe in some detail "JOIN," an income maintenance system which is proposed as an alternative to current policy. This program includes wage subsidies, public service employment, and income supplements for one-parent families.

The third paper reviews the evidence concerning the impact of a range of existing public employment programs and notes that this impact depends critically upon the extent to which federal funds displace state and local funds in the provision of public services. The historical analysis of the Works Progress Administration stresses the effect upon the agency of inherent contradictions in its goals: that of providing relief and that of providing work. Among the lessons of the WPA for current policy-makers is that "a choice has to be made between quantity and quality of public employment." The final paper involves a theoretical analysis of wage supplement programs which comes to the following conclusions:

- The benefits resulting from a wage subsidy program are likely to go almost entirely to workers. It is unlikely that a wage subsidy program will make it possible for firms to reduce their wage payments.
- A wage subsidy which helps low-skill workers may have a negative effect on the wage rate of semiskilled workers. However, the size of such a negative effect is likely to be small.

As is indicated in the above summary, the content of paper #19 will be of more interest to those seeking to develop alternatives to current income maintenance policies than to those seeking to more precisely define the concept of poverty.

U.S. Congress, Joint Economic Committee. Studies in Public Welfare, Paper #20, Handbook of Public Income Transfer Programs: 1975. Washington, D.C.: U.S. Government Printing Office, 1974.

(XII)

The Studies in Public Welfare series represents perhaps the most recent effort at "comprehensive and nonpartisan review of all phases of the nation's system of welfare-related programs." In all, twenty papers were prepared between 1972 and 1974 under the auspices of the Congressional Joint Economic Committee, Subcommittee on Fiscal Policy, under the leadership of subcommittee Chairman Martha Griffiths.

Paper #20 is a reference document giving a detailed description of the features of AFDC and 38 related income transfer programs, focussing on such topics as eligibility criteria, benefit computation procedures, work requirements, benefit amounts, and so forth. As such, it provides the basis for comparing the poverty-related criteria for program eligibility in the AFDC program with similar definitions in such other income-tested programs as Supplemental Security Income, pensions for widows of veterans, assistance to Indians, Medicaid, Department of Housing and Urban Development income-tested housing programs, and the food stamp program.

The conclusions of the paper are directed more to the public policy-maker than the student of the definition of poverty, but can be briefly summarized as follows:

It is no longer possible--if indeed it ever was--to provide a convincing rationale for the programs as they exist in terms of who is covered and who is excluded, benefit amounts, and eligibility conditions. No coherent rationale binds them together as a system.

U.S. Congress, Senate Committee on Labor and Public Welfare, Subcommittee on Employment, Manpower, and Poverty. Toward Economic Security for the Poor. Washington, D.C.: U.S. Government Printing Office, 1968.

(II, X)

A report of the subcommittee's "Examination of the War on Poverty,"--a comprehensive evaluation, based on seven months of hearings, of OEO's anti-poverty programs. Poverty is defined; the poor are described; and recommendations are made on creating employment opportunities, skill development and job placement, income support for the elderly, income support for families, and action strategies.

*U.S. Congress, Senate Select Committee on Equal Educational Opportunity. _The Financial Aspects of Equality of Educational Opportunity and Inequities in School Finance_. Washington, D.C.: U.S. Government Printing Office, 1972.

(V, VI)

This Committee print contains two reports which discuss the inequities of school finance. The first article summarizes present fiscal inequities, reviews their causes and related court decisions, and concludes with a series of recommendations; the second "examines the impact of recent school finance decisions and proposed revenue sharing programs, with particular attention to the problems of large urban schools." Both papers describe and document startling disparities in per pupil expenditures and pupil-teacher ratios which exist between states, between central cities and suburbs, and within school districts. Attention is given to contrasting problems faced by rural areas which lack an adequate tax base and whose high need parallels the urban situation.

U.S. Congress, Senate Select Committee on Nutrition and Human Needs. _Nutrition and Human Needs: Part 1--Hunger and the Income Gap_. Washington, D.C.: U.S. Government Printing Office, 1970.

(XI)

Between 1968 and 1970 the American federal budgetary expenditures for food aid jumped 300%, from $650 million (which satisfied only 15% of statistically recognized need) to $1.9 billion. Nonetheless, as the Reverend Jesse Jackson of the Southern Christian Leadership Conference testifies before the Senate Select Committee on Nutrition and Human Needs, grave problems still confront the poor. "The welfare system was not designed by the poor. Welfare was necessary because of the greed of men at the top who were frightened at the nation's economy and withheld their money... People, white and black, are malnourished and starving on government subsidized farms when it would be illegal for them to raise their own food." In the past year, while 69.9% of the federal budget was inclined toward the Vietnamese, only 12.2% was spent toward the health, education, and welfare of the citizens of America. President Nixon's $1600 income maintenance program is not a realistic improvement over a $500 a year welfare program because it is neither sufficient to relieve nor to solve the problems of poverty.

Other testimony is given by Mayor John Lindsay of New York City and others on food stamp programs, welfare, and other projects.

U.S. Congress, Senate Subcommittee on Housing and Urban Affairs of the Committee on Banking, Housing and Urban Affairs. Hearings: Oversight on Rural Housing Programs, November 19, 20, and 21, 1974. Washington, D.C.: U.S. Government Printing Office, 1974.

(V)

The Hearings before the Senate Subcommittee on Housing and Urban Affairs concerning rural housing programs. The Hearings were held over a period of three days during which time the Subcommittee called over twenty-five witnesses. Supplementing the testimony of the witnesses are additional statements and data which were incorporated into the report. All aspects of rural housing in America were covered including those of Indian, migrant, and elderly populations. Specific case studies and statistical data are given to support witnesses' testimony.

U.S. Congress, Senate Subcommittee on Rural Development of the Committee on Agriculture and Forestry. Rural Housing: Needs, Credit Availability, and Federal Programs. Washington, D.C.: U.S. Government Printing Office, March 1975.

(V)

A report issued by the Committee on Agriculture and Forestry concerning rural housing. Major topics covered include rural housing conditions and needs; housing credit availability in rural areas including variances in mortgage terms in those areas vs. urban areas; federal programs for rural housing; and progress toward congressional objectives. An important fact concerning the housing of the poor which the report stresses is that both DHUD and FmHA programs do not reach many poverty-level families, although both Congress and various administrations have indicated that these families should receive priority in housing programs.

U.S. Department of Agriculture. Household Food Consumption Survey, 1955. Report #16. (November 1961).

(II, IV)

An evaluation of dietary levels in the United States in 1955 based on the National Research Council's recommended allowances for calories and eight nutrients. According to these recommended levels, 48% of U.S. households had inadequate diets in 1955. The report describes the frequency of inadequacy among nutrient groups and holds that calcium and ascorbic acid are most likely to be in short supply.

A comparison with earlier studies made in 1936 and 1942 reveals that significant improvements occurred in nutrient levels of city and low-income diets, especially between 1936 and 1942.

The study explores differences in diet patterns by region and by urbanization. The findings reveal that diets in the South generally have a lower nutrient level than those in the North and West. Farm diets furnished more nutrients, except in vitamins A and C, than city diets.

Finally, the report demonstrates that age, income and level of education are significant factors affecting dietary adequacy.

United States Department of Agriculture, Economic Research Service. Impact of Job Development on Poverty in Four Developing Areas (by John A. Kuehn, et al.). Agricultural Economic Report No. 225. Washington, D.C.: United States Department of Agriculture, June 1972.

(VI)

Direct economic impacts of job development in new and expanded plants in four developing areas within Arizona, Appalachia, the Mississippi Delta, and the Ozarks were estimated. Approximately 25 percent of all jobs in these plants in 1970 were held by employees whose households had been poor. About 16 percent of the total jobs were held by persons whose households escaped poverty by finding employment in the new or expanded plants.

The present discounted value of the increase in employee's salaries was $12,880. Migrants competed directly with residents for the new jobs, but not on a large scale. Previously poor residents got 22% of the new jobs and previously poor migrants got 4% of the new jobs. Over all, residents held approximately 77% of the new jobs and migrants and people returning to the area held the remainder. The families of one-third of the previously poor employees who found employment in new or expanded plants remained poor. Higher salaries, multiple wage earners or both would be necessary to remove these people from poverty. There was considerable variation in the impact of new jobs among the four areas.

(Partially taken from the article)

*U.S. Department of Agriculture, Economic Research Service. Rural People in the American Economy. Agricultural Economics Report No. 101. Washington, D.C.: U.S. Government Printing Office, 1966.

(V)

This paper discusses the adverse impacts of economic development on those who are "left behind." In particular, economic progress in farming has hurt the small farmer who is unable to expand his enterprise to reach the level of efficiency of large mechanized farms. This results in unemployment and underemployment. This in turn leads to further adverse economic impacts in and near rural areas. Not only does the rural population suffer economically, but there is abundant evidence that quantity and quality of education, training, health, housing, welfare programs, and anti-poverty efforts are inferior in rural areas. Additionally, access to public and private services is limited. Despite advances being made to support rural Americans, this study concludes that more needs to be done.

U.S. Department of Commerce, Bureau of the Census. "General Social and Economic Characteristics." Chapter C of U.S. Census of Population 1970; V.I., Characteristics of Population, Part 1, United States Summary, Section 1. Washington: 1973.

(VI)

This is a systemization of general social and economic data collected from samples of 5, 15, and 20 percent of the population. The data are shown for the U.S. as a whole. Some historical data are provided for census years from 1900 or later. Data cover the following subjects:

1) Nativity; place of birth; country of origin; parentage; citizenship; and mother tongue.
2) Residence in 1965; year moved into present house.
3) School enrollment; years of school completed; vocational training.
4) Veteran status.
5) Marital status and history; family composition; fertility.
6) Employment status, weeks worked, and activity five years ago; place of and transportation to work; occupation, class, and industry of workers.
7) Income, earnings, and poverty status.

In addition, separate tables provide selected data for Negroes and persons of Spanish "heritage" for areas with specified populations of these groups. These data are also available for each state.

(Partially taken from Congressional Information Service, American Statistical Index 1974: Annual and Retrospective Edition)

U.S. Department of Commerce, Bureau of the Census. Revision in Poverty Statistics, 1959 to 1968. Current Population Reports, Series P-23, No. 28. August 12, 1969.

(III)

"This report describes modifications in the definition of poverty which were adopted in 1969.... These two modifications change the method of adjusting the poverty threshold for annual cost-of-living fluctuations and alter the poverty income differential between farm and nonfarm families. This report shows the effect of the revised definition on estimates of the number of families and persons below the poverty levels for the years 1959 and 1967. Data for the year 1968 based on the revised poverty definition are also presented."

U.S. Department of Commerce, Bureau of the Census. U.S. Census Population: 1970, Subject Reports: Low Income Population, PC(2)-9H. Washington: 1973.

(XI)

"A report presenting statistics for the U.S. on the social, economic and housing characteristics of the population, by poverty status in 1969. Data are estimated based mostly on a 15% sample of the population." Statistics are presented on the following characteristics by poverty status:

- Social Characteristics--residence, birthplace, race, migration/mobility, single years of age, family characteristics, characteristics of civilian male veterans, and educational enrollment and attainment.
- Economic Characteristics--employment status and educational attainment, work disability, vocational training, selected income/earnings measures, occupation, earnings, earners and income.
- Housing Characteristics--tenure; value and rent-income ratio; selected equipment; year moved into unit and year structure built; units and stories in structure; persons in unit; plumbing and heating equipment; and persons per room.

This volume includes two technical tables: "poverty cutoff and weighted average threshholds at the poverty level in 1969, and families and unrelated individuals with one or more times of income allocated by ratio of total income in 1969."

(Partially taken from American Statistical Index 1974: Annual and Retrospective Edition, Abstracts)

U.S. Department of Commerce, Bureau of the Census. U.S. Census of Population: 1970, Subject Reports: Migration Between State Economic Areas, PC(2)-2E. Washington: 1972.

(VI)

A report presenting statistics on the movement of persons 5 years old and over between State Economic Areas (SEA's). Data are shown also for Negro migrants in SEA's with a Negro population of specified size.

The focus of this report is on detailed streams of migration; therefore, the only characteristics shown for migrants are age, sex, and race. Extensive cross tabulations of social and economic characteristics will appear in other 1970 census reports on migration.

(Taken from U.S. Department of Commerce, Bureau of the Census. Catalog of Publication: 1970-1972.)

U.S. Department of Commerce, Bureau of the Census. U.S. Census of Population: 1970, Subject Report: State Economic Areas, PC(2)-10B. Washington, D.C.: 1972.

(VI)

A report presenting statistics from the 1970 Census of Population on general social and economic characteristics of the inhabitants of each of the 510 State Economic Areas (SEA's). The report represents a consolidation of selected tabulations published for counties in the PC(1)-C series of reports for the various States.

Data cover the total population, the Negro population, persons of Spanish heritage, and the rural population, and provide statistics on general, social, and economic characteristics; employment and industrial characteristics; educational and family characteristics; and occupation and income. All data are for 1970.

The four appendixes: (a) describe the various area classifications (e.g., urban and rural residence, counties, State economic areas), and explain the residence rules used in counting the population; (b) provide definitions and explanations for the subject report; (c) provide information on sources of error in the data, sampling variation, ratio estimation, and editing procedures; and (d) summarize the data dissemination program of the 1970 census.

(Taken from U.S. Department of Commerce Bureau of the Census Catalog of Publications: 1970-1972.

*U.S. Department of Health, Education, and Welfare. "Characteristics of State Public Assistance Plans Under the Social Security Act," (SRS) 74-21215. Washington, D.C.: U.S. Government Printing Office, 1973.

(V, XII)

Outlines characteristics for each state's public assistance plans for Old Age Assistance (OAA), Aid to the Blind (AB), Aid to the Permanently and Totally Disabled (APTD), and Aid to Families with Dependent Children (AFDC). Focus is on provisions affecting individual's eligibility for money payment. Contains separate appendix with definitions of 'need' and listing of disregards.

U.S. Department of Health, Education, and Welfare. "Funds, by Source, Expended for Public Assistance Payments," (SRS) 74-04006. Washington, D.C.: U.S. Government Printing Office, July 15, 1973.

(V, XII)

Totals and breakdowns of federal and state/local expenditures for assistance payments, administration, services, and training in 1972. Separate tables for each of the four assistance categories (Aid to the Blind, Aid to the Disabled, Old Age Assistance, and Aid to Families with Dependent Children) and for emergency assistance indicate federal/state matching fund percentages.

U.S. Department of Health, Education, and Welfare. "Recipients of Public Assistance Money Payments and Amounts of Such Payments, by Program, State and County," Publication No. 74-03105. Washington, D.C.: U.S. Government Printing Office, 1973.

(V, XII)

Tables show number of recipients and amounts of payments by county for general assistance and the four categories of assistance for which federal funds are available.

U.S. Department of Health, Education, and Welfare. Recipients of Public Assistance Money Payments and Amounts of Such Payments, By Program, State and County: February, 1975. DHEW Publication No. (SRS) 76-03105. Washington, July 1975.

(XII)

This volume is the county data book on public assistance receipts for the report month of February, 1975, and is made up of data multilithed from State reports. According to the Monthly Labor Review the rate of unemployment in January and February 1975 -- 8.2 percent -- was the highest rate recorded for the entire post-World War II period. Unemployment rates are shown for 66 counties and cities with populations exceeding 500,000, of which 28 had unemployment rates above the national rate.

In February, 1975, in the cities of Boston, Baltimore, and Philadelphia, over 16% of the city populations received Aid to Families with Dependent Children (AFDC) or state administered general assistance (GA). Of the implications of such high rates, the volume states: "The impact of higher unemployment rates nationally during the past year on the program of AFDC cannot be gauged without also taking into consideration characteristics of the population in large urban areas; that is, the proportion of the population with low incomes, the racial or ethnic makeup, the median age, and other demographic factors that are interrelated with the economy. However, widespread unemployment will diminish the amount of resources families have to meet living expenses, and lack of opportunities for part-time and/or unskilled jobs will especially adversely affect female-headed families in which the mother is the primary wage earner and children's contributions augment family resources." A tabulation is included showing the proportion of populations receiving assistance under AFDC in 78 larger urban areas in the U.S. For these areas, rates of unemployment are also shown. Also discussed are the receipt and implications of unemployment insurance, and figures of State administered GA are shown.

U.S. Department of Health, Education, and Welfare. A Report on Measurement and the Quality of Life. Washington, D.C.: January 1973.

(XI)

A staff report clarifying the nature of theoretical and practical difficulties in measuring social well-being. Of importance to policy analysts, politicians, and social scientists are quantitative comparisons of aspects of the social welfare so that government policies may be adapted to improve the quality of life.

The report presents recent and current endeavors in approaching the task, then discusses obstacles which impede progress. Finally, possible approaches to changing the intensity or direction of present efforts are briefly delineated.

The conclusions which emerge from the report are that:

- There is at present a very substantial effort, both here and abroad, devoted to improving measurement of social conditions and social welfare.
- There is no immediate prospect of a dramatic breakthrough in achieving intellectually respectable broad-gauge measures of the quality of life. The realistic expectation is for gradual improvements in measuring particular problem areas (e.g., health, poverty, environment) rather than any grand synthesis.
- Efforts in this area have been hampered primarily by two factors. First, we are largely ignorant of the causal mechanisms underlying social behavior, and thus of what to measure, and find it difficult to quantify even when we know what we want. This makes the development and linkage of unambiguous quality of life measures extraordinarily difficult. But progress is possible. Second, we do not have a theoretical basis to aggregate individual measures to enable us to measure objectively whether and to what degree the world is a better place today than yesterday. Progress is not likely since ultimately arbitrary judgments are at stake.

(Partially taken from the Introduction)

*U.S. Department of Health, Education and Welfare. Toward a Social Report. Washington, D.C.: U.S. Government Printing Office, 1969.

(XI)

A report on various non-economic aspects of U.S. social welfare, intended as the first step toward the development of a comprehensive set of social indicators. Although Americans are healthier than they were in 1900, the U.S. lags behind many other developed countries in health. Intergenerational upward mobility is as great or greater than ever for white Americans. Opportunity for Black Americans is greatly restricted; upward mobility or even maintenance of father's high status is strikingly low, even if background factors are taken into account. United States per capita income is the highest in the world and is rising, with the distribution of income practically unchanged in 20 years. The poor numbered 40 million in 1960 and 26 million in 1967.

Pollution, science and art, crime and alienation are also considered in the report.

*U.S. Department of Health, Education, and Welfare, Medical Services Administration. "Characteristics of State Medical Assistance Programs Under Title XIX of the Social Security Act." Washington, D.C.: U.S. Government Printing Office, 1970.

(V)

Outlines characteristics of individual state's Medicaid programs. Reports on scope of coverage, scope of medical and remedial services provided, and eligibility criteria for each state. Also covers administration and financing procedures.

U.S. Department of Health, Education and Welfare, National Institute of Child Health and Human Development, Center for Population Research. Rural Urban Migration Research in the United States by Daniel Price and Melanie Sikes. Washington, D.C.: Government Printing Office, 1975.

(VI)

An annotated bibliography of books and articles on the subject of rural to urban migration in the United States, including over 1200 items. This book also contains a synthesis of the research covered by the bibliography. The synthesis addresses six major areas: sources of migration, selectivity of rural-urban migration and its effects on rural areas, the decision to migrate, adjustment of migrants and effects on urban areas, return migration, and needed research.

U.S. Department of Health, Education, and Welfare, Office of Income Security Policy and Office of the Assistant Secretary for Planning and Evaluation. "The Impacts of Inflation and Higher Unemployment: With Emphasis on the Lower Income Population." Technical Analysis Paper No. 2, October 1974.

(III)

The purpose of this paper is to analyze the size and distribution effects of higher unemployment and inflation on the economic status of several types of households, especially the poor and elderly. It was found that the burden of unemployment falls mainly on the poor, although the earnings losses are very unevenly distributed even within a given income class. The effects of inflation on the well being of various subgroups were examined in four areas: the cost of living, wealth, taxes and income source.

During periods of mild inflation, the cost of living effect was evenly distributed across income classes. During the recent, more acute inflation, the price increases faced by the poor have been 20% higher than those faced by middle income groups. Inflation has caused a redistribution of wealth away from the very rich and the poor towards middle income groups, although wealth "losses among the poor are concentrated among a small number and for most they are negligible." During an inflationary period, the real burden of taxes can increase because the parameters of the tax system are defined in money instead of real terms. Thus a monetary income that keeps pace with inflation represents a drop in real income because of higher proportional taxes. "This effect is proportionately larger for lower and higher income taxpayers than for those in the middle income ranges." The effect of inflation on income sources is complex. In general, families that depend on employment income lose during inflation if wages do not rise fast enough to compensate for price increases and the tax effect. Transfer income has tended to rise with inflation but usually with a lag, and overall, this rise has not been uniform. In some states, inflation has caused substantial real losses to transfer recipients.

U.S. Department of Health, Education, and Welfare, Public Health Service. "Age Patterns in Medical Care, Illness and Disability, U.S., 1968-1969," (HSM) 72-1026. Washington, D.C.: U.S. Government Printing Office, 1972.

(V)

Statistics on the use of medical services and the extent of illness and disability in the population by age, with emphasis on the health status of persons 65 years and over. Based on data collected in household interviews during the period 1968-1969.

(Taken from the pamphlet)

U.S. Department of Health, Education, and Welfare, Social and Rehabilitation Service. "Medicaid and Other Medical Care Financed from Public Assistance Funds, Fiscal Year, 1971." Washington, D.C.: U.S. Government Printing Office, 1972.

(V)

Discusses magnitude of increase in medical care expenditures, 1970-1971. Charts show breakdown of expenditures on medical services by type of service and by group served (OA, AB, AD, AFDC, children under 21, and other adults). Tables demonstrate range among states in expenditure per inhabitant (aggregate figures broken down by basis of eligibility and by type of service).

U.S. Department of Labor, Bureau of Labor Statistics. "Additional Results from Latest Survey of Consumer Expenditures Released by BLS." Washington: May 15, 1975.

(III)

A press release reporting the latest (as of 5/15/75) results from the 1972-73 Consumer Expenditure Survey. This release expands on the release of 4/16/75 (also annotated) entitled "The 1972-73 Consumer Expenditure Survey--Some First-Year Diary Results."

Selected weekly expenditure data are presented for U.S. families classified by income, family size, age of head, region, occupation of head, housing status, urbanization area, race, education, and family composition. For each classification of families, expenditure data are presented for 18 categories of food purchased for home consumption and a category for food consumed away from home. Selected non-food expenditures, some of which are frequently purchased in grocery stores, are presented, including housekeeping supplies, personal care products and services and non-prescription drugs and medical supplies. Expenditures for energy, specifically gasoline, gas and electricity, and other fuels (primarily home-heating oil) are also included.

These data were developed from one component of the 1972-73 Consumer Expenditure Survey--the first-year diary. The diary data presented were collected over the period July 1972 to June 1973 from more than 10,000 families in the U.S. which kept daily records of their expenditures for two 1-week periods.

(Partially taken from press release)

U.S. Department of Labor, Bureau of Labor Statistics. <u>The Concept of Part-Year Families in Consumer Expenditure Studies</u>, by Ann Erickson. CES Research Note No. 1. Washington, October 1968.

(IV)

The term "part-year family" refers to families (consumer units) in which all members belonged to a consumer unit which was in existence only part of the survey year, or in which some members joined or left a consumer unit which was in existence only part of the survey year. The existence of part-year units creates problems for researchers in consumer economics because if these units are not identified, expenditures for some persons may be reported twice.

This report reviews the history of the treatment of part-year families in Bureau of Labor Statistics surveys, describes the part-year families interviewed in the 1960-61 sample of urban families, and estimates the effect that part-year expenditures have in aggregate for urban families. "The measurement adjustments for part-year units are comparatively small and there is little objective basis for evaluating the completeness of the information.

Since processing the data requires either special machine instructions or hand tabulations, the cost of contacting the families and collecting and processing the 1960-61 schedules probably exceeded comparable costs for a major metropolitan area with a sample of 375 addresses. The analysis of the past year's schedules did show, however, that their estimates of the value of goods and services received as gifts added to substantial totals."

U.S. Department of Labor, Bureau of Labor Statistics. Consumer Credit in Consumer Expenditure Surveys, by Michael A. Carlson. CES Research Note No. 7. Washington, April 1970.

(III)

"The expanding volume of consumer credit and its cost to the consumer, the loss of wages through garnishment, and the number of personal bankruptcies resulting from over-extended buying raise questions about the reporting of purchases on credit in future consumer expenditure surveys conducted by the U.S. Bureau of Labor Statistics. Since consumers can use credit in lieu of current income for more and more types of purchases, it is important in studying family living conditions to know how much and what kind of credit different types of families use to achieve and maintain their level of living....

"At the end of 1968, consumers owed more than $113 billion for goods and services bought on credit. This total, which was over and above their home mortgage debt, was equivalent to more than a fifth of total personal consumption expenditures of $534 billion in the United States in 1968. Since the Bureau's 1960-61 Survey of Consumer Expenditures (CES), the volume of consumer credit outstanding has virtually doubled and has risen at a substantially faster rate than personal consumption expenditures....

"The Bureau's efforts to collect information on the amount and cost of credit in its 1960-61 CES revealed the complexity of the problem and consumers' confusion about how much they were paying for the credit service. The Bureau's past procedures in identifying and measuring the use of consumer credit and the provisions of the new legislation that are relevant to future expenditure surveys are outlined in this paper....

U.S. Department of Labor, Bureau of Labor Statistics. Consumer Expenditures and Income, Urban U.S. 1960-61. Supplement 3--Part A to BLS Report 237-238, July 1964.

(II,VII)

Contains information on family spending patterns in the United States, 1960-1961. Consumer groups classified by family size and income after taxes, and by family size and location of families residences inside or outside Standard Metropolitan Statistical Areas. (Generally, expenses are recorded in specific categories.)

U.S. Department of Labor, Bureau of Labor Statistics. *The Consumer Price Index: A Short Description*. Washington: 1971.

(III)

A simple explanation of the Consumer Price Index. "The CPI is a statistical measure of changes in prices of goods and services bought by urban wage earners and clerical workers including families and single persons." The index is computed by dividing the price of an average "market basket" in the current period by the price of that basket in a base period (currently 1967) and multiplying times 100:

$$I_{i:o} = \frac{\Sigma(q_o p_i)}{\Sigma(q_o p_o} \times 100$$

The "market basket" and the locations where pricing is made are chosen so that the samples are as representative as possible. Sampling and measurement (reporting) error still exist, but the index is considered to be sufficiently accurate for most of the practical uses made of it. In 1966 the Bureau of Labor Statistics began making available seasonally adjusted indexes for groups of items that are subject to significant seasonal price fluctuations. This report also includes two tables: 1) population weights and pricing schedules for cities used in computing the CPI, and 2) the December 1963 relative importance and number of items prices for groups and services priced for the CPI.

U.S. Department of Labor, Bureau of Labor Statistics. *Employment and Earnings Monthly*. Washington, D.C.: 1954-present.

(X)

A monthly report issued by the Bureau of Labor Statistics which contains aggregate data on U.S. labor-related activities during the previous month. Each report contains the following regular monthly data: household data (employment, unemployment and participation in the labor force); quarterly averages; establishment data (employees on payrolls, hours and earnings, labor turnover, job vacancy areas); and unemployment insurance data. In addition, each report contains a summary of employment and unemployment developments during the previous month and a description of the survey methodology which was used to collect the data. In addition to the regular monthly data enumerated above, special features appear in most of the issues, as shown below:

	Jan.	Feb.	Mar.	Apr.	May	June	July	Aug.	Sept.	Oct.	Nov.
Household data											
Annual averages	x										
Revised seasonally adjusted series and current seasonal factors		x									
Quarterly averages: Seasonally adjusted data Persons not in labor force Vietnam Era war veterans	x			x			x			x	
Establishment data											
National annual averages: Industry divisions (preliminary)	x										
Industry detail (final)			x								
Women employment (National)		x			x			x			x
National data adjusted to new benchmarks										(1)	
Revised seasonally adjusted series and current seasonal factors						(2)					
State and area annual averages					x						
Area definitions					x						

[1] The issue that introduces the establishment data adjusted to new benchmarks varies. The October 1972 issue marks the introduction of March 1971 benchmarks.

[2] Revised data introduced in June 1973.

*U.S. Department of Labor, Bureau of Labor Statistics. "Estimating Equivalent Incomes or Budget Costs by Family Type." Monthly Labor Review 83 (November 1960): 1197-1200.

(IV)

A "scale or equivalent income" is developed which indicates the amount of relative income required by families of different composition to maintain the same standard of living. The scale values are presented for six different family sizes cross classified by five family types (a specification of the age of the oldest child) and four age-of-head classes. "The scale is based on the assumption that families spending the same proportion of income on food have attained equal levels of living." The procedure used here assumes a consumption function that makes food expenditure proportional to the square root of income. The proportionality constant for each family category considered is approximated by calculating the averages of income and food expenditure in those categories, using data in the Bureau of Labor Statistics Survey of Consumer Expenditures for 1950. These relationships then determine the relative income required by different family types spending the same proportion of income on food. A family of four with the oldest child between 6 and 16 years and family head between 35 and 55 years is used as the base category. The scale values derived compare favorably with earlier measures for two and three person families. Higher values for five and six person families "appear to reflect a trend to greater expenditures for teenage and near teenage children in 1950."

U.S. Department of Labor, Bureau of Labor Statistics. Family Income in Consumer Expenditure Surveys, by George V. Spraggins and Caroll Downey. CES Research Note No. 8. Washington, May 1970.

(VII)

"Before undertaking another nationwide Bureau of Labor Statistics survey of consumer expenditures, income, and savings, the Bureau's Division of Living Conditions Studies decided to review the definitions of income and the distinctions between money income and non-money income. This review led to consideration of the desirability and possibility of modifications in survey practices that would take account of recent trends in types and sources of income and, hopefully, improve comparability with the Office of Business Economics national income and product accounts....

"In recent years two opposing trends have developed that complicate studying a family's level of living in terms of the customary relationship between expenditures and money income during the period surveyed. On the one hand, a larger share of employees' compensation is employer payments into insurance and welfare programs to protect employees and their families against the economic hazards of illness, accidents, or unemployment, and against loss of income after retirement... On the other hand, families expand consumption from current income by buying an increasing variety of goods and services on credit." This report looks at both money and non-money income in a large number of categories and makes several recommendations for revising the methods of reporting various types of both money and non-money income in upcoming consumer expenditure studies surveys.

U.S. Department of Labor, Bureau of Labor Statistics. Gifts and Contributions in Consumer Expenditure Surveys. CES Research Note No. 6. Washington, March 1970.

(VII)

"Gifts and contributions appear on both sides of the accounts of most families -- they give and, in turn, receive gifts. How these gifts and contributions have been recorded and classified in the Bureau of Labor Statistics' Consumer Expenditure Surveys has varied with the type of gift. As part of the research on the concept of non-money income to be used in the comprehensive expenditure survey in the 1970's, it is pertinent to review the reporting and classification of gifts and contributions in the Survey of Consumer

Expenditures, 1960-61 (CES), and to relate the information obtained to its uses in revision of the Consumer Prices Index (CPI) and in comparisons with the Office of Business Economics' (OBE) national accounts estimates and with the Internal Revenue Service reports on itemized contributions.

"Gifts and contributions given to organizations or to persons outside the consumer unit, were not classified as a family expenditure in the 1960-61 CES tabulations but were a separate category with subgroups...The following recommendations are made for collecting and tabulating information on gifts and contributions in the pilot surveys:

1. Continue the 1960-61 procedures for reporting and classifying cash gifts and contributions.
2. Collect and tabulate the dollar value of goods and services given to persons not in the family at a level of detail compatible with requirements for reconciliation with OBE's Personal Consumption Expenditures and for research in connection with revising weights for the CPI.
3. Identify items received without direct expense to the family by source, i.e., employer, welfare agencies, other persons.
4. Concentrate on measuring the type and frequency of such non-cash items received by the family and, for a limited number, experiment with questions to determine the family's knowledge of their cash value."

*U.S. Department of Labor, Bureau of Labor Statistics. Handbook of Labor Statistics. Washington, D.C.: U.S. Government Printing Office, 1971.

(V, XII)

The Bureau of Labor Statistics (BLS) lower budget has three components which might include some publicly-provided (or subsidized) goods: transportation, housing and medical care. Only in transportation are regional differences in the level of services recognized and included in the cost statistics. Their procedure is to calculate the cost of automobile ownership and apply 100 percent of it to the nonmetropolitan cost-of-living, 50 percent of it to the cost-of-living in New York, Boston, Chicago, Philadelphia, and other metropolitan areas. Sixty-five percent was applied to the cost-of-living for automobile owners and 34% for nonowners. Average rental levels undoubtedly include the subsidies implicit in public housing. Since the BLS lower budget is above the Medicaid cut-off level, medical insurance costs are assumed to be borne privately.

U.S. Department of Labor, Bureau of Labor Statistics. How the Government Measures Unemployment, Report 418, 1973.

(X)

This report describes the methods used by the Bureau of Labor Statistics in measuring unemployment. Unemployment statistics are based on a monthly sample of approximately 47,000 households or 1 in every 1,300 households throughout the country. The sample is designed to reflect urban and rural areas, industrial and family differences, and geographical divisions of the country in the same proportion as they occur in the nation as a whole. Each person interviewed is classified as either employed, unemployed, or not in the labor force. Employed persons consist of:

- People who did any work for pay or profit during the survey week
- People who worked at least 15 hours for no pay in a family enterprise
- People who were temporarily absent from their regular job because of illness, vacation, industrial dispute, bad weather, or various personal reasons.

Unemployed persons are:

- People who did not have a job during the survey week and who actively sought work during the previous 4 weeks
- People who were not working and were waiting to be recalled to a job from which they had been laid off
- People who were not working and were waiting to report to a new job within 30 days.

People not in the labor force consist of:

- People under 16 and inmates of institutions
- People who have no job and are not looking.

This latter group is subdivided according to whether they are: housewives, students, retired people, the disabled, and other. 'Other' is comprised of: people who like to work only at certain times of the year, people who don't want to work, and people who believe they can't get a job.

Since the unemployment rate fluctuates with the seasons, seasonal adjustments are made.

A different method is used to determine local unemployment. This is described.

Underemployment, called "the percent of labor force time lost" expresses the total man hours lost through unemployment and through shortened work weeks as a percent of the totally available manhours.

U.S. Department of Labor, Bureau of Labor Statistics. Imputed Income from Owner-Owned Housing, by George V. Spraggins. CES Research Note No. 4. Washington, June 1969.

(XI)

"Imputed income from owner-occupied housing is an estimated value of the services received by people for living in their own homes that are not measured by their cash outlays for housing. It is not money income that can be used for the purchase of food, clothing, or other consumer items. However, it is a type of non-money income that allows the homeowner to enjoy a higher standard of living accomodations than the renter having an equivalent money income." This report is a reexamination of the implications of the treatment of imputed income from owner-occupied housing in its measurement of family income and expenditures for housing.

"Of the four major items of nonmoney income identified in national accounts series, imputed rental income from owner-occupied nonfarm housing is the most important. In 1967, it accounted for about $13 billion, or 2 percent of the national income. Next was the imputed value of services furnished without payment by financial intermediaries, which was estimated to be $9.1 billion. Food and shelter received as payment-in-kind totaled $2.7 billion. Food and fuel produced and consumed on farms, the last item, has declined steadily in importance from a high of $2.8 billion in 1947 to about $700 million in 1967."

U.S. Department of Labor, Bureau of Labor Statistics. Medical Care Expenditures in Consumer Expenditure Surveys, by Alice L. Bynum. CES Research Note No. 2. Washington, February 1969.

(XI)

This report reviews the measurement of medical expenditures in Consumer Expenditure Surveys made by the Bureau of Labor Statistics, and evaluates the relative importance of various insurance and other programs that assist families in paying for medical care. "The purpose of the review and evaluation is to help in making decisions on collecting medical care costs to families in the 1970's that will provide (1) continuity with earlier family expenditure surveys, and (2) the identification of details essential for multipurpose tabulations and analysis of medical expenditures as required for the 1970's....

"In 1966, families paid directly (i.e., out-of-pocket) for less than half of the total spent for personal health care. These payments would be reported as family expenditures in the customary way." Employer's contributions for health insurance premiums, if considered a form of nonmonetary compensation, would be added to the family's income and to its expenditures for health insurance. While determining the dollar value of health insurance may pose problems, especially if the employer paid the entire premium, counting only the family's expenditures (including deductions from pay) for health insurance could result in a significant gap in personal consumption expenditures for health. "Furthermore, the underreporting of health insurance expenditures would be concentrated among wage and salary workers covered by employee health-benefit plans and this group includes families from whose expenditure patterns the weights for the Consumer Price Index have been obtained."

U.S. Department of Labor, Bureau of Labor Statistics. "The 1972-73 Consumer Expenditure Survey--Some First-Year Diary Results," by Julius Shiskin. Washington, April 16, 1975.

(III)

A press release announcing the publication of partial results of the 1972-73 Consumer Expenditure Survey. The release includes a paper presented by Julius Shiskin, Commissioner of Labor Statistics, at a meeting of the American Marketing Association in April 1975. He discusses the data collecting and processing methodology of the Survey. (These are discussed in greater detail in Monthly Labor Review articles by Shiskin and Carlson annotated for this section.) Tables of statistics are also presented on the variation in consumption expenditures by family income, family size and age of head. Some of the more important findings are that beef accounts for about 15% of the average family's home food budget, the amount spent on food away from home rises steeply as income rises, the amount spent on gasoline is 50% of direct energy purchases, younger families spend more on gasoline than older families, and expenditures on gasoline are more than one fourth of the amount spent on food at home.

U.S. Department of Labor, Bureau of Labor Statistics. Personal Insurance in Consumer Expenditure Surveys, by Alice L. Bynum. CES Research Note. No. 5. Washington, July 1969.

(III, VII)

"Personal insurance in the 1960-61 Survey of Consumer Expenditures (CES) covered the family's out-of-pocket payments and deductions from pay for life insurance, social security, and public and private retirement plans. As social security deductions and provisions for insurance and pensions as "fringe benefits" of employment increase, these financial protection for the family can expand without commensurate increases in family income or disbursements as recorded in the 1960-61 CES. Also, introduction of Medicare raises the question of whether social security deductions should be allocated between "personal insurance" and "health insurance" in the next CES.

"This report reviews the treatment of personal insurance in previous Bureau of Labor Statistics surveys and in the Office of Business Economics estimates of national accounts, examines trends in public and private insurance and retirement programs, and makes recommmendations for measuring personal insurance in the CES in the 1970's." It is recommended that CES data on personal insurance continue to include employee contributions for social security and be expanded to include employee contributions for life insurance, for private and for Federal and other government retirement and pension plans, for health and welfare plans, and for temporary disability or income maintenance insurance. No change is proposed for treatment of unemployment insurance or Workmen's Compensation.

U.S. Department of Labor, Bureau of Labor Statistics. Recreation Expenditures: Definition and Measurement in Consumer Expenditure Surveys, by Ana P. Lavallee. CES Research Note No. 3. Washington, May 1969.

(XI)

"The Survey of Consumer Expenditures, 1960-61 (CES) showed a decline in the relative importance of recreational expenditures by urban families to 4.0 percent of their current consumption expenditures from 4.4 percent in 1950. This finding came at a time of continued expansion in those socio-economic factors generally associated with the demand for recreation, namely: (1) increasing leisure time in the form of a shorter work-week, paid holidays, paid vacations; (2) better transportation and greater mobility; (3) rising levels of total, real, and discretionary income; and (4) pension and retirement programs that encourage earlier retirement.

"This unexpected downtrend can be attributed to problems of defining and measuring recreation to take account of changes in its character... It is the purpose of this paper to (1) review current definitions of recreation and the magnitude and economic impact of major recreational "growth" items now classified in other expenditure categories; and (2) develop proposals for an alternative classification of major types of recreational activities by purpose or use....

"Two guidelines to be observed in changes to measure recreational expenditures more completely are: (1) to improve comparability with Office of Business Economics's classification of personal consumption expenditures and (2) to provide bridges to measure historical trends in CES expenditure categories, paying particular attention to requirements for the Consumer Price Index and Standard Budget. It is believed that these objectives can be attained by (1) collecting and publishing sufficient detail for certain expenditures so that they can be identified and combined as needed for comparability; and (2) devising a coding system that will simplify alternate classifications of the data."

U.S. Department of Labor, Bureau of Labor Statistics. Relative Importance of Components in the Consumer Price Index 1972-73. Washington: 1974.

(III)

This report presents two tables: 1) the relative weights in the national CPI for December 1972 and December 1973 for groups, subgroups and selected items; and 2) the relative importance of groups and subgroups of items in U.S. cities overall and in 23 selected SMSA's. ("The relative importance of a component of the CPI is its expenditure of value weight expressed as a percentage of all items.") About every 10 years (1960-61, 1972-73), the BLS revises the "market basket" of goods that they price to determine the CPI. Between revisions, the quantity and quality of priced goods are not changed so changes in the CPI only reflect price changes. Therefore, changes in the relative importance data only reflect changes in the relative prices of items. Since the pattern of consumption will undoubtedly change over a decade and since relative consumption of items will change as relative prices change, the relative weights do not show the percentage of overall consumption expenditure the average family spends on each item in the current year. They show the percentage a family would have spent at current prices if the mix and quantity of consumption in the current year was identical to the consumption in the base year (the year of the last revision of the "market basket").

*U.S. Department of Labor, Bureau of Labor Statistics. "Revised Equivalence Scale for Estimating Equivalent Incomes or Budget Costs by Family Type." U.S. Department of Labor Statistics Bulletin, 1570-2. Washington, D.C.: U.S. Government Printing Office, November 1968.

(III,IV)

Explains derivation of revised family equivalence scale (measuring relative income required by families differing in composition to maintain equivalent levels of consumption). Scale based on assumption that families spending an equal proportion of their income on food have attained an equivalent level of total consumption. Therefore, the equation used to derive income equivalencies expresses a functional relationship between income after personal taxes and food expenditures. Income adjustments are built in for size and type of family and age of family head.

Applying the formula to empirical data reveals that age of family head and age of oldest child are important factors in determining the range of changing income requirements.

U.S. Department of Labor. Sub-Employment in the Slums of Boston. Washington, D.C.: U.S. Government Printing Office, 1968.

(X)

A description of unemployment patterns in a Boston ghetto area. National unemployment measurements are utterly irrelevant in this area. A sub-employment index is used which includes assessments of those working part time, although they are looking for full-time work; those working full time but receiving low wages; the labor force dropouts who are not working and have given up looking for a job; and those who are known to be present in the community but who do not show up at all in a survey. The unemployment rate for the South Boston ghetto area in 1968 was 6.8% but the subemployment rate was 24.2%. Increases in the gross national product would do little to affect this area. Unemployment is thought to be primarily a story of inferior education, no skills, police records, discrimination, unnecessarily rigid hiring practices, and hopelessness.

U.S. Department of Labor, Bureau of Labor Statistics. Survey of Consumer Expenditures 1960-1961, Consumer Expenditures and Income: Total Northeastern Region, Urban and Rural. BLS Report No. 237-89. May 1965.

(III)

This report is one of five presenting data on consumer expenditures and income collected jointly by the Bureau of Labor Statistics and the U.S. Department of Agriculture from families and single consumers living in urban and rural areas throughout the United States. Comparable reports in this BLS and USDA series cover the North Central, Southern and Western regions, as defined by the Bureau of the Census, and a summary report covers the entire urban and rural United States. These reports for the total population combine data previously issued in reports for separate levels of urbanization, including the joint reports for rural nonfarm families for 1961, the Bureau of Labor Statistics' reports for urban families for 1960-61 and the Department of Agriculture's reports for rural farm families for 1961. Tabulations for nonfarm (urban and rural nonfarm) families for 1960-61 are presented.

This report also contains data on the variation in expenditures by selected family characteristics; definitions of categories used; and an explanation of the sample design, the methods of collection and processing of data, and weighting systems used for U.S. and regional average.

(Partially taken from report)

U. S. Department of Labor, Bureau of Labor Statistics. "Three Standards of Living for an Urban Family of Four Persons, Spring 1967." U.S. Department of Labor _Bulletin_ 1570-5, 1969.

(III, IV)

Summarizes the attempt by the Bureau of Labor Statistics to develop three budget levels based on a uniform market basket of goods and services--a moderate budget and budgets higher and lower than that level. Empirical data on patterns of consumption used in determining kind and quantity of items in the three standard-of-living budgets as well as in establishing various levels of cost at those levels of living are presented.

Explores intercity differences in costs, quantity, and types of items required in the budget. Observes that, of the major components in the budget, shelter and transportation contribute most to inter-city variations resulting from differences in quantities and prices.

Presents detailed description of methods and sources of data used for estimating quantities and prices for major budget components.

* U.S. Department of Labor, Manpower Administration. _The Pre-Retirement Years: A Longitudinal Study of the Labor Market Experience of Men_. Washington, D.C.: Vol. 1: 1970; Vol. 2: 1970; Vol. 3: 1973.

(IX)

A four-volume study of the labor market experience and behavior of middle-aged men over a five-year period. Empirical work is based on data from the National Longitudinal Survey. In Volume 1, basic data on labor force participation, employment status, and attitudes is presented and discussed. Volumes 2 and 3 emphasize the causes of changes in the levels and distribution of social and economic variables over the survey period. The data indicates that movements in and out of poverty are common. Between 1965 and 1968, 45% of poor whites (using Social Security definition) and 39% of poor Blacks had escaped poverty; 2% of whites and 40% of Blacks newly entered poverty during the period. Turnover, it is noted, decreases with family size.

*U.S. Department of Transportation. _1972 National Transportation Report_. Washington, D.C.: 1972.

(V)

The 1972 National Transportation Report (NTR) is the first in a series of reports on the nation's transportation system and the planning alternatives of federal, state and local governments for improving the system in the future. The report provides estimates of investment needs and program priorities as seen by the states, local governments, and the private sector; analyzes selected issues; and provides guidelines for future action.

One of the special issues considered is the transportation needs of the disadvantaged including the elderly, the handicapped, the poor, the unemployed and the young. In both urban and rural areas these groups suffer from a lack of mobility due to the following reasons:

- they cannot afford or are unable to drive an automobile;
- they cannot afford public transportation;
- they reside in areas poorly served by public transportation;
- the design and service features of public transportation pose difficult health, maneuverability or orientation problems for them.

In spite of the fact that lack of car ownership often makes the poor dependent upon public transportation, transit service for the poor tends to be inadequate. The 1972 NTR cites the 1963 Census of Transportation which indicates the lowest income groups had the highest percentage of workers with no public transportation service available and the longest distance to a transit line. Programs to increase the mobility of the poor and unemployed have included reverse commuter experiments, to provide public transportation to carry low-income city residents to suburban jobs. Approximately 59% of these experiments were judged to be successful providing benefits estimated at between $3 and $30 per week in additional income for each rider.

*U.S. Department of Transportation. 1974 National Transportation Report: Summary. Washington, D.C.: December 1974.

(V)

Like the 1972 National Transportation Report (NTR), the 1974 NTR provides an assessment of the present state of the U.S. transportation system and a discussion of alternatives for improving transportation in the future. In considering the mobility of the poor, two issues appear important: Chapter IV's discussion of transit use and income, and Chapter V's discussion of the significantly urban location of planned public transportation capital expenditures.

Chapter IV indicates that a larger proportion of trips by persons whose family income is less than $3,000 in 1970 occurred on public transportation than for other income groups. One reason for this is that about 83 percent of SMSA households with annual incomes less than $3,000 indicated that public transportation was six blocks or less from their homes. In addition, while public transportation accounted for 7.2% of home-to-work trips for all households, it accounted for 13% of home-to-work trips by households with under $3,000 annual income.

Chapter V indicates that planned capital investment in public transportation is concentrated in the larger urbanized areas. Between 1972 and 1990, areas over one million in population will account for 83.5 percent of planned public transportation capital expenditures. This would tend to indicate that no significant investments in public transportation are expected in rural areas, thus perpetuating the mobility problems of the rural poor.

U.S. National Center for Health Statistics. Report of the International Conference on the Perinatal and Infant Mortality Problem of the U.S., June 1966. U.S. Public Health Service Publication #1000, Series 4, No. 3.

(XI)

Article notes two points of concern about the infant mortality rate in the United States: (1) a virtual halt in the rate of decline of infant mortality after a long period of rapid decline; (2) the unfavorable position of infant mortality compared with that of many other countries, whereas fifteen years ago infant mortality in the U.S. was about the lowest in the world. Now only in Denmark and the Netherlands do the rates continue to decline. In Denmark specially trained nurses are provided during the first year to supervise infants under one year in private homes. In the Netherlands the low infant loss rate is mainly attributed to a relatively long tradition of infant care in the family unit supplied by district nurses, a welfare center and supported by elementary social security and a rising standard of living. In the U.S. it is noted that there has been an influx of lower income and higher infant mortality risk groups in the large cities.

Various aspects of the infant mortality problem are considered. Also established is a positive association between low-income and fetal and neonatal mortality, especially in the United States, England and Wales.

Comparison of infant mortality rates among countries is difficult due to varied registration and statistical practices.

(Poverty and Health in the United States)

U.S. Office of Management and the Budget, Statistical Policy Division. Social Indicators 1973. Washington, D.C.: U.S. Government Printing Office, 1973.

(XI)

A compilation of statistics on eight areas of U.S. social conditions. Life expectancy has risen slowly; the numbers of the ill and disabled are shown; the confidence in one's ability to obtain good health care was best correlated with income. Violent crime and fear of assault showed increases, while robbery rates dropped slightly after a long rise. Education continued to spread; achievement was higher among whites and those with educated parents. While unemployment remains high, working conditions are improving. Blacks and especially women have lower earnings within job categories. The long-run steady rise in median income seems to be leveling off, while the distribution of income remains stable. A downward trend in the number of impoverished Americans since 1959 reversed itself in 1969. Substandard housing was being steadily eliminated. The use of time is shown. Demographic data concludes the volume; both birth and death rates have been falling steadily but the population of the U.S. will continue to grow for as long as they project (50 years).

Urban Systems Research and Engineering. Employment Growth in Rural Areas. Prepared for the Office of Economic Opportunity. Cambridge: 1973.

(VI)

This study analyzes rural economic growth in 6 multi-county substate regions defined by the OEO as the "spheres of influence" of a small city (population in 1970 less than 110,000). Two cities were chosen from each of three different areas: the Ohio Valley, the Gulf Coast and the West Texas Plains. The study developed five conclusions which are relevant to federal rural development policy: 1) Rural economic growth and development is dominated by national rather than local firms. 2) Economic development can occur in rural areas without significantly helping the poor. 3) Economic development in the study areas can be attributed to an expansion of local industries that is greater than the national experience for those particular industries. 4) Substate regionalism is useful for rural economic development policy research and implementation. Of the 21 regional systems that exist, the state-designated substate planning and development districts should be used. 5) The Rural Development Act of 1972 contains some provisions which can aid rural economic development and others which will be largely ineffective. Since rural development depends on national companies, the Act's provisions for rural industrial finance assistance will have little impact. Financing assistance for essential community facilities can help indirectly but not directly. Regional substate planning can be helpful; however, all potentially helpful provisions are inadequate.

(Partially taken from the report)

Urban Systems Research and Engineering, Inc. Evaluation of Medicaid Spend-Down: Administrative Analysis and Methodology and Three Case Studies. Prepared for U.S. Department of Health, Education, and Welfare, Social and Rehabilitation Service, 1975.

(V)

Three case studies present an analysis of state administrative mechanisms and procedures for the implementation of spend-down programs. The focus is on the context in which states exercise discretion in exercising policy options afforded them. Specific policies considered include administrative structure, benefit levels, eligibility levels, eligibility periods and retroactivity provisions, policy dissemination, field supervision and eligibility staff training. Among implementation procedures considered are intake methods, income determination, card issuance, redetermination, and enrollment methods. Specific structures devised by states can have a measurable effect on program's participation rate.

Urban Systems Research and Engineering, Inc. Evaluation of Medicaid Spend-Down; Recipient Survey Analysis. Prepared for U.S. Department of Health, Education, and Welfare, Social and Rehabilitation Service, 1975.

(V)

Presents findings of a survey of Medicaid recipients. Explores predictive aspects of Medicaid spend-down experience and assesses effectiveness of spend-down program in meeting the health care needs of categorically-related persons with extraordinary medical bills whose incomes exceed the level for financial assistance.

Data collected from county welfare offices and interviews with Medicaid applicants (spend-down and non-spend-down). Interview form designed to elicit socio-demographic, economic, behavioral and health services utilization information.

Relevant to a study of differences among states in scope and quality of their Medicaid programs as reflected in recipient responses and attitudes toward care provided. Variation among states in structure of spend-down programs shown to have significant effect on financial and health care impact of the program.

Uzawa, Hirofumi. "Preference and Rational Choice in the Theory of Consumption." In Mathematical Models in the Social Sciences, edited by Ken Arrow. Stanford, California: Stanford University Press, 1959.

(III)

The purpose of this paper is to study the logical foundations of the theory of consumer behavior. Assuming rational consumer behavior, preference relations are defined as irreflexive, transitive, monotone, convex and continuous relations over the set of all conceivable commodity bundles. A choice function associates prices and incomes with those commodity bundles that the consumer chooses subject to budgetary restraints. Samuelson shows that almost all properties of the choice functions derived from preferences are consequences of the so-called Weak Axiom of Consumer Behavior:

> If at the price and income of situation 0 commodity bundle x^1 could be chosen but commodity bundle x^0 actually has been chosen, than at the price and income of situation 1 at which commodity bundle x^1 is chosen it is impossible to choose commodity bundle 0.

But this has been shown to apply only in the case of two commodities. Houthakker postulated that a necessary and sufficient condition for a choice function to be derived from a consumer's preference is the Strong Axiom of Consumer Behavior:

> If a finite sequence of commodity bundles x^0, x^1,... x^s each commodity bundle is revealed preferred to commodity bundle x^{t+1} (t=0,1,..., s-1), then the commodity bundle x^s is not revealed preferred to commodity bundle x^0.

This article shows that for choice functions with certain qualitative regularity conditions, Samuelson's Weak Axiom implies the Strong Axiom. This suggests that the whole theory of rational consumer behavior may be built on the basis of Samuelson's Weak Axiom of Consumer Behavior.

(Partially taken from the article)

Vadakin, James G. <u>Children, Poverty, and Family Allowances</u>. New York: Basic Books, Inc., 1968.

(IV)

Family allowances are "systematic payments made to families with dependent children, either by employers or by the government, for the primary purpose of promoting the welfare of such children." This fast, efficient, nonbureaucratic system is meant to redistribute income and to eliminate the discrepancy between family income and need. Additional children mean additional need, and family income must increase commensurately, or the economic and social status of its members will be impaired.

The book's initial chapter acquaints the reader with the general philosphy and method of family allowances, after which the socio-economic status of children in the United States will be viewed against this background. Subsequent chapters summarize the attention given to family allowances to date; trace the history and development of the system throughout the world, showing the present status of these programs and the Canadian scheme in particular; and analyze shortcomings of our existing income maintenance system. Finally, a family allowances plan for the country is outlined, showing benefits, costs, administrative provisions, correlation with existing measures, advantages, and other relevant factors.

Valentine, Charles A. <u>Culture and Poverty: Critique and Counter Proposals</u>. Chicago: The University of Chicago Press, 1968.

(II,XI)

The poor have never been adequately studied by social scientists. The author shows how such studies could be done and outlines a program for the reduction of poverty. Valentine takes issue with the culture of poverty theory and its exponents, feeling that they have blamed poverty on the poor and discouraged efforts to wage war on poverty.

Poverty is traced to middle-class behavior toward the deprived. Most studies of the poor, particularly the urban poor, have been made from insufficient evidence. Such studies have usually relied on statistics supplied by census takers, police, and social workers. New ethnographic research to be made by anthropologists living among the poor is called for. In this way the needs and motivations of the poor and the structure of their society could be studied by well-tested methods.

The book sets forth proposals to grant the poor power over the resources needed to overcome poverty. This would involve special rights and positive discrimination in favor of the most disadvantaged groups. The goal would be the reduction of poverty in the United States.

Van Dusen, Roxann A. "Problems of Measurement in Areas of Social Concern." Monthly Labor Review 97 (1974): 17-18.

(XI)

A review of the U.S. Government published collection of statistics entitled Social Indicators, 1973. The volume is organized around eight major social areas: health, public safety, education, employment, income, housing, leisure, recreation and population. Van Dusen finds the effort worthwhile, but wonders if this collection of statistics could be made more valuable. Should Social Indicators, 1973 attempt a broad picture of society generally, or focus on those societal elements for which goal consensus exists? To whom should these national reports be addressed? And should they not be accompanied by an interpretative text?

Vickrey, William. "Resource Distribution Patterns and the Classification of Families." Studies in Income and Wealth 10 (1947).

(VII)

This paper makes two major points. The first is that for many purposes, a classification of income by equivalent adults (children= fraction of adult) summarizes data more accurately than a classification by family. The second is that expenditure is a better proxy for living standards than annual income. Both of these points are controversial and there are no less than four long comments on the paper. These comments, by Alice Hansen, Margaret Reid, Dorothy Brady, and Jerome Cornfield, are for the most part negative. It is pointed out that the use of an equivalent adult scale loses information, blurs the distinction between family size and income (because the two are not independent), and ignores economies of scale in family size. Several points are made about the use of consumption as a measure of well-being. High consumption levels are associated with dissavings which distorts the link between expenditures and income at the high end (of consumption). The use of expenditure would place small, wealthy families and large poorer families at the same level. Consumption is not a good variable at both its high and low levels because it varies a lot at these extremes. Finally, the plight of the poor forced to dissave and go into debt in order to survive would be hidden by the use of an expenditure standard instead of an income standard.

*Vietorisz, T.; Mier, R.; and Giblin, J. "Subemployment: Exclusion and Inadequacy Indexes." Monthly Labor Review (June 1975): 3-12.

(X) ,

This article analyzes several alternative subemployment indices and suggests some alternative measures which use subemployment rates to identify economic hardship. The unemployment rate had traditionally been the most common indicator of financial hardship, but a number of alternative indices have been proposed because of the inadequacy of the unemployment rate. The problem with these alternatives is that they measure different phenomena, and thus yield vastly different results. What is needed is a range of alternative measures whose purposes and methodologies are linked to specific alternative policies. The major differences among existing proposed indices are differences as to who should be included in the index and in the definition of adequate income. The authors classify proposed indices into three groups:

1) An Exclusion Index which measures the lack of individual opportunity for finding a job at a proper level of remuneration

2) Inadequacy Index which measures the inadequacy of earnings to provide a decent standard of living

3) An Underutilization Index which measures the wasted potential labor supply in both a quantitative and qualitative sense.

Vogel, Ronald J., and Morrall, John F. "The Impact on Medicaid of State and Local Health and Hospital Expenditures, with Special Reference to Blacks." Journal of Human Resources 8 (Spring 1973).

(V)

A simple demand and supply model is proposed to "explain" the wide variations in state and local government expenditures on health and hospitals and to assess the impact of Medicaid in satisfying the health need of Blacks. The model shows that a large percentage of the variation can be explained and that Blacks tend to demand and evidently receive a higher proportion of public health care on the basis of their income than one would expect. The discriminatory effects of Medicare are more than offset by a combination of Medicaid and state and local spending on health care, although the continuing racial health gap indicates that state and local spending has not offset the wide differences between Blacks and whites in private and Medicare spending.

(Journal of Human Resources)

Walinsky, Adam. "Keeping the Poor in Their Place: Notes on the Importance of Being One-up." In New Perspectives on Poverty, edited by Shostak and Gomberg. Englewood Cliffs, New Jersey: Prentice-Hall, Inc. 1965.

(II)

A different orientation towards poverty definition. The poor are defined as "not-middle-class" and their existence is important to the sense of security of members of the middle-class. The desire to preserve one's gains by denying them to others has been heightened by a general loss of middle-class security. With a general decline in the significance of work, symbols of consumption--housing, education, etc.--have become important. People whose work is meaningless except as it allows them, by earning money, to differentiate themselves from the poor oppose large-scale employment projects; instead they support transfer payments at a level too low to allow recipients to compete for status in housing or education.

Wallich, Henry. "Inequality and Growth." In Inequality and Poverty, edited by Edward L. Budd. New York: Norton & Company, 1967. (Selection from his book, The Cost of Freedom.)

(II)

The question of equal versus unequal income distribution is examined here in terms of the "functional" criterion of greater welfare for all. "Economic equality...is not an end in itself. It is only a means, designed to reduce poverty; perhaps it is not the most effective means." Thus economic growth, seen as a benefit to the whole society, is given the role of tempering the demands for equality that a simpler model might prescribe. A competitive labor market that induces people to use their skills to best advantage and the incentives that reward labor performance and risk-taking all serve economic growth and at the same time demand some differentiation of income. It is assumed that a desire for Veblen's "invidious distinction" provides the real motivation; so that differentials of reward are important, not absolute levels. The growth demands of industry provide another argument for inequality, since the savings of wealthier individuals are typically the source of needed investment. Finally, a cultural-intellectual elite or perhaps more palatably a "leadership" elite is considered beneficial. The conclusion is that the real problem consists in determining exactly how much inequality is required. There is a need for more specific analysis of the relation between degrees of inequality and the objectives that inequality is thought to serve.

Wan, T., and Tarver, J. "Socioeconomic Status, Migration and Morbidity." Social Biology 19 (1972):51-59.

(XI)

Data from the 1967 Survey of Economic Opportunity conducted by the Bureau of the Census are used to determine what socio-economic factors influence health (morbidity). The measure of morbidity used is the number of work limiting chronic conditions in a particular population. The authors argue that social strains adversely effect health. Among the strains they examine are socio-economic status (SES) and migration-residence status. They find that higher rates of morbidity are likely to be found in aged persons, those with low SES levels, non-white and rural to rural migrants. In general, morbidity is slightly lower for non-migrants than for migrants. Migrants with rural backgrounds have substantially higher morbidity rates than migrants or non-migrants with urban backgrounds. Urban to urban migrants and urban non-migrants were substantially more healthy than rural to urban and rural to rural migrants, but rural to urban migrants were slightly more healthy than rural to rural migrants.

Warren, Martin, and Berkowitz, Sheldon. "The Employability of AFDC Mothers and Fathers." Welfare in Review 7 (July-August 1969): 1-7.

(IX)

This article describes the results of an employability survey of 100 California AFDC mothers and fathers. A panel of experts rated the employability of each case and put it into one of four classes. The four classes used were:

1. capable of earning a living for self and dependents,

2H. capable of partially supporting self and dependents with probable earnings in excess of half of AFDC payments,

2L. capable of partially supporting self and dependents but probable earnings are less than half of AFDC payments, and

3. totally unemployable.

The results show that roughly one-half of all individuals receiving AFDC in California are capable of full or significant partial self-sufficiency. The principal obstacles facing AFDC mothers looking for work are child care, limited work skills, lack of a previous work history, poor personality traits, and insufficient education. The principal obstacles facing the unemployed AFDC fathers are an arrest record, poor job adjustment, limited skills, negative personality traits and an insufficient work record.

* Watts, Harold. "An Economic Definition of Poverty." In <u>On Understanding Poverty</u>, edited by Daniel Moynihan. New York: Basic Books, 1968.

(II)

Watts presents a strict economic definition of poverty, intended for administrative application. Income, not consumption, is his measure of poverty since income captures the household's command over goods and services without imposing an arbitrary ideal market basket. His welfare measure is the ratio of a family's permanent income to its total needs. While this ratio still divides families between poor and non-poor as it exceeds or falls short of 1 (one), it preserves the notion that a family barely above the line is not much better off than one below it. By taking the log of this ratio as his welfare index, Watts recognizes the fact that poverty becomes a more and more pressing problem the farther below the poverty line a family is.

*Watts, Harold W. "The Iso-Prop Index: An Approach to the Determination of Differential Poverty Thresholds." <u>The Journal of Human Resources</u> 3 (Winter 1967): 3-18.

(III, IV)

An index is constructed to determine equivalent incomes for families in different circumstances on the assumption that families spending the same proportion of income on food, or on some group of basic necessary commodities, enjoy an equivalent standard of living. This basis for determining equivalent income has been used before (study by the Bureau of Labor Statistics, 1960, for example); however in this paper the Engel curves, and hence the iso-proportional indices derived from them, are differentiated not only by family size and age of family head but by geographic region and urban-rural designations as well. Moreover, it is assumed that the basic form of the Engel function, which determines the amount of income spent on a given commodity, can be factored into independent family size and location components. Therefore any given differentiations of family situation can be separated out and an index can be derived which reflects only variation in one specific circumstance, such as urban/rural location or geographic area, while all other variables are held constant. The parameters in the assumed form of the Engel function were estimated by means of a regression using data from the 1960 Survey of Consumer Expenditures. Regressions using limited subsets of the income distribution, comparable for the different family circumstances, were found to be more appropriate to the assumption of equal income elasticity for all Engel curves than those regressions using data from the whole distribution.

Watts, Harold W. "Long-Run Income Expectations and Consumer Spending." In Studies in Household Economic Behavior, edited by Thomas F. Dernberg, Richard N. Rosett, and Harold W. Watts. New Haven: Yale University Press, 1958.

(VII)

This study brings empirical evidence from cross-section surveys to determine whether households base their consumption and saving decisions on expected future income. Since actual measurement of long-run expectations is difficult, data on current income, age, occupation, education, race, and location are used as proxy measures under the assumption that these variables are systematically related to expectations of future income. The results provide some indication, though not overwhelming, that savings decisions are based on expected future earnings.

Watts, Harold W. "The Measurement of Poverty--An Exploratory Exercise." Institute for Research on Poverty, Reprint No. 42, 1962.

(II)

The general structure of the rule for measuring poverty is divided into two parts. One component, a "threshold function" establishes a poverty line (which may vary for different families); and a second component uses this threshold value to determine some poverty measure. The purpose here is to see what the consequences are for the distribution of poverty if one tries alternate specifications of these two components. The poverty line rule used by the OEO (Office of Economic Opportunity) is approximated by a function which distinguishes farm and non-farm location (farm thresholds are three-fourths of non-farm for equivalent families) and which begins with a base of $1000 and adds $500 for every family member regardless of age. Variations of the threshold function which are examined include an alternative that adds to the $1000 base $350, $600, or $750 depending on age and another option which retains the constant $500 per person allowance but introduces a geographical correction factor. Both the geographic correction and the age of family member adjustment are based on a Bureau of Labor Statistics study which assumes equivalent living standard when equivalent portions of income are spent on food. (This study is annotated elsewhere.) Of the "poverty measure" functions, the simplest is that which specifies the measure as the total number of people in families below this respective poverty thresholds (or as a variation, below 1.5 times their poverty threshold). The "poverty gap" function takes the measure as equal to the amount of money that would be required to bring the income of all "poor" families up to their appropriate threshold values (or up to 1.5 times their threshold). This measure gives an added weight to those poor farther below the threshold, and this weight increases in a linear fashion. Also, one non-linear measure is examined which attempts to capture the diminishing marginal utility of income. Three threshold variations and five measure variations result in fifteen different indicators which are applied to 1960 census data. The relative distribution of poverty by race, family type, work experience, and geographic region is compared for these alternatives. In terms of the threshold component, only the geographical variant showed much effect in terms of the distributions, and this effect was only the obvious change in the geographical distribution itself. The variation in the measuring function was important for all the distributions. "Having shown that such changes can make an appreciable difference, it becomes doubly important to investigate the alternatives more fully."

Waud, Roger N. "Inflation, Unemployment and Economic Welfare." American Economic Review.

(III)

If wages are not completely flexible, thus allowing equilibrium at less than full employment, anticipated inflation does not have an unambiguously bad effect on "feasible welfare." The expectation of inflation has different effects on the three main objectives of economic policy. (1) It moves the economy towards full employment. (2) It moves the economy from the desirable position of "full liquidity" ("a situation where the opportunity cost of holding money is nil"). (3) It may have a positive effect on attempts to achieve a real rate of interest consistent with an optimum rate of economic growth. The traditional tools of monetary and fiscal policy are probably not capable of achieving more than one of these goals. Nevertheless, the government's ability to reduce the opportunity cost of holding money, by paying interest on money, increases the possibility of simultaneously achieving all three goals.

*Wayland, Sloan R. "Old Problems, New Faces, and New Standards." In Education in Depressed Areas, edited by A. Harry Passow. New York: Teachers College Press, 1966.

(XI)

Urban educational problems of today are in reality new expressions of century-old problems. As such, more careful analysis is needed to sort out features of urban groups which are functions of class position and immigrant status from those features which are asserted to be a function of a particular subculture. For instance, a great deal which has been attributed to the subculture of the Negro (i.e., Moynihan Report) should be associated more with factors of class position and difficulties stemming from recent migration to the city from the country. Wayland also argues that the perceived contrast between urban depressed and other classes has been sharpened because America has succeeded in raising the standards of living for all classes.

Wedderburn, Dorothy, ed. Poverty, Inequality and Class Structure. London: Cambridge University Press, 1974.

(II)

A collection of essays on measuring poverty, case studies on poverty, and class consciousness. Contributors include economists, sociologists and political scientists. The focus of the essays is on poverty in industrialized societies, particularly Great Britain.

Weeks, Christopher. Job Corps: Dollars and Dropouts. Boston: Little Brown & Co., 1967.

(X)

An historical review of the Federal anti-poverty program entitled "Job Corps." During the Johnson Administration, Sargent Shriver campaigned hard for the inclusion of a residential job training and educational enrichment program for low-income teenagers. As one of the 10 programs to come out of the Equal Opportunity Act of 1964, Job Corps' main thrust was focused at improving the mobility of the teenager at the bottom of the economic ladder. Weeks examines some of the program's problems during the first two years of operation. Job Corps centers, administered by universities and non-profit organizations, tended to have greater absenteeism, high dropout rates, and more financial problems than centers run by corporations. One survey on the effectiveness of the program indicated six dropouts for every Job Corps graduate. Weeks concluded by explaining that the country still needs a Job Corps, but that the problem it must face is itself.

Weisbrod, Burton A. "The Economics of Poverty: An American Paradox." In The Economics of Poverty, edited by Burton A. Weisbrod. Englewood Cliffs, New Jersey: Prentice-Hall, Inc. 1965.

(II)

An introduction to a series of essays concerning poverty, this essay uses the commonly accepted measure of family income as its index for the determination of poverty. The Johnson Administration figure of $3000 as the income level below which a family can be said to live in poverty, as well as the concept of income in general as a useful measure of poverty, are discussed in terms of their relative merits for measurement and policy.

Among families with incomes of less than $3000 in 1962, 69% of those families were still at that income level in 1963, and two-fifths of the remaining 31% had incomes of less than $4000. However, if, instead of the $3000 figure, the measure of family income at a level which is less than half of the national median family income is used as the measure of poverty, then the net percentage of American families in poverty has not declined from 1947 to 1962. Among the problems which arise in trying to set income level as an adequate definition of poverty are: a measure which adjusts for family size, and which accounts for assets and non-money income, will exclude many aged, particularly farm-based, families and will increase the relative number of poverty children and Blacks classified as poor; and a measure which includes medical needs and income prospects will increase the relative number of aged classified as poor.

*Weisbrod, Burton A., and Hansen, W. Lee. "An Income-Net Worth Approach to Measuring Economic Welfare." In Institute for Research on Poverty: Discussion Papers, 1968.

(II,VII)

This paper presents an empirical measure of economic welfare, called economic position, which integrates current money income and current net worth both to determine to a significant degree the economic position of a consumer unit. The distribution of income and the distribution of net worth differ. It would be less important to integrate these two distributions were it not for these differences. Income is a flow, while net worth is a stock; thus, in order to merge the two, it is necessary to convert net worth into a flow by translating it into an annuity. The economic position of a consumer unit--individual, family, or household--should be measured as the sum of: (1) the unit's current annual adjusted income; and (2) the annual lifetime annuity value of the unit's current net worth. The most notable result of using the new measure is its impact on the economic position of the aged, who, by this measure, are better off than they would be according to the current income measure. This result arises from the interaction of income, net worth holdings, and life expectancy.

(Poverty and Human Resources Abstracts)

Weiss, L., and Williamson, J. "Black Education, Earnings, and Interregional Migration: Some New Evidence." American Economic Review 62 (June 1972): 373-383.

(VI)

This article discusses the returns to education for blacks and the interaction of black education and black migration. The authors found that the inferiority of southern black schools cannot account for the poverty of black migrants to the North. Apparently, the overall effect of urban ghettos is more harmful to black economic progress than their rural origins. It was found that black returns to education in 1967 were as high as those experienced by whites in 1960, and that there was a great increase in the returns to black education in the sixties at all educational levels. Furthermore, the elasticity of income with respect to experience for young blacks increased significantly over the decade. Weiss and Williamson conclude that "increased investment in black education will generate further economic progress for the black population relative to the white."

Welch, Finis, and Rosen, Sherwin. "A Note on the Estimation of Labor Supply." Journal of Human Resources 7 (Winter 1972): 104-111.

(II)

Welch and Rosen examine the validity of a study conducted by Christopher Green and Alfred Tella that indicated national output declines stemming from work disincentives and that these need to be included in the evaluation of anti-poverty policies. They find the study adequate in both its methodological and conceptual approaches. The failure to consider all existing and prospective income redistribution alternatives for families and the absence of any real association between income structure and earnings which produces a regression fallacy are the two weakest points highlighted by the authors. They then compare Green and Tella's results to a random model. Results indicate that wage rates for families with and without nonemployment income varied by more than the income class differentials using the new model, and that in order to earn more one must work more. The authors belief that stratification by income is misleading is confirmed.

Wertheimer, Richard F. The Monetary Rewards of Migration Within the U.S. Washington, D.C.: The Urban Institute, 1970.

(VI)

Migration from the South to the North and from rural to urban areas yields substantial economic gains. The earnings differentials are about $800 a year and $600 a year respectively, although disaggregating the population of migrants indicates that there are large differentials within these two groups. In general, during the first few years after migrating, migrants experience very little monetary gain, but after 5 years, migrants have earnings equal to those of northern and urban non-migrants of the same education, age, race and sex. Discounted average annual returns are higher for younger migrants than for older migrants. "The average annual return of migrating at age 30 is less than half of the return of migrating at age 20" (using a 10% discount rate). Nonwhites appear to gain more from migration than whites, but female heads of families and unrelated women experience no earnings gain from migration.

Wetzel, James R., and Holland, Susan S. "Poverty Areas of Our Major Cities." Monthly Labor Review 89 (October 1966): 1105-1110.

(II,X)

"Hidden by the national averages of record employment and low unemployment is a different--and dismal--picture of the unemployment situation for both white and Negro workers in the slum areas of large cities. The urban poor live in a world characterized by frequent periods of unemployment between menial and unrewarding jobs. In March, 1966, the average unemployment rate for workers living in poverty areas of big cities was 7.5 percent--about double the rate for the United States as a whole." For the same month, the 12.1 million persons 14 years old or more in the big city poverty areas accounted for 16% of the populations of those cities. Of these 12.1 million, 42% are Black, and 56% of the big city Blacks live in poverty areas. Black men accounted for 100,000 of the 150,000 labor force non-participants in city poverty areas, and the Black unemployment rate in the poverty areas was 1.5 times that for whites in those areas. Moreover, the white employment situation in the poverty areas was more favorable than the Black employment situation even in non-poverty areas.

Poverty area dwellers, especially Blacks, are concentrated in less secure, desirable, or rewarding jobs. Occupational distribution for poverty areas is nearly 50% blue collar, 28% white collar, and 23% service, as compared to 33% blue collar, over 50% white collar, and less than 12.5% service in non-poverty areas. It would require over 600,000 full-time jobs to reduce the level of Black unemployment to the level for whites in non-poverty areas, but even this would not in itself be a sufficient remedy because of the nature of Blacks' jobs.

Whitley, J.D. "Mortgages: The Case for Index-Linking." <u>National Institute Economic Review</u> 70 (November 1974): 75-79.

(III)

This article argues that mortgage payment schedules and interest on building society deposits should be linked to an inflation index. Present mortgages involve fixed money repayments, so that during a period of inflation, real payments are concentrated in the first few years. If a bank sets a rate of interest on mortgages high enough to maintain a positive real rate of return throughout the repayment term, the interest, especially in the initial periods, would be prohibitively high for many prospective home buyers. In order to keep mortgage rates down and still allow building societies and savings and loan associations to make a profit, the government sets limits on interest paid by those savings media which are competitors of building societies (i.e., full service banks). This penalizes short term savers by paying them an artifically regulated, below-market interest rate, thus, creating an unstable and sometimes insufficient supply of mortgage funds. Linked mortgage payments would set fixed <u>real</u> repayments. Market rates of interest could be charged, but by rearranging payments through time, initial real repayments would be lower. This would allow more people to enter the housing market, despite higher overall nominal repayments. At the same time, the market interest rates would ensure an adequate supply of mortgage funds without penalizing small savers.

Wilber, George L., ed. <u>Poverty: A New Perspective</u>. Lexington, Kentucky: University of Kentucky Press, 1975.

(II,V,VI,XI)

"There are deeply rooted dimensions of poverty--not well understood or recognized--which respond slowly to treatment... A major contention in this book is that these fundamental dimensions of poverty--not merely their correlates--need to be recognized and understood. Poverty should not be viewed merely as an economic predicament but as a 'system of measurable poverties,' of which low income level is only one."

The essays which are included deal with: determinants of poverty, poverty indicators as indicators of social welfare, migration and poverty, social services for the residential and migrant poor, and achievement motivation and poverty. An emphasis of the book is that by looking for "villains" who are responsible for poverty, social scientists divert themselves from reality. Rather, researchers should look toward conflicting objectives which exist in different sectors of society. Problems are not solved precisely because we do not know how to solve them in light of these conflicting objectives.

Wilber, G.L. "Systematic Indicators of Regional Poverty." _Growth and Change_ 3 (July 1972): 11-15.

(VI)

This article develops a framework for evaluating regional poverty. The framework is built on the following seven properties of poverty: (1) resource poverty--a scarcity of necessary natural resources; (2) norm poverty--a lack of important social attitudes such as a "degree of achievement" norm; (3) poverty of information--inadequate mass media and education; (4) social class poverty--rigid class distinctions and low upward mobility; (5) facility and service poverty--insufficient public services; (6) economic poverty--a scarcity of important economic resources such as labor and capital, or the inability to mobilize existing resources; and (7) policy poverty--inadequate government policy. An understanding of poverty in a region can be reached by defining these properties and analysing the ways in which they interact.

Wilcock, Richard. "Who Are the Unemployed?" In _In Aid of the Unemployed_. Baltimore, Maryland: Johns Hopkins Press, 1965.

(X)

An overview of the unemployment data collection process and an analysis of those classified as unemployed. The major sources of unemployment data, the requirement to be counted as unemployed and the number and characteristics of the unemployed are described. Wilcock finds the unemployment rate to be highest among teenagers, Blacks, the least educated, and manual and service workers. Although Wilcock could find no current series of data (1963) that provided information on the incomes of the unemployed, a number of special reports are cited which conclude that unemployment is high among the poor. One report indicated that about half of the jobless poor in 1961 were family heads responsible for other persons. A geographical look at unemployment shows some high pockets of unemployment in the nation and only few areas of satisfactorily low levels of unemployment. Wilcock concludes with a review of the recommendations made by the President's Committee to Appraise Employment Statistics. Among these are the inclusions of part-time workers, information on the number of hours of work wanted, and data on the incentives required to promote those not in the labor force to return.

Will, Robert, and Vatter, Harold. Poverty in Affluence. New York: Harcourt, Brace and World, Inc., 1970.

(II,V,VI,X)

A collage of short articles on the social, political and economic dimensions of poverty in the United States. Selections on regional differences in poverty are presented by the AFL-CIO Economic Policy Committee, Dorothy Newman, the Presidential Advisory Committee on Rural Poverty, and Oscar Ornati. The first two authors describe the poor in the urban setting. Poor housing, deteriorating neighborhoods, high rents, the increase of urban unemployment and suburban industrial migration are elements discussed in these passages. The third piece is concerned with the rural poor and how the changes in rural America have left this group of deprived individuals without much hope for the future. Ornati discusses the South's regional disadvantage as it relates to the incidence of poverty. By examining the 1960 Census data Ornati finds residing in the South, especially the rural South, to be a definite disadvantage.

Also discussed in this collection of works on poverty are the inadequate health services offered the poor and the added transportation costs facing the urban poor in order to maintain employment.

Will, Robert E., and Vatter, Harold G. "The Unemployed and the Underpaid." In Poverty in Affluence. New York: Harcourt, Brace and World, 1965, 109-117.

(X)

"The Unemployed and the Underpaid"--A section on "casual and chronic unemployment" presents statistics on levels of extended unemployment and repeated periods of joblessness in 1966. Discusses effects of improved economic conditions on employment rate during years of economic upturn, 1961 to 1966. Notes that expansion of work force during that period had greater impact on long-term unemployment relative to periodic unemployment. Policy implications of this observation point to aiding chronically unemployed to find jobs that offer continuity of employment.

The concept of sub-employment (the problem of low earnings) is discussed in the next section. Statistics reveal that the employed poor are a larger problem in terms of numbers than the unemployed poor; in 1966, the number of subemployed was 6.7 million as compared with 2.4 million with 15 or more weeks of unemployment. This problem is most severe for Blacks.

The last piece in this section addresses the problems of those who are willing to work but not seeking jobs. A Department of Labor study in 1966 revealed that one out of every ten men and women without work wanted jobs. Reasons most often cited for not looking for work included ill health, family responsibilities, school attendance, or discouragement with the job market.

Willie, Charles V., and Rothney, William B. "Racial, Ethnic, and Income Factors in the Epidemiology of Neonatal Mortality." American Sociological Review 27 (1962): 522-526.

(XI)

A study "to determine whether infant mortality rates, particularly neonatal mortality rates, vary by racial and by ethnic neighborhoods when socio-economic status is held constant."

The study population consisted of four racial and ethnic neighborhoods--Negro, Native White, Italian, and Polish--all in the lowest socio-economic area of Syracuse. The authors are careful to differentiate between family income and socio-economic status, the latter relating to occupation, housing level, and education. While socio-economic status is held constant, family income is not.

The findings indicate that Negro and Native White populations have similar infant mortality rates when socio-economic status is held constant; rates differ between white native-born persons and other Caucasian neighborhoods of similar status. Therefore, the hypothesis that suggests that racial factors contribute to variations in the distribution of neonatal mortality by residential neighborhoods is not validated. However, while the association between neonatal mortality and economic circumstances is diminishing, a critical income level was found to exist above which there is little association between neonatal mortality and family income.

Wilson, Stan B. "Social Stratification and Academic Achievement." In Education in Depressed Areas, edited by A. Harry Passow. New York: Teachers College Press, 1966.

(XI)

A report on the effects of social stratification and of segregation on the academic attainment of elementary school children. While gross differences in scholastic achievement can be accounted for in part by family backgrounds, subcultural factors and other environmental factors, these are not the whole story. Watson suggests that we look at the school itself as a contributing factor in achievement. As students progress through junior and senior high school, those from middle-class schools tend to be assigned to the academic stream while pupils from the lower-class schools are placed in general or vocational programs. Using sociometric data, Wilson specifically points to the tendency of schools to homogenize standards, particularly through the influence of teacher expectations and peer group pressures. Teachers in the lower-class schools did not set as high standards nor did they concern themselves as much as teachers in the middle-class schools with "bringing the children up to grade level." Looking at peer group pressures in lower-class schools, he found lower expectations of success and of further education.

Wilson, V.E. "Rural Health Care Systems." Journal of the American Medical Association 216 (June 7, 1971): 1623-1626.

(V)

Health care delivery in rural areas is seriously constrained by fundamental supply and demand problems. Inadequate income limits demand, while scarcity of health facilities and shortages of health manpower restrict supply.

Author notes encouraging developments on the income dimension. Movement by the federal government towards establishing national health insurance and assuring a floor under family income could stimulate effective demand for health services for rural areas.

Possible solutions to supply problems could be provided by innovative use of existing community and health care centers. Consolidated schools in rural areas could be used as outreach mechanisms and channels for volunteer support. Further, community mental health centers which have shown remarkable ability to penetrate rural areas could be models for broader delivery systems.

Lastly, broad measures are needed to raise the quality of rural life. Rural areas must be revitalized to attract new manpower.

Windham, Douglas M. Education, Equality, and Income Redistribution. Lexington, Massachusetts: Lexington Book, 1970.

(II)

"The net effect of the state-financed post-secondary education system in Florida is regressive in that it redistributes income in favor of the wealthy." Windham tests this hypothesis by examining the tax incidence on different income groups in Florida during fiscal year 1967-68 and comparing these results to an earlier study in California. This is accomplished by distributing the costs of public higher education in Florida among income groups based on their local-state-federal tax share available for support of public higher education. The benefits are determined by quantifying the investment sum equal to the present value of an income group's lifetime earnings attributable to the subsidized education. The difference between these two (benefits and costs) is the short run effect of the tax system. The long run effect is measured by the difference between the investment potential lost through paying taxes and the investment subsidy gained by paying for a portion of the student's education. The major conclusion is that while some lower class members are able to obtain subsidies, as a whole, lower income classes would be better off without a public education system. The poor in Florida through regressive and proportional state taxes are paying for a good that the rich receive more of. Windham also indicates that Florida is not atypical in that respect.

*Winegarden, C.R. "The Welfare 'Explosion': Determinants of the Size and Recent Growth of the AFDC Population." Journal of Economics and Sociology 32 (1973): 245-256.

(V, IX)

An attempt to identify the factors directly responsible for the relative size of the Aid to Families with Dependent Children (AFDC) population. The amount of the welfare grant is singled out for closest scrutiny. Two models of multiple regression analysis are used on data from the 50 states. The first has the purpose of explaining interstate variation in the relative levels of the AFDC population in the initial quarter of 1971, when the national total reached an all time high. The second is designed to reveal reasons for the interstate differences in the growth rate of the AFDC rolls during the preceding 2 years, a period characterized by recession and expansion of the welfare population. Winegarden's conclusion: neither the average amount of the welfare grant nor its rate of increase positively influences the relative size or growth rate of the AFDC population. This study supports the contention that a more generous scale of assistance payments would not result, in and of itself, in a larger or more rapidly growing dependent population.

Wingo, Lowdon. "Issues in a National Urban Development Strategy for the United States." Urban Studies 9 (1972): 3-27.

(V,VI)

National urban growth policy, which became part of national policy with the enactment of the National Housing and Urban Development Act of 1970, has its origins in the vigorous advocacy of Johnson's Secretary of Agriculture, Orville I. Freeman. The New Federalism of the Nixon Administration implies a national "hands off" policy with respect to local development, and so conflicts with this new legislation. However, defining the public ends of such a policy and relating to appropriate means will require some considerable improvement in the state of knowledge available to policy makers. The shape of such a policy model can be dimly seen to integrate some key constructs of urban economics, including settlement patterns, urban externalities, internal migration, and important urban markets, such as those for land, labour, housing and transportation.

(Taken from the article)

Winston, Gordon C. "An International Comparison of Hours of Work." *Review of Economics and Statistics* 48 (February 1967): 28-39.

(VIII)

This article provides an empirical test of the relationship between income and per capita hours of work per week. The test involves the use of data from 47 countries, and it conclusively shows that as per capita income goes up, the number of hours worked per week goes down. This negative relationship is statistically very strong, though small; per capita hours worked will decline roughly 1% for every 10% increase in per capita income.

Although income is the strongest determinant of the numbers of hours worked, it is not the only one. The state of aggregate demand (measured by the unemployment rate) is another important determining factor. As unemployment increases, the number of hours worked per capita decreases (as firms cut back on both hours and personnel).

Wippler, Reinhard. "Leisure Behavior: A Multivariable Approach." *Sociologia NeerLandica* 6 (1970): 51-67.

(VIII)

The article presents a multivariate approach to measure the social determinants of leisure behavior. Wippler introduces 50 independent variables associated with leisure behavior and tests a number of hypothesized relationships among them. Variables included social background, social status, social mobility, religious denomination, political orientation, and work related information. The "contrast" hypothesis, which predicted "that strains in work are conducive to contrasting leisure behavior," was not supported by the results. Education and occupation level were found to be the best indicators of leisure behavior. High education level meant more cultural participation in leisure time, and differences in occupational prestige had a strong correlation to social and political participation. When these two variables were held constant, income alone could not account for leisure activity variations. Whippler concluded that as the society becomes more educated, urbanized, secularized, and hedonistic, future leisure activity will become more diverse, more informal, more physically passive, more practical, and less religious.

Woodbury, Robert Morse. "Economic Consumption Scales and Their Uses." *Journal of the American Statistical Society* 39 (December 1944): 455-468.

(VII)

A thorough discussion of consumption scales as a means of ranking families by economic welfare. These scales are used to equate the needs of different sized families by relating either the needs (nutrition scales) or the consumption (consumption scales) of individuals of different ages and sexes to a common standard. The article discusses the methodology of the eleven scales that had been proposed before 1944 and then compares them. They are generally similar, though later scales tended to give higher values to children (they were worth a larger fraction of an adult) than earlier ones. The article concludes with a discussion of areas in need of further work, particularly non-food, non-clothing scales and the problem of standardization.

"Worker's Budgets in the U. S.: City Families and Single Persons, 1946 and 1947." Bureau of Labor Statistics *Bulletin* #972, 1948.

(III,IV)

Discusses derivation of Bureau of Labor Statistics' City Worker's Family Budget. CWFB represents an attempt to develop a comprehensive list of goods and services which approximate a "modest but adequate" living standard. The content of the budget is based on consumption patterns, and quantities are determined by a "quantity-income elasticity" technique. The standard achieved by the budget encompasses certain social and psychological needs as well as material well-being.

Yinger, L. Milton. "Contraculture and Subculture." <u>American Sociological Review</u> 25 (October 1960): 625-635.

(II,VI,XI)

Current sociological work makes extensive use of the concept of subculture--in the analysis of delinquency, adolescence, regional and class differences, religious sects, and other topics. In the study of these areas, sociologists' understanding has been increased by seeing norms that vary from more general standards as manifestations of distinctive sub-societies. However, the term subculture is used in several different ways. Over 100 sources are reviewed which show that three clearly different meanings of subculture are found. A new term "contraculture" is suggested in order to distinguish between normative systems of sub-society and emergent norms that appear in conflict situations.

(Partially taken from <u>American Sociological Review</u>)

Yoshihara, Kunio. "Demand Functions: An Application to the Japanese Expenditure Pattern." <u>Econometrica</u> 37(1969): 257-274.

(III)

In a theoretical discussion of the derivation of demand systems from utility functions, Yoshihara finds that if the income elasticity is not unity for all commodities, the utility function will not be homogeneous. Of four demand systems often used in empirical studies, only Stone's linear expenditure system and Houthakker's indirect addilog system were acceptable on theoretical grounds. Stone's system explains the pattern of Japanese demand far better than Houthakker's.

Zeckhauser, Richard J. "Optimal Mechanisms for Income Transfer." American Economic Review (June 1971).

(II)

A model is posed in which a representative non-poor citizen derives positive utility from the increased welfare of the poor and, within limits, from the increased hours of work performed by the poor. The costs of a given welfare program are presumed to have a negative influence on utility. The representative poor man's utility increases with income and decreases with hours worked. The problem investigated here is what kind of welfare program should the non-poor citizen construct in order to maximize his utility knowing that the poor man's response will be to maximize his own utility. Assuming a general form for these functions and specifying a wage rate makes it possible to plot together the indifference curves for these two representative citizens and to compare the implications of various welfare programs. Negative income tax and income maintenance both entail positive marginal tax rates and are distinguished from transfer programs which have negative marginal tax rates. It is found that, at a given cost, the negative tax rate transfer plans are superior to the other two general programs in that they result in more income for the poor and greater labor time. A scheme is presented for selecting the Pareto optimal transfer plan which might be seen as the best outcome of a cooperative solution. In this case, the transfer plan line is tangent to indifference curves of both representative citizens. It is acknowledged that the two-person analysis presented here would presume similarity of wage rate and employment opportunities if applied to a larger group. Where this assumption would not be appropriate (e.g. handicapped, aged), it is suggested that more than one transfer program would be appropriate.

*Zimbalist, Sidney. "Drawing the Poverty Line." Social Work 9 (1964): 19-26.

(II,IV)

The article reviews British and American efforts to determine a minimum standard of living. At the turn of the nineteenth century Booth and Rowntree made a systematic study of poverty in England, using a simple poverty line based on physical necessities. In 1907 American researchers More and Chapin independently set poverty lines of $800-$900 based on observed expenditures.

Minimum budgets are based on subjective cultural standards and assume that low-income families spend their income with a high degree of skill. The contrary is often true.

A formal minimum budget was first applied to relief grants in 1913. This was the Chicago Standard Budget--used in Chicago until the late forties.

The best-known budgetary yardstick today is the "City Worker's Family Budget" prepared by the Bureau of Labor Statistics. This budget is not a poverty measure. Through survey techniques it estimates "the total cost of a representative list of goods and services considered necessary by 4-person city families..." It locates the "point on the income scale where families stop buying more and more" and start buying either "better and better" or something" less essential to them."

Since food comprises one-third of a typical family's expenditures, Orshansky calculated a poverty line by tripling the cost of the Department of Agriculture's economy food plan. A more refined method would take differing family circumstances into account in setting a poverty line.

(Poverty and Human Resources Abstracts)

Zimmerman, Carle C., and Frampton, Merle E. Family and Society. New York: D. Van Nostrand Co., 1935.

(II, III, VII)

This investigation into the sociological basis of poverty and well-being begins with a presentation of European Le Playist and Engelian types of analyses as they pertain to the relationship between family form and condition, and social structure and behavior. Ozark families are then studied in terms of their "systems of living" in which income and social conditions combine to produce a standard of living. A poor Ozark family is analyzed for factors of family background, education, income, diet, housing, property, pride, social habits, social mobility, family stability, and physical and moral well-being, and the following conclusion is reached: "Judging this family on the basis of its standard of living and its general mental ability, it would be on the relief rolls in any urban or commercialized agricultural area. The position of the family is, however, quite the opposite. It is socially prosperous although not economically prosperous. The chief reason for the success of this family...lies in the social organization of which it is a part."

INDEX

Chapter II. Historical Definitions of Poverty: An Overview

INDEX

Chapter III. Index Numbers

INDEX

Chapter IV. Adjustments for Family Size and Composition

INDEX

Chapter V. Regional Cost of Living Differences as a Function of Public Sector Differences

INDEX

Chapter VI. Regional Cost of Living Differences as a Function of Private Sector Differences

INDEX

Chapter VII. Wealth/Assets and Consumption as Measures of Poverty

INDEX

Chapter VIII. Is Leisure a Resource?

INDEX

Chapter IX. Determinants of the Turn-over Rates of Poor Families

INDEX

Chapter X. Social and Economic Proxies for Poverty

INDEX

Chapter XI. Social Indicators

INDEX

Chapter XII. State Administration Definitions of Poverty

For Product Safety Concerns and Information please contact our EU representative GPSR@taylorandfrancis.com Taylor & Francis Verlag GmbH, Kaufingerstraße 24, 80331 München, Germany

Batch number: 10726009

Printed by Printforce, the Netherlands